THE ART OF DIALOGUE IN JEWISH PHILOSOPHY

The Art of Dialogue in Jewish Philosophy

Aaron W. Hughes

INDIANA UNIVERSITY PRESS
Bloomington and Indianapolis

This book is a publication of

Indiana University Press
601 North Morton Street
Bloomington, IN 47404-3797 USA

http://iupress.indiana.edu

Telephone orders 800-842-6796
Fax orders 812-855-7931
Orders by e-mail iuporder@indiana.edu

The paper used in this publication meets the minimum requirements of American National Standard for Information Sciences—Permanence of Paper for Printed Library Materials, ANSI Z39.48-1984.

Manufactured in the United States of America

Library of Congress Cataloging-in-Publication Data

Hughes, Aaron W., date
The art of dialogue in Jewish philosophy / Aaron W. Hughes.
p. cm.
Includes bibliographical references and index.
ISBN-13: 978-0-253-34982-8 (cloth : alk. paper)
ISBN-13: 978-0-253-21944-2 (pbk. : alk. paper) 1. Philosophy, Jewish. I. Title.
B755.H765 2008
181'.06—dc22

2007024494

1 2 3 4 5 13 12 11 10 09 08

l, r, m

Man communicates himself to God through name, which he gives to nature and (in proper names) to his own kind; and to nature he gives names according to the communication he receives from her, for the whole of nature, too, is imbued with a nameless, unspoken language, the residue of the creative word of God, which is preserved in man as the cognizing name and above man as the judgment suspended over him. The language of nature is comparable to a secret password that each sentry passes to the next in his own language, but the meaning of the password is the sentry's language itself. All higher language is a translation of lower ones, until in ultimate clarity the word of God unfolds, which is the unity of this movement made up of language.

WALTER BENJAMIN,
"ON LANGUAGE AS SUCH AND ON THE LANGUAGE OF MAN"

CONTENTS

ACKNOWLEDGMENTS

Research for this book was made possible by the generosity of the Social Sciences and Humanities Research Council of Canada (SSHRC), which provided me with a Standard Research Grant for the years 2004–2007. The Lady Davis Fellowship Trust at the Hebrew University of Jerusalem gave me much-needed time and energy to think about this project at a crucial stage in its development with a faculty fellowship during the 2005–2006 academic year. I would also like to acknowledge the support and encouragement of Zev Harvey, my colleague in the Department of Jewish Thought at the Hebrew University.

Versions of several of these chapters were presented at the Hebrew University of Jerusalem, Ben Gurion University of the Negev, the Oxford Centre for Hebrew and Judaic Studies, University of Kentucky, New York University, Penn State University, the C.N.R.S, the Goethe University in Frankfurt am Main, and the Zagreb Institute of Philosophy. I am grateful for the invitations to speak at these institutions, and would like to thank all of those who gave me much-needed feedback at early stages, lending further support to my argument that dialogue is a central component in the practice of Jewish philosophy. All mistakes in what follows are solely my own.

More specifically, I would like to thank Ross Brann, Almut Sh. Bruckstein, James Diamond, Dan Frank, Gad Freudenthal, Zev Greis, Steven Harvey, Haim Kreisel, Oliver Leaman, Tony Levy, Michael Lundell, Sarah Pessin, James Robinson, Hava Tirosh-Samuelson, Vladimir Stoupel, Steven Wasserstrom, Elliot Wolfson, and Marie-Elise Zovko. At the University of Calgary I would like to acknowledge Virginia Tumasz, Eliezer Segal, Pierre-Yves Mocquais, and Rowland Smith, all of whom have supported my work in Jewish Studies. Last, but certainly not least, I am grateful to and for Lisa A. Hughes, who read many versions, both in whole and in part, of this study.

THE ART OF DIALOGUE IN JEWISH PHILOSOPHY

1
EXPANDING THE CANON OF JEWISH PHILOSOPHY: TOWARD AN APPRECIATION OF GENRE

If Alfred North Whitehead is correct and the history of Western philosophy is but a footnote to Plato, then in much of this history we encounter a struggle for the proper literary form to present philosophy. How, for example, does one portray a living, philosophical encounter in a written text? Unlike many difficult and often highly unliterary works of philosophy that would come after him, Plato's dialogues remain a testament to the portrayal of philosophy as a way of life. The fine balance that Plato strikes between the philosophical and the literary permits entry into a narrative that unfolds in front of the reader, thereby allowing him or her to struggle actively with the ideas presented within. Although the philosophical dialogue would in the centuries after Plato go in and out of vogue, the spirit illuminating it—the encounter between antagonistic views, the attempt to convince another of the incorrectness of his or her arguments, and an ultimate resolution—sought to breathe life into a written text.

What follows examines this genre in medieval and early modern Jewish philosophy. Unlike many analyses, this study does not focus on disembodied ideas or arguments, but on a particular genre, the dialogue, showing how it was deployed, geographically and temporally, by a number of different authors. My operating assumption is that a text's contents cannot be neatly separated from its form. By tracing a particular genre through time and space, locating various examples in specific contexts, I hope to pose and subsequently answer a series of questions: Why did various authors choose this genre as opposed to others? What did the dialogue allow a particular thinker to accomplish that other genres did not? How are the literary features of the dialogue used to construct a philosophical argument? What, in turn, is the nature of the relationship between Jewish philosophical dialogues and those composed by non-Jews? The answers to such questions will, I trust, contribute to our appreciation of the dynamics of Jewish philosophical writing.

The literary dialogue was but one of several genres that Jewish thinkers employed to articulate their philosophical programs. By philosophical dialogue I mean nothing more than a series of narrative exchanges between two or more distinct characters whose conversations revolve around a number of philosophical issues. These dialogues usually take place in a particular narrative setting, and through the various exchanges, we witness the development of not only a set of philosophical arguments but also the protagonists' personalities. This genre conveniently allows an author to present a particular argument, raise a number of counterarguments to it, and subsequently refute such counterarguments, thereby providing a natural venue for the philosophical enterprise.[1]

A closer examination will also reveal that Jewish philosophical dialogues tended to be composed at times when this genre was relatively popular in larger non-Jewish cultures. In the Jewish philosophical dialogue, then, we witness both a Jewish response to non-Jewish ideas, and a convenient narrative setting whereby we can get a better sense of the social and polemical production of Jewish philosophy. An analysis of this genre reveals that dialogues are not just about the ideas contained within, but that these ideas tend to constellate around a number of literary, aesthetic, and rhetorical features. These features, far from marginal, are often as important as the actual contents of the work.

Informing this study is the desire to contribute to the expansion of our understanding of Jewish philosophy—its genesis, its dissemination, its relationship to literature and literary creativity—by studying what James T. Robinson calls its "secondary forms."[2] The examination of medieval Jewish philosophy, still primarily indebted to the ideals and categories of *Wissenschaft des Judentums,* is based on a number of premises that are regarded as axiomatic. These include putting prime emphasis on ideas, often divorced from specific textual contexts. A good example of this is the *Kuzari* by Judah Halevi, in which, despite his claim at the beginning of the work that he does not necessarily agree with everything the character of the *ḥaver* will say, the tendency is to discuss the views of this character as if he were simply Halevi's mouthpiece.[3]

Another feature of the *Wissenschaft* model is its focus on great men (e.g., Halevi, Maimonides, Gersonides) and their great texts (e.g., *Kuzari, Guide of the Perplexed, Wars of the Lord*). Yet, as great as these thinkers were and as brilliant and important as their treatises are for understanding the history of Jewish philosophy, this approach only tells part of the story.[4] Often left unanswered are questions such as the following: How did these "great works" take hold in various Jewish cultures? How did other Jewish thinkers, the so-called "epigones," react and respond to such texts?[5] An examination of secondary forms enables us to begin to answer such questions by understanding the various ways in which philosophical ideas were received and subsequently disseminated to a larger reading public.

Two caveats are in order at the beginning of this study. First, some kind of definition of what I mean by *Jewish philosophy* is in order.[6] Jewish philosophy is a modern term; none of the thinkers discussed in this study, with the possible exception of those mentioned in the epilogue, would have employed it, considered themselves to have been "Jewish philosophers," or engaged in an activity we today recognize as "Jewish philosophy." Despite this, it is nevertheless possible to identify a phenomenon for heuristic purposes regardless of whether acknowledged or mentioned by the object of study. In the present case, one can define Jewish philosophy as the reading of Jewish sources (e.g., the Bible, the Talmud, midrashim) through philosophical lenses inherited from non-Jewish cultures. The benefits of employing the term *Jewish philosophy,* it seems to me, far outweigh those of not using it. This definition, however, immediately alerts us to the fact that philosophy is not autochthonous to Judaism. It proclaims Jewish philosophy as a response, whether positive or negative, to larger non-Jewish intellectual forces. In many ways, the present study supports this thesis: when Jewish philosophers wrote dialogues they often did so to respond to dialogues written by non-Jews.

Secondly, I have no intention of denigrating studies of Jewish philosophy that focus solely on elucidating the content of texts. This approach has been too valuable and important to make into a straw man. Indeed, a quick perusal of the reference notes to the present study will reveal to just what an extent my debt is to such work. A study that focuses on secondary forms, in other words, can only take place after the elucidation of so-called "primary forms." The present work, then, naturally builds upon, expands, and hopefully will reinform such studies by showing further the richness and beauty of Jewish philosophical texts.

As I argued in my previous book, *The Texture of the Divine,* there has been a tendency in studies devoted to Jewish philosophy, especially in the medieval period, to gravitate toward the "grand" themes of the Western intellectual tradition: metaphysics, ontology, epistemology, and ethics.[7] While there is certainly nothing inherently wrong with such an approach, it tends to marginalize other features of this tradition, such as aesthetics, poetics, and rhetoric. *The Art of Dialogue in Jewish Philosophy* seeks to contribute further to these traditionally marginalized fields by examining the important nexus between philosophy and literature. Many of the thinkers discussed in this work did not consider themselves to be simply philosophers. For instance, all wrote poetry and/or other forms of literature. As poets or as litterateurs, all were surely aware of, consciously or otherwise, the literary and aesthetic conventions that governed artistic creativity in their respective cultures. I work on the assumption that these literary, artistic, and aesthetic sensibilities left traces within their philosophical compositions, and that these are retrievable.

Furthermore, dialogues, when read properly, function as windows through which we are able to examine both a specific author in addition to the broader community of which he was a part. Consequently, the various debates that arise in these dialogues are not simply theoretical, but reflect the various religious, intellectual, and social issues of the day. These issues were often extremely vitriolic, for at stake was Judaism's orientation to other cultures. For instance, what texts should Jews read? Should non-Jewish scientific sources play a role in the Jewish educational curriculum? All of the authors analyzed in this study confront and essentially attempt to mediate these various tensions. For example, when Halevi rebels against the dominant intellectual and spiritual reading of Judaism offered by his contemporaries, he does so not as an individual but as a spokesperson for what he considers to be the authentic Jewish tradition. Or, when Isaac Polleqar composes a dialogue between an astrologer and a philosopher, he does so not simply because it makes for a quaint or entertaining conversation but because he saw astrology as antagonistic to free will, one of the hallmarks of his rational understanding of religion. The astrologer, in other words, is not simply a literary character but a metonym for an ideology that Polleqar regarded as insidious, and one that, based on his vitriol, must certainly have made significant inroads in contemporaneous Jewish culture.

The dialogue thus becomes an important locus through which we are able to confront firsthand the dynamics, often nonphilosophical, behind the composition of Jewish philosophy. Yet although virtually all were written as responses, we should not however assume that the reasons behind each text's composition were necessarily the same. These responses could be subversive, as in the case of Halevi, showing how non-Jewish philosophical ideas—themselves expressed in dialogue form—threaten Jewish authenticity. His response is to overturn the rules of the genre by employing terms and categories in ways that defy contemporaneous literary expectations. Others, most notably Judah Abravanel, employed the genre because they really had no choice: the dialogue was such a popular genre in Renaissance Humanism, following the rediscovery and translation of the Platonic corpus, that it became one of the primary vehicles whereby philosophers expressed their ideas, especially those on love. In order to absorb and ultimately respond to such ideas, Abravanel had to use this genre. That he did so and that his own dialogue became a best-seller is a testament to both his literary and philosophical abilities.

A Brief History of the Dialogue in Judaism

Judaism possesses a venerable and ancient tradition of dialogue, at least broadly conceived. Indeed, one could quite easily argue that the history of the Jewish people from antiquity to the present is essentially the story of a series of dialogues and silences between God and Israel. The covenantal relationship, in other words, is one that is based on two sides communicating to each other through time. However, much like the notion of dialogue in modern Jewish philosophy, this idea of God and Israel engaged in a constant conversation is a concept or process, and not necessarily a literary encounter portrayed using a particular genre. The one real exception is the book of Job wherein we encounter a literal dialogue that revolves around a number of philosophical themes such as theodicy, freedom of will, suffering of the righteous, and so on, including often ambiguous resolutions to such issues. Not surprisingly, then, many Jewish philosophers, beginning with Saadia Gaon (882–942),[8] gravitated to the book of Job and read it as a philosophical dialogue dealing with God's providential relationship to humans.

Moreover, the phenomenon of disputation and literature plays a central role in the various sources of rabbinic Judaism (e.g., Talmud, midrashim). Many of the stories that appear in the Babylonian Talmud, as Jeffrey L. Rubenstein has well noted, gave the sages an opportunity "to ponder the tensions inherent in their culture, not an easy means of resolving them."[9] Much like the philosophical dialogues examined here, a proper understanding of rabbinic stories is contingent upon the broader literary, historical, and intellectual environments in which Jews found themselves (i.e., those of late antiquity).[10] Despite the prevalence for both disputation and stories, the existence of literal dialogues is relatively rare in this literature. One important exception, however, is the series of exchanges between Rabbi Judah the Prince and the enigmatic Antoninus, believed to be a Roman governor or emperor.[11] In these dialogues, the two characters discuss a number of issues that we could loosely label as philosophical (e.g., when life begins, the afterlife).

Despite examples such as Job and the dialogic encounters of Rabbi Judah and Antoninus, there is no evidence that when Jewish philosophers decided to compose dialogues they looked to this body of literature. For example, although Jewish philosophers wrote commentaries to Job, they rarely focused on the dialogic aspect or aspects of the work. They were, in other words, primarily interested in the contents of the work, and not its form.

A more likely candidate for the composition of Jewish philosophical dialogues would seem to be Plato. As generally acknowledged today, Plato is the true master of the philosophical dialogue. His creations are so effective precisely because they are not monologues, wherein an author expatiates at length on a single topic, but are a series of living encounters between moral agents.[12] The reader is drawn into these encounters and, much like the slave boy in *Meno*,[13] comes to the realization that he or she already possesses knowledge, only that it has yet to be articulated.[14] Socrates, in other words, helps not only his companions, but also the reader, both to clarify and to order what they already know. As literature, Platonic dialogues enable the reader to take an active role in the treatise. Plato thus succeeds in engaging, arousing, shocking, and amusing the reader,[15] thereby permitting him or her to make intellectual progress as the work unfolds.

Despite such an obvious precursor to medieval Jewish dialogues, it seems highly unlikely that Jewish or medieval thinkers had firsthand knowledge of the Platonic corpus. In a landmark essay from 1940, Franz Rosenthal argues that complete translations of Platonic dialogues,

> according to the information obtainable from Arabic Bibliographies, were made very rarely. Not a single one of them has come down to us, and the character of those quotations which we have before us, never seems, as far as we can now judge, to afford grounds for the slightest probability that we are concerned with the remains of a pure and complete text of a Platonic Dialogue.[16]

It would seem that the majority of Platonic texts that reached the Arabs did so by way of Galen's summaries.[17] Islamic and Jewish philosophers, then, had knowledge of the contents but not necessarily the original forms of the *Sophist, Cratylus, Euthydemus, Statesman, Timaeus, Laws*,[18] and *Parmenides*, in addition to a paraphrase of the *Republic*.[19] Another important source for knowledge of Plato came from the compilation of his sayings included in *Nawadir al-falasifāʾ wa al-ḥukamāʾ* (Anecdotes of Philosophers and Sages) by Ḥunayn ibn Isḥāq (809–893). These latter sayings, however, often had no relation to Plato's actual works. On the contrary, they became convenient ways to attach a famous name to various sayings that circulated in the Islamicate world.[20] Even though knowledge of the form of the Platonic dialogues seems to have been wanting in the medieval Islamicate world, the figure of Socrates played an important role in the literature associated with this period. This, however, was neither the Socrates of history nor the Socrates of the Platonic dialogue. To use the words of Ilai Alon,

> On the one hand the original Greek Socrates, whoever or whatever he was, as described and alluded to by Plato, Xenophon, and Aristophanes, was

> vaguely remembered, and on the other hand, some new traits, entirely alien to him, were added throughout the centuries of the existence of that legend. Socrates's name seems to have been known by many Arabs, and the details of his biography were often regarded as an ideal to be imitated.[21]

The Socrates of medieval Islamicate civilization was thus a pliable symbol that could be used either to uphold certain values deemed religiously significant or to show the danger of philosophy to religion. Of especial significance for understanding the former were numerous pithy sayings attributed to Socrates in which he celebrates earthly death (e.g., "Think lightly of death, for its bitterness lies in fearing it")[22] or stresses various ethical principles (e.g., "A king, seeing Socrates wearing a worn-out woolen garment during a festival, said to him, 'I wished you had adorned yourself on such a day.' Socrates said to him, 'No ornament is more beautiful than justice, for it is one of the intellect's noblest faculties.'").[23] Even the anti-rationalist al-Ghazālī (d. 1111), although generally critical of Socrates as a pagan and a philosopher,[24] nonetheless favorably quotes anecdotes attributed to him about the fleeting nature of this world.[25]

So, despite the modern importance of the Platonic dialogue to Western thought, it is highly unlikely, if not outright impossible, that the Platonic method of composition would have influenced anyone in this study prior to Judah Abravanel. Before Renaissance Humanists began their translation project of the Platonic corpus, only a small number of garbled Platonic translations existed.[26] It was only in Abravanel's generation, then, that we witness the first full-scale editions and translations of Plato's dialogues. This is not to say that the character of Socrates did not play a role in the philosophical or even the popular imagination before the Renaissance, only that the ideas of Plato did not circulate in dialogue form. The result is that only those Jewish thinkers after Abravanel would have had access to the full Platonic corpus. For example, Moses Mendelssohn, early in his career, intended to translate certain of these dialogues into German. Moreover, although his *Phaedon* rewrites or updates for a German-speaking audience Plato's dialogue of the same name, in places, especially at the beginning, it virtually copies its Platonic model word for word.[27]

If the origins of the Jewish philosophical dialogue can be found neither in biblical literature nor the Platonic corpus, then it would seem that we would have to look elsewhere for its origins. Yet, I argue that there really is no point of origin for Jewish philosophical dialogues because when Jews wrote them they were responding to non-Jewish dialogues written at roughly the same time. Moreover, as with the quest for "origins" more generally, even if we could pinpoint with any degree of accuracy the origins of these dialogues, it would not necessarily follow that we would understand the dynamics of this genre any better.

Having said this, though, it seems likely that some of the earliest non-Jewish dialogues that Jews would have encountered originated not from the Greek-speaking world, but the Arabo-Islamic one. One of the earliest examples of an Islamic dialogue is Abū Ḥayyān al-Tawḥīdī's (ca. 930–1023) record of a debate between the grammarian Abū Saʿīd al-Sīrāfī (d. 979) and Abū Bishr Mattā b. Yūnus (d. 940).[28] Mattā b. Yūnus, one of the teachers of al-Fārābī, argues in this dialogue that logic is a universal science and thus is central to clear thinking; al-Sīrāfī, who by all accounts wins the debate, counters that logic is not universal, but a Greek linguistic habit, and consequently unnecessary for Arab speakers, who have all they need in the rules of Arabic grammar.

In addition, the first dialogue studied below—Halevi's *Kuzari*—was composed in an Arabo-Islamic environment, within which certain subcultures used the genre of the dialogue to articulate their religious, spiritual, or intellectual programs. One of the primary groups to employ the dialogue was that of the Ismaʿilis, who seem to have inherited the genre, as they did many other phenomena, from various esoteric groups of late antiquity.[29] In particular, certain treatises in the *Corpus Hermeticum* were written as dialogues, wherein gods reveal esoteric and philosophical truths to their pupils. The actual chains of transmission of this literature from late antiquity to the early Islamic world are, however, very difficult to reconstruct, primarily owing to the fact that it is virtually impossible to know what exactly the earliest Ismaʿilis were reading and, equally importantly, in what literary forms or genres.[30]

Another important and early Islamicate dialogue may be found in the debate between animals and humans in the Ismaʿili-influenced *Rasāʾil Ikhwān al-Ṣafāʾ* (Epistles of the Brethren of Purity).[31] This work, in addition to various proselytizing works composed by Ismaʿili missionaries designed to appeal to the philosophically inclined, would have circulated throughout Muslim Spain.[32] It would seem that these dialogues—and not biblical, rabbinic, or Platonic ones—served as the immediate influence on the composition of Jewish philosophical dialogues. Individuals such as ibn Gabirol, Baḥya ibn Paquda, and Abraham ibn Ezra seem to have composed their dialogues under the sphere of influence of this Ismaʿili philosophical spirituality. Judah Halevi, on the other hand, composed his dialogue as a way to subvert this sphere of influence. When Jews wrote philosophical dialogues, to reiterate, it was a response to non-Jewish dialogues. And although these non-Jewish dialogues may well have drawn inspiration from Plato, Cicero, or Augustine, until the Renaissance Jewish thinkers seem neither to have known nor to have had ready access to such texts.

A Preliminary Contextual and Literary Analysis

Most premodern philosophers do not tell us why they have chosen to write in a particular genre. Of all the dialogues examined below, only Halevi informs us of such details, although his rationale—to retell imaginatively the factors leading to the fabled existence of a Jewish kingdom somewhere in the Caucasus—is not particularly informative when it comes to answering the question of why a dialogue as opposed to some other genre (e.g., epistolary treatise). Since all of the authors are silent on this issue, let me suggest some features that dialogues presented to an author, and why such features might have naturally lent themselves to the philosophical enterprise. As will become obvious in the following chapters, each dialogue was written in response to local internal and external forces, and I certainly have no intention of insinuating that these forces were identical in each text that I examine. However, it does become possible to illumine a number of features that revolve around most, if not all, of the dialogues discussed here. Before examining each of the dialogues chronologically, then, let me articulate certain features, commonalities, and issues that I will subsequently reintroduce as heuristic devices in subsequent chapters.

Although these treatises are dialogues in the sense that they deploy a series of textual interactions between two or more characters in a specific setting, it is important not to assume that all of the dialogues function in the same manner. To this end, I have given each of the chapters a subtitle that I contend accurately reflects the specific contents of each particular work. These subtitles do not so much reflect a typology of Jewish philosophical dialogues as they capture the main theme or themes of the work in question.

Having said this, though, it becomes obvious fairly quickly that the earliest dialogues are highly polemical in intent. The *Kuzari, Iggeret ha-Vikuaḥ,* and *Ezer ha-Dat* all involve polemics between a character who is, at least ideologically, related to the author of the text and one or more characters who hold opposing positions. All of these dialogues involve the protagonist successfully convincing these antagonists that he alone holds the correct view on any given topic. Often, once the original antagonist accepts that his prior convictions are incorrect and that his protagonist's arguments are well founded, the dialogue moves from polemics to conversation. This leads to the further elucidation of a number of key issues that were briefly touched upon in the initial polemical exchange.

The two later dialogues, the *Dialoghi d'amore* and *Phaedon*, however, lack this polemical tone. The main characters in these two works tend to interact in more friendly terms. That is, the antagonists do not hold radically different ideological perspectives, but function as characters whose dialogical interactions with the protagonist bring the intellectual encounters to completion. Ideological antagonists of the earlier dialogues thus give way to conversational partners in the later ones. Indeed, in the case of the *Dialoghi* we are not even sure who the protagonist is. Although the natural assumption is that it is Philo, as the text progresses we see that it is actually the *female* character of Sophia, someone who is unwilling to accept truth on the authority of the past, who embodies most fully the traits of a Renaissance thinker. In Mendelssohn's *Phaedon*, Socrates does not debate Sophists in order to show their ignorance and their logical inconsistencies; rather, he converses with his disciples on his deathbed, trying to convince them of the soul's immortality and providence.[33] Finally, in the epilogue we will see how the concept of dialogue is replaced by that of dialogic, a principle that no longer requires the literary genre that is the subject of this study. In modern Jewish philosophy, then, it is the spontaneity of the dialogic encounter that gives way to an authentic relationship with others and ultimately God.

All of the dialogues that appear in this study publicize, popularize, or disseminate philosophical teachings to as wide an audience as possible. They do this primarily by encoding philosophical ideas in a pleasing literary form. By giving a philosophical treatise various characters, a plot, and a setting, philosophers create texts that work on a number of different levels. A philosophically inclined reader is able to encounter in such a treatise a work of philosophy; a more literary-minded reader is able to see in the same text a work of literature. It is, however, mistaken to ignore one of these aspects at the expense of the other; for it is ultimately the intersection of philosophy and literature that is not only one of the hallmarks of these dialogues, but the main reason for their popularity. Perhaps nowhere is this more evident than in the extreme, almost uncanny, popularity that Judah Abravanel's *Dialoghi d'amore* and Mendelssohn's *Phaedon* enjoyed—not so much among Jewish audiences, but among non-Jewish ones.

The subject of chapter 2, the *Kuzari* of Judah Halevi, shows how a thinker used the dialogue to subvert treatises written by his contemporaries who, not surprisingly, articulated their own visions of Judaism in dialogues. The genre, then, enabled Halevi to portray an intellectual encounter, especially in the first book of the *Kuzari*, wherein a philosopher, a Muslim, a Christian, and a Jew put their cases before a king who sits as an independent judge.[34] The speeches that Halevi puts in the mouths of the non-Jewish characters are, unbeknownst to them, full of irony and humor, making for a highly entertaining encounter between a number of antagonists. In these encounters, the audience undoubtedly discerns the erroneous claims to monotheism made by various subcultures through Halevi's skillful use of literary terms and tropes.

It is probably no coincidence that other thinkers used such literary and often highly entertaining features of the dialogue to popularize their rationalizing agendas. Increasingly in the thirteenth and fourteenth centuries, this genre became intertwined with the Maimonidean controversies, which witnessed a vitriolic struggle for what Jewish culture should look like.[35] Accordingly, dialogues—in addition to sermons and philosophical biblical commentaries—played a large role in disseminating Maimonidean principles to various audiences that neither understood Arabic nor were trained in the technical dimensions of philosophy. For example, Shem Tov ibn Falaquera composed at least two treatises, *Iggeret ha-Vikuaḥ* (The Epistle of the Debate) and *Sefer ha-Mevaqqesh* (The Book of the Seeker), as dialogues. The former work—a dialogue between a philosopher and a rabbinic scholar—allowed Falaquera to justify, on legal grounds, the importance of the study of philosophy.[36] The latter work, in contrast, is a series of dialogues between a student and various teachers who represent the medieval philosophical curriculum. This dialogue both popularizes the study of philosophy and functions as an encyclopedia of the various Aristotelian sciences. In like manner, Polleqar composed his highly literary *Ezer ha-Dat* in the form of a dialogue in order to defend Maimonideanism against, inter alia, astrology and kabbalah, two tools that were used by the philosophically sophisticated Abner of Burgos to justify his apostasy.[37] The dialogue became a convenient way for Polleqar to refute, point-by-point, Abner's arguments, and also to show others the philosophical principles behind this refutation.

Even a work such as Judah Abravanel's *Dialoghi* has an important pedagogical function. Here it is important to remember that Abravanel was one of the earliest Jewish thinkers to write in Italian,[38] and was also one of the first Jews to engage seriously and systematically with the main tenets of Renaissance Humanism. His *Dialoghi d'amore,* written in a highly literary and engaging style, reaches out to as broad an audience as possible, both Jewish and non-Jewish, in order to show that the rational truths associated with the Renaissance were not only the same as, but also derived from, those of the Hebrew Bible. In order to be a good Jew, then, one had to embrace Renaissance ideals, which are ultimately no different from the ideals of Judaism.

Mendelssohn's *Phaedon* also plays an important role in the popularization and dissemination of philosophical ideals. In rewriting Plato's work of the same name, Mendelssohn was able to articulate in a highly literary fashion many of the themes of eighteenth-century natural religion (e.g., the soul's immortality). This pleasing literary style, its poetic prose, and the fact that it was one of the first works of the German Enlightenment written in the form of a dialogue undoubtedly led to the general popularity of the work.

All of the authors thus saw in the dialogue a convenient mechanism to formulate and subsequently popularize philosophical principles. Moreover, all of these authors popularized such principles in response to what they considered to be pressing social issues. In other words, dialogues were not just philosophical texts, but were also convenient vehicles for articulating various forms of Jewish authenticity, whether particularistic in the case of Halevi, or universalistic in the case of the others. Yet even those emphasizing the universalistic element of Judaism nevertheless still felt compelled, as I shall show throughout this study, to stress that it was only in Judaism that one truly encountered such universalism.

Dialogues also allowed various authors to present an argument in an artificially controlled or, perhaps even better, an ideal environment. The dialogue thus enabled an author to bring together a series of opinions, arguments, ideas, or ideologies that were opposed to his own and put them in the mouth of a literary antagonist over which the author had ultimate control. Although these literary antagonists may, on occasion, surprise us with the deftness of their arguments or the quality of their responses, the victor and the ultimate outcome of polemical dialogues are never in any real doubt.

On one level, this feature makes these dialogues seem artificial. The antagonists' arguments are often too easily deflated or mocked in these textual settings, when in reality the situation was probably much more precarious or vitriolic. This is not to say that we do not get glimpses of the reality behind these textual encounters. The best example of this may be found in Falaquera's *Iggeret ha-Vikuaḥ* when the *ḥasid,* the character who embodies the rabbinic-legal tradition, threatens the philosophical protagonist, the philosopher or *ḥakham,* with "excommunication" (*nidui*) if he does not agree with his arguments or finds them too far removed from mainstream rabbinic positions. The threat of excommunication was a central feature of the Maimonidean controversies, with adherents on opposing sides using it on their adversaries. Although this example from Falaquera is really an exception to the rule, this is not that surprising given the fact that dialogues functioned as important vehicles of dissemination. These texts, in other words, had to have clear resolutions if they were to popularize philosophical teachings. For example, there cannot be any doubt at the beginning of the *Kuzari* which monotheism the king will adopt. Likewise in *Ezer ha-Dat,* the strict determinism of the astrologer (a stand-in for Abner of Burgos) cannot be seen to trump the freedom of will of the philosopher (a stand-in for Polleqar).

Furthermore, Halevi makes the philosopher who appears briefly at the beginning of the *Kuzari* into an individual who makes a complete mockery of the king's dream.[39] Whereas the king wants to know how to improve his actions (*aʿmāl*) so that they may be brought into harmony with his proper intentions (*niyyāt*), the philosopher's response is completely insensitive to the king's plea:

> There is no favor or dislike in [the nature of] God, because he is above desire and will. A desire intimates a want in the person who feels it, and not until it is satisfied does he become complete. . . . God, therefore, does not know you, much less your intentions or actions [*niyyāt wa-aʿmāl*], nor does he listen to your prayers or see your movements.[40]

By putting these words into the philosopher's mouth, Halevi quickly, and one could say all too easily, dismisses the philosopher from the dialogue (in much the same way that he will do with both the Christian and the Muslim).[41]

Another clear example of how the dialogue enables an author to dispose of antagonistic positions may be found in Polleqar's highly sarcastic dismissal of astrology. Following a lengthy and often acrimonious exchange between a philosopher and an astrologer, the latter subsequently admits that all of his instruments and predictions were meant to give him respect and a high social standing. This reversal is extreme and is essentially confined to *Ezer ha-Dat.* Not nearly as extreme is Falaquera's *Iggeret ha-Vikuaḥ,* wherein the *ḥakham* manages to convince the *ḥasid,* using a variety of legal arguments, that the study of philosophy is required for pious Jews, in addition to being legally binding.

Halevi informs us at the beginning of the *Kuzari* that we should be cautious of assuming a simple correspondence between an author of a dialogue and his main character.[42] Although we tend to equate the *ḥaver* with Halevi, the *ḥakham* with Falaquera, or the various characters who espouse philosophy in *Ezer ha-Dat* with Polleqar, there is not necessarily a one-to-one correspondence between author and main protagonist. Because of this, I spend considerable time in each chapter delineating the various characteristics and personalities that the authors give to their textual protagonists. Sometimes it seems that these characters are based loosely on actual individuals, for example, Abner of Burgos in the case of the various antagonists in Polleqar's *Ezer ha-Dat.* In a similar way, the debate between the *ḥakham* and the *ḥasid* in Falaquera's *Iggeret ha-Vikuaḥ* seems to have been based on real epistolary debates between David Kimḥi and Judah Alfakar.[43]

Other characters that we encounter in these dialogues are mythic or allegorical. Halevi's *Kuzari,* much like Mendelssohn's *Phaedon,* claims to retell past encounters, although updated for a contemporary reading public. Despite such a claim, however, Halevi primarily creates ex nihilo the mise-en-scène, debates, and subsequent conversations between the Khazar king and the various spokespeople with rival claims on monotheism. Halevi thus gives an amorphous story a firm narrative articulation, which enables him to make his case for a particular reading of Judaism. In the same manner, Mendelssohn uses Plato's dialogue of the same name to update Socrates' arguments, in addition to putting new arguments in the mouth of Socrates in order to formulate his own position on natural religion.

In like manner, it is also important to take into account the narrative settings of the dialogic encounters between characters. Rather than regard these settings as haphazard or simply a matter of convenience, I contend that they play a role in the actual contents of these works and contribute to the emergence and subsequent unfolding of the work's argument.

Although not all of the dialogues are concerned with the settings in which the encounters take place (e.g., *Iggeret ha-Vikuaḥ*), the majority are. Falaquera's other work examined here, *Sefer ha-Mevaqqesh,* for example, follows a seeker of knowledge who, in his quest, moves from teacher to teacher in the search for wisdom. This seeker spends considerable time with each teacher before moving on to the next. During each encounter, we are given brief descriptions of that teacher's workshop and place of employment, or receive an account of their duties.

In like manner, in the *Kuzari* all of the spokespeople for rival monotheisms must come to the king's court in Khazaria in order to make their case. This gives way, as other have duly noted,[44] to a situation in which the Khazar king, occupying a position of secular authority, judges presumably with equanimity between these rival religious claims. Moreover, the fact that he chooses Judaism, the "despised" religion, adds to Halevi's argument that only in rabbinic Judaism does there exist a "spiritual" authenticity deriving from the historical bond between God and Israel.

The author who spends the most detail on creating and describing various settings is Isaac Polleqar. The various dialogues recounted in *Ezer ha-Dat* take place in a number of significant venues. For instance a "young" man (*naʿar*) who is a philosopher and an "old" man (*zaqen*) opposed to philosophy acrimoniously debate the true nature of Judaism, the proper reading of Jewish sources, and the place of non-Jewish science in Jewish education. To add to the intensity of the circumstances and to show just what is at stake in their debate, all of this takes place on the cobbled streets of Jerusalem. Moreover, in a debate between an astrologer and another philosopher everything occurs in an open market where the astrologer, with his astrolabes and compasses displayed before him on a table, pitches his wares to a willing crowd. That the philosopher must debate the astrologer in front of this crowd tells the reading audience to just what an extent astrology had taken hold in Jewish society of the fourteenth century. That the philosopher ultimately triumphs before such an inhospitable crowd is certainly no coincidence and is indeed symbolic of the philosopher's place in society. Moreover, when the astrologer admits he is defeated, he joins the philosopher in debating the crowd.

Even when the setting is not described in any particular detail, it can be equally effective. Juxtaposed against the rich descriptions of Polleqar is Abravanel's virtual silence on where the dialogic encounters between Philo and Sophia take place. In particular, we are privy to a series of intimate conversations between a female, presumably unmarried, and a male, also presumably single, in some kind of private setting in which they are not interrupted.[45] The subsequent teasing and provocative dialogue that emerges out of this undefined setting adds to the erotic tensions and innuendo, in turn contributing to the philosophical discussion of love as both a cosmic and a sensual principle.

Although inherent to the genre is a certain artificiality, we must also attune ourselves to the many surprises that can and do occur in these dialogues. The author, then, does not simply manipulate the conversation between characters to move the treatise in a particular way. Indeed, one of the great surprises at the end of the *Kuzari* is that it is ultimately the rabbi who is transformed and, based on his dialogue with the king, comes to the realization that the *intention* (*niyya*) to move to Israel is not enough, but that he must *act* (*ᶜamala*) on this intention.

In the dialogues of Falaquera and Polleqar, we encounter textual records of living debates that shook Jewish cultures of the day. Although, as noted above, the outcomes of these dialogues are never in serious doubt, the genre puts on display various characters' emotions, revealing just what was at stake in these discussions. I mentioned above the threat of the ban raised by Falaquera's *ḥasid,* a threat that was very much a part of the Maimonidean controversies of the age. Likewise the various antagonists who oppose philosophy in *Ezer ha-Dat* are not straw men, whose arguments can be easily dismissed. Although the astrologer ultimately capitulates, the strengths of some of his arguments linger. This undoubtedly is because if we scratch the surface of this astrologer we find the problematic figure of Abner of Burgos.

Similarly, the character of Sophia in the *Dialoghi* does not simply feed convenient questions to Philo to move the dialogue along; she has a personality of her own and often disagrees and debates with Philo.[46] Sophia, then, is not just a convenient textual strategy, but a character in her own right, one who significantly contributes to the philosophical discourse.[47] Indeed, the end of the *Dialoghi* has Philo still requesting from Sophia that she fulfill her "obligation" to him for his lessons on the discourse of love (*pensa di pagare tu a me li debiti che amore ragione e virtú t'obligano*).[48] The sexual tension between the characters, despite the lengthy discussions of love and desire as philosophical principles, remains.

As mentioned above, the study of dialogues enables us to get a sense of the various forces behind the composition of Jewish philosophical texts. Moreover, as will become clear in detail throughout this study, all of these dialogues were written not just for the reasons listed above, but primarily to provide a distinctly Jewish response to non-Jewish ideas, many of which were themselves written and disseminated in the form of dialogues. These non-Jewish ideas and genres—whether developed by Ismaᶜilis, apostates to Catholicism, Renaissance Humanists, or Enlightenment thinkers—made impressions, sometimes positively, other times negatively, on Jewish philosophers. If non-Jews had not expressed their ideas in dialogue form, then perhaps Jews would have been unlikely to have composed dialogues. This, in turn, raises larger issues for the production of Jewish philosophy, issues to which I shall return, time and again, in the following chapters.

Selection of Dialogues

I have chosen these dialogues either because I could not easily ignore them or because, it seemed to me, they had been unduly neglected in the main narrative of Jewish philosophy. The perfect example of the former is Halevi's *Kuzari,* easily one of the best-known texts in the Jewish philosophical canon, despite the fact that it mounts a sustained critique of the philosophical program of his day. Another example of a well-known dialogue that I examine is Judah Abravanel's *Dialoghi d'amore.* This work, however, is more problematic in the study of Jewish philosophy. As I shall show in detail in chapter 5, although relatively well known, its Jewish "credentials" are often questioned. How can a treatise written in Italian and that hardly mentions Jewish concerns be a work of Jewish philosophy? I contend that it is a very Jewish dialogue, and that it also enables us to witness one of the earliest Jewish responses to the "universalism" of the Renaissance. Although not interested in *explicitly* interpreting Jewish sources in the light of the Renaissance, Abravanel nevertheless mounts a Jewish response to the claims of Christian Humanism.

I have also chosen to look at a number of dialogues that are often marginalized or left out of the unofficial canon of Jewish philosophy. Probably the best example of this is the work of Isaac Polleqar. His *Ezer ha-Dat*, perhaps the most elaborate of the dialogues examined here, has for the most part been ignored in the modern study of Jewish philosophical texts. A few years ago one could have made the same case with respect to Falaquera. However, the pioneering studies of, inter alia, Steven Harvey[49] and Raphael Jospe[50] have gone a long way to making him a fairly well known thinker. The chapter that I devote to Falaquera builds upon the work of these scholars by focusing upon his use of dialogue and the various relationships that develop between the textual protagonists.

A different example of a relatively ignored text, although for other reasons, is *Phaedon* by Moses Mendelssohn. This work, the product of his optimistic youth, is usually overlooked in favor of his more "Jewish" works such as *Jerusalem* or his preface to and German translation of Manasseh ben Israel's *Vindication of the Jews*. Even more so than Abravanel's *Dialoghi*, *Phaedon* makes no explicit reference to Judaism or Jewish sources. Indeed, if we did not know that its author was Jewish, we would *apparently* have no reason to believe that this treatise had anything whatsoever to do with Judaism. I try to make the case that it is possible to read *Phaedon* as a work of Jewish philosophy because in it we encounter, albeit in an underemphasized manner, a number of the themes and issues that will receive full attention and elaboration in Mendelssohn's later, more explicitly Jewish works.

A brief examination of the dates of all of the authors discussed in this study reveals that all lived in distinct Jewish cultures in the medieval and early modern periods. This wide geographic, temporal, and spatial framework enables me to examine the various localized contexts behind the production of such texts. I wanted to choose a set of texts with such a broad time frame and with disparate geographic environments in order to look more generally at Jewish philosophy than would be possible by examining one text or a set of texts within a particular historical moment. By examining the texts that I do, I hope both to follow a genre as it exists in various Jewish cultures and to provide meaningful generalizations about the genesis and dissemination of Jewish philosophy.

Any study that examines a particular set of texts leads almost inevitably, and perhaps justifiably, to this question: Why these texts and not others? Or, what about this additional text; surely it also contributes to the study of "x"? Let me try to offset some of this potential criticism and explain why I have examined these particular texts, and why I have opted not to include others. I should begin by saying that the scope of the present study is modest, and my greatest hope is that my contribution will encourage both new studies and a new appreciation of those dialogues not discussed here. Indeed, rather than regard this study as an end, I offer it as a point of departure for further exploration.

Dialogues proved to be a fairly popular genre among Jews of the medieval and early modern periods. This study represents an analysis of but one instance of this genre, that of Jewish philosophical dialogues. I have chosen, then, not to examine Jewish dialogues that are not philosophical. Although admittedly the line between a philosophical dialogue and a nonphilosophical dialogue can be very fine or even blurred, I do not examine important dialogues such as the highly literary *Taḥkemoni* by Judah al-Ḥarizi (1165–1225)[51] or the historical *Shevet Yehudah* by Shlomo ibn Verga (1460–1554).[52]

Perhaps more provocative is my omission of a number of dialogues that have a distinct philosophical content. One text in particular that I do not examine in any detail is the *Fons Vitae* or *Meqor Ḥayyim* ("Fountain of Life") by Shlomo ibn Gabirol (1021–ca. 1058). The primary reason for this lacuna is that, despite the fact that he uses a dialogue to record a conversation between a master and a disciple, the challenge is not an integral part of the work. The disciple conveniently supplies questions to the master, who subsequently clarifies matters for the student.

In fact, so contrived is the dialogue in this treatise that Shem Tov ibn Falaquera, who translated the work into Hebrew, seems to have concluded with Abraham ibn Daᶜud (ca. 1110–ca. 1180) that "perhaps if [the *Meqor Ḥayyim*'s] contents were refined, [ibn Gabirol's] words could be included in [a treatise that is] less than one tenth of that treatise."[53] When Falaquera translated the work, he chose—despite the fact that he himself wrote philosophical dialogues—not to retain the dialogue form but simply to summarize the main points.

Despite the fact that I do not spend much time on ibn Gabirol's *Meqor Ḥayyim*, I do, however, examine it in the chapter devoted to Halevi's *Kuzari*. In particular, I argue that Halevi composed his magnum opus, an informed and sustained critique of the philosophical enterprise, in the form of a dialogue because many of his Jewish contemporaries who were interested in tuning Judaism in a philosophical key did so using precisely the same genre. So, whereas ibn Gabirol's provides a fairly wooden dialogic exchange, we witness in Halevi's *Kuzari*, especially in the first book and in the conclusion, a dramatic and dynamic dialogic exchange between characters. Halevi thus does on the level of genre what he does on that of content.

Perhaps the other obvious example that I have chosen not to examine in detail is *Ḥai ha-Olamim* by Yohanan Alemanno (1435–ca. 1504). This work, written just prior to Judah Abravanel's *Dialoghi*, is a dialogue between two characters, one influenced by Maimonidean philosophy and the other by some of the new trends provided by the Renaissance (e.g., rhetoric). The subsequent debate is wide-ranging and encyclopedic,[54] and its main concern is the various stages of human development, showing how the various sciences lead to human perfection. There are several reasons why I do not go into any detail with this treatise. Primary is that, from a literary perspective, Abravanel's *Dialoghi* is a much more interesting work, and therefore allows me to investigate in greater detail than Alemanno's dialogue could the intersection between philosophy and literature. Secondly, the fact that the *Dialoghi* is written in the Italian vernacular as opposed to Hebrew, the language of *Ḥai ha-Olamim,* permits me to ask important questions on the nature of Jewish philosophy—for whom was it written? What are some of its literary intentions? How was it received in a non-Hebrew-speaking world?—than would be possible if I were to examine texts written solely in Hebrew. Thirdly, and intimately related to this last point, unlike *Ḥai ha-Olamim,* the subsequent afterlife of the *Dialoghi d'amore,* in both Jewish and non-Jewish cultures, makes this one of the most widely read works of Jewish philosophy in the premodern world.

Another possible lacuna in this study is that I have not chosen to examine in detail the role of dialogue and the dialogic in modern Jewish philosophy. The thought of philosophers such as Franz Rosenzweig (1886–1929) and Martin Buber (1878–1965) abounds with the concept of dialogue; in particular, how humans communicate with one another, and, through this communication, how they experience the divine presence. Indeed, Buber's entire notion of "I and Thou" (*Ich und Du*) is essentially a philosophy of dialogue.[55] The main reason that I have chosen not to analyze this phenomenon in modern Jewish philosophy is because in it the *concept of* dialogue tends to replace the *composition of* actual dialogues. The dialogic, in other words, takes precedence over the dialogue. This is not to say, however, that modern Jewish philosophers did not write dialogues. The young Buber, for example, wrote *Daniel,* a dialogue between the main character and a series of individuals, as a way to articulate his notion of authenticity. Despite the literary quality of this work, it does not seem to have played a major role in his subsequent philosophical system. In the epilogue to this study—"From Dialogue to Dialogic"—I briefly trace this metamorphosis.

Method, Aims, and Scope

Recent years have witnessed the critique of intellectual history as a study devoted solely to "great men," "great ideas," and/or "great texts" often at the expense of various marginalized groups (e.g., women, slaves, freedmen).[56] Intellectual history, according to this argument, is irrelevant at best because history is more than just the interests of elites, and at worst the perpetrator of various forms of imperialism against the disenfranchised. Increasingly, intellectual history is overlooked in favor of other disciplines within the humanities—such as social history, cultural studies, gender studies, queer theory, etc.—that seek to give voices to the traditionally voiceless. I certainly have no intention of polemicizing against such disciplines; indeed, I think that they have much to offer the study of philosophy and intellectual history. And, in the chapters that follow, I do not hesitate to embrace and use features from many of these disciplines in order to illumine, from a variety of perspectives, a set of philosophical texts. Despite this, however, intellectual history can and should play an important part in any interdisciplinary approach that seeks to understand premodern Jewish culture in all of its diversity.

Writing, be it literary or philosophical, is, to use the words of Daniel Boyarin, "one practice among many by which a culture organizes its production of meaning and values and structures itself."[57] My aim in what follows is not simply to read medieval philosophical texts as contributions to philosophy, but to connect such texts to the literary mechanisms by which specific Jewish cultures mediated (and continue to mediate) various social, cultural, and intellectual concerns. To regard such texts simply as the products of elites is to ignore the beliefs and cultural practices of Jews. As David Biale has argued,

> the intellectual elite does not exist in isolation, just as daily life does not remain in its own mute universe, unencumbered by intellectual reflection. . . . Those who produce cultural objects, whether written, visual, or material, can never be isolated from the larger social context, the everyday world, in which they live, just as those who belong to this larger world are not immune to the ideas and symbolic meanings that may be articulated by intellectuals. The relationship between text and context ought rather to be seen as the relationship between different types of texts, rather than between the "ideas" of elites versus the "material" reality of the wider society.[58]

In many ways, the charge that intellectual history emphasizes "elite" culture at the expense of "material" or "nonelite" culture risks reifying each term at the expense of nuance. Many of the thinkers examined in this study, for example, certainly belong to "elite" culture in the sense of their education, rabbinic training, and livelihood. Despite this, however, they all had concerns that were not far removed from the so-called "nonelites." The great majority of philosophers in Jewish history wrote both for other philosophers and also for nonphilosophers. Ibn Ezra, Maimonides, Gersonides, to name but a few of the biggest names of Jewish philosophy, all wrote treatises, including biblical commentaries, designed to introduce science into the traditional Jewish education curriculum.[59] In so doing, Jewish philosophers became important cultural mediators, not only between various Jewish communities and the larger cultures in which they found themselves, but also between Jewish and non-Jewish ideas.

The history of Judaism, at least until the contemporary period, is essentially the history of encounters and responses, both positive and negative, of Jews to non-Jews, non-Jewish ideas, cultures, and categories. Since Jewish philosophers essentially read Jewish sources using interpretive lenses derived from non-Jews, we are often able to witness in their writings some of these *initial* encounters and responses. Yet such ideas did not remain reified in philosophical texts, but were often filtered into nonphilosophical sources through a variety of mechanisms. One of the primary vehicles for such dissemination was through secondary forms. An in-depth study of one of these particular genres thus has the potential if not to break down the lines between "elites" and "nonelites," then at least to blunt their edges. In philosophical dialogues, we are able to apprehend the various modalities by which "elites" attempted to communicate to "nonelites," or by which traditionally conceived epigonic thinkers bridged the gap between the so-called "great" philosophers and nonphilosophers.

Even though I would be the first to admit that we encounter Judaism not just where there are Jewish texts, but also Jewish bodies, the study of premodern Judaism is, for the most part, confined to written sources (be they biblical commentaries, philosophical treatises, or tax records). The following study works on the assumption that philosophical texts are not only worthy of study, but that they also provide insights into larger social and cultural issues, ones that might otherwise be difficult to access. Yet, to analyze philosophical texts without proper consideration of their manifold cultural, gendered, and socioeconomic contexts gives us a potentially unbalanced or artificial reading. This is not to say that texts are simply the sum of their contexts, but that such texts can never be fully understood apart from them.

This study has several aims. The first is to trace a particular genre across time and space, showing various similarities, continuities, differences, and discrepancies. At the same time, however, what follows is not an explicit comparison of these dialogues but a rich contextual analysis of each one. It makes little sense to compare or contrast explicitly texts written hundreds of years apart from one another, which are produced within cultures with radically different literary, philosophical, and aesthetic sensibilities. On the contrary, I have found it much more profitable to devote a particular chapter to a specific dialogue that I regard as fundamental to the Jewish philosophical culture of that age. I subsequently describe "thickly" each dialogue, embedding it within its immediate Jewish and non-Jewish contexts. When it does seem possible to compare and/or contrast certain features among these dialogues, especially for the sake of nuance, I proceed cautiously.

Second, this study, although devoted to the genre of the dialogue, is also in many ways a comparative study of Jewish cultures.[60] Each dialogue exists within a specific cultural setting and makes use of the codes and conventions of that culture. As a result, we can envisage these texts as local sites of contention between Jewish and non-Jewish encounters. We thus witness a number of tensions, concerns, and fractures that faced a particular author, including the larger society of which that author was a part. Read in this manner, these dialogues function as part window and part mirror. As a window, they let us peer into these texts in order to apprehend a number of communal, cultural, intellectual, and religious debates, since more often than not the dialogues are between individuals with distinct ideological readings of what Judaism is or should be. As part mirror, they in many instances let us ultimately see the author's own point of view reflected in the dialogue, trying to convince us, the audience, that his reading of Judaism is the correct one.

Third, I would like to think that this examination could be read not only as a specialized study on a specific genre, but also as a new introduction to Jewish philosophy. I say "new" because most standard introductions to Jewish philosophy move rapidly from great thinker to great thinker, and from great text to great text, taking only the barest approach to larger concerns. Unlike such introductions, the present work focuses on a relatively small number of thinkers and texts, and opts to provide rich descriptions of these texts—how they interact with, struggle with, and respond to other texts, both Jewish and non-Jewish—over the course of six centuries of Jewish philosophical writing. As a result, we are able to witness the production of philosophical texts in terms of the ideas contained within, but also in relationship to a complex web of social, cultural, religious, and "nationalist"[61] features.

As should be clear from a quick glance at the table of contents, each chapter is devoted to a dialogue written at a particular moment within a distinct Jewish culture. As I mentioned above, I conceptualize each dialogue as a microcosm, one that contains any number of tensions, ideologies, or concerns that faced a particular community. In doing this I am certainly neither attempting to reduce the dynamics of an entire culture to one text nor to suggest that cultures are accessible solely through the textual or philosophical record. However, I do contend that the dialogues under discussion here permit us to conceptualize and understand, on a local level, some of the main intellectual, social, and religious sites of contention that, historically, Jews struggled with or with which they were preoccupied.

One might well object that I apply the term *dialogue* retroactively to an assortment of texts that lack any real inner cohesion.[62] Evidence here could be drawn from the fact that most of the authors did not explicitly call their works "dialogues," which raises the point that it might be artificial to employ modern terms and concepts such as *genre* to medieval texts. In addition, authors of later dialogues rarely, if ever, mention their antecedents. Although there exist a number of interesting relationships between the various authors examined here—for example, Shem Tov ibn Falaquera summarized dialogues of his predecessors; during the Renaissance there was a renewed interest in Halevi's *Kuzari;* one of Mendelssohn's teachers in Berlin, Israel Zamosc, wrote a line-by-line commentary to the *Kuzari*—one still has to ask whether or not these commonalities suffice to speak of a distinct genre of philosophical writing.

Yet, even if these authors would not have recognized their works as belonging to a specific "genre," the fact remains that all, for one reason or another, wrote treatises wherein various characters debate with one another to clarify and elaborate upon a philosophical point or argument. In what follows, I employ terms such as *dialogue* and *genre* heuristically to uncover and analyze not only the reasons behind the composition of a set of texts, but equally importantly to show the dynamics within these texts. Granted that certain of the commonalities that exist between them would not have been intended at the time of each dialogue's genesis, looking at them from the vantage point of the modern period makes it difficult to deny that they do not exist.

Although medieval conceptions of genre may well differ from modern understandings, medieval philosophers were familiar with and employed a number of distinct literary forms (e.g., allegories,[63] *summa,*[64] axiomatic works,[65] commentaries[66]) in addition to the dialogue.[67] Whether or not they actually conceived of these literary forms as genres is difficult to say. Despite this, I am comfortable in employing terms such as *genre* and *dialogue* because even if the actual terms did not exist, the conceptual and literary techniques behind them certainly did. I thus agree with Peter Heath, who, in his study of allegory in Islamic philosophical writing, argues that the

> theoretical question of the extent to which it is proper or useful to employ western critical terms for works of Islamic literatures is a general problem that can be resolved only by a comparative use of such terms in ways that are sensitive to the limits of the conceptual analogy. I use the term *allegory* here in reference to the Islamic tradition because I believe that the concept, and more

> important, its praxis have their own indigenous histories. My aim is not to distort our understanding of this historical tradition by indiscreetly applying concepts borrowed from western literature but rather to employ them carefully in order to explore literary techniques and historical permutations that developed in the Islamic world.[68]

So even though the authors examined here may not have employed the term *dialogue* to describe their mode of writing, it nonetheless becomes possible to isolate a number of literary features that their works share. For this reason, I employ the term *dialogue* to speak collectively about this constellation of literary features. All the while, however, it is important to be conscious of the fact that each one of these authors uses the genre to respond to a number of external features that were not necessarily shared by either his predecessors or those who will come after him.

The chapters below replicate a similar structure. Each begins by situating a particular dialogue in its historical, social, and intellectual environments. This enables me to problematize the issues relevant to the Jewish cultures in which these texts were produced. What, for example, were the pressing intellectual and religious issues of the day? What was going on in the larger societies in which Jews found themselves? How did these societies, or perhaps more accurately their intelligentsias, conceptualize the relationship between philosophy and literature? This, in turn, permits me to set the stage for an analysis of the dialogue in question.

After examining these various contexts, I situate the author of each dialogue against this backdrop. I should add, though, that for the chapters on Halevi and Mendelssohn, two of the most important philosophers in the Jewish philosophical "canon," much has been written. I have no intention of retelling their life stories here. However, with some of the thinkers—most notably Polleqar and to a lesser extent Falaquera and Judah Abravanel, who have not been subject to the same biographical studies—I have chosen to go into more detail.

The final part of each chapter moves from the global framework in which each author lived and wrote to the particular text in question. Here I am concerned with analyzing the intersection of the philosophical and the literary. As such, I go into considerable detail examining the literary dimensions of each dialogue. In particular, I focus on the nature of the various characters, the way they interact with each other, and the tone of their dialogic encounters. These literary dimensions, in turn, enable me to show how the content of the work slowly emerges.

This approach permits both the contextualization of each dialogue within a complex set of broader concerns, and also the conceptualization of these dialogues as a genre. I am well aware that close to six hundred years separate the dialogue in chapter 2 from that in chapter 6, with the result that these texts may resist such classification. Despite this, I persist in the attempt because even though Halevi's *Kuzari* may seem to have nothing in common with Mendelssohn's *Phaedon,* both of these texts represent literary attempts to confront a set of intellectual concerns facing particular Jewish communities. Even though Halevi may ultimately have responded differently than Mendelssohn to the intellectual trajectories of his day, both authors nevertheless sought to articulate their visions of what Judaism was or should be, using philosophical arguments and literary techniques that they inherited from their non-Jewish contemporaries.

In this introductory chapter, I have tried to accomplish two things. First, I hope to have called attention to the importance of genre in both the creation and subsequent dissemination of Jewish philosophical writing. In so doing, I argued that a focus solely on content risks overlooking the literary and other nonphilosophical dimensions both within and behind the composition of philosophy. The content of the dialogues discussed in the coming chapters emerges not only through the ideas presented by a textual spokesperson who is often considered to be the author himself, but also through a series of dialectical encounters between characters, the exchange and interchange of ideas, literary devices that frame the encounters, and various settings. Attention to these manifold details enables us to not only appreciate these literary dialogues as philosophical treatises, but also to situate them in light of concerns that are not just philosophical.

Secondly, I have begun to establish a series of features around which many of the dialogues discussed in this study constellate. Although these dialogues were produced in distinct Jewish cultures and only make full sense when contextualized in them, these features nevertheless permit careful generalizations. Although each text invites an understanding of the intersection of the literary and the philosophical on its own terms, taken as a whole they lead to a new appreciation of a distinct genre of Jewish philosophical writing. To begin this appreciation, the following chapter examines arguably the most famous of all Jewish dialogues, philosophical or otherwise: Judah Halevi's *Kuzari.*

2
JUDAH HALEVI: THE DIALOGUE OF SUBVERSION

THE DEFINING FEATURE OF MEDIEVAL ISLAMICATE[1] COURTIER CULTURE was that of *adab*. This term, although difficult to translate, constellates around the myriad of social graces, literary tastes, and ingenuity in manipulating language associated with the ideal of cultured living.[2] Jews living within the orbit of Islam naturally gravitated to this ideal, reframing their understanding of Judaism in its light. In al-Andalus, viz., Muslim Spain, Jewish intellectuals assimilated Arabic paradigms of beauty, rhetoric, and eloquence, which led to the emergence of Jewish philosophy and science, Hebrew poetry, poetics, and rhetoric. It was into this cultural context that Judah Halevi (1075–1141) was born and subsequently raised, and he used its intellectual and literary categories to express himself until his fiftieth year.

At the age of fifty, Halevi, in theory if not always in practice, turned his back on what he perceived to be the inauthenticity of Judeo-Arabic cultural forms.[3] This, in large part, stemmed from his disillusionment with the dominant spirituality of his day—articulated most prominently in various Islamicate subcultures such as Sufism, Ismaʿilism, and other groups influenced by Neoplatonic hermeneutics—which bifurcated reality into the exoteric and the esoteric, the *ẓāhir* and the *bāṭin*, respectively.[4] Such groups were predicated upon spiritual elites initiated into the divine secrets, elites who claimed access to the esoteric dimensions of religion; the rest of humanity, lacking such initiation, was confined to the superficial level. Initiation, therefore, was based on how to read properly, be the material a text or reality itself. In its most extreme form, this initiation was based on a spiritually informed reading that was, more often than not, in conflict with the literal reading.

Whereas various Islamicate subcultures emphasized the esoteric over the exoteric, belief over action, inner core over outer husk, Halevi emphasizes the latter of each of these dichotomies and, in the process, claims that it is in the physical, embodied performance of the divinely revealed commandments that one attains the purity of experience. Judaism, on Halevi's reading, is superior to all of its competitors because it alone affords a harmonious relationship between thought and praxis. Halevi thus reads against the grain of the eleventh-century zeitgeist by arguing that Truth is located not in the deepest levels of texts or reality, but on the surface, open for all to access.

Halevi's interest in these dichotomies becomes evident in the opening pages of the *Kuzari.*[5] Here the Khazar king—the ruler of the mythico-historical Khazaria[6]—has a series of dreams,[7] informing him that his religious intentions (*niyyāt*) are fine but ultimately misplaced because they lack fulfillment in proper action (*ᶜamal*). To repair this disjuncture the king seeks to embrace a monotheistic religion, which will presumably provide him the appropriate framework with which to harmonize his intentions and his actions. After disappointing encounters with a philosopher,[8] a Muslim (i.e., a Sunni), and a Christian, the king decides, despite his initial *intention,* to invite a Jew to his court. The *ᶜamal* of inviting the Jew, in other words, is at odds with his initial *niyya* that Judaism has nothing to offer. This relationship between intentions and actions, appearances and reality, *on all levels of the narrative,* is central to Halevi's unfolding argument in the *Kuzari.* Indeed, all four of these terms—intentions, actions, appearance, and reality—are not used haphazardly. On the contrary, they were deeply contested terms in various religious and intellectual circles of the eleventh- and twelfth-century Islamicate world. In employing these terms and, in many cases, resignifying them, Halevi consciously enters into a particular discourse and, in so doing, frames his defense of Judaism in such a manner that would have a maximum impact on his contemporaries.

That Halevi chose to communicate his ideas in a dialogue is especially significant. This genre was a well-established literary form that various Islamicate subcultures used to make cases for their exclusive claims to religious authority and gnosis. It was particularly popular among Ismaᶜili missionaries, many of whom employed dialogues to disseminate their Neoplatonically inspired brand of Islam. Ismaᶜilism was an extremely proselytizing sect in Islam, and was predicated on an oath-based system of allegiance to a living imam, who alone was regarded as possessing the keys to proper religious understanding. In addition, Ismaᶜilis stressed intention (*niyya*) over action (*ᶜamal*), and the esoteric (*bāṭin*) over the exoteric (*ẓāhir*). The key to maneuvering successfully between these dichotomies was an appropriate hermeneutical system (*taʾwīl*). This Ismaᶜili- or Ismaᶜili-inspired system proved popular among Muslim and Jewish intellectuals who appreciated its presentation of religion using philosophical terminology and categories.[9]

The genre and literary setting of the *Kuzari* allows Halevi to mount a full-scale justification and defense of Judaism, its rituals and beliefs, and its perceived lowly state among the nations. Unlike Maimonides and other rationalists, Halevi sought the eternal truths of Judaism not in the universal claims of philosophy, but in the particularities of Jewish history and the dynamics of its inner experience. That Halevi chose to mount his defense in the form of a dialogue is not coincidental. Since Halevi was one of the most gifted secular and religious poets of his generation, and given that the *adab*-ideal of proper expression was central to Jewish Andalusi literary composition, we should be cautious of separating the form of the dialogue from its content.[10] This, in turn, produces a series of questions that revolve around the form of the *Kuzari:* Why would Halevi decide to compose his grand defense of Judaism in the form of a dialogue? What did the dialogue allow Halevi to accomplish that other literary genres could not? Is his dialogue in direct or indirect conversation with other dialogues, either Jewish or non-Jewish?

Judah Halevi: Life and Times

Halevi[11] was born in either Toledo (al-Andalus) or Tudela (Christian Spain),[12] in the year 1075. Regardless of his birthplace, he soon made his way to the Castilian court in search of fame and fortune among its Jewish literary circles. Impressed with the poetic gifts and promise of this aspiring young poet, Moshe ibn Ezra (ca. 1055–1138) invited him to Granada.[13] There, Halevi became the darling of the Jewish literati: his poetic brilliance, facility with prosody, and ability to manipulate language quickly ensured for him a prominent place within the pantheon of distinguished Andalusi Jewish poets. He also became an important court physician and respected leader of the Jewish community.[14] Halevi spent much of his youth and middle age mesmerized by the universal poetic and intellectual currents associated with Arabo-Islamic Neoplatonism, creatively framing Judaism in the light of its categories.

By the age of fifty, however, Halevi began to turn his back on the ideals and practices that defined the elite culture of which he was so intimately involved. His disillusionment with its poetic manners and forms,[15] and its intellectualist mooring of Judaism, led him to renounce an entire way of life. On one level, then, Halevi was a product of the rich Judeo-Arabic culture,[16] yet on another level his life reveals the ambiguity of this symbiosis at the points at which it was increasingly fragile and most vulnerable:

> They congratulate him for being in the service of kings
> Which to him is like the worship of idols.
> Is it right for a worthy and pious man

To be glad that he is caught, like a bird by a child,
In the service of Philistines, Hittites, and descendents of Hagar
His heart is seduced by alien deities
To do their will, and forsake the will of God,
To deceive the Creator and serve His creatures.[17]

As this poem makes explicit, Halevi refuses to connect authentic Jewish existence to the slavish imitation of Arab and Islamicate values. True piety could no longer be defined, as it was for so many of Halevi's Jewish contemporaries, as a set of universal, ahistorical ideals provided by a generic and spiritualized Neoplatonism. In its place, Halevi crafts his magnum opus, the *Kuzari*, as a peon to Jewish particularism, an indictment against attempts to read Judaism in the light of such universal categories. Ironically, however, Halevi composes his defense of Jewish particularism in the Arabic language, using the Arabo-Islamic categories of his day. Yet if we frame the *Kuzari* as a "dialogue of subversion," a sustained attempt to deconstruct a particular reading of religion in general and Judaism in particular, the language and genre of the treatise need not surprise us.

Halevi wrote his magnum opus over a period of at least twenty years. Not surprisingly, we witness in the *Kuzari* the changing attitudes of an individual to the dominant paradigms of Andalusi Jewish culture.[18] Although he began the work while still living in al-Andalus, he completed the work in Egypt in 1140, just before he made his way to the land of Israel.[19] This rather lengthy period of composition has led some to conclude that the final version of the *Kuzari* was hastily put together in an "uncrafted and disconnected manner."[20] Yet the very fact that the *Kuzari* is the product of one of the most creative and distinguished of the medieval Jewish poets should mitigate against such a reading.

Shlomo Pines has argued that in order to understand the generation of the *Kuzari* it is necessary to examine its language, especially the genealogy of certain terms that Halevi employs to make his case. Many of these terms, Pines demonstrates, were borrowed from various Islamicate subcultures, in particular that of the Ismaᶜilis, and subsequently resignified.[21] In a more recent version of this thesis, Diana Lobel has shown that the manner in which Halevi articulated the importance of religious experience was derived from his use and adaptation of terms derived from circles of Islamic mysticism, or Sufism.[22]

I follow the lead of Pines and Lobel, and argue that since Halevi did not compose the *Kuzari* in a vacuum, it becomes necessary to contextualize it within the literary, intellectual and cultural web of the eleventh and twelfth centuries. To insure as wide an audience as possible for his sweeping indictment of the Judeo-Arab synthesis, he would not invent a new genre; rather, he would have employed one that was familiar to his contemporaries. So although the *Kuzari* is certainly a Jewish work, its vocabulary, categories, and terms of reference are ultimately derived from Arabo-Islamicate cultural, intellectual and aesthetic contexts. My goal here is to demonstrate that the *Kuzari*, a timeless classic of Jewish thought, presents a pleasing and well-crafted argument that subverts, in its use of genre no less than in its contents, the dominant intellectual and religious paradigms of the day.

The Role of Dialogue among Isma^c^ilis

Since the Isma^c^ilis loom large in much of what follows, it becomes necessary to situate them briefly in their appropriate historical and cultural contexts. As a group, they seem to have coalesced at some point after the death of the sixth Shi^c^i Imam, Ja^c^far al-Ṣādiq (d. 765).[23] The early leaders of the movement organized secretly in response to the Abbasid dynasty, which the Isma^c^ilis considered to be illegitimate. Through the establishment of *dā^c^īs*, religiopolitical missionaries and propagandists, Isma^c^ilis spread their message throughout the Islamic world. Eventually they established a state, known as the Fāṭimid Empire, in Egypt in the mid-tenth century, with the so-called "golden age" of Isma^c^ilism generally acknowledged to have occurred in the late tenth and eleventh centuries.

In terms of intellectual history, the Isma^c^ilis functioned as an important conduit between late antique esoteric circles and the early Islamic world.[24] Much of their teachings centered on the *dā^c^ī* who functioned as the intermediary between the imam (the mystico-political head of state) and his followers. This intermediary role was often explained using Neoplatonic terminology of emanation (*inbi^c^āth*), the universal intellect (*al-^c^aql al-kulliyya*), and the universal soul (*al-nafs al-kulliyya*). Neoplatonism also played a large role in Isma^c^ili cosmology,[25] prophetology, and eschatology, with appropriate understanding of religion and religious phenomena predicated upon an understanding of the theoretical sciences.[26] The *dā^c^īs* often incorporated philosophical theory into their preaching, which was often well received by intellectual elites throughout the Islamic world, as witnessed, inter alia, in the autobiography of Avicenna (980–1037).[27]

One of the defining characteristics of the Isma^c^ilis was their distinction between the esoteric (*bāṭin*) and exoteric (*ẓāhir*) dimensions of reality. In many circles the Isma^c^ilis were known pejoratively as the *bāṭiniyya* (Esotericists). Their knowledge was secret, and it was forbidden for initiates to disclose it to those who were not part of the elect. Although writing in the thirteenth century, the words of the Isma^c^ili Naṣīr al-Dīn al-Ṭūsī (1201–1274), in the introduction to his spiritual autobiography are relevant: "For intelligent people there is no secret that has to be kept more hidden than the secret of belief and religious doctrine. Indeed, what harmful consequences would follow if the ordinary, ignorant folk were to become aware of these things requires no explanation."[28]

Al-Ṭūsī further emphasizes that to prevent such secrets from getting into the hands of the masses, he will write in such a manner that only like-minded individuals can understand. This practice of concealing and revealing at the same time would prove to be popular throughout the medieval Islamicate world, and would be a staple of Jewish philosophical literature in al-Andalus, as can be witnessed in the works of Abraham ibn Ezra (e.g., his famous phrase, *ha-maskil yavin*) and Maimonides (e.g., in the epistle dedicatory of his *Guide of the Perplexed*).[29]

Although very little work has been done on the reception of Ismaᶜili texts in Muslim Spain,[30] let alone their circulation in Jewish intellectual circles, their ideas were widely known, disseminated either through various esoteric circles (e.g., ibn Masarra),[31] writings of heresiographers (e.g., ibn Ḥazm),[32] or informed critics of philosophy (e.g., al-Ghazālī).[33]

In disseminating their ideas, Ismaᶜilis made prominent use of the dialogue genre, which they employed in at least two ways. The first was to refute those hostile to their particular interpretation of Islam. This was done by recounting real or imagined disputations (*munāẓarāt*). Probably the best-known example of this may be found in *Kitāb al-ᶜalām wa al-nubuwwa* by Abū Ḥātim al-Rāzī (d. ca. 934).[34] This dialogue recounts the debates between the author and the "atheistic" physician/philosopher, Abū Bakr al-Rāzī. This use of the dialogue to recount a religious or theological disputation would also become popular among non-Ismaᶜili Muslim writers, such as al-Shahrastānī's *Kitāb al-milal wa al-nihal,* especially in the debate between the primordial monotheists (*al-ḥunafāʾ*) and the Sabians (*al-ṣābiʾa*).[35]

In addition to this disputative function of the dialogue, Ismaᶜili authors appreciated the genre's dialectical component. This allowed them not only to elucidate and clarify certain topics that were central to the movement, but also to communicate esoteric topics to like-minded individuals. A number of Ismaᶜili dialogues, for instance, include textual oaths (*ᶜahd*) that, as I shall discuss in greater detail below, appear to be narrative homologues of what went on in the actual secret sessions (*majālis al-ḥikma*) of various groups.[36] Within this context, literary dialogues take the place of the actual "sessions," and work in such a manner that they convey the secret, inner dimensions of the Quʾrān, the law, and reality itself. Important dialogues that work in this manner include *Kitāb al-ᶜālim wa al-ghulām* (The Book of the Master and the Disciple) by Jaᶜfar ibn Manṣūr al-Yaman (d. 914),[37] and the *Kitāb al-munāẓarāt* by Ibn al-Ḥaytham (d. ca. 950).[38]

In order to appreciate fully the *Kuzari* as a literary dialogue, it becomes necessary to connect it to this broader milieu. Where and how does Halevi use, diverge from, and subvert the generic features employed in Ismaʿili dialogues? For instance, and as I shall discuss in greater detail below, he subverts the relationship between action and intention, and the exoteric and esoteric, that played such an important role in Ismaʿili hermeneutics and cosmology. Similarly, unlike Ismaʿili esotericism, which tends not to take revelation at face value, the Khazar king unhesitatingly accepts the literal contents of his dream/revelation, and it is for precisely this reason that the subsequent dialogue unfolds. Finally, unlike Ismaʿili dialogues which often culminate in conversion at the end of the narrative, we are informed of the Khazar king's conversion at the very beginning of the *Kuzari.* Interestingly, and also breaking with the expectations that we find in Ismaʿili texts, at the end of the *Kuzari* we witness the *ḥaver*—the person supposed to be doing the "initiating"—transforming his own views on the relationship between intention and action. As far as I am aware, the person doing the initiating in Ismaʿili texts never undergoes such a transformation.

Halevi thus breaks with a number of the generic and literary features that we encounter in Ismaʿili dialogues. In the following section, I suggest that Halevi was not only familiar with these various dialogues, but that he also used his own dialogue to confront these other works on their own terms. The genre of the dialogue thus provided him with a ready-made and convenient form to articulate his own construction of Judaism, one that was the polar opposite of those—whether Ismaʿilis or Jews under their sphere of influence—who employed dialogues to advance their own esoteric claims to religious truth. For instance, whereas the Ismaʿilis stressed a quasi-mystical, esoteric take on religion, Halevi upholds an exoteric reading of the Jewish tradition; whereas they emphasize the proper intention of religious devotion over its actual praxis, Halevi does the opposite; and whereas the Ismaʿilis directed their teachings toward an initiated intellectual elite that was focused on the spiritual authority of the living Imam, Halevi's reading of Judaism is one that stresses the entire Jewish people as the spiritual elite.

Halevi, Ismaʿilis, and the Kuzari as a Dialogue of Subversion

ʿamal *versus* niyya

As mentioned above, Halevi begins his *Kuzari* with a dream sequence in which an angel appears to the Khazar king informing him that the intention (*niyya*) behind his religious orientation is appropriate, but that his ritual actions or devotions (*aᶜmāl*) are not. These two technical terms form the centerpiece of the beginning of the work, and it is the dissonance between them that informs Halevi's intended desire to compose the work. In the opening page of the work, for example, we read:

> [The angel] said to [the king]: "Your intention [*niyya;* pl. *niyyāt*] is pleasing to God, but your action [*ᶜamal;* pl. *aᶜmāl*] is not." Yet he was so zealous in the cult of the Khazar religion, and with a pure and sincere *niyya* he devoted himself to the *aᶜmāl* of the temple and the offering of sacrifices. Yet the angel came again at night and said to him: "Your *niyya* is pleasing, but your *ᶜamal* is not."[39]

Halevi's use of these two technical terms are the opposite of their employment in Ismaᶜili texts. For the Ismaᶜilis, the *aᶜmāl* of Islam are the various religious observances and obligations revealed through the divine law (*sharīᶜa*) and incumbent upon all Muslims (e.g., prayer, fasting, almsgiving). It is the goal of the *dāᶜī,* however, to encourage initiates to penetrate beyond simple observance in order to contemplate the spiritual truths (*ḥaqāʾiq*) that exist behind such actions. Not coincidentally, most Ismaᶜili treatises begin with an elucidation of the differences between intentions and actions. In the beginning of his *Kitāb al-yanābiᶜ* (Wellsprings of Wisdom), for example, al-Sijistānī (d. ca. 980) informs like-minded initiates of the dual nature of divine law:

> Then Muhammad took upon the Command of God, Almighty is He, both as its messenger and as the conveyor of His wisdom. Thus, accordingly, he composed his Law [*sharīᶜa*] in a double manner: one relating to the arrangement and organization of situations that combine souls with locations; and the other dealing with purely spiritual knowledge and divine wisdom [*al-ḥikma al-ilāhiyya*]. Human beings, both the learned and the ignorant, rely on him because what he conveys to them of the light of the Word of God, the Most High, conforms both to the *physical situation of unlearned men and to the refined thoughts of educated scholars.*[40]

Although not a dialogue per se, al-Sijistānī here juxtaposes two classes of individuals, the ignorant and the scholars, and describes how the Law imposes different obligations upon each. Educated scholars, viz., the spiritual elite, must move beyond mere performance of the Law to an appreciation of the appropriate spirituality behind it. According to al-Sijistānī, "works" are those duties, obligations, and observances that Islam imposes upon its believers in order to systematize and regulate appropriate social and communal behavior. They are, by definition, exoteric (*ẓāhirī*) acts. Such acts, in other words, represent the lowest common denominator of belief, functioning as a springboard with which to dive deeper into spiritual matters.

This rather stark juxtaposition between action and belief is reinforced in other Ismaᶜili dialogues. At the beginning of *Kitāb al-ᶜālim wa al-ghulām,* al-Yaman has a group of those who seek after knowledge ask one who is already initiated:

> **Seekers:** You have liberated us by helping us to know an affair [*amr;* of such great importance] that we are obligated to show our gratitude to you for three reasons: our thanks to you for having called us to that [religion]; our thanks for the knowledge [*ᶜilm*] to which you directed us; and our thanks for the works [*aᶜmāl*] you ordered us to perform. So explain to us what one ought to do who wishes to show his thankfulness. . . . Then inform us about the rights and duties that are obligatory for us among the ordinances of religion [*ḥudūd al-dīn*]; and about what is obligatory for the seeker in his questioning, and for the person who is sought, in his responding to that. And let us know as much as you can easily express about the ways of the righteous and the proper behavior [*adab*] of the seekers.
> **The knower:** Now the affair to which I called you all is that which God has bestowed as an honor for His servants . . . [What follows] are the way-stations of "the people of true understanding" [Qurʾān 2:269; 3:7, etc.][41]

This passage again signals a bifurcation between obligatory duties and actions of average Muslims and those that are supererogatory, those that are the provenance of righteous individuals (*al-ṣaliḥūn*). This is, in many ways, the exact opposite of what we find in the *Kuzari:* al-Yaman's treatise works on the assumption that the seeker already understands and performs the proper religious works, but that he lacks the proper spiritual intentions that lead to an understanding of the secrets (*asrār*) behind such actions. This is in keeping with Ismaᶜili cosmology which is predicated upon spiritual hierarchies, through which the initiate must ascend. Al-Yaman's employment of the term *adab* is significant here. On the one hand, this term, as I indicated above, refers to the cultural norms that define proper social behavior; on the other hand, it can also refer to the proper orientation of the initiate toward spiritual matters.[42] In the subsequent dialogue, the master informs the disciple that his actions are fine, but that his intentions are wrong because they are those of the ignorant.[43] The rest of the narrative witnesses the disciple's initiation into the spiritual tradition and his subsequent change in intention.

This, of course, is the polar opposite of Halevi's account. In the *Kuzari* the angel that appears to the king informs him that his intentions are fine, but that his actions leave much to be desired. For Halevi, unlike the Ismaᶜilis, it is the external rituals of religion that, paradoxically, represent its spiritual depths. As a consequence, access to spiritual truths is not confined to initiated elites, but must be open to the entire Jewish people. Halevi thus frames his work using the same genre (e.g., a dialogue), the same terminology (e.g., actions versus intentions), and a similar narrative structure (e.g., a potential disciple asking a potential teacher about their difference) as the Ismaʿilis. Unlike them, however, Halevi gives all of these phenomena a completely different interpretation by making true religious experience contingent on proper physical ritual, something that has to be accessible to the entire community.

Halevi follows this section with the statement that the perceived dissonance between belief and intention led the king to become a Jew. Unlike Ismaʿili dialogues that often culminate in conversion at the end of the narrative, we are informed of the king's conversion at the very beginning of the *Kuzari*. Halevi is able to do this because external action must be tantamount to proper worship. The king, in other words, converts to Judaism and then undertakes a series of conversations with the *ḥaver*, whereas the Ismaʿili initiate must undergo a series of spiritual exercises to learn about esoteric matters and only after this can the initiate have the proper intention. Unlike Ismaʿili initiates, the Khazar king already possessed the proper intention before his conversion to Judaism. What Judaism offers him, though, is the proper physical and bodily outlets to bring his actions into harmony with his intentions. This becomes even clearer once the king speaks to both the Muslim and the Christian delegates, neither of whom so much as mentions action. Both tell the king what they believe, but only the Jew connects this belief to observance as found in the divine law (*sharīʿa*).

ẓāhir *versus* bāṭin

The Ismaʿilis connected the relationship between action and intention to that between the outer or exoteric (*ẓāhir*) form of religion and its inner or esoteric (*bāṭin*) core. This dichotomy did not refer simply to the dual level of the Qurʾān and its proper interpretation, but was also conceived to encompass all levels of reality. We see this clearly, for example, in *Kitāb al-ʿālim wa al-ghulām*, wherein a disciple who has just received an oath of initiation (*ʿahd*) is subsequently instructed into these esoteric secrets. In a lengthy monologue describing these secrets, we encounter the following statement:

> **The knower:** It is the same way with the outer [*ẓāhir*] aspects of the religious paths and all other things: they only subsist through the inner, spiritual religion [*dīn al-bāṭin*], because it is their light and their essential meaning. . . . Nor does the inner aspect subsist except through the outer aspect, because that is its covering and the sign pointing to it. Now the outer aspect is the distinctive mark of this lower world, which can only be seen through that; and the inner aspect is the distinctive mark of the other world, which can only be seen through that.[44]

Implicit in the distinction between the *ẓāhir* and the *bāṭin* is the need for a spiritual guide who can help the initiate negotiate the mysteries and various gradations of reality. On one level, then, we can read the Ismaʿili dialogue as a textual replacement for the physical presence of an actual *dāʿī*. The text, in other words, functions as a guide, and the master-disciple relationship recounted in the dialogue becomes a metaphor for the text and the reader.[45] For this reason, the text itself takes on the attributes of the *ẓāhir/bāṭin* distinction:

> **The knower:** Now our speaking about this could go on and be greatly expanded. But when one is speaking of wisdom, because of its preciousness and the purity of its substance, the longer one's reply is, the more the point becomes hidden; the later part makes you forget the beginning. For part of the light of wisdom can obscure another part, just as the light of the sun veils and weakens the light of the moon and the stars.
> **The young man:** But don't you see that in this lower world—in which He created those creatures whose essence is so marvelous, so immense in their sheer numbers, from the first to the last—people differ concerning it?
> **The knower:** . . . No one ever really condemns this lower world except for the totally ignorant.[46]

It is within the context of this distinction between the *ẓāhir* and the *bāṭin* that we need to situate Halevi's discussion. For him, this dichotomy is an artificial one; in its place, he emphasizes not the inner or esoteric dimension of the law, but its external fulfillment. In Book Two, for instance, the *ḥaver* claims that "he who accepts the commandments without scrutiny or argument is better off than he who investigates and analyzes."[47] This theme is picked up in Book Three, a book that is critical of those opposed to the pious acts of the believer.

> **The king:** I have speculated about your authority [*amrakum*] and understand that God desires your survival [*ibqāʾkum*], and that He appointed the sabbaths and the holy days [*al-asbāt wa al-aʿyād*] among the strongest means of preserving your spark and luster. . . . All of these are divine commandments that are incumbent upon you [*kullihā awāmir ilāhiyya muʾaqqada ʿalakum*] . . .
>
> . . .
>
> **The ḥaver:** The best [*al-khayr*] among us fulfills the precepts from this divine law [*al-sharīʿa al-ilāhiyya*]—circumcision, sabbaths, holy days, and the legal necessities [*lawāzim al-mashrūʿ*] that come from God. He refrains from forbidden marriages, using mixtures in plants, clothes and animals, keeps the years of release and jubilee, avoids idolatry or the search for knowledge [*ṭalab ʿilm*] without prophecy by means of *urim ve-thummim* or dreams. He does not listen to the soothsayer, or astrologer, or magician, augur, or necromancer. . . .[48]

Whereas Ismaʿili dialogues are interested in analyzing the appropriate *bāṭin*-based understanding of such actions, Halevi is content to allow such actions to remain at the *ẓāhir* level. In other words, the pious and observant individual should have no need to inquire into the mystical and esoteric properties of divinely revealed rituals. The fact that they are divine and revealed from heaven should suffice for such an individual. Later on in Book Three, the *ḥaver* elaborates on this point in response to the Khazar king's question about the Karaites.

> **The king:** I would now like you to tell me about the Karaites and their beliefs, which seem more pious [*al-taᶜbbud akthar*] than those of the Rabbanites. I have heard that their arguments are superior and better [*arjaḥ wa-akthar*] when it comes to [understanding] the literal level of the Torah [*nuṣūṣ al-taura*].
> **The ḥaver:** Did I not already say that arbitrariness [*al-taḥakkum*], rational discernment [*al-taᶜaqqul*], and conjecture [*al-takharruṣ*] concerning the Law [*al-sharīᶜa*] do not lead to the pleasure of God. If this were the case then dualists [*al-thanawiyya*], materialists [*al-dahrīyyūn*], worshipers of spirits [*aṣḥāb al-rūḥāniyyāt*], those who withdraw to mountain tops [*munqitaᶜūn fī al-jibāl*], and those who burn their children [*awlādahum bi'l-nūr*] all desire to approach God. We have, however, said that one cannot approach God except by His commands [*awāmir Allah*].[49]

The commandments are holy because they form the core of divine revelation, not because they are subject to esoteric manipulation by any self-styled spiritual elite. Although in the following passage the *ḥaver* has the Karaites in mind, his criticisms extend to all who prefer to seek out the "true" or spiritual meanings of the commandments as opposed to engaging in their actual observance:

> I have already said to you that rational discernment [*al-taᶜaqqul*], arbitrariness [*al-taḥakkum*], and those who do try to discern religious observances [*ibāda*] for the service of heaven may appear more diligent [*akthār ijtihādan*] than those who perform the service of God exactly as is commanded [*maʾmūr*]. However, the latter are at ease with their uncritical faith [*istarāḥu taqlīdahum*], and their souls are calm like one who lives in a city and does not fear destruction. The former, however, are like stragglers in the desert, who do not know what may happen.[50]

The *ẓāhir–bāṭin* distinction that forms the pivot around which Ismaᶜili cosmology and textual interpretation revolves was one that many Jewish philosophers also found attractive. For instance, the distinction between the body and the soul, outward appearance and inner understanding formed the foundation upon which much of medieval Jewish philosophy was constructed.[51] In challenging this bipolarity, Halevi signals his displeasure with the conception of religion among his contemporaries. A true understanding of religion, for him, does not reside in an esoteric dimension that is only loosely connected to what covers it; on the contrary, and paradoxically, Halevi equates the inner dimension of Judaism with the proper action of its outer dimensions. The *ẓāhir,* according to Halevi's reading, becomes the *bāṭin.*

taʾwīl

Since Ismaʿili reality and textuality revolve around the distinction between the *ẓāhir* and the *bāṭin,* this necessitated an appropriate hermeneutical system to ascertain their interdependency. Correct interpretation (*taʾwīl*) is institutionalized in the living Imam, someone deemed by his followers to be infallible (*maʿsūm*) based on his descent from the prophet and his own personal charisma.[52] The goal of such interpretation, in the words of al-Sijistānī, is the ability to differentiate between the outer husk of revelation (*tanzīl*) and its living, inner core. The *tanzīl* is composed of "subjective items and restricted phrases beneath which there are hidden meanings. *Taʾwīl* on the part of its master puts all of these into a proper context and extracts from each phrase what is intended."[53]

It is the goal of the imam, or in his place, his spokesmen, the *dāʿīs,* to inform the initiated of the *bāṭin* by means of the authority granted to them through divine inspiration. For example, in his *Wellsprings of Wisdom,* al-Sijistānī compares the act of *taʾwīl* to the various degrees of water:

> The Prophet [*al-nāṭiq*] resembles water in all of its states because from him comes all wisdom and knowledge and from him flows the holy law that is appropriate to the people of his era. As in the water there occurs the clash of waves that are destructive and deadly for creatures, so also in the outward realm of the Prophet the waves of wicked and harmful dissension arise. The utility of the water is greater on the inside [*bāṭin*] of things than the outside [*ẓāhir*]. As water eternally rises and falls without pause, so too the Prophet continually rises upward to the level of the Follower in order to gather from that being his allotment of the [divine] Word and then [descends] to communicate this to those lesser than he.[54]

Here al-Sijistānī argues that the exoteric and fixed level of Scripture is the locus of confusion and dissension, and only within its deeper levels does the initiate truly abide and find spiritual fulfillment. The Prophet of the age is the one who ascends to the higher levels of the universe and is thereby charged with bringing appropriate interpretation (*taʾwīl*) to his believers. In *Kitāb al-ʿālim wa al-ghulām,* al-Yaman provides the following dialogic exchange between two characters:

> **Abū Mālik:** If he is like the superior with respect to revealed inspiration [*waḥy*] and obedience, why is he called the subordinate?
> **Ṣāliḥ:** Because of his obedience to the superior and his need for him.
> . . .

> **Abū Mālik:** Now the messenger on whom [revelation] has been sent down has certainly shown his truthfulness through the knowledge of the unseen which is in his [revealed] book. But what indicates that the person who has been given this inspired interpretation [*ta*ʾ*wīl*] also has with him that knowledge of the unseen which would bear witness that he has also been given a revealed inspiration [from God], so that he ought to be obeyed instead of someone else—just as one is obliged [to obey] the person to whom [the book] has been sent down."
> **Ṣāliḥ:** Through his inspired interpretation he brings knowledge from heaven and a "clear sign" [Qurʾān 75:19] from "the heavenly host" [37:8; 38:69], and the book bears witness to him [and his role] in that regard.[55]

This individual, according to the Ismaʿilis, is the living Imam who possesses the keys to unlock the authoritative interpretation of the Qurʾān and, by extension, of the entire universe. There thus exists one person in every generation who possesses the proper authority to make the secrets of the Qurʾān accessible to the believers.

Halevi, however, is opposed to locating any authoritative interpretation, much less *the* authoritative one, in a single, living individual. If there are no fixed rules by which *ta*ʾ*wīl* operates, this interpretation is constantly changing and, thus, potentially antinomian. Juxtaposed against the Ismaʿili claim, Halevi argues that the entire community of Israel was present at Sinai and, by extension, all of the Jewish people share in the ability to engage in proper interpretation, something that can only be grounded in tradition not an individual. An individual who lays claim to authority based on an amorphous charisma, be it a living Imam or a Greek philosopher, is fallacious and becomes dangerous to the community of believers. For example, Halevi is adamant that the role of Moses is neither that of a divine Imam (à la Ismaʿilism) nor that of the perfect philosopher (à la Jewish philosophical tradition). The *ḥaver* argues:

> For the Torah is more pure [*aṭhar*], more magnificent [*abhar*], more resplendent [*ashar*], subtler [*arfa*ʿ], and more beneficial [*anfa*ʿ]. If there were no Israelites there would be no Torah. They are not set apart on account of Moses [*wa-lam yufaḍḍalu min ajli mūsā*], but Moses was set apart on account of them. The divine love dwelt among the descendants of Abraham, Isaac, and Jacob. The election of Moses [*ikhtiyār mūsā*] was to link [his] blessing [*al-khayr*] to them by means of him.[56]

With this passage, the *ḥaver* claims that Israel is a sacred community not because of Moses or any other individual, but because of the very nature of its peoplehood. Moses himself derives his special prophetic status because of Israel, not vice versa. For the entire Jewish people, as Pines has argued,[57] share in the elect category (*ṣafwa*) inherited to them through Adam and the patriarchs:

The king: It is strange [*gharīb*] that you possess an authentic account of the creation of the world [*ṭarīq mutaḥaqqiq li-khalīqa al-ʿālam*].
The ḥaver: Surely we reckon according to it, and there is no difference [*lā ikhtilāf*] between the Jews of Khazar and Ethiopia in this respect.
The king: What date do you consider it at present?
The ḥaver: Four thousand and nine hundred years. The details can be demonstrated from the lives of Adam, Seth, Enoch to Noah, then Shem and Eber to Abraham, then Isaac and Jacob to Moses. These [individuals] possess a connection [*ittiṣālahum*] to Adam on account of his purity [*ṣafwa*]. Each of them had children who were like empty vessels when compared to their fathers because the divine influence did not unite with them [*lam yittaṣalu bi-hum amr ilāhi*]. This account occurs through sainted persons [*al-ilāhūn*] who were individuals and not a group, *until Jacob gave birth to the twelve tribes, who all united to the divine influence* [*kullahum yaṣilun li-l-amr al-ilāhi*].[58]

All of Israel, according to this passage, share in and inherit the charisma and spiritual superiority of their ancestors. The entire community, taken as a whole and not as individuals, have no need of any sort of authoritative hermeneute. Moses, as part of the Jewish people and not as someone distinct from them, becomes a primus inter pares. Unlike the living imam of the Ismaʿilis, the Jewish people possessed Moses, the person who brings the revelation (*tanzīl*), but not the esoteric secrets of this that are grounded in *taʾwīl*. Whereas the Ismaʿilis have *taʾwīl*, the Jews possess an authoritative tradition. Further evidence of this may be found in *Kuzari* 4:3, an extended monologue on the part of the *ḥaver:*

This name [i.e., the tetragrammaton] distinguishes us because no one knows the truth of its inner meaning except us [*ḥaqq maʿrifatiha ghairnā*]. . . . This name [*ism*] is among the group of excellent qualities [*jumla al-faḍāʾil*] that distinguishes us.[59]

Halevi here, as in so many other places, denies the epistemological foundations of esotericism. The key to unlocking the Torah does not reside in any individual who lays claim to charismatic authority; rather, the secret of the Torah is paradoxically not a secret, it is open to the entire Jewish people.

This notion of *taʾwīl* carries into the genre of the Ismaʿili dialogue. Explicit in the interchange between the master and the disciple, the initiated and the uninitiated, is that the former possesses both the secrets of the tradition and the correct hermeneutical framework to ascertain such secrets. The Ismaʿili dialogue, in many ways, mirrors the living encounter between master and disciple. It does on a textual level what the *dāʿī* does on a personal one, viz., the genre of the dialogue imparts something of the hidden order of nature to willing and like-minded individuals. For Halevi, however, there can be no such thing as an authoritative interpretive framework existing solely in living individuals. Such a framework can only exist within the living tradition of the Torah and the *halakhah*. This framework, moreover, is not based on esoteric knowledge, but on traditional belief and practice. The encounter between the king and the *ḥaver*, therefore, revolves around the latter teaching the former that, paradoxically, Judaism at its most "esoteric" is actually Judaism at its most "exoteric."

*Textual Initiation (*ᶜahd*)*

A central component of early Ismaᶜilism was the oath of initiation (*ᶜahd*) into the secrets of the group.[60] The dialogue played an important role in this process because of its ability to use multiple voices, and to reveal and conceal information at the same time. The Ismaᶜili dialogue thus archives the initiation between a master and a disciple. In his dialogue entitled *Kitāb al-munāẓarāt*, for example, ibn al-Ḥaytham, a tenth-century *dāᶜī*, puts the following words in the mouth of one of his protagonists:

> Following that [the *dāᶜī*] summoned me to the faith and he gave permission for our colleague whom he had summoned before me to enter into his presence. Thus, they joined in the *daᶜwa*. When it was time for the oath [*ᶜahd*],
> **the dāᶜī:** "Know, may God have mercy on you, that this oath is a sunna [example] from God in respect to His people and His servants. God took it from His prophets, and each prophet took it from his own community.
>
> . . .
>
> **me:** By God, O by God, I had never heard this and yet I have read all that reached us concerning the teachings of the sects and the many doctrines of both heretics and believers.[61]

As Ismaᶜili missionary activity spread rapidly throughout the Islamic world, the textual oath became a convenient way of passing on esoteric secrets, for only those with appropriate understanding were able to penetrate into the depths of the narrative. In his *Kitāb al-ᶜālim wa al-ghulām*, for instance, al-Yaman weaves this textual initiation into the very fabric of his dialogue.

> **The Knower:** . . . I shall repeat the oath [*ᶜahd*] to you and impose its obligation upon you.
> **The young man:** Yes, ask of me whatever you would like. I am not hesitant about your opinion, nor will I violate your tradition.
> **The narrator:** So the Knower began to recite the oath [*ᶜahd*] to the young man, and he slowly repeated it and bound himself by it. The young man could not control himself because of his emotions, and his tears were streaming down because of the intensity of that moment, until [the Knower] brought him to the end of the oath. . . . Then he finished his praises and became silent, and the Knower began his explanation and clarification.[62]

Although the actual contents of the oath are not, and indeed probably could not be, revealed in a narrative setting, the dialogue nonetheless describes the effects of it in such a manner that imitates the actual initiation that every individual already would have gone through. The actual oath, according to the above passage, is followed by the subsequent elucidation of the secrets of the tradition.

Halevi's dialogue, on one level, is similar to those composed by his Isma^cili contemporaries. Like them, his dialogue unfolds around the close relationship that develops between a master and a disciple, the latter of whom must be instructed in the doctrines of a religious tradition that he is unfamiliar with. Significantly, though, for Halevi a proper understanding of Judaism does not reside in any sort of esoteric initiation or gnosis, but in the very praxis of the commandments. Halevi's concern is not with solitary individuals who seek access into the spiritual truths of Judaism. On the contrary, the king's "initiation" occurs through membership in the Jewish people. This is not immediately apparent to the king:

> **The ḥaver:** . . . and prayer [*al-duʿā*] [must be recited] for a group or in a group or for an individual who takes the place of a group. But this does not occur in our time.
> **The king:** Why is this? If everyone read his prayers for himself, would not his soul be purer and his mind less abstracted?
> **The ḥaver:** . . . A person who prays but for himself is like him who retires alone into his house, refusing to assist his fellow citizens in the repair of their walls. . . . He, however, who joins the majority spends little, yet remains in safety, because one replaces the defects of the other. . . . For the relation of the individual is as the relation of the single limb to the body.[63]

The individual who is interested in salvation through gnosis, according to Halevi, threatens to undermine the entire community. In its place, Halevi's soteriology can only come from membership in the group and the observation of Jewish ritual. This is the opposite of Ismaʿili soteriology, which revolves around the spiritual gap that opens up between what a text literally says and what it esoterically means. Halevi, on the contrary, argues that the true secrets (i.e., the proper observation and performance of the divine commands qua action) are revealed to all, not simply to a spiritual elite:

> one cannot approach God except through God's commands [*awāmir Allah*], and there is no path [*sabīl*] to the knowledge of God's commands [*al-ilm bi-awāmir Allah*] except by way of prophecy [*ṭarīq al-nubuwwa*], and not by means of speculation and reasoning [*qiyās wa-aqūl*].[64]

Unlike his Ismaʿili contemporaries, Halevi downplays any sort of textual initiation between the text's narrative and the reader. The only form of initiation is that which makes one a member of the Jewish people. We witness this in the *Kuzari* when the king and his vizier convert to Judaism.[65] Although this "initiation" is done in secret and is originally kept secret, Halevi informs us that this was done so that they could prepare their countrymen to accept it. What Halevi does here is show us that even among the Khazars there is not a spiritual elite;[66] indeed, the entire country is invited and encouraged to embrace Judaism.

As I close this section, it is once again worth reiterating that Halevi employs the genre of the dialogue as a means of entering, and ultimately subverting, a larger discourse in the Islamicate world. Of especial concern is his attempt to undermine contemporaneous theories of spirituality that are infused with a generous dosage of philosophical speculation. The form and genre of the dialogue, in other words, enabled him to create a narrative encounter between living individuals with, at least initially, opposing viewpoints. Even though Halevi all too easily dismisses the philosopher, the Christian, and the Muslim from the narrative, the spiritual claims of the Ismaᶜilis remain, and Halevi returns to these claims again and again. Yet, in using both the genre of the dialogue and in resignifying a series of highly contested terms, Halevi seeks to articulate the superiority of Judaism, at least as he defines and understands this tradition.

Dialogue in Medieval Jewish Neoplatonic Literature

It is important to remember that Neoplatonism was not simply a philosophical system, but was predicated on a concept of revelation that claimed to offer its practitioners or adherents a form of salvation.[67] Precisely because Neoplatonism provided an understanding of religion grounded in reason, it proved attractive to philosophical elites. Whereas religious worldviews often provided naive or simplistic models of the natural world, Neoplatonism established a spiritually informed cosmology that gave a rational account of the universe based on a system of emanative causality. Ismaᶜili cosmology, based on the *ẓāhir–bāṭin* distinction, ultimately relied on that of Neoplatonism, thereby providing the framework in which intellectuals could articulate and discuss religion in an attractive manner.

I have argued in this chapter that one of the primary vehicles by which this discourse was articulated in the ninth- and tenth-century Islamicate world was through the genre of the dialogue. Even though Halevi's *Kuzari*—on the levels of genre, structure, terminology, and contents—subverts such dialogues, we should not overlook the inroads that such a generic *bāṭin*-based spirituality made among Andalusi Jews. Nowhere is this more evident than in the character of the philosopher that we encounter at the beginning of the *Kuzari*. This individual, for instance, stresses the importance of purifying one's soul, understanding the sciences and all of their truths (*al-ʿulūm ʿalā ḥaqāʾiqihā*), attaining the level of the angels and ultimately eternal life.[68] In addition to such theoretical knowledge, he emphasizes the importance of proper intention, ethical behavior, and action. The philosopher's worldview, then, is predicated on purification, knowledge of eternal truths, and, ultimately salvation. For Halevi, this is ultimately much more insidious for Judaism than the worldviews provided by Christianity or Islam (at least in its non-Ismaʿili variety) since the generic type of spiritually infused thought of the philosopher does not require irrational assent to either the incarnation of Jesus or the language of the Qurʾān.

In the space that remains I would like to examine briefly some of the main dialogues written by Halevi's Jewish contemporaries. My goal is not to provide an in-depth or sustained textual comparison of these works or even necessarily to examine their contents; on the contrary, I hope to do no more than call attention to the importance of the formal structure of the dialogue for various Jewish thinkers as they articulated different conceptions of Judaism. These dialogues, written under the influence of "Neoplatonic ecumenism," would have been, for Halevi, just as dangerous if not more so that those written by non-Jews.

It is difficult to imagine that someone like Halevi, despite his later remonstrations, had not completely absorbed the rules, written and unwritten, governing Andalusi literary production. In the case of the Ismaʿili dialogues discussed above, it is fairly obvious that Halevi employed the same terminology as the Ismaʿilis, but that he did so by making important twists. It becomes much more difficult, however, to show on a textual or philological level that the *Kuzari* was in direct conversation with dialogues written by Jewish Neoplatonists, even though socially he knew and interacted with such individuals. None of these dialogues, for example, employs the terms *niyya* and *ʿamal*. As a result, I am less interested in showing here how the *Kuzari* subverts these dialogues than in juxtaposing them, showing how it is probably no coincidence that Jewish Neoplatonists, a group that Halevi was extremely critical of, framed their articulations of Judaism using the genre of the dialogue.

The *Fons Vitae* of ibn Gabirol (1021–ca. 1058) represents one of the earliest and most sustained attempts by a Jewish philosopher to engage with the tenets of Neoplatonism. It is presented in the form of a dialogue, one that, like many of the dialogues discussed above, presents a master who leads his disciple to a proper understanding of the universe. Even though he does not frame the opening of his work using the distinction between *niyyāt* and *aʿmāl,* let us keep in mind the dramatic opening sections of the *Kuzari* as we read the beginning of ibn Gabirol's *Fons Vitae:*

> **Master:** Thanks to your natural ability and diligence, you possess the requisite strength to proceed in the study of philosophy. Let us begin with you telling me about matters that are dear to your heart, and then we will eventually arrive to the most important question of all, viz., "Why was man created?" The form of our conversation will be the following: question and answer according to the rules of logical disputation.
> **Disciple:** How can we order our questions and answers according to these rules without talking on and on? Perhaps you should clarify matters before this? If you want to follow the rules of logical disputation in all that follows, then the work will be long and the toil great.[69]

Without even getting into the contents of this work, it is readily apparent that we here encounter none of the dramatic backdrop that we do in the *Kuzari.* On the contrary, the master informs the disciple that the latter is ready to begin the study of philosophy, and that the rules of the conversation to follow will be those that govern all logical disputations. In the subsequent exchanges we witness the student asking all the questions and the master answering them. To cite but one example:

> **Disciple:** Is there an end [*takhlit*] to human existence?
> **Master:** Why shouldn't there be? For everything [*ha-kol*] conforms to the will of the great one.
> **Disciple:** Please explain this to me.
> **Master:** Since the will is the divine strength, it supplies everything and keeps everything apart. It is impossible that something can occur without it.
> **Disciple:** How is this so?[70]

This exchange is typical of the book as a whole. The disciple constantly feeds convenient questions to the master to move the conversation along. Other sections of the work involve lengthy monologues on the part of the master, in which the disciple becomes little more than a passive recipient of his teachings.[71] The role of the dialogue between the main characters, as I argued in the previous chapter, has little to do with the emerging thesis of the *Fons Vitae* and is not particularly integral to major arguments of the work.

Although it is difficult to prove with certainty that Halevi had the *Fons Vitae* in mind when he composed his dialogue, he certainly would have known of the work and its contents. I simply note that one of the most engaged works of Neoplatonism written by a Jew was done so in al-Andalus, that ibn Gabirol was a noted poet and litterateur, and that he wrote his work using the form of the dialogue. It is probably no coincidence that, especially given the highly literary and competitive Andalusi culture, Halevi presents at least the opening of his *Kuzari* using a much more dramatic narrative and employing characters that undergo changes in their personalities.[72] We can, admittedly cautiously, read Halevi's interesting use of the generic features of the dialogue form in the opening section of the *Kuzari* as offering an alternative, both philosophical *and* aesthetic, to ibn Gabirol's dialogue.

Another example of a dialogue composed by an Andalusi Jew is *Ḥay ben Meqitz* by Abraham ibn Ezra (1089–1164). Even more so than the *Fons Vitae,* it is difficult to know whether or not Halevi would have had access to this work. Even though ibn Ezra and Halevi were friends and, according to some accounts, related by marriage, they share radically differing conceptions of Judaism and the place of philosophy within it.[73] It seems highly likely, for example, that Ismaᶜili cosmology had a significant role in ibn Ezra's thought,[74] and, much like ibn Gabirol, he emphasizes the universalism of Judaism as opposed to its particularism. In the following exchange between the unnamed protagonist and his celestial guide, Ḥay ben Meqitz, we encounter the former's initiation into the secrets of the universe:

> He said: "Drink the water from its source
> The fluids flowing from its well!
> In it your fractures will be healed
> Your limbs will be dressed
> You will have wings
> To fly into the heavens."
> I drank from the water of life
> The water that gives life to souls
> My pains and my afflictions left me . . .
> My sickness was cured.
> He reached out his hand and grabbed me
> Lifting me from the depth of the spring.[75]

Although ibn Ezra does not employ the Ismaᶜili term *ᶜahd* here, his account certainly seems to imply some form of initiation. For only after the unnamed protagonist has undergone the baptism in water is he able to continue on his heavenly journey, one that will ultimately culminate in a vision of the divine presence. From the perspective of Halevi, the encasing of a generic Neoplatonic spirituality within a Jewish and Hebrew idiom would have been extremely dangerous. The ritual purification of an initiate that enabled him or her to see the structure of the universe more clearly would undoubtedly remind Halevi of Ismaᶜili or Ismaᶜili-inspired practice.

As a final example, let me briefly focus on *Kitāb al-hidāya ilā farāʾid al-qulūb* (The Book of Direction to the Duties of the Heart) by Baḥya ibn Paquda (ca. 1040–ca. 1080). Baḥya is, on one level, in agreement with

Halevi: the ultimate moment of the true believer is suprarational, mystical. In other words, philosophical speculation can only take the believer so far, at which point ratiocination must give way to total submission in the service of God. It is this type of spiritually informed worship, Baḥya informs us, that becomes the duty of every Jew, not just the obligation for spiritual or philosophical elites. This type of worship emerges not from philosophical sciences, but from the divine Law.[76]

However, unlike Halevi, Baḥya situates his work in the realm of "metaphysics,"[77] thereby signaling that the inward "duties of the heart" are contingent upon knowing the structure of the universe and the place of humans within this structure. The "duties of the heart," in other words, can only be deduced from the unity of God. Here Baḥya employs a number of theological–philosophical arguments common among *mutakallimūn* ("Muslim theologians") to conceptualize God's unity.[78] In addition to such theological arguments, Baḥya is particularly indebted to the mystical speculation of Sufism, or Islamic mysticism. Nowhere is this more evident than in his chapter devoted to asceticism (*zuhd*), which Baḥya regards as "the purpose of the Law."[79] Despite the extreme piety in Baḥya's treatise and the centrality of the Law within it, we nevertheless witness, at least from Halevi's point of view, the interpretation of Judaism through foreign categories.

Since neither time nor space permits a full-scale analysis of Baḥya's rich work, I shall confine remarks to the part of the work that is written in the form of a dialogue. In chapter 3, Baḥya recounts a dialogue between the soul and the intellect concerning the true nature of happiness:

> **The soul:** What is the evil food to which I am accustomed?
> **The intellect:** It is the blameworthy trait that overcame you from the beginning, and the forces that strengthen it.
> **The soul:** What are the components of this trait and what are the forces that strengthen it?
> **The intellect:** Your blameworthy traits are many, but their origin and beginning are two: first, love of bodily pleasures. . . . these you have acquired from your evil neighbor, the body . . . The second is your love of leadership and honor . . . these cause you to be ungrateful to your Benefactor.[80]

Baḥya's dialogue here gives priority to the rational faculty as the locus of determining what ails the soul. Whereas Halevi's dialogue is all about getting the Khazar king to relinquish the intellectual worship of God and, in its place, to engage in the proper physical actions of worship, Baḥya implies that the intellect is still paramount in the religious life:

> **The soul:** The finesse and subtlety of this matter is so great that you have made me despair of grasping its meaning, and now you console me. Please reveal to me also the secret of my place in this world and the purpose of my

> stay on it. Bring me closer to an understanding of divine determination and justice, as briefly as possible, so that I will not be like the man who does not know the right way that leads to his good . . .
>
> . . .
>
> **The intellect:** The secret is that the Creator formed you out of nothing, among the other spiritual entities created by Him. Intending to raise your position, He elevated you to the level of His chosen favorites who are near to His light, all as a manifestation of His grace and benevolence toward you. . . . [God] gave you two chosen viziers. . . . The first vizier is the mind, which directs you in the way of God's satisfaction; the second vizier is the instinct, which seduces you and leads you to the things which arouse the anger of your Lord and Creator.[81]

For Baḥya, the life of meditation and thinking is ultimately superior to one of mere action. Like his near contemporaries, ibn Gabirol and ibn Ezra, he grafts philosophy and rational speculation onto the religious life. In Halevi's eyes, Baḥya's religious and theoretical orientation is no different from that of all the other Jewish thinkers who came under the orbit of Ismaʿili-inspired Islam.

On a philological level, it is difficult to know whether or not Halevi was responding directly to these dialogues written by Jewish Neoplatonists. Yet on a phenomenological level, it becomes possible to speculate that the types of readings offered by the likes of ibn Gabirol, ibn Ezra, and Baḥya ibn Paquda—all expressed using dialogues—would have been extremely problematic to Halevi. Any attempt to rationalize Judaism according to intellectual paradigms imported from non-Jews or any desire to undermine traditional Jewish praxis was, for Halevi, tantamount to the subversion of Judaism. Keeping in mind the highly competitive literary environment in al-Andalus, it would seem that Halevi chose to compose his magnum opus using the generic and formal characteristics of the dialogue in order to offer a religious, aesthetic, and intellectual alternative to other dialogues in circulation.

Conclusions

This chapter has focused on arguably the most famous Jewish dialogue ever composed, Halevi's *Kuzari.* Yet rather than regard the genre of the work as somehow secondary to its content or as a marginal feature of the work, I have argued that Halevi's desire to compose his elaborate defense of Judaism in the genre that he does is highly significant. The form of the work reinforces its content. Just as the contents of the *Kuzari* attempt to carve out a unique place for Judaism and the Jewish people using the Arabic language and the noetic categories of various Islamicate subcultures, especially those of the Ismaʿilis, the genre of the work does exactly the same thing. In other words, Halevi consciously adopted a genre that various subcultures used to articulate their claims to religious authenticity and superiority in order to make the same claims for Judaism.

Yet the *Kuzari* subverts the expectations of the genre by putting primary emphasis on the opposite poles (e.g., *ʿamal* over *niyya; ẓāhir* over *bāṭin; tanzīl* over *taʾwīl*) than that which other competing subcultures stressed. In so doing, Halevi constructs a dialogue that counters those written not only by Ismaʿilis but also by Jewish intellectuals who chose to tune Judaism in an Ismaʿili key. Whereas ibn Gabirol and Baḥya provide fairly wooden dialogues, Halevi, especially at the beginning of his work, provides a dynamic encounter between various individuals representing claims to truth in his own day. Moreover, by the end of the dialogue, the *ḥaver,* the person responsible for instructing the king, undergoes a dramatic "conversionary" experience when he realizes that he must depart for Israel, a journey that Halevi himself undertook.

In the general history of Jewish philosophy, the composition of philosophical texts, especially after the death of Maimonides (d. 1204), moves out of the Islamicate world into that of Christian Europe. In this new context, Jewish thinkers began to focus on and debate the merits of the place of philosophy in Judaism. The writings of Maimonides now became a catalyst for a series of vitriolic encounters between those for and against the introduction of non-Jewish wisdom into the Jewish educational curriculum. Jewish thinkers who were in favor of introducing philosophy into this curriculum now began to write in Hebrew and less technically so that all Jews could be introduced to the merits accrued by the study of philosophy. Chapters 3 and 4 seek to document the tensions associated with this, once again focusing on the genre of the dialogue.

3

SHEM TOV IBN FALAQUERA: DIALOGUES OF RECONCILIATION AND DISSEMINATION

In the dominant narrative of Jewish intellectual history, the transition from Halevi to Shem Tov ben Joseph ibn Falaquera (ca. 1225–ca. 1295) could not be more dramatic. If Halevi is regarded as one of the ablest critics of philosophy, Falaquera is seen as one of philosophy's most important popularizers and disseminators.[1] Whereas Halevi is generally considered to be one of the most creative and original Jewish thinkers, Falaquera is widely regarded as "unoriginal."[2] If Halevi is praised as one of the bright lights of Andalusi "Golden Age" poetry, Falaquera's poetry, if mentioned at all, is usually deemed mediocre at best.[3] Despite such differences, however, both had a surprising amount in common. Both were what Ross Brann felicitously calls "compunctious poets." That is, at a certain point in their careers, each *apparently* renounced poetry in general and their poetic writings in particular as superfluous products of youth.[4] Yet, despite intentions to the contrary, neither could entirely give up the poetic art. Most importantly for my study, though, is the fact that Falaquera, like Halevi before him, chose to express at least part of his large oeuvre using the genre of dialogue.

Falaquera's use of the dialogue contributes further to our understanding of the genre because he employs its literary structure and generic characteristics in ways that differ from Halevi. Whereas the latter, it will be recalled, wrote his *Kuzari* to subvert Isma^cili dialogues and, in the process, offer an authentic Jewish response, in the present chapter we shall see how the dialectic component inherent to the genre contributes to the resolution of antagonistic positions. Here it is important to remember that Falaquera lived during a period of extreme polarization that revolved around the role of philosophy in Judaism. Falaquera found the genre conducive to mediating the acrimonious debates between traditional Judaism and the emerging philosophical discourse by showing their points of intersection and mutual compatibility.[5] Yet, it is also important to realize that this mediation was primarily textual. That is, the genre permitted a convenient literary forum to air debates and seek their resolution when, in reality, such resolution was often impossible.

In addition to the genre's ability to mediate between opposing views, we will also encounter in this chapter the ways in which certain thinkers adopted dialogues to popularize and disseminate philosophy. The generic structure of the dialogue, then, was conducive to teaching those with little formal scientific education about how philosophy could contribute to a better understanding of religion and religious truths. In other words, when an author made his protagonist a philosopher, the various questions that other characters put to him provided a forum for providing nontechnical descriptions of philosophy, in addition to expounding upon the relationship between faith and reason *in a nonthreatening or nonantagonistic manner.* Often such dialogues tend to be artificial because the author has ultimate control over what questions could be asked or not.

To elucidate such features, this chapter focuses on Falaquera's *Iggeret ha-Vikuaḥ* (Epistle of the Debate) and *Sefer ha-Mevaqqesh* (Book of the Seeker). These two works serve different purposes and it is likely that Falaquera had distinct, though ultimately overlapping, audiences in mind when composing them. The former work recounts a debate between a learned pietist (*ḥasid*) and a philosopher (*ḥakham*). The pietist, trained in law but ignorant in matters of philosophy, accuses the philosopher of unbelief. As I shall explore in much greater detail below, the philosopher succeeds in demonstrating to the *ḥasid* that there exists a fundamental harmony between the truths of philosophy and religion. Yet the very fact that the study of philosophy had to be defended is worthy of note and, as such, the *Epistle of the Debate* provides an important narrative setting of the Maimonidean Controversies that wracked the Jewish communities of northern Spain and southern France during the 1230s. Falaquera seems to have written this work as an attempt to offer an ideal solution to a debate that in reality had none.

The *Book of the Seeker,* on the other hand, is often described not as a dialogue proper, but as an "encyclopedia."[6] Although the term itself is anachronistic, scholars of medieval Christianity and Judaism agree that the term *encyclopedia* can be used accurately to refer to a "well-ordered, easy-to-use, comprehensive account of already existing information."[7] The medieval encyclopedia, then, represented an attempt to order knowledge with the explicit aim of educating and edifying as large an audience as possible. It was probably no coincidence that the thirteenth century not only witnessed the emergence of Jewish encyclopedias, but was also the "age of encyclopedias" in Christianity.[8]

Within this context, the *Book of the Seeker* recounts the story of a young man's search for knowledge. The first part of the book records his conversations with a series of individuals who claim practical knowledge (e.g., a merchant, a warrior, a physician, a poet), and the second part of the work involves the seeker's conversations with those who claim expertise in theoretical knowledge (e.g., a mathematician, an astronomer, and a philosopher). The central features, including shortcomings, of each discipline are described through the dialogic exchanges between the seeker and these various individuals, as is the amount of time that should be spent mastering each craft or science. By the end of the work, then, the seeker has accomplished what he had set out to do: he has discovered the taxonomy of the various branches of knowledge, the major principles of each branch, and the appropriate length of time that should be devoted to mastering each one.

Both the *Epistle of the Debate* and the *Book of the Seeker*, as is typical of the genre as whole, provide eyewitness accounts of the various debates and concerns facing Jewish communities at a particular historical moment. In the thirteenth century, these debates and concerns revolved around what constituted authentic Jewish knowledge and, in particular, the sources from which one derived this knowledge. Conservative thinkers regarded philosophy, with its origins in Greek thought and elaboration in Arab culture, as "foreign" and "heretical." To those who saw value in the study of philosophy, its method provided a way to mine the biblical text by putting it in counterpoint with larger truth claims. Falaquera played an important role in these debates because, as a nonradical philosopher, he saw the harmony between religion and philosophy. The dialogues discussed here show exactly how he conceived of this harmonistic relationship.

Maimonidean Controversies: A Brief Overview of the "Second Phase"

The Maimonidean Controversies revolved around the reception, role, and function of Maimonides' writings in a number of Jewish cultures.[9] Although the Maimonidean Controversies reached Jewish communities in many countries, the epicenter was northern Spain and Provençe.[10] The reasons for this, according to Bernard Septimus, result from the intersection of two distinct Jewish cultures:

> The explosive change of atmosphere in the old debate over rationalism coincides with a shift in arena. Previously, the controversy had been carried on solely within the confines of Judeo-Arabic culture. Now, with Spain's

> entry into Europe, the talmudic culture of Franco-German Jewry became aware, for the first time, of Spanish philosophical rationalism. Two sharply contrasting interpretations of Judaism were brought into abrupt confrontation, with the result that the controversy over rationalism took a more vehement turn.[11]

With the transmission of Judeo-Arabic philosophical terms and categories into regions that had been primarily versed in talmudic and rabbinic study, we essentially see, depending upon the viewpoint, either the collision of or the synergy between two different worldviews, two different understandings of what Judaism was or should be. Yet, almost immediately after the introduction of philosophy by, inter alia, the ibn Tibbon family,[12] its principles and methods caught on rapidly and became popular.[13] Provençe subsequently became the locus of the Hebrew translation movement and thus the new center of Jewish philosophical activity taking the place of its antecedent, al-Andalus.[14] One of the primary ways that philosophy was disseminated in this period, however, was not through technical treatises of philosophy but through what James T. Robinson calls "secondary forms,"[15] which included encyclopedias, philosophical Bible commentaries, and philosophical sermons preached in the synagogue.[16] To this list, as this chapter and the following one will demonstrate, we also need to add the philosophical dialogue, a genre that played an equally crucial role in introducing philosophical concepts in a pleasing literary form.

Despite the controversy stirred up by the translation of Maimonides' *Guide of the Perplexed* into Hebrew in 1204, the first half of the thirteenth century witnessed philosophy make major inroads into the culture of educated Jews in northern Spain and Provençe. This dissemination and popularization concomitantly led to what is known as the "second phase" of the Maimonidean Controversies, which focused primarily on the issue of what constituted authentic Jewish education; in particular, what role, if any, philosophy should play in this curriculum.[17] One individual in particular who was opposed to philosophy playing any role whatsoever in Jewish education was Rabbi Solomon ben Abraham of Montpellier (ca. 1170–1234), who on the one hand publicly defended Maimonides owing to his stature in rabbinic matters, but on the other attacked those Maimonideans who were less interested in *halakhah* and who disseminated the study of philosophy in Provençe, among them, the ibn Tibbons and their followers.[18] Rabbi Solomon appealed successfully to the Jewish communities of northern France, a different jurisdiction with a different sociology and history, to ban the study of philosophy because the study of such texts, written by non-Jews, was regarded as calling into question the veracity of the biblical narrative and other traditional Jewish sources.[19]

This ban (*ḥerem*), however, did not go unchallenged. Jewish communal leaders of Narbonne and Lunel in southern France accused Rabbi Solomon and his followers of superstition and ignorance and, with the support of Rabbi David Kimḥi (1160–1235), subsequently issued a counter ban.[20] Matters only intensified, however, when someone denounced Maimonides' *Guide* and *Sefer ha-Madda*, the first book of his *Mishneh Torah*, to the church authorities in Montpellier. That the Church would become involved in the role of philosophy in Judaism only makes sense when it is remembered that during this period the ecclesiastical authorities were greatly concerned with the spread of Aristotelianism in the Christian university curriculum. In 1210, for example, Aristotle's natural science (e.g., his physics and metaphysics) was banned at the University of Paris, and in the same year all of the works of David of Dimant were publicly burned.[21]

As a result, the Church apparently saw fit in 1232 to burn parts of Maimonides' works.[22] The involvement of the Christian authorities set, as will become clear in the following chapter, a dangerous precedent and one from which it would prove virtually impossible to escape.[23] Although the full weight of this Christian involvement in Jewish affairs would not occur for another generation, the internecine conflict among Jews—bans, counter bans, ad hominem attacks, and anonymous accusations circulating in the form of letters—intensified.[24] And even though these vitriolic attacks would eventually subside, the controversy over the role of philosophy in Jewish culture would remain, culminating in 1305 when Rabbi Solomon Adret banned the study of philosophy for those under the age of twenty-five.[25]

Despite the fact that Falaquera would only have been in his teens during the height of the Controversy of the 1230s, the mutual anger and recriminations of both sides would undoubtedly have left their mark on him. Although he never seems to have taken a commanding or public role in his support for the Maimonideans, most likely owing to his desire to show the harmony between faith and reason, he did issue one public letter on behalf of the Maimonideans, wherein he writes:

> I see in these days of nonsense a great evil, one in which flattery emerges and hearts fragment. There are many fools who study [only] the chapter headings [of books] of science [*ḥokhmah*], but not their depths. They are spoiled and their hearts jealous. They write about our master [Moses ben Maimon] in order to make a name for themselves, pretending that they are strong in faith [*emunah*].[26]

Yet, before I attempt to understand Falaquera's entry into these debates and his desire to seek a détente, it is first necessary to examine the little that we do know about his life and times.

SHEM TOV BEN JOSEPH IBN FALAQUERA: LIFE AND TIMES

Shem Tov ben Joseph ibn Falaquera[27] was born ca. 1225 in northern Spain or Provençe.[28] Although he seems to have been descended from one of the wealthiest and noblest families in Tudela, Falaquera, at least according to his poetry, seems to have been quite poor.[29] Most likely he made his living as a physician, perhaps leading a peripatetic life in much the same manner as the protagonist in the *Book of the Seeker.* As mentioned in the previous section, despite his investiture in the teaching of philosophy, he did not play a major role in the Maimonidean Controversies and, therefore, this probably attests to the fact that he was not a major public figure. It seems, then, that Falaquera preferred to reconcile philosophy and religion not in the acrimonious public arena, but behind the scenes, especially in his various writings that were meant for public consumption.

In addition to his philosophical works, which I shall mention shortly, Falaquera was, if we are to take his claims seriously, a poet of some renown.[30] He boasts that he had composed "over 20,000 poetic stanzas, with only about 10,000 of them written in permanent form."[31] If this is an accurate statement, then the bulk of these stanzas have unfortunately not survived. Later in his life, he publicly renounced his poetry as immature, the product of the folly of his youth. We see this most clearly in his autobiographical introduction to the *Book of the Seeker.* There, Falaquera writes:

> As I began to approach twilight, the sins of my early years, which had been red as crimson, have turned white as wool, and their stains have faded. The stars of boyhood's dawn have darkened as I have passed middle age. Youth, like a dream, had flown by, since frightening experiences have made the years fleet away. . . . When my years passed the midpoint of seventy and the fortieth year drew near, my conscience compelled me to forsake the gay poetry of my companions and friends and to refrain from ridiculing the "miser whose knavish ways are evil" [Is 32:7], and to muzzle my lips to prevent their flattery of wealthy men and aristocrats.[32]

Falaquera here renounces poetry, in much the same manner as Halevi had before him, and signals his desire to devote his energy to a more rewarding and authentic form of literary expression. Also like Halevi, there seems to be a fundamental tension between the theoretical desire to desist from the composition of poetry and the actual ability to carry this out.[33] Falaquera, like Halevi, did indeed continue to write poetry and even his last surviving work, *Mikhtav ʿal devar ha-Moreh* (Letter Concerning the *Guide*), contains verse. Yet here the similarity ends. Even though Halevi and Falaquera may have employed the same literary trope, that of the "compunctious poet," each renounced the composition of poetry for different reasons: whereas Halevi sought out religious authenticity in the uniqueness of the Jewish experience, Falaquera locates this authenticity in the study and dissemination of the universal truths of philosophy. Not coincidentally, both chose to express their ideas in dialogue form.

Falaquera, however, is better known for his philosophical works. In a survey of Falaquera's writings, Raphael Jospe lists eighteen philosophical treatises,[34] the overwhelming majority of which are commentaries[35] on or the "popularization" of other philosophers' works. Such titles include his *Moreh ha-Moreh* (Guide to the *Guide*)[36] an explication of certain passages from Maimonides' work, one that was used by virtually all later commentators. This work would subsequently play an important role in the study curriculum of Renaissance Jews and Christians, the former of which would have undoubtedly included Judah Abravanel.

In addition to his philosophical activities, Falaquera was also an important translator. He translated into Hebrew, inter alia, selections from the *Book of Five Substances* (*Liqquṭim mi-Sefer ha-ʿAẓamim ha-ḥamishah*) by Pseudo-Empedocles,[37] in addition to selections from Shlomo ibn Gabirol's Arabic *Meqor Ḥayyim*, known as *Liqquṭim mi-Sefer Meqor Ḥayyim*.[38] This last work, as I mentioned in chapter 1, is particularly interesting because despite the fact that ibn Gabirol originally wrote this treatise as a dialogue, Falaquera did not see fit to retain this genre when he rendered it into Hebrew.[39] Although many of Falaquera's "selections" are identical to those found in the *Meqor Ḥayyim*, several are longer, including examples and/or expansions not found in the original.[40] Moreover, the overwhelming majority of the selections found in the *Liqquṭim* are those of the teacher, not the disciple,[41] giving further corroboration to my comments in the previous two chapters, viz., that even though the *Meqor Ḥayyim* is written as a dialogue, it employs the genre artificially and that the dialogic exchange between the master and the disciple adds little to the actual content of the work. That Falaquera opted not to retain the dialogic form of this treatise further attests to this.[42]

Falaquera, however, is perhaps best known for his philosophical "encyclopedias," works that, as mentioned above, were defined by their comprehensiveness, clear organization, and ability to provide the potential reader with a quick and easy set of references. Falaquera wrote three of these works: *Reshit ḥokhmah* (Beginning of Wisdom),[43] *Deʿot ha-Filosofim* (The Opinions of the Philosophers),[44] and, most importantly for my purposes, the aforementioned *Book of the Seeker.*

At the end of his main philosophical dialogue, *Iggeret ha-Vikuaḥ*, the philosopher—here clearly the mouthpiece of Falaquera—informs the pietist that he will compose three books that will help him better understand the aim and intentions of philosophy, only two of which I will mention here:

> **The philosopher:** I will open for you a gate unto wisdom. If your opinion agrees with these opinions, then you will resolve to come inside the holy temple and "you will be changed" and you will become "another man [1Sam 10:6]. If not, you will return to your first state.
> **The pietist:** And what will this gate be?
> **The philosopher:** I will write a small book for you, and I will divide it into three parts. The first part will be on knowledge for the improvement of virtues [*tikkun ha-middot*]. In the second part I will enumerate the sciences [*ḥokhmot*] for you, and I will inform you of the intention [*kavanah*] of each one of them, of the parts of every science and about which matter it speaks and what its use is. The third part will be to explain that philosophy is necessary for the attainment of true happiness [*ha-hatzlaḥah ha-amitit*]. I will call this book *Reshit Ḥokhmah*. . . . And yet still I will write for you a third book on the opinions of the philosophers about the beings, and they are the beliefs for which the true philosophers have brought demonstration, and, according to the philosophers' view, the perfect pietist [*ḥasid shalem*] must make them our beliefs. I will call this book *De'ot ha-Filosofim* . . .[45]

The goal of the encyclopedias, according to this passage, is to inform the person who is firmly grounded in religion that he or she has nothing to fear from the philosophical sciences. This position is one that functions as a leitmotif throughout most of Falaquera's writing: a commitment to Judaism and to philosophical truth is mutually compatible, not antagonistic. The generic features of the dialogue further contribute to this compatibility because in the *Epistle of the Debate* we quite literally watch the *ḥasid* transform before our eyes, from someone who was initially opposed to philosophy to someone who comes to the realization that philosophy may actually deepen religious faith. The give-and-take exchanges that comprise the dialogue permit the author to offset some of the potential criticisms leveled against the philosophical enterprise and subsequently refute them.

Iggeret ha-Vikuaḥ: The Reconciliation of Faith and Reason

Falaquera wrote the *Epistle of the Debate*—whose full title is *Iggeret ha-Vikuaḥ, Be-Ve'ur ha-Haskamah ʿasher bein ha-Torah ve ha-Ḥokhmah* (The Epistle of the Debate, An Explanation of the Agreement between the Torah and Philosophy)—fairly early in his intellectual career, prior to the composition of his other major philosophical works.[46] Typical of the majority of philosophical literature produced in Provençe during the first half of the thirteenth century, it is not a technical treatise. Rather it is, to use the words of Steven Harvey, "a delightful dialogue . . . neither impenetrable nor boring to the uninitiated, but rather inviting and captivating."[47]

Falaquera's goal in the work is, as he himself admits at the beginning of it, to demonstrate to as wide an audience as possible the fact that the Law commands Jews to study philosophy, which, when properly understood, does not negate or contradict the truths of religion. Such a general methodological framework has led many to point out similarities with Averroes' *Faṣl al-maqāl* (The Decisive Treatise),[48] incidentally not composed as a dialogue, a work which Falaquera seems to have been familiar with since he quotes from it in some of his other treatises.[49] In the beginning of the work, for example, Falaquera, speaking in his own words, explicitly argues that

> the purpose of this epistle, which is written by way of allegory and figure [*ha-mashal ve ha-melitzah*], is to explain that the study of the true sciences [*ha-ḥokhmot ha-amitiot*] by whomever is worthy of them and whom God in His mercy has favored with an intellect to discover their depths is not prohibited from the point of view of our Law [*torateinu*], and that the truth [*ha-emet*] hidden in them does not contradict a word of our belief [*emunateinu*], as the fools think who are void of truth and disagree with this.[50]

The work, then, has a fairly explicit aim, one that is further attested to in the very structure and style that Falaquera chooses to mount this defense. The dialogue, as we will see throughout this study, is a convenient genre to exploit, and ultimately resolve, the tension between two diametrically opposed positions. It enables the author to raise viewpoints and ideologies that are not his own with an eye toward reconciling them.

The *Epistle of the Debate* is written in a clear and simple Hebrew, most of which is composed in a rhyming prose that was popular among contemporaneous Jewish literati.[51] In addition, Falaquera also intersperses throughout the work biblical and rabbinic phrases, undoubtedly to convince further the skeptical reader that the Bible and philosophy are not opposed to one another. Finally, Falaquera does not digress from his task at hand, thereby refusing to overcomplicate matters. When the pietist asks the philosopher to explicate an idea, the latter refuses if he feels that it will take him too far from the main path of the work.[52]

Falaquera, or at least the philosopher who acts as his mouthpiece, keeps matters simple, concise, and direct. Anything else would recreate on a textual level the social vitriol and religious strife of the Maimonidean Controversies. Falaquera's goal, on the contrary, is to neutralize these Controversies by attempting to demonstrate to a potential antirationalist in a convincing and sensitive manner that philosophy is not necessarily what its despisers claim it to be.[53] The result is, as the title of Steven Harvey's critical edition states explicitly, an excellent "introduction" into philosophy and the philosophical sciences for those inexperienced in such matters.

Yet, like Halevi before him, Falaquera was an artist and an aesthete, someone who was indebted to and defined by the literary canons of al-Andalus.[54] We should accordingly pay attention to the genres that he uses to compose his works. As I have argued numerous times throughout this chapter, however, at a fundamental point the similarities between Halevi and Falaquera begin to break down. Whereas the former composed his dialogue to confront and ultimately subvert Ismaᶜili dialogues, the latter does not have the same subversive intent. If Halevi sought to resignify the same terminology and categories as the Ismaᶜilis, Falaquera's goal was nevertheless equally difficult: to write an engaging dialogue that would convince the unconvinced. Each author, therefore, had to marshal all of his literary and poetic skills to achieve his task.

This need to convince the skeptical can be witnessed clearly in two features of the work. First, nowhere in the *Epistle of the Debate* does Maimonides' name appear. This is significant because the figure of Maimonides, whether real or imagined, was the pivot around which so many of the debates revolved. The critics of philosophy can essentially be placed in one of two camps: those who refused to criticize Maimonides, but felt free to criticize his renegade followers;[55] and those who were equally critical of Maimonides and all who followed his rationalist program.[56] In not mentioning the name of Maimonides, then, Falaquera opts to move the debate beyond the ad hominem attacks that had played such a large role in the Controversy of the 1230s. He thus tries to extricate individuals or even individual works (e.g., the *Guide*) from the turmoil and instead focus on and explain the issues rationally.

The second rhetorical feature of the *Epistle* that Falaquera employs to convince his readers is found in the descriptions of the two main characters in his debate. The pietist is described as one

> who meditated day and night on the Law [*torah*], who engaged always in the study of Scripture [*miqra*], who negotiated the disputes of Abbaye and Raba[57] and made "a path in the mighty waters" [Is 43:16] of these difficulties, who was meticulous in [the performance of] the light commandments as well as the weighty ones, and who walked in just ways.[58]

The pietist, in other words, is not described in a mocking tone. On the contrary, he is described as pious, engaged in Torah study, and diligent in proper religious practice. His opponent, the philosopher, is also described respectfully:

> The second was a scholar, who at times engaged in the study of the law [*torah*] and at times in the study of science [*ḥokhmah*], who divided his time between reading about what is forbidden and permitted, and reading the books of the scholars [*sifrei ha-ḥakhamim*] who endeavored to investigate the secrets of wisdom [*sodot ha-tushiah*] and who looked into the philosophical books, and who withal "pondered, and sought out, and set in order" [Qoh 12:9] his virtues according to the Law [*torah*] and set straight his ways according to the commandments of the Sages, may their memory be blessed.[59]

Significantly, the philosopher is not someone who devotes all of his time and energy to matters of philosophy. Falaquera is sure to include in his description the fact that the philosopher is also a religious man, someone who studies *both* the law and science, learning the true nature of the world from *both* philosophical and Jewish sources.

Immediately, then, we do not encounter two individuals who are necessarily or mutually opposed to each other. They both share a commitment to the religious law and scripture. Where they differ, however, is in the place and role that philosophy plays in this commitment. For the philosopher, philosophy obviously plays a very important role since it is that which supports the key tenets of religion. For the pietist, at first blush, philosophy plays the opposite role: it threatens to undermine religious faith. The subsequent dialogue between the two individuals, as we shall presently see, is one in which the philosopher must and ultimately does show the pietist that the real danger resides in the faulty knowledge of what philosophy is and what it can (and cannot) do. Moreover, the philosopher is also quick to note that an incorrect understanding of religious beliefs equally threatens to undermine a true understanding of religion.

In choosing these two characters, Falaquera seems to have had in mind two particular individuals who took opposing positions in the Maimonidean Controversy of the 1230s: R. David Kimḥi and R. Judah Alfakar.[60] These two individuals were engaged in a series of epistolary exchanges regarding the place of philosophy in Jewish education, with Kimḥi in support of philosophy and Alfakar opposed to it.[61] Rather than focusing on the animosity that appears in the actual correspondence between these two individuals, however, Falaquera essentially "rewrites" the nature of their literary encounter. To use the words of Steven Harvey,

> In his desire to show the harmony between Torah and philosophy, Falaquera had to rewrite history, or at least revise the outcome of the controversy and, thereby, have the Scholar of his debate accomplish what Kimḥi and the other Maimonideans could not.[62]

Falaquera thus attempts to neutralize the venom of the actual Controversy by creating a literary debate in which two protagonists do not attack each other, but engage in a civil conversation. Indeed, unlike the historical Controversies, Falaquera's *Epistle* has a clear and specific resolution. Not coincidentally, it is a resolution in which the philosopher ultimately has the last word, and in which the opponent of philosophy comes to understand that philosophy is necessary for a proper understanding of religious faith.

However, just so that we do not forget the sociological and intellectual contexts in which he composed the work, Falaquera reminds us what is at stake when he has the pietist threaten the philosopher with a ban (*nidui*) if he does not like what the philosopher has to say:

> **The philosopher:** May God lead you, O pietist, to His truth, may He broaden your intellect, and may the foreskin of our ears and our minds be circumcised. Please be so kind to tell me what your opinion is about what we said yesterday.
> **The pietist:** May God return you, O philosopher, from the perplexing path of philosophy to the words of the law and the halakhah. It appears to me that your words are sophistical, ugly within though beautiful on the outside. You incline from the path of the Law in your inclining toward the words of the philosophers. I warn you that if, Heaven forfend, your words are heard any more in my presence, I will decree a ban [*nidui*] upon you![63]

Interestingly the pietist threatens the philosopher with such a ban only *after* he feels that the philosopher has gotten the best of him owing to the latter's superior logical and rhetorical skills.

The role and function of tradition serves as a leitmotif that runs throughout the debate between the pietist and the philosopher. As was the case for the Maimonidean Controversies, at stake was how one acquires knowledge of truth:

> **The Philosopher:** Now if concerning these things man desires to know their truth and is not satisfied with tradition alone until he knows their cause and their reason, how much more is this the case with the things that are the foundations [*yesodei ha-yesodot*] and the roots of roots [*ʿikkarei ha-ʿikkarim*], whose reasons man must seek a way to know, and which he must apprehend in truth, not accidentally. This is not necessary for all men, but for the one who is meticulous in his faith and endeavors to ascend to the rank of the perfect man and conceive what he conceives by way of the intellect [*ha-sekel*], not by way of the imagination [*ha-dimiyon*]. As for the others who do not perceive this degree, tradition without their knowing the reason is sufficient.
> **The Pietist:** In your opinion, who showed the philosophers in the first place the paths that lead to truth, and who awakened them since there were not prophets among them?
> **The Philosopher:** He who awakes them is God, may He be blessed, in His bestowing upon them the intelligibles among which are the true universal premises. . . . God, may He be blessed, gives to him whom He loves a discerning mind to investigate by means of these intelligibles the true reality of the

> beings. Therefore, the sages may their memory be blessed, arranged that man ask for them in the beginning of the petition for his needs in his prayer.[64]

In this exchange, the philosopher couches his response to the pietist in both philosophical and religious terms. Philosophically, he argues that those who are capable are required by law to use their intellects to investigate the nature of first principles for themselves. However, he also claims that, religiously, this knowledge ultimately derives from God, and that one can only seek out the knowledge of intelligibles if one is "meticulous in one's faith." Interestingly, and here we see the selective aspect of the genre, the philosopher downplays the tension between faith and reason here by leaving out the role of the Active Intellect in the noetic process. Many critics of philosophy, most notably Halevi, faulted the philosophers for making God only indirectly involved in human cognition by relegating his role in this process in favor of the last of the emanated intellects. At the end of his response here, the philosopher even goes so far as to claim that the sages of old had philosophy in mind when they composed the fourth benediction of the *amidah*.[65]

The pietist begins to be intrigued by the scholar's argument, but is still unconvinced that the Torah explicitly encourages philosophical study:

> **The Pietist:** If the matter were as you mentioned, why did the Law not exhort us to seek these ways? Why did the prophets, peace be upon them, and the Sages, may their memory be blessed, not exhort us to engage in the study of these sciences?
> **The Philosopher:** I will show you that we are indeed exhorted about the knowledge of the true sciences [*ha-ḥokhmot ha-amitiot*] that inform us of the existence of the Creator, may He be exalted, and His unity, and that inform us of true reality of His creatures. I will show you this from the Law, from the Prophets, from the Hagiographa, from the words of the Sages, may their memory be blessed, and from reason [*shiqqul ha-daʿat*].
> **The Pietist:** If you will show me this with clear proofs, then I will know that the truth [*emet*] is with you.[66]

The philosopher then explains that he cannot immediately inform the pietist of the secrets of philosophy because the present venue is not conducive to such a disclosure. The beginning student of philosophy, and we shall see this reinforced in the conclusion to the *Book of the Seeker*, should not immediately be taught the truths of philosophy, especially metaphysics. The philosopher implies that the first step for such a student must be apprehending how the traditional sources of the Jewish tradition encourage the study of such sciences:

> **The Philosopher:** We find in many places that [the Sages] used to engage in the study of mathematical disciplines, such as geometry, as they mention in the order of *Zera'im*, and astronomy in their investigation into the cycles, and arithmetic is necessarily prior to astronomy in study. We find that Samuel

> was an expert in astronomy as he said, "The paths of heaven are as well-known to me as the streets of Nehardea" [*BT Berakhot* 58b]. . . . You should know that if these sciences were forbidden, they would not be permitted to the few and to the greats among our Sages.[67]

Since both philosophy and the Torah encourage the individual to gain knowledge of the created world, the philosopher, following Maimonides, here argues that one must seek out this knowledge wherever one can find it, be it in traditional Jewish works or in non-Jewish treatises:

> **The Philosopher:** one must be assisted in [ascertaining the true knowledge of things] by what the ancients have said about it. There is no difference whether these ancients were from our nation or not. Now since the ancients among the philosophers spent their time investigating the true proofs and endeavoring to distinguish them from those that are not true, it is therefore necessary when we want to apprehend the thing by means of the intellect, that we examine their books written about this matter. What there is in them of the truth we accept; what is not true and what contradicts a word of our Law, we reject and do not think about it. We need their books since the books of our Sages, may their memory be blessed, written on this matter were lost.[68]

Contextualizing this passage against the larger trends in the Maimonidean Controversy of the 1230s is helpful. As I mentioned above, central to this Controversy was the role and place of non-Jewish texts in the Jewish curriculum. For those opposed to the study of philosophy, the prime target was precisely the type of works that the philosopher here mentions. Yet, the philosopher rebuts these claims in two ways. First, he argues that ascertaining the ultimate truth is essential to both Judaism and philosophy. Because there cannot be different types of ultimate truth, it becomes necessary to use any tools and methods at one's disposal. Even a nonrationalist, the philosopher implies, must use reason or the arguments that such a person uses will be the subject of scorn and mockery by his opponents. This is, for instance, exactly how the pietist felt after his initial conversation with the philosopher, just before he threatened him with a ban. It is also in keeping with Halevi's argument that logic and mathematics were irrefutable, but that metaphysics was owing to its imprecision.

Secondly, and most importantly, the philosopher argues that the use of such "foreign" wisdom is neither as infelicitous nor as transparent as it first appears. On the contrary, the ideas that are ultimately to be found in such books are not foreign at all; rather, one finds in them the traces of Jewish ideas and concepts that have been lost.[69] Moreover, wherever and whenever the Torah and science appear to be antagonistic, it is either the result of the Torah not being understood properly, or of a particular scientific idea being corrupted in its transmission from the Jewish world to the non-Jewish world.

Unlike many of his contemporaries in Provençe, including Samuel ibn Tibbon (ca. 1165–1232)[70] and Isaac Albalag (d. ca. 1300),[71] Falaquera did not believe in revealing the truths of philosophy to all and sundry. Although he certainly, like Maimonides before him, saw his vocation as raising the general level of Jewish worship by connecting it to intellectual perfection, he was also conscious of the potential problems that revealing esoteric truths to all could cause. We witness this in the following exchange:

> **The Pietist:** I see that most of those who engage in the study of these sciences fall into bad ways and make light of the commandments, and some of them deny the Law, and they are men of vice. I see that these sciences are not useful for them in straightening their ways, but rather harmful to their souls. They are the cause of them going astray.
> **The Philosopher:** Know, O Pietist, that these sciences, and especially the divine science, cannot be endured by the mind of every man. Just as bread and meat cannot be endured by the body of a child or a sick person, but only by the healthy, so these sciences can be endured only by an exceedingly correct mind and a soul that has first been accustomed to virtues and that has labored in the mathematical sciences, whose intention is to exercise the soul. . . . there are among those who engage in [the sciences] those who fall into bad ways, know that this is not a result of the science, but rather of their inferior temperament and their evil desire. . . . This does not occur to them [the philosophers] alone, but you will find this among many of those who study the Law that they are more evil than the ignoramuses.[72]

Here the philosopher and the pietist agree that that philosophy is not meant for everyone. Only an individual who is virtuous, grounded in the teachings of religion, and who undergoes the proper propaedeutic sciences should study philosophy. Such prerequisites ideally guard the potential philosopher from going astray. The philosopher adds that this is as much a danger for philosophy as it is for those learned in religious law.

Finally, as we approach the end of the dialogue, the pietist gradually gains a new understanding of the aims and goals of philosophy. In particular, he comes to the realization that philosophy is not tantamount to unbelief, and that all philosophers are not by definition Epicureans (*epikorsim*). Philosophy, when properly defined and its goals correctly understood, is not the enemy of true belief, but the buttress of such belief:

> **The Pietist:** What you said is new to me, and if it is as you said, then I know that I erred in how I regarded [the philosophers].
> **The Philosopher:** Please be so kind, O Pietist, to tell me about this.
> **The Pietist:** I regarded them as heretics and Epicureans. I thought that their books were irreligious, that whoever reads them would have no share in the World to Come.
> **The Philosopher:** You erred greatly! You entertained a suspicion against the worthy. The Epicurean is an extremely impudent man, and he believes that

God, may He be blessed and exalted above such a thought, is not present in the world, and that the soul dies after the death of the body. The true philosophers [*ha-filosofim ha-amitiim*]—and these are the ones to which I always refer—bring strong and true proofs for the refutation of [the Epicurean's] belief. They make known with these proofs that there is a God in the world and that the soul remains after the separation from the body. . . .

The Pietist: Please be so kind as to tell me briefly what is the purpose [*takhlit*] of philosophy according to the philosophers.

The Philosopher: "How good and how pleasant" [Ps 133:1] is what you ask. Know that its purpose according to them is to liken themselves to God, may He be exalted, as much as within human power.

The Pietist: It seems to me that this is close to what is written in our Law: "To love your God, [to hearken to His voice,] and to cleave unto Him" [Dt 30:20].[73]

By the end of the dialogue, we learn that the debate between the philosopher and the pietist was based on the pietist's, not the philosopher's, incorrect belief. The pietist misunderstood the true nature of philosophy, whereas the philosopher was well acquainted with the true nature of religion. In fact, the debate ends with the understanding that there is, in fact, no actual debate between the two positions. Faith and reason are in harmony with one another so long as the former is not based on naive belief, and that the latter is not an extreme version of Aristotelianism.

If we use the *Epistle of the Debate* as a torch to illumine the Maimonidean Controversies, we see that Falaquera implies that the solution does not reside in extremes, neither completely with the philosophers nor completely with the antirationalists, but somewhere in the middle. It is this synthetic dimension of the dialogue that allows opposing views to be mediated. Falaquera, then, chooses to emphasize those dimensions of the genre that allow for synthesis. And it is precisely within this middle position—wherein philosophy and law, truth and religion, coincide—that Falaquera seeks to carve out a niche for his dialogue and provide a solution to the problems plaguing Jewish communal life in the thirteenth century. The target audience of the work, then, is not the budding philosopher, who already knows the truths that reside in science, but the potential critic of philosophy, the so-called "open-minded" antirationalist, viz., that person who is opposed to philosophy but not to the extent that his opposition blinds him to reason. Having convinced this person, at least textually in the dialogue, that philosophy is worthy of study, Falaquera moves in his later work to the next stage, that of disseminating philosophy to as wide an audience as possible. At the end of the *Epistle of the Debate* the philosopher informs the pietist that he will open a "gate of wisdom" (*shaʿar be-ḥokhmah*). It is precisely this gate into which Falaquera's *Book of the Seeker* provides an entry.

Sefer ha-Mevaqqesh: The Dissemination of Philosophy

If the aim of the *Epistle of the Debate* was to neutralize the indictments of the antirationalists and thereby to show the ultimate consensus between philosophy and religion, *Sefer ha-Mevaqqesh* (The Book of the Seeker) begins where the previous work ends. Written after the *Epistle of the Debate,*[74] *The Book of the Seeker* takes for granted the harmony between faith and reason that the previous work established. Consequently its main focus is not whether philosophy and religion can coexist harmoniously, but in providing an introduction into the various sciences that comprise the philosophical curriculum. *The Book of the Seeker,* then, responds directly to the main question posed in the Controversy of the 1230s: what should the place of non-Jewish learning be in Judaism? Although not included in the list that the philosopher says that he will compose for the pietist at the end of the *Epistle of the Debate,* it nonetheless functions in much the same manner as the other encyclopedic works mentioned in that context, most notably, *Reshit Ḥokhmah.*

The main purpose of the *Book of the Seeker,* like that of his other encyclopedias, is to present and disseminate the various sciences to as wide an audience as possible. Falaquera himself writes in the introduction to the work:

> I am determined to compose a treatise that will teach men the proper path [*ha-derekh ha-yeshara*], how to distinguish between sacred and profane, bringing them forth from darkness unto light. The contents of this work, which accords with the teachings of the Torah, have been built upon a foundation of poetry [*yesod ha-shirim*] to aid the reader to recall them for many a long day. "I have laid the book's foundation with sapphires" (Is 52:1) and divided it into two parts, arranging the first section in the words of poets, using the rich language of rhetoricians, and composing the second part according to the words of the truly wise by supporting it upon pillars of prose based upon the maxims and parables of sages.[75]

Yet there are a number of important differences between this work and Falaquera's other encyclopedias. Many of these differences are the direct result of the *Book of the Seeker* being written in the form of a dialogue, a literary form that Falaquera did not employ in his other encyclopedias. First, although all of his other encyclopedic works are not particularly technical, they nonetheless lack the literary features that play such a major role in this work. Unlike these other encyclopedias, the *Book of the Seeker* provides a literary introduction to philosophy, functioning almost as an "encyclopedia of an encyclopedia." Secondly, and intimately related to the previous point, the *Book of the Seeker* is written, at least in part, in a rhyming prose. This technique, a subject to which we shall return in chapter 4, is an important feature of didactic and pedagogical works. By employing such prose, and also by turning throughout to poetic interludes and other rhetorical devices, Falaquera seeks to maintain the interest of the reader, especially the nontechnical one. Here it is crucial that we not lose sight of the fact that the primary intent of such literature is to entertain while also educating. Thirdly, unlike his other encyclopedias, Falaquera includes not only the various sciences in the *Book of the Seeker,* but also a variety of other professions and crafts (e.g., those of the soldier, wealthy man, physician, and poet).

These three features are perhaps related to the fact that there is a distinctly autobiographical tone to the *Book of the Seeker,* something that is especially in evidence in Falaquera's ambiguous relationship to poetry in the work. Interestingly, Falaquera employs rhyming prose only for the first of the two books, which not coincidentally culminates in the dialogue between the seeker and the poet.[76] After the debate with the poet, who in many ways functions as a symbol for Falaquera's youth, the narrator informs us that:

> This concludes the first section of the treatise. These are my final words of poetry. From this day on I have no share in poems and no part in songs. It is time to seek the Lord, for He, in His kindness, will teach me the proper way and guard me against verbal transgression. Amen.[77]

Following this, we witness Falaquera's "last" words of poetry. And indeed the tenor of the second book is completely different. Although still written in a clear and simple prose, missing is the rhyme, the rhetorical niceties, and the poetry. Brann argues, convincingly in my opinion, that Falaquera had to make such a dramatic break with his poetic past in order to demonstrate to the reader that poetry, especially the social graces and manners that it implies, must ultimately give way to the life of reason and the philosophical method.[78]

Unlike the other dialogues examined in this study, the *Book of the Seeker* does not provide an engaged and lengthy conversation between two protagonists. Rather, it gives us a series of vignettes between the seeker and those from whom he believes that he can learn. So, though not technically a dialogue, this work nevertheless offers a highly literary and engaging account of the true end of human life, viz., the constituents of human felicity. Even though I have devoted my main analysis of Falaquera's use of dialogue in this chapter to the *Epistle of the Debate,* the *Book of the Seeker* merits brief examination here.

The work itself begins with a description of the seeker about to set out on a quest in search of understanding. This is a fairly common trope in Islamicate literature, where it is known as *ṭalab al-ᶜilm:* literally "the search for knowledge." This seeker is described in generic terms because, in order to make the quest more believable, he must be everyone in general, yet no one in particular. Like Halevi's king of the Khazars, the seeker is described as possessing the correct intention (*kavanah*), but is in need of the proper actions to actualize this:

> They said that there was a youth in a country, his days were young but his understanding mature. His entire intention [*kavanah*] was to seek out and investigate knowledge [*ḥokhmah*]. All who knew him formerly called him the seeker [*ha-mevaqqesh*]. He never left the tent of knowledge [*ḥokhmah*], seeking out the noble virtues and qualities, avoiding the extremes and remaining on the straight path. [His goal was] to dwell in the shade of the wise. Swift like an eagle, he pursued the truth [*emet*] and those who claimed to possess it; strong as a tiger, he persevered upon [truth's] door, ready to die for it. He endeavored to know the truth of things and to understand on his own terms. Therefore, he opened his heart to the words of every man and weighed everyone's sayings [judiciously]. Whenever he heard something he only assented if it accorded with the intellect [*ha-sekel*]; if not, he did not allow [the utterance] to enter his ear, in which case it became difficult in his eye.[79]

What follows is a series of encounters with a variety of individuals who claim to possess knowledge concerning the true nature of human happiness. These individuals are, in the order that the seeker meets them: a rich man, a warrior, a craftsman, a physician, a pious individual who teaches ethics, a grammarian, a poet, a religious (and nonphilosophical) Jew, a Jew versed in both religion and philosophy, a mathematician, a geometrician, an optician, an astronomer, a musician, a logician, a physicist, and finally a philosopher. The seeker spends a set amount of time with each of these individuals,[80] learning and describing, for the reader's benefit, their crafts and contribution to scientific knowledge. The main exceptions are the rich man and the warrior, whom the seeker considers vain and ignorant, but are undoubtedly mentioned because people generally perceive money and honor to constitute happiness.

The structure of the seeker's encounter with each of these individuals follows a similar pattern. The seeker first challenges the person, who then defends his art or craft, followed by a series of questions by which the seeker tries to understand, and ultimately to point out the weaknesses of, each person's livelihood. Upon departing from each person, the seeker requests additional information, signaled by the phrase "advise me," essentially asking for a summary of the person's art or craft.

To illustrate, let us examine the seeker's encounter and subsequent dialogue with the physician. After he follows the physician on his daily routine of house calls, observing him make various diagnoses and cures, the following exchange occurs between them:

The Seeker: My soul yearns for your wisdom and "I present my supplication" [Dan 9: 20] before you that you may tell me the main principles [*roshei peraqim*] of medicine, its scope [*gader*], and some of its subdivisions [*miqiẓat mi-ha-helaqim*].
The Physician: The scope of this profession is the knowledge of human conditions that make for either health or sickness. It teaches one how to maintain health or, in the case of illness, how to cure the malady.
The Seeker: If this is so, is it always efficacious in preserving health, removing, sicknesses, and preparing remedies?
The Physician: The physician does, indeed, investigate ways to preserve the patient's health and to cure his sickness, performing all his actions in accordance with the requirements and teachings of his profession; then he hopes that his work will bear fruit.

. . .

The Seeker: Does the physician have absolute knowledge in his profession or is his diagnosis conjectural? Can he clearly demonstrate his accuracy, or does this lie beyond him?
The Physician: Know that most medical teachings are based upon logical assessment of the patient's condition, and knowledge in the profession consists of estimate and conjecture. Inasmuch as this profession is conjectural, it is impossible for the physician to be free of error, and he can err, even if he is the rank of Hippocrates. . . .[81]

Here the physician informs the seeker of the principles that define his profession and that guide him in his conduct. Although not strictly speaking an exact science, medicine is based on observation, general principles that constitute health and sickness, and how, if necessary, to cure the latter if nature itself does not.[82] There follows a series of exchanges in which the seeker asks the physician to elaborate further on his profession by responding to twelve particular questions that he has. For example, the seeker asks, "Why do stones develop in the kidneys of children, but in the bladders of adults?"[83] To which the physician proffers an explanation based on the bodily humours, and the natural heat and cold in these organs. Following these questions,

The Seeker studied books of medicine with the physician and attended the sick together with him. When he decided it was time to leave the physician. [At which point the following conversation occurred.]
The Seeker: Master healer, give me advise [before I depart].
The Physician: "Guard your health by eating only to the point of satiety, and not to excess. Refrain from sloth by sufficient exercise."[84]

This pattern of exchange is repeated time and again. One of the more interesting exchanges takes place at the end of the first book when the seeker encounters a poet. In many ways, as suggested above, this encounter represents a meeting between Falaquera's old and new selves, the one who engaged in poetry as a youth, and the "compunctious poet" of old age.

When the seeker first meets the poet, the seeker describes the poetic craft in the following positive terms:

> Then he came upon a poet whose mouth was filled with precious and lofty expressions, and whose heart abounded with poetic visions [*ḥazon ha-shir*]. A man of words and an abundance of praises, one who pondered, studied and arranged parables [*meshalim*]. His melodies were like honey and butter; his lips dropped sweet words and honey flowed from his poems. He filled lips with laughter and tongues with shouts of joy when he uttered his words, and oil gushed as from an oil press when he spoke, and when he opened his mouth in song "the lame would leap like a deer and the dumb tongues sing for joy" [Is 35–6].[85]

Yet this ability to manipulate language and potential to make anything sound pleasing leads the seeker to make a familiar Platonic critique of the poetic arts. The seeker thus moves from this positive assessment to an accusation that the poet is a person of deceit and lies, someone far removed from the lofty heights of rationality. Here it is important to remember that Falaquera speaks as a reformed poet, and it is precisely this confrontation with his past that, according to Brann, makes the narrative encounter between the seeker and the poet one of the most interesting in the entire book. Moreover, this is all the more strange because Falaquera does, after all, compose the entire first half of the *Book of the Seeker* in a rhymed prose that is replete with poetic meter.

The seeker himself sheds light on this paradox when he arrives at his customary question-and-answer exchange with the poet. In this exchange we may witness Falaquera's intention to compose the work.

> **The Seeker:** Why do they say that the craft of poetry has a strong effect on the masses [*hamon*] and that a poetic rebuke affects them deeply? And why are the admonitions and praises of the prophets couched in the language of poetry?
> **The Poet:** The reason for this is that poetry is based on imitation [*ha-dimui*], and that the masses [*ha-hamon*] form their opinions based on such imitation. They use poetic language when they speak with someone whom they want to perform some action, or to accustom this person to do something. This person may have no deliberation [*ʿiyyun*] in his actions; therefore it is necessary that they stimulate his imagination [*dimiyon*] concerning that which they want this person to do. Hence his imagination must be stimulated in the desired direction. In which case, imagination takes the place of deliberation. For this reason, poetical compositions are needed to embellish and adorn various concepts.[86]

The imagination, according to the poet, is required to teach those who are ignorant about truths that they would otherwise be unable to access. According to the poet, imitation—the craft of poetry and prophecy—is essential to establishing order. Yet, as the seeker had earlier pointed out, this is precisely wherein the danger of poetry resides: in its ability to stimulate the imaginations of the masses, it is potentially dangerous because it can have the opposite effect, viz., stimulating them to do that which is harmful.

At the beginning of the question-and-answer section, the poet says to the seeker: "'Ask probing questions' (Is 7:11), for I have a reply for every query."[87] Yet when it comes to the seeker's fourth and final question—on why poetry can so easily make a person err—the poet has no answer.[88] The poet, in other words, may be able to stimulate the imaginative faculties of the masses, but he is ultimately unable to understand how he does this. And, it is precisely the ignorance of his own craft, according to the seeker (and Falaquera), that makes the poet so dangerous to philosophy, the subject matter of the second part of the work.

The dialogue between the seeker and the poet takes us to the heart of the *Book of the Seeker.* It is certainly no coincidence that Falaquera ends the first book with this exchange. For poetic language is crucial to reaching out to those who are unlearned in philosophy; it is what can teach them a modicum of truth, and in Alfarabian terms, make them productive members of the perfect state.[89] Yet, ultimately, if one is to take the next step, to move from being vaguely interested in philosophy to becoming a student of philosophy, one must transcend poetry. This is, according to Falaquera's introduction to the work, what he himself did, and what he wants others to do. In order to move from the first book, that of the propadeutic crafts (e.g., grammar, ethics), to the second, that of philosophy (e.g., astronomy, metaphysics), one must leave poetry behind.

The final dialogic exchange that I shall focus on here is that between the seeker and the philosopher, which is the ultimate scene in the treatise. Despite the importance of philosophy in the work, indeed metaphysical truths are the apex of the seeker's quest—the dialogue between the seeker and the philosopher is paradoxically the shortest of any recounted. Yet there may very well be good reasons for this since, as the philosopher argues, he cannot reveal the truths of metaphysics to anyone, only to those who have the requisite intellectual background.

Falaquera sets up the dialogue in the following manner:

> After all of these encounters, the seeker knew that all of those with whom he had argued did not grasp the [ultimate] end that he himself desired, and [realized] that their opinions were useless when it came to answering his questions. He also realized that some of them, despite hearing the king's voice, were unable to enter into the king's courtyard and, therefore, could not see his face; some were able to stand in the courtyard; others stood by the king's gate; yet others knocked on the door, yet found it locked to them. Then the

> seeker desired to speak with someone who was perfect in his virtues [*middot*], superior to all others, one who desired to transcend all of the axioms [that the others had established], and one who was different from all other humans because he alone could grasp his creator and cleave to him. This person is called in the Greek language, "the philosopher" [*ha-filosof*], viz., one who loves wisdom [*ḥokhmah*].[90]

This passage, with its equation of various degrees of knowledge with a king's courtyard, recalls Maimonides' parable of the palace in *Guide* III.51.[91] Moreover, it informs us that it is the philosopher alone who desires knowledge of, and therefore only he who truly understands, the true nature of intelligibles. The philosopher subsequently informs the seeker that

> You will not find your desired end [*takhlit*] among these others, because their opinions only represent levels to attain this end. The truth is that human felicity [*hatzlaḥat ha-adam*] [resides] in grasping his creator and cleaving to him. This is impossible except by way of the knowledge of created beings [*nivraim*] and in the conception of unity, which is the cause of all created beings. This science is called the "divine science" [*ḥokhmat ha-elohut*].[92]

Unlike the exchanges with the other figures in the book, the seeker does not attempt to expose contradictions in the philosopher's thought. Indeed, one of the reasons that the dialogue between them is so brief is precisely because the seeker asks none of the questions that, as in the case of previous encounters, were ultimately meant to stump his interlocutors by showing the weaknesses of their crafts and professions. This implies, then, that the arguments of the philosopher, at least compared to the other crafts and sciences, are ultimately unassailable. One of the few exchanges that takes place between the seeker and the philosopher is the following:

> **The Seeker** (in his heart): This is similar to what Moses, upon whom be peace, says, "The Rock!—His deeds are perfect."
> **The Seeker** (to the philosopher): I request that you answer some of my questions that I have about this science.
> **The Philosopher:** I am unable to do so! Philosophers command that we not reveal the secrets of this science. But, you can read the books that they composed on this topic, especially the *Metaphysics,* which will explain to you all that you do not know and you will come to understand the truth.[93]

This exchange is interesting for a number of reasons. First, we witness the seeker say one thing "in his heart" (*bi-libo*), and something different verbally to his interlocutor. Secondly, what he says "in his heart" is that the philosopher's words correspond to what he already knows from the Torah. As with the *Epistle of the Debate,* then, Falaquera again shows the basic and fundamental compatibility between philosophy and religion. Thirdly and finally, unlike the other dialogic exchanges where the interlocutor agrees to answer the seeker's question, here the philosopher refuses outrightly. If the seeker wants to learn the various dimensions of metaphysics, the philosopher informs him, he will have to study them in Aristotle's book of the same name, and as elaborated by the commentaries written about this work. There are, the philosopher intimates, no short cuts to understanding this science.

Structurally, the ending of the *Book of the Seeker* resembles that of the *Epistle of the Debate* in that both imply that even though the book has ended, the study of philosophy has only just begun. Whereas the latter treatise ends with the philosopher promising to write the pietist books that deal with the philosophical sciences, which would of course include treatises like the *Book of the Seeker*, the former ends with the philosopher informing the seeker that philosophical secrets can only be passed on through the master–disciple relationship.

The seeker agrees to spend three years with the philosopher, during which time we learn that the philosopher "answered all his questions."[94] When he goes to take his leave of the philosopher, the seeker asks his customary question, "advise me," to which the philosopher responds:

> I advise you to find for yourself a place to study, seclude yourself there and learn. You will need to learn much from psychology [*ḥokhmat ha-nefesh*], about the senses and perception, the intellect and ideas. You will also need to learn [more] about mathematics. But the majority of your energy should be [expended] in the divine sciences, and their ends. After these words, I can tell you that all that you see with your eyes in this world is opposed to the apprehension of the creator, most high, and [prevents you] from cleaving to him.[95]

Since the first book ended in such a dramatic fashion—with the seeker renouncing poetry—the manner in which the second book ends also merits attention. In particular, I draw attention again to the fact that the dialogic encounter with the philosopher is so brief and structurally unlike those of the others in the book. This, I have tried to argue, is because Falaquera intimates that his book has taken the reader as far as it can. It has offered to the ideal reader a convenient and highly usable introduction to the crafts and sciences. The onus is now upon the ideal or interested (if they are in fact different) individual to set aside the work and seek out a teacher or series of teachers. The ultimate end of this education will be, as the philosopher informs the seeker, an understanding of divine intelligibles so that the reader will reach human felicity: knowing his or her creator and cleaving to him.

Moreover, the ending of this work also implies that the philosophical life is ultimately a solitary one. Perhaps in light of the Maimonidean Controversies, Falaquera returns to the model articulated most forcefully in the Andalusi philosophical tradition by ibn Bājja and his *Governance of the Solitary*. The Philosopher in Falaquera's work informs the seeker that his best recourse is to isolate himself in order to prefect himself, not to involve himself in matters of state and society. Perhaps this is the path that Falaquera himself chose, and that his silence on so many of the social, intellectual, and religious conflicts of his day is the outcome of this position.

The crucial difference in terms of dialogue between the *Epistle of the Debate* and the *Book of the Seeker* resides in the fact that whereas the former is an attempt to mediate between opposing views, the goal of the latter is to teach component parts of philosophy to one without technical training. These two features inherent to the genre are complementary in the case of Falaquera: only after he has shown the reader that philosophy and law are not necessarily antagonistic to each other can he take him or her through a dialogic journey through the various sciences that comprise the philosophical curriculum.

Conclusions

This chapter has presented two dialogues that further our understanding of the composition of Jewish philosophy. Whereas Halevi's dialogue, as we saw in the previous chapter, was written in response to what he perceived to be foreign ideas and concepts, including their infiltration into Judaism, Falaquera's dialogues reveal how a thinker sought not to counter, but actually to spread such ideas among his coreligionists. According to Falaquera, like so many of those influenced by philosophy, only these sciences could inform the true understanding of religion and the religious life. For him, the genre of the dialogue provided the most convenient way to disseminate rational teachings to as wide an audience as possible. In particular, the nontechnical and literary dimensions of the genre invited those not previously trained in the various sciences to encounter philosophy for the first time.

Falaquera's use of these dialogues sheds further light on the genre because we once again see in them—in their genesis, intention, and the desire for subsequent dissemination—some of the important reasons behind the composition of Jewish philosophy. In particular, we encounter first hand in *Iggeret ha-Vikuaḥ* a cultural and intellectual struggle between two competing visions of what Judaism should look like. These competing visions, to reiterate, were not simply part of an academic debate, but represented a *Kulturkampf* in the thirteenth and fourteenth centuries. Within this context, both philosophy and those engaged in its production sought various means at their disposal to convince others that their way of life was not opposed to religion, but that it actually upheld and secured it. Jewish philosophy, in other words, was not just about philosophers writing technical treatises to other like-minded individuals; on the contrary, we see in the work of scholars such as Falaquera how these philosophers were engaged in showing others, particularly nonphilosophers, that not only was philosophy not atheistic, but that it actually possessed the keys to unlock the secrets of religion.

In the decades following Falaquera's death, however, matters did not dramatically improve for either philosophers or the study of philosophy. In 1305, for example, Rabbi Solomon Adret banned the study of philosophy for those under the age of twenty-five. This new offensive was in part related to the rise and growing popularity of Zoharic kabbalah in northern Spain and Provençe, in addition to the popularity of analogous disciplines such as astrology and magic. These threats to philosophy—kabbalah, magic, an uninformed and literal understanding of religion—form the backdrop against which the subject of chapter 4 takes place.

4
ISAAC POLLEQAR: THE DIALOGUE OF DISPUTATION

Of all the dialogues discussed in this study none exploits the genre as effectively as Isaac Polleqar's *Ezer ha-Dat* (Support of the Faith).[1] Much like Falaquera, Polleqar (fl. mid-fourteenth century) wrote his magnum opus in the rhyming prose that was so popular among Andalusi literati. The structure of the treatise provides a series of dialogues, often with a central one introducing others that further elaborate on the original theme. Moreover, interspersed throughout the dialogues are poetic summations and colorful digressions that engage and maintain the interest of the reader. As in Falaquera's work, we once again witness the genre disseminating a rational agenda in a popular and easily accessible form for those not necessarily trained in the technical study of philosophy.

The work's literary quality, however, has not secured a place for Polleqar in the canon of medieval Jewish philosophy. As is the case with Falaquera, if and when Polleqar is mentioned his name is usually coupled with terms such as *epigonic* or *unoriginal*.[2] Creative imagination and literary skill are, as I mentioned in chapter 1, not virtues to which *Wissenschaft* categories have traditionally afforded pride of place. Yet, as I am trying to make clear throughout this study, originality is too often associated in the study of medieval Jewish philosophy with a thinker's contribution to physics, ethics, or ontology. If we widen our definition of what constitutes originality to include phenomena such as aesthetics, poetics, or the dynamic interchange between philosophy and literature, we can expand our notion of what constitutes Jewish philosophy, thereby gaining a clearer and broader understanding of how Jews struggled with, interacted with, and disseminated philosophical ideas. Within such an expanded purview, Polleqar's *Ezer ha-Dat* should emerge as one of the most striking exchanges between philosophy and literature that medieval philosophy has bequeathed to us.

We know very little about Polleqar[3] other than the fact that he flourished in the middle of the first half of the fourteenth century in northern Spain and that he was engaged in a number of literary and more than likely face-to-face exchanges with his former teacher, Abner of Burgos (1270–1347). Abner, more familiar to students of medieval Jewish history,[4] converted to Christianity sometime in the early 1320s, taking on the name Alfonso de Valladolid. Abner looms large in *Ezer ha-Dat,* with every chapter of the work responding in some way to Abner's attacks on his former coreligionists. In these attacks, Abner appealed to kabbalah, astrology, determinism, rabbinic *aggadot,* and criticism of philosophy both to justify his conversion to Christianity and to adumbrate the intransigence of those Jews who did not follow him to his new religion. We cannot, however, simply write Abner off as an apostate. He was a very serious thinker who struggled intellectually with the ideas that Jews of his generation inherited from the Maimonidean tradition, ideas that he ultimately found inadequate and with which he associated Isaac Polleqar. The debate between the two individuals, then, is not simply that between Jew and apostate, but also that between the Arabo-Islamic philosophical tradition associated with Maimonides and the new Scholastic paradigm. In many ways, Abner and Polleqar were speaking entirely different languages.

We should not lose sight of the fact that Polleqar lived, both temporally and spatially, at a time of great transition on the Iberian peninsula in general and Castile in particular. Internally, as I mentioned at the end of chapter 3, the fourteenth century witnessed, inter alia, the rise of Zoharic kabbalah in Gerona, and Solomon ben Adret's ban in 1305 against the study of physics and metaphysics before the age of twenty-five. Whereas Falaquera had lived during the early stages of the Maimonidean controversies, Polleqar was living during their heyday, with anti-Maimonideans increasingly adding to their arsenal the emerging doctrines of kabbalah and finding additional support in the ban.

Externally, the Jews of northern Spain and southern France increasingly found themselves under increased legal and spiritual pressure from the Church.[5] This pressure came primarily from the recently intensified commitment to convert Jews to Christianity. Historically there were many reasons for this, including the increased number of Jews making their way from al-Andalus into northern Spain and southern France, a sense of Christian triumphalism, and the rise of a Christian bourgeoisie class, which desired to encroach upon traditional Jewish interests and occupations.[6] From roughly the end of the twelfth century on, these Jewish communities came under intense missionary pressure. Such pressures were manifested in anti-Jewish polemics that often culminated in officially sponsored religious disputations, about which I will say more below. Many of those employed to dispute Jewish leaders on behalf of the Church were apostate Jews, individuals extremely knowledgeable about Jewish sources and rabbinic method.

It is against this backdrop of internal and external pressures, especially as manifested in the disputation literature, that we need to situate *Ezer ha-Dat*. Polleqar is, first and foremost, a rationalist, and is, thus, highly critical of those who attempt to subvert a rational understanding of Judaism.[7] These included, but were not necessarily limited to, kabbalists, astrologers, and those who relied too heavily on rabbinic sources without grounding such knowledge in the rational sciences. The *Ezer* thus functions as an ideal "transcript" of a debate between a rationally infused Judaism against, to use the words of Halevi, its "cultured despisers."

Central to this disputative quality of *Ezer ha-Dat* is the specter of Abner of Burgos. Although Abner is the main antagonist in the work, he is for all intents and purposes a silent one. In many ways he had to be. For Polleqar to aim a direct critique at a Jewish convert to Christianity, especially a high-profile one who occupied an official position in the Church, would have been politically inexpedient to say the least. Most Jewish anti-Christian polemics were intended for internal consumption,[8] and if a devastating Jewish critique of Christianity would fall in the wrong hands the consequences could be severe. This is especially the case with Abner who, in some of his later writings, implied that Jews should be forcefully encouraged to embrace Christianity.[9] Even though Polleqar does not criticize Abner directly, the primary polemical thrust of his work undermines the various ideological principles that Abner used in his justification to apostatize. In many ways such a critique is more devastating because, fugue-like, it constantly revisits the same theme with increasing tempo, thereby creating a sustained and multi-pronged attack. In other words, rather than spend all his time and energy attacking one person, Polleqar succeeds in undermining all those who use similar arguments. Implicit in his discussion, then, is the idea that all those who subscribe to kabbalistic, astrological, or uninformed rabbinic principles could end up like Abner of Burgos.

Here, it might be worth examining in greater detail the role, function, and place of the theological disputation in medieval Christian society. Such disputations were one of the primary ways that the Church sought to show the Jews their intransigence. These official disputations, often public events, were meant to show the Jews both their errors and the potential windfalls that they might receive should they adopt the dominant faith. Such disputations, however, were anything but interfaith dialogues between equal partners. To use the words of Robert Chazan:

> These proceedings were not convened as a fair and equal exchange of views on religious truth; they were set in motion by the Christian side as a means of confronting Jews with the truth. The Jewish side was rigorously restricted to defending itself against the Christian thrusts that were at the heart of the encounter.[10]

The Christian disputants were almost always Jewish apostates who were familiar with the intricacies of rabbinic thought. Such disputations ended in, for example, the mass burning of the Talmud in Paris in 1240. One of the most famous of these disputations, that of Barcelona in 1263,[11] about which I shall have more to say below, would have occurred during Polleqar's lifetime and was one that, undoubtedly, left an impression on Jewish communities of northern Spain. Despite the "famous" disputations of Paris, Barcelona, and Tortosa (1413–1414),[12] there most likely also existed various "local" versions of these disputes.[13] There is even some evidence that Polleqar himself might have been a participant in such a public disputation with Abner.[14] Moreover, we also know that Abner was involved in a "public" (i.e., forced) debate with a "Rabbi Joshua."[15]

The literary dialogue proved to be a convenient and remarkably consistent genre used in both Jewish and Christian polemical literature. Christian authors frequently resorted to this genre, often using a Christian character to show a Jew the error and stubbornness of his ways in failing to recognize, inter alia, the messiahship of Jesus. One of the earliest of such dialogues was the *Dialogue with Trypho* composed by Justin Martyr (d. ca. 165). In this work a Christian tries to convince a Jew, Trypho, that the Jew misreads his own book and fails to see the foreshadowing in it that points to Jesus.[16] Other well-known examples of such anti-Jewish polemic include, but are certainly not limited to, the tenth-century *Altercatio Aecclesie contra Synagogam,* the eleventh century *Dialogus Petri and Moysi* by the apostate Petrus Alfonsi,[17] in which his pre- and postconversion personalities debate with each other. Other important dialogues include the twelfth-century *De Peccato Originali* (On Original Sin) by Odo of Tournai,[18] and the thirteenth-century *Libre del Gentil e los tres savis* (The Book of the Gentile and the Three Wise Men) by Ramon Llull (ca. 1231–1316).[19]

Christian polemicists were not the only ones to exploit the genre. Many Jewish thinkers also used dialogues to defend Jewish readings and hermeneutics in light of Christian claims.[20] Polemical dialogues were particularly popular in the intellectual circles of northern Spain and southern France during the twelfth and thirteenth centuries. Well-known dialogues include *Sefer ha-Berit* by Joseph Kimḥi (1105–1170),[21] *Milḥamot ha-Shem* by Jacob ben Reuben (fl. late 12th century),[22] and the *Milḥamet Miẓvah* by Rabbi Meir bar Simon (fl. mid 13th century).[23] The best-known polemical dialogue composed during this period is the *Vikuaḥ Barcelona* by Moses ben Naḥman (also known as the Ramban or Naḥmanides, d. ca 1270).[24] In this work, Naḥmanides recounts his version of the events that took place during the Barcelona disputation, at which he was the main Jewish disputant.

It is within this context of polemical exchanges and religious disputations that, I contend, we need to situate Polleqar's dialogue. Like the works mentioned in the previous paragraphs, *Ezer ha-Dat* uses the genre of the dialogue to create a textual setting in which a character, often representing the author himself, debates and argues with others who hold positions that are somehow regarded as wrong, misinformed, or pernicious to true belief. The dialogue allowed Polleqar to dispute and ultimately refute the various positions that Abner used to justify his apostasy. But even more than this, Polleqar also uses the disputative function of the dialogue to articulate his own reading of Judaism, one that was rationally informed, critical of mysticism, and one wherein faith and reason, when properly understood, need not contradict each other. So, if on one level we read the *Ezer ha-Dat* as a response to Abner, we must also, on another level, read it, much like Falaquera's *Iggeret ha-Vikuaḥ*, as an attempt to articulate and disseminate a philosophical understanding of the Jewish tradition.

Isaac Polleqar: Life and Times

The late thirteenth and early fourteenth centuries witnessed an increased deterioration in the Jews' legal and economic status, and the concomitant rise of a strong and self-assertive Christian bourgeoisie class throughout the communities of northern Spain.[25] This deteriorating situation led, for example, to a blood libel in the Castilian town of Saragossa in 1294, restrictions put on Jewish moneylenders in Burgos in 1321, and, in Castile more generally, a "disturbance of public order [that] often led not only to destruction of Jewish lives and properties, but also, as a means of escaping the wrath of assailants, to numerous conversions."[26]

As is so often the case in times of social turmoil, Castile was intellectually vibrant. Thirteenth-century Castile, especially Gerona, witnessed the birth of Zoharic kabbalah in the work of Moses de León (ca. 1240–1305),[27] with other notable kabbalists in the area including Joseph Gikatilla (1248–ca. 1325), who was also part of the circle responsible for the composition/redaction of Zoharic literature.[28] According to Scholem, there also existed a fairly "sizable number" of kabbalists in Burgos,[29] which seems to have been the birthplace of both Abner and Polleqar. Both of these individuals reveal contrasting attitudes to the kabbalah: whereas Abner positively cites kabbalistic principles to argue for divine plurality in the form of the trinity,[30] Polleqar was extremely critical of such principles, criticizing them for their irrationality.[31]

As far as Polleqar's biography is concerned, we know virtually nothing. We do know that he lived during the first half of the fourteenth century, and, according to Yitzhak Baer, "was a member of a wealthy family resident in Burgos and other northern Castilian cities."[32] He seems to have been a physician by profession, and, like several other contemporaneous Jewish philosophers from Castile, he was a former student and friend of Abner of Burgos.[33] So, despite Abner's subsequent critique of rationalism, he seems to have subscribed to it at an earlier period in his life. In his *Teshuvot la-Meḥaref* (Refutation of the Blasphemer), Abner writes to Polleqar:

> When you were a diligent [student] in my academy I loved you like my own soul, and even if you have betrayed and kicked [me] and forgotten everything in your pride and high-mindedness, I am still your teacher, even against your will.[34]

The little that we do know about Polleqar is intimately connected to his polemical exchanges with Abner. Despite the acrimonious debate between them, Polleqar's identity remains intertwined with that of Abner. For Polleqar is primarily known in the history of Jewish thought as the individual who tried, successfully or unsuccessfully it is not quite clear, to defend Judaism against the charges of Abner.[35] Because Abner plays such a large role in both Polleqar's life and in the unfolding of *Ezer ha-Dat,* it is worth examining his biography with the hope that it might cast additional light on the protagonist of this chapter.

Abner was a physician and, from the context of the passage just cited, apparently the head of some kind of philosophical academy in Burgos. He was also an individual who seems to have been constantly wracked by doubts about the Jewish tradition, especially its perceived lowly status when compared to Christianity.[36] According to Baer, he was shaken to the core by the outbreak of messianic speculation that occurred in Castile in 1295, in which two men, claiming to be prophets, said that a blast from the Messiah's shofar would sound at the end of Tammuz. On the anticipated date, according to legend, the community appeared in white at the local synagogue and crosses began to appear on their clothes.[37] Many of those who witnessed the "miracle" came to him for medical advice. Roughly twenty-five years later he had, according to the work in which he justified his conversion, *Milḥamot ha-Shem* (which survives only in Spanish translation as *El Libro de las Batallas de Dios*), a similar vision.[38] Connecting his vision to those he had heard about in 1295 is what ultimately seems to have led him to convert to Christianity, when he would have been in his sixties. At this point in his life he moved to Valladolid, and became known as Maestre Alfonso, where, most likely owing to his heterodox opinions on will, he occupied a fairly minor rank office of sacristan in the Church.[39]

The story does not end here, however. Abner becomes a difficult individual to classify. This difficulty, in many ways, stems from the paradoxical assessment of Baer. On the one hand, he claims that Abner was the individual who "fathered the ideology of apostasy which was destined . . . to bring wrack and ruin upon Spanish Jewry."[40] As a *social* type, then, many regard Abner as one in a long line of apostates to Christianity (e.g., Petrus Alfonsi, Pablo Christiani), who subsequently used their new status to proselytize against their former coreligionists.[41] There is ample proof for this in the historical record as Abner's writings were frequently used by later apostates and by Christian-born polemicists.[42]

Yet, on the other hand, Baer was fascinated, if not obsessed, with the figure of Abner, identifying on one level with the latter's critique of philosophy as pernicious to an authentic Jewish experience.[43] As an *intellectual* type, then, Baer argues that Abner had an important effect on subsequent Jewish thought.[44] Those who follow this trajectory regard Abner as an important thinker in his own right, one who developed a highly original philosophical argument that stressed the role of will and determinism.[45] Although I shall discuss this in greater detail below, suffice it to say now that Abner's theory of will, his employment of kabbalistic and rabbinic principles, combined to create a potent critique of rationalism that would exert an influence on subsequent Jewish thinkers such as Ḥasdai Crescas (ca. 1340–1411).

As mentioned in chapter 1, the story of Jewish philosophy is more fluid than we are accustomed to admit. Since no thinkers examined here would have regarded themselves as Jewish philosophers, what do we do with Abner? Despite his conversion to Christianity, was Abner an important Jewish philosopher? In many ways, of the two thinkers, Polleqar and Abner, it was the latter who was the more "interesting" and "original" thinker. Moreover, it was Abner who would, despite his conversion and call for the forced proselytization against Jews, paradoxically exert the greater influence on subsequent Jewish thought.

Regardless, though, the subject of this chapter remains Polleqar. And it is in his work, *Ezer ha-Dat,* that we encounter one of the most interesting and elaborate dialogues in the history of Jewish philosophy. What follows examines this work in greater detail, showing how Polleqar conceived of and exploited the genre.

Ezer ha-Dat: A Summary and Structure of a Debate

Historically, we have a vague outline of the contours of the debate between Abner and Polleqar. We know, for instance, that Abner composed his *Minḥat Qenaʾot* (Offering of Jealousy) as a response to at least three different treatises composed by Polleqar, treatises which he subsequently recycled in *Ezer ha-Dat*. Abner waited for a response from Polleqar to the aforementioned work and when one finally came to him, an unnamed work which Abner dubs *Iggeret ha-ḥarefut* (the Epistle of the Blasphemer), it was actually a work that Polleqar had written much earlier. In response to this work, Abner nevertheless composed his *Teshuvot ha-meḥaref* (Refutation of the Blasphemer).[46] Shoshanna Gershenzon suggests that after this, Polleqar seems to have withdrawn from this series of literary encounters.[47] Yet near the end of his own life, after the death of Abner, Polleqar nonetheless decided to compose *Ezer ha-Dat*, which is essentially a compilation of three of his earlier treatises against Abner, in addition to two new ones. Polleqar's magnum opus thus represents a final attempt to respond to the charges that Abner had leveled against Judaism.

As mentioned above, we have to regard Abner as the silent antagonist of *Ezer ha-Dat*. Although he is mentioned by name only a few times in the work,[48] his presence looms large. Every chapter is connected, in some way, shape, or form to his debate with Polleqar. *Ezer ha-Dat*, as I shall show in this section, takes the opposite position on virtually every principle that we know Abner used in his criticism of Judaism. Abner based his critique on (1) Jewish obduracy, (2) a reliance on key rabbinic *aggadot*, (3) a critique of philosophy, (4) the employment of astrology, and (5) the use of kabbalah. Polleqar, in contrast, mounts his refutation on (1) the establishment of key rational principles of Judaism, (2) a need to interpret certain *aggadot* allegorically, (3) a defense of philosophy, and a critique of both (4) astrology and (5) kabbalah. Every chapter of the *Ezer ha-Dat* picks up and elaborates upon each of these issues in greater detail.

Whereas books two and four of the *Ezer* seem to be independent creations, books one, three, and five are most likely expanded or updated versions of earlier treatises.[49] In this section, I briefly summarize all of the books that comprise *Ezer ha-Dat;* I provide these summaries not only because the treatise as a whole is so little known, but also to show the interlocking structure of the books that comprise it. In subsequent sections, however, I confine my analysis to books two and three because of their elaborate use of dialogue.

Book one of the *Ezer* most likely represents a new version of his *Teshuvot Apiqoros* (Response to a Heretic), a non-extant treatise devoted to articulating the central principles of Judaism most likely in response to Abner's critique. As included in *Ezer ha-Dat*, this book includes eight chapters, each one defending and elaborating upon a particular principle of faith:[50] what constitutes the essence (*mahut*) of Torah; the perfect nature of the Torah, which was given to the tribe of Jacob; the perfection of Mosaic prophecy; the importance of the world to come; the significance of exile (*galut*); the messianic age that will occur at a later date; the true meaning of *aggadot* (nonlegal material in rabbinic literature); and how to understand the meaning of the sages.[51]

Book two recounts the debate between an old man who is adamantly opposed to "Moabite and Hagaritic sciences,"[52] and a young man who holds that philosophy (*ḥokhmah*) is the key to religious perfection. After sparring in this manner for some time, the old man seeks to have the younger one arrested so he hauls him in front of a wise king. As in Halevi's *Kuzari*, the king is presumably a symbol of fair and impartial adjudication, someone to judge who is correct when it comes to true belief. The king, to the surprise of all, rules in such a manner that strikes a middle ground between the two antagonistic positions. He claims that God

> guides us according to two paths, so that we do not walk in darkness. The first path is that of perfect theoretical wisdom; the other is that of God's perfect religion. The first imprints in the soul the forms of the intelligibles that are found in existing things, and also that of the separate forms. The second seeks to straighten the deeds in our hands, and to direct our actions toward good and beautiful works, which bring about the perfection of [our ability to engage in philosophy]. However, there is no perfection in deeds alone, if the intellect cannot grasp the intelligibles and combine them. . . . Therefore, one needs the two paths to attain perfection: obligatory action and theoretical science. Wisdom cannot exist outside of Torah, for in it everything is brought to light. A religious person without philosophy in his soul is lost, because people of the earth are not righteous. In truth, the Torah is a prolegomenon and a preparation to draw the potential intellect to its actuality, and to cleave to it and to unite with [the Active Intellect]. Whosoever ascends to this level reaches eternity and this is the world to come.[53]

Thinking that the dialogue has come to an end, the narrator returns home; however, there he encounters another individual who is antagonistic to philosophy, and a new dialogue begins. This presumably allows Polleqar to revisit and visit anew certain key principles. This second dialogue provides a far-reaching discussion of many of the central themes for which the philosophers were criticized (e.g., function of prayer, creation of the universe, miracles).

The third book is probably a later version of his *Be-Hakhashot ha-Iṣtaginut* (On the Refutation of Astrology). It is worth pointing out here, and it is a subject to which I shall return below, that Abner relied heavily on determinism to justify his conversion and to point out the obduracy of his former coreligionists. Whether or not he would have framed this in terms of astrology or astral magic, this at least is the way that Polleqar understood the debate.[54] This book revolves around a dialogue between a philosopher and astrologer, in which the astrologer after a fairly lengthy debate realizes the errors of his ways and decides to renounce astrology as a false science and adopt the worldview of the philosopher.[55] The book ends by shifting to another dialogue between the narrator, presumably Polleqar himself, and an old man who, in turn, recounts another dialogue regarding the absurdities that result from people believing in astrology.

Book four, also believed to be an independent work, is not written in the form of a dialogue. Instead, Polleqar provides a list of those who are the enemies of true Judaism: (1) those who ignore philosophy, yet think that they are the true "guardians" of religion; (2) the kabbalists who presume to lay claim to an ancient and unadulterated message; (3) those who elevate the laws of nature to a position equal or superior to God; and (4) those who believe in magic and are subsequently led into idolatry. Not without significance, Abner used arguments from (1), (2), and (4)—especially if we take the latter to refer to a form of astrology—in his variegated and multipronged attacks on Judaism. Moreover, Abner also accused the philosophers (of which Polleqar was a part) of denying the will of God and substituting it with the laws of nature.

The fifth and final book is most likely a later version of the nonextant *Iggeret ha-Tiqvah* (The Epistle of Hope). In the version that exists in *Ezer ha-Dat,* we encounter a dialogue between a living person and a soul that has shed its body. The person who is alive attempts to convince the soul that the pleasures, both sensual and intellectual, enjoyed while alive far surpass anything that could await one on the other side of death. After a prolonged debate, the angel Gabriel arrives and decides in favor of the soul.[56]

From this summary of the *Ezer ha-Dat,* it should come as no surprise that Polleqar's treatise is a broad-ranging defense of a rationally based Judaism against various internal and external critiques. The fact that it is written in the form of a dialogue, in light of the role that this genre plays in contemporaneous polemical literature, as I shall discuss in greater detail below, alerts us to the fact that we should contextualize the *Ezer* as a form of disputation literature. Accordingly, the work also shares certain features with both Halevi's *Kuzari* and Falaquera's *Sefer ha Mevaqqesh.* In light of the former, the *Ezer* is an attempt to subvert certain non-Jewish cultural trends (e.g., astrology) that have been appropriated into Jewish culture; and, in light of the latter, we should understand Polleqar's work as an attempt to disseminate rational teachings to those not necessarily schooled in the philosophical sciences.

Contextualizing *Ezer ha-Dat:* Dialogue as Literary Disputation

The late thirteenth century, to reiterate, was a period of confrontation between Judaism and Christianity, not only literally in the form of Church-sanctioned disputations, but also textually through the popular genre of polemic literature.[57] This century also witnessed, as Jeremy Cohen argues, the increasing encroachment of the Church on the actual practice of Jewish worship.[58] This included engagement with the Talmud, the banning of certain parts of the Jewish liturgy, and the forced imposition of listening to pro-Christian sermons in the synagogues on Jewish sabbaths and festival days.

The Iberian peninsula, in particular, was a hotbed of Church-sponsored activity to convert the Jews to Christianity. For example, Raymond Martini (d. 1290) composed his massive *Pugio Fidei,* a work that redefined the concept of Jews as "witness people." For Martini, "the Jews have no positive function in Christendom . . . they constitute the worst enemy of the Church. . . ."[59] In fact, Cohen argues that Martini engaged in public disputations with Shlomo ben Adret (the Rashba, ca. 1235–1310).[60] Another important individual in this anti-Jewish polemic was Ramon Llull (ca. 1231–1316), who spent his career affiliated with the Aragonese court, and who made it his life work to convert "infidels" (Jewish or Muslim) to Christianity. In 1299, Llull received official permission from James II of Aragon to enter Jewish synagogues and to force Jews to listen to his sermons. Moreover, he wrote a dialogue, *Libre del Gentil e los tres savis* (The Book of the Gentile and the Three Wise Men), in which he recounts, in a form that recalls at least superficially Halevi's *Kuzari,* a conversation between a Jew, a Christian, a Muslim, and someone who wants to choose a monotheistic faith. Although not an overly zealous work, Llull nevertheless is unsympathetic to the Jewish interlocutor.

As mentioned above, Jewish polemicists also saw great value in the literary form of the dialogue. This is because the genre enabled them to respond directly to and subsequently rebut Christian charges. It also allowed them to do this in a highly entertaining and dramatic way that would have had great appeal to a reading audience. The best-known literary account that presents a Jewish response to these disputations was composed by Naḥmanides, a participant in the Barcelona disputation.[61] His *Vikuaḥ* is a post factum response to the disputation; owing to its importance, a brief examination of it might help illumine certain feature of Polleqar's *Ezer ha-Dat.* There exists a significant debate in the secondary literature as to how to read the *Vikuaḥ.*[62] I recount this debate here because it seems to me that this argument can equally be applied to an understanding of how to make sense of and contextualize *Ezer ha-Dat.*

Perhaps the most extreme view is that offered by Baer, who argues that Naḥmanides essentially presents a tendentious account in the *Vikuaḥ,* one which we should not regard as historically reliable, but as a work of propaganda.[63] Hyam Maccoby, taking the opposite approach, contends that there is no good reason to doubt the accuracy of the *Vikuaḥ* and, therefore, we should, lacking alternative evidence, regard it as a transcript of the actual disputation.[64] Striking a middle ground between these two approaches is the more sophisticated reading offered by Robert Chazan, who argues that it is impossible to reconstruct the actual events of the Barcelona disputation from either the *Vikuaḥ* or the Christian account of the debate. Rather, he claims that it is necessary to try to understand the literary structure and organizational patterns employed by each account.[65] On this reading, Naḥmanides' account offers one version of the event, admittedly an idealized one, but one that nonetheless reflects what *he would have liked to have happened* at the disputation. The text, in other words, was meant for internal consumption and, thus, it becomes a central device in the dissemination of arguments to counter anti-Christian polemic to a larger reading audience. Chazan further argues, correctly in my opinion, that the genre of the dialogue greatly aided in this dissemination due to its use of dramatic tension, simple yet effective use of language, and overall clear and indisputable conclusion of who won the encounter.[66]

This literary-historical analysis of the primary literature surrounding the Barcelona disputation is helpful when it comes to understanding Polleqar's *Ezer ha-Dat.* Central is the idea that we need not necessarily regard the written account of a disputation as a transcript or verbatim literal account that is composed post-factum. Going even further than this, I would argue that a textual account of a disputation need not have a literal historical precedent. In the *Ezer ha-Dat,* for instance, we encounter a series of literary disputations between a proponent of true belief and a series of its critics, all of whom represent distinct aspects of Abner's multipronged polemic. Even though Polleqar would probably not have engaged in a literal dispute with these antagonists, the genre of the dialogue nevertheless enabled him to create a literary setting to polemicize against these antagonists regardless of whether such a dialogue ever actually occurred in real life.

Polleqar's account shares a number of literary qualities with Naḥmanides' *Vikuaḥ.* First is the flair for the dramatic that we encounter in Polleqar's work, which, as I already suggested, functions as a textual strategy to maintain the interest of the reader. He does this through the genre of the dialogue (which I shall examine in more detail in the following section), and also by providing a rich context and backdrop against which each disputation takes place. The result is the formation of a dramatic setting that articulates the immediate contexts of each encounter. This, for example, is the way he frames the debate between the living individual and the soul that has departed the body in Book five:

> After I turned my heart from the affairs of this world to matters of the precious world . . . I called out [for a teacher] but could not find one. . . . [then] I saw a man standing, a cane at his side. There was great beauty in his eyes, and a glory in the form of his face . . . his appearance was like that of an angel of God. I approached him, thinking to myself that perhaps this is the man who will illumine my darkness and heal my wound . . . He said to me, "what are you doing here? From where do you come? . . . Follow me to a large and fortified city where we shall spend the night among the graves. There I shall reveal to you the secrets [that you desire]." He arose and walked with me from there to Mount Gilboa . . . until we came to the place that he had mentioned, to the graves of desire. The sun turned to night, and between two graves he pitched his tent. . . .[67]

From here Polleqar relates how these two individuals became privy to an argument between two souls arguing whether or not they should debate in the presence of two eavesdropping humans. The old man subsequently engages in a debate with one of the souls on the nature of what constitutes human felicity. Polleqar thus masterfully combines three dialogues—between the master and disciple, two souls, and a living individual and a soul that has shed its body—in order to create and sustain a dramatic and multifaceted encounter on the nature of human happiness.

However, Polleqar also employs various devices that we do not encounter in Naḥmanides' work. Whereas Naḥmanides' prose is direct and straightforward, Polleqar employs both rhyming prose and metered poetry. In the following example, for instance, the old man, a critic of philosophy, uses verse that essentially summarizes or encapsulates his prose narrative that will follow:

> Young man, listen to me and I will advise you
> So that you do not act foolishly as I once did.
> Clean out your ears and listen, open your eyes and see
> Do not fall into a pit of ruin as I did.
> In the days of my youth I too was convinced that
> The mortal intellect could grasp everything and in this act lay my purity.
> Greek wisdom opened up before me
> Her gates welcomed me and I approached.
> Her words were smooth and enticing

I spent some time in her house and then departed.
Because God came to my aid
He freed me and I apologized.
I began to heed those who told me that to seek knowledge
One must follow the Prophets and there I walked.
From them I learned the divine secrets,
Which I glanced at in His appearances and then I understood . . .
You are always speaking foolishness; in vain do you conduct your mouth.
Tohu [Chaos] comes forth from your lips . . .[68]

Just in case the reader should miss the central point of each narrative exchange, Polleqar provides a poetic summary of key passages in the debate. He does this not only at the end of each book, but also often incorporates poetry into the dialogue to provide another take on the prose discussion of each author.

One of the greatest virtues that the genre of the dialogue affords is that in the literary encounter—perhaps unlike the living disputation on which they were ultimately modeled—one's own side always emerges victorious. In this regard, polemical literature must always have a victor. As a result, Polleqar ensures that there is a clear winner at the conclusion to each one of his literary disputations. The culmination of each dialogue clearly states in what position, or sometimes even in what combination of positions, the truth resides. This succeeds in creating a clear resolution to the tension that is built up in each debate. For instance, at the end of the disputation between the philosopher and the astrologer, the astrologer admits his complete and utter defeat:

> **The astrologer:** Blessed is the teacher to humankind whose knowledge saved me from worthless belief and who guided me from my errors and mistakes. [You prevented me] from believing in sick and corrupt opinions and guided me from ignorance. I thank you for your words and for strengthening me in the truth of your faith . . . you prevented my foot from stumbling, and since you have illumined me with the light of your intellect, I have renounced my astronomy![69]

If only all disputations ended so neatly with the antagonist to true belief completely renouncing his opinion and embracing the opinions of the protagonist. The philosopher responds to his former disputant:

> Then [the philosopher] composed a poem out of an abundance of happiness, and he praised and acclaimed God. When he finished the reciting and praising . . . he walked over and approached [the former astrologer]. He said to him, "God's mercy reached out to me and He led me from darkness to light, and He guided me from error and restored me. . . ."[70]

As a result, the philosopher and his newly won disciple meet the wrath of the crowd in front of which they were disputing:

> After hearing this, the crowd [*hamon*], comprised of fools and those with weak intellects, gathered around them. The dozy and those already asleep said, "What is this that the two of you utter from your mouths; your logic is nonsense to our devoted beliefs. You know you do not speak the truth because we are asleep in the bosoms of our beds, we are quiet and restful in our laziness. . . ."[71]

The philosopher and the ex-astrologer must now briefly dispute with the audience about the ills of astrology! Both the philosopher and the astrologer then recite a poem in which they praise the virtue of action over determinism: one is only rewarded based on one's deeds, not based on some ambiguous revolution of the stars or planets. Hearing this, the crowd, now called *kahal* as opposed to *hamon*,[72] agrees with the two and they also praise God. So after a fairly grueling debate between the astrologer and the philosopher, indeed a debate in which each character, in turn, is allowed to have the upper hand, Polleqar makes it very clear at the end that there is no doubt as to the victor.

In addition, Polleqar, like Naḥmanides before him, introduces additional participants in the discussion in order to heighten the dramatic effect. A prime example comes from the fifth book of *Ezer ha-Dat,* when Gabriel appears near the end of the disputation to reconcile the views of the two disputants:[73]

> After the two speakers had spoken at length, each had quarrelled and dominated in turn, the one tried to trick the other, and the other tried to be too wise. With each trying to humiliate the other, suddenly Gabriel arrived, awesome and terrifying to all present. I recognized his appearance immediately though I had never seen him before; he was truly sanctified by God. He said: "Listen to my words and prick up your ears to my rebuke."[74]

Following this, Gabriel lists three levels of human life in ascending order of importance. The first level consists of a life that is completely unconcerned with matters of the intellect, making due solely with material things. The second order of life consists of those individuals who have the capacity to reason but, for a variety of reasons, choose not to. The third and final level consists of those humans who are engaged in constant intellectual contemplation, and have reached a state of conjunction with the Active Intellect (*ha-sekel ha-poʿel*). This is, he informs the disputants, the level of the prophets.

Having heard the dispute between the two souls, and the comments of Gabriel, the original narrator of the dialogue returns to decide in favor of the arguments of the soul that had departed the body. For only "the soul that is separated from matter" can, according to him, truly grasp God.[75] So the narrator, who at the outset of the dialogue was in search of guidance from a master, is at the end of the dialogue able to become an arbiter in two competing views regarding true human happiness.

A caveat, however, is in order before I conclude this section. Despite the production and consumption of these dialogues that recount disputations and that "successfully" defended Jewish belief, the fact of the matter is that very little changed—historically, legally, or socially—for Jews. Public disputations were still held, missionary activity only increased, and the general plight of Jews dramatically increased throughout the fourteenth century, culminating in the murderous riots of 1391.[76] Despite this, the Jewish polemical dialogue of this period, a genre in which we must certainly include Polleqar's *Ezer ha-Dat,* provides a literary setting, admittedly an idealized one, wherein Jewish thinkers could respond to the charges leveled against their tradition. Even if they did not change the actual social conditions regarding Jews, dialogues nevertheless provided the valuable service of creating a set of narratives to which other Jews, contemporaneous or in subsequent generations, could go in order to articulate responses to various intellectual and religious pressures exerted by non-Jewish society.

EZER HA-DAT AS DIALOGIC ENCOUNTER BETWEEN POLLEQAR AND ABNER OF BURGOS

In the final section of this chapter, I shall examine in greater detail two of the dialogic exchanges that play a large role in *Ezer ha-Dat.* The first is a disputative encounter between a distinguished older talmudist and a handsome young philosopher that occurs in book two. The second exchange takes place between an astrologer and a philosopher in book three. Both of these exchanges will reveal how Polleqar conceived of the literary structure and form of the dialogue, in addition to illuminating the scope and nature of his broader dispute with Abner of Burgos.

The first debate, between the talmudist and the philosopher, revolves around what constitutes the nature of true religious belief. As we shall see, Polleqar strikes a middle position, one that is ultimately critical both of the talmudist's naive faith and of the philosopher's extreme skepticism when it comes to religion. In the previous book of the *Ezer,* Polleqar had divided human knowledge into two general categories, both of which are derived from the Torah. The first he calls "knowledge of man" (*yidiʿat ha-adam*), and the second "knowledge of one's soul and its telos" (*yidiʿat nafsho ve-takhlit aḥarito*).[77] The first type of knowledge involves affirming principles such as God's incorporeality and denying that God is a bodily power, whereas the second type concerns the intimate relationship between the human soul and God, and that the *telos* of this relationship is the intellectual love of God. In this regard, Polleqar is quick to imply that these two types of knowledge can also be found in the books of Aristotle.[78] For Polleqar, then, there need be no discrepancy between religious and philosophical belief. The key to proper belief, according to Polleqar, is the fundamental synergy between religion and philosophy, faith and reason. A naive belief in either the truths of philosophy or of religion is dangerous, and it is precisely this charge of naive belief that Polleqar levels, albeit indirectly, at Abner.

The second dialogue consists of a debate between an astrologer and a philosopher. Astrology, especially its emphasis on causal determinism, played a large role in Abner's justification of his apostasy. In this dialogue, Polleqar accordingly sets out to undermine the arguments of the astrologer, and instead articulates a concept of will that makes room for human choice. Much of the debate in this dialogue, as we shall see, revolves around the proper interpretation of key biblical passages, especially that of Qoheleth. This debate concerning proper interpretation, and concomitant hermeneutic framework, was a central feature to both internal and external religious debates in the thirteenth and fourteenth centuries.

The dialogues that we find embedded in *Ezer ha-Dat* thus provide us with a window through which we can glimpse at various social, religious, and intellectual tensions that beset Jewish communities in northern Spain at the beginning of the fourteenth century. Despite the often humorous and sarcastic tone that Polleqar gives to the various characters, these debates were, as we saw in the previous chapter, extremely vitriolic. For what was at stake was ultimately what Judaism should look like.

The Resolution of a Dialogue between Philosophy and Religion

Polleqar opens the second book with a description of his visit to Jerusalem. One day, walking around its cobblestone streets, he comes across a crowd of men and witnesses a strange sight:

> Two men were quarreling and jesting back and forth, each one trying to overtake the other. One was a venerable old man, his hair a distinguished gray. . . . his appearance was glorious and proper, his stature was tall and he was wrapped in a prayer shawl. . . . the second was a handsome youth, beautiful to the sight, and all looked admiringly at him. His countenance shone like pearls, his complexion like roses, and his lips were a beautiful red.[79]

Although both men are initially presented favorably—with the older one, a critic of philosophy, described in terms that are the exact opposite of his younger antagonist—this quickly gives way to caricature. Whereas the critic is elderly, distinguished, wrapped in a prayer shawl, the philosopher is young, arrogantly relying on his good looks, and unadorned with religious paraphernalia. At the outset, then, Polleqar personifies religion and philosophy as radically opposed to each other. Perhaps the critic of philosophy is described in a manner that would have been clearly modeled on Abner, who was not only the senior of Polleqar, but also someone who gravely misunderstood the philosophical sciences, something that ultimately led to his apostasy.

After expatiating on the greatness of God, the Torah, tradition, and the chosenness of the Jewish people, the old man turns to his junior and accuses him of being influenced by the philosophers:

> **The old man:** The philosophers are grave sinners, who mock our wisdom, speaking a foreign language, that of the Moabites and the Hagarites. Their opinions are strange, their books are irreligious, and their compositions are all derived from foreign sources, namely, Greek wisdom, which is that of the *Epikorsim*. . . . they attempt to uproot and refute the foundations of true belief [*emunah*].[80]

The young man, however, gives just as good as he receives, in turn accusing the old man of speaking without wisdom (*ḥokhmah*), and intimating that the old man is a fraud who is full of malicious intent.

> **The young man:** . . . The [halakhic] dispute between Abbayeh and Raba is but a trifle when compared to the greatness of *maʿaseh merkabah.* Perhaps one of the great sages of Israel may have said, "*ḥokhmah* destroys Torah." Yet others certainly encouraged the study of the theoretical Sciences. . . . For [science] allows us to judge and understand matters that we do not automatically know. . . . Without these sciences how are we to differentiate between truth and falsity? . . . How can the eunuch judge about matters of sexual passion?[81]

The subsequent debate between the two gets to the heart of the struggle between rationalism and traditionalism in fourteenth century Jewish cultures of northern Spain and Provençe. The vitriol surrounding the Maimonidean controversies that we witnessed in the previous chapter has not disappeared in the early fourteenth century. Typical of the intractable debate is the following exchange:

> **The old man:** . . . Aristotle, the Greek unbeliever with whom [the young man] is in alliance[82] denies the religion of God. . . . It is prophecy that allows one to apprehend hidden matters that the intellect cannot grasp. Torah is all that one needs. It provides an account of the chariot, the secrets of the heav-

ens, the difference between "upper water" and "lower water" [i.e., in Genesis 1:7], the secret of the *urim* and *thumim*. . . . what is above and below, before and after. I understand that which is hidden and concealed, the green line that surrounds the world, lofty and hidden matters, and the viscous stones. I understand the secret of Adam and Eve . . . of Metatron, of Gabriel and the other angels, of the *Sefer Yetsirah,* of *gematria,* of *Keter* [first of the sefirot] and of *Atarah* [tenth of the sefirot]. . . . Now why don't you tell me about your sciences. Where are your miracles and wondrous deeds? What is the profit for us in all of your sciences? It is no exaggeration to say that there is none except in the customary and habitual occurrences in the world of nature, which we perceive with our eyes and ears every day![83]

The young man: The philosophers grasp hidden things, but do so honestly and completely, because the intellect is like a spring and a fountain, in which the unknown is evident from what is known. The philosopher is able to do this because he is able to understand the middle term, and bring it to light. He is able to connect the great to the small, and join them so that the answer to every question is derived syllogistically. The philosopher is, thus, able to negotiate around every obstacle. The prophet, however, is able to grasp the essence [*ʿinyan*] of things, but he does not know how this grasping takes place, or why it appears to him. If you were to ask him anything about it, he would be unable to respond because he does not know its path. Prophecy does not occur except in the imaginative faculty. Do not imagine that it occurs in the rational faculty. . . . Because of this, a wise man once said, "A *ḥakham* is better than a prophet." . . . A prophet cannot teach to another the quiddity of his prophecy.[84]

Here the issue between the two disputants revolves around the nature of true knowledge. For the talmudist, such knowledge derives solely from the Torah, which alone suffices to teach the believer all that he or she needs. Moreover, he intimates that this is true knowledge because it is a knowledge that does not necessarily conform to sensual experience. He argues that although the philosophers claim that they have true knowledge they are unable to tell us about that which we cannot perceive. The talmudist obviously has in mind the mathematical and physical sciences, but not metaphysics.[85] The philosopher, however, takes the opposite position: philosophical knowledge is superior because it is predictable and based on syllogistic reasoning. In an extreme position for medieval philosophers, he claims that although the prophets have strong imaginative faculties, they are ignorant when it comes either to the source of their knowledge or about teaching it to others.

I could certainly cite many more examples of such exchanges in the subsequent dialogue between the two characters. Rather than do this, however, I shall instead focus on the ultimate resolution between the extreme positions of the talmudist and the philosopher. Here it is important to mention that we should not simply regard the young philosopher as a stand-in for Polleqar, since for the latter, unlike the former, philosophical and religious truths mutually reinforce each other.[86] This comes to the foreground in the introduction of the character of a king, someone to whom the two quarreling parties go in order to seek arbitration. After listening to both sides of the debate, the king responds to the interlocutors:

> Listen to me and I will give to you the words of wisdom, and the sayings of grace I will make known to you. 'Listen to what I say and this will be your consolation' [Job 21:2]. Know that God created us, mixing us from the best of the elements. He created us so that we could receive the highest form, which is the *ṣelem elohim.* The two worlds—the upper and the lower, the light and the dark—are joined together in man, who clings to God and praises Him. The best part of us is the light of the intellect, which extricates us from the mask of stupidity. In this part of us, man lives and does not pass away. By it, he is renewed and does not become worn out. It enables him to glow in the light of the stars and allows him to ascend to a level of [the angels], who are eternal and who live forever. However, if he turns to the side that is from the darkness of his body, he will chase after the "muddy" light of his own image. He will wear out and die; he will descend to hell and be unable to ascend. From an abundance of pity, divine providence is upon us to guide us and to put us on the correct path, lest we become lost in our wickedness. It guides us according to two paths, so that we do not walk in darkness. The first path is that of perfect theoretical wisdom; the other is that of God's perfect religion. The first imprints in the soul the forms of the intelligibles that are found in existing things, and also that of the separate forms. The second seeks to straighten the deeds in our hands, and to direct our actions toward good and beautiful works, which bring about the perfection of [our ability to engage in philosophy]. However, there is no perfection in deeds alone, if the intellect cannot grasp the intelligibles and combine them. It is impossible to imprint them and see in the mirror [i.e., the imagination] all the opposing forms, whereas its impurity is in its marginality, until it bathes and cleanses its impurities and dross. Therefore, one needs the two paths to attain perfection: obligatory action and theoretical science. Wisdom cannot exist outside of Torah, for in it everything is brought to light. A religious person without philosophy in his soul is lost, because people of the earth are not righteous. In truth, the Torah is a prolegomenon and a preparation to draw the potential intellect to its actuality, and to cleave to [the Active Intellect] and to unite with it. Whosoever ascends to this level reaches eternity and this is the world to come.[87]

Then, just in case his ruling is not properly understood, the king summarizes it in poetic form:

> With religion, you purify your soul from impurities
> You increase its purity by the commandments.
> It becomes like a polished mirror
> Reflecting purity and not dross.
> When you bathe in its waters your sins are removed
> If in your deeds you walk its paths.

Aim to grasp the ways of God
    And all of the intelligibles.
Bring science into your soul
    After you have mastered the ways of religion.
Then you will rejoice in the sight of Shaddai
    And increase the length of your days.
For religion without science is impossible
    Much like a meal devoid of food.[88]

Despite the king's ruling, which attempts to harmonize the truths of philosophy and religion, the matter does not end here. After the narrator (*maggid*) returns home from his journey, he encounters the wrath of an unnamed individual who picks up a similar line of argumentation that we had previously found in the old man's critique. Only now the dialogue turns on the role of the Islamic philosophers, and key philosophical principles such as will and creation. In this, the unnamed disputant uses the very words of the philosophers to undermine their arguments in the same manner that al-Ghazālī did before him:

> **The unnamed disputant:** The Muslim sage, Abū Ḥāmid al-Ghazālī, composed a treatise [called] the *Incoherence of the Philosophers,* and in it he revealed the [weaknesses] of their arguments and destroyed the wickedness of their ideas. Al-Ghazālī knew that [the philosophers] were lying blasphemers . . . who undermine creation, deny the will of God, and his ability to act freely. . . . They also destroy faith [*emunah*] . . . because [according to them] the Creator can neither move nor change, He cannot hear the call of the supplicant, nor does He reward the righteous or punish the sinner. Every philosopher is a danger. They sin in believing that God cannot know particulars or grasp individual human beings, only the species of things, or that He know the particular in a general way. Every human being [according to them] is solitary and wanders [without guidance], like sheep without a shepherd. Each individual walks without purpose, [leaving things to] chance because they are devoid of knowing custom or guidance. . . . how can you compare a philosopher to a Baᶜal-Torah, one an apostate and the other a man of righteousness?[89]

After this outburst, the text introduces an individual named Isaac, perhaps Polleqar speaking in his own name.[90] Regardless, he responds to the man's diatribe:

> **Isaac:** How can you claim to help when you have no strength? Without courage you claim to come to [someone's] aid. You have no wisdom, but try to offer advice. . . . Although you mentioned Abū Ḥāmid [al-Ghazālī], you failed to cite Abū Walid [Ibn Rushd] who wrote *The Refutation of [al-Ghazālī's] Refutation,* in which he removed the fundamentals from [al-Ghazālī's] arguments, and showed that it was [al-Ghazālī's] intention to deceive. . . . Also Rabbi Isaac ben Albalag overturned [al-Ghazālī's] claims and refuted the details of

his arguments, thereby explaining his errors in his commentary to the *Intentions of the Philosophers*.[91]

Following this, Isaac gets at what he considers to be the centerpiece of those who criticize philosophy: the role of God's ability to act in the world. Isaac informs his textual antagonist:

> **Isaac:** Let me instruct you in the fundamentals of religion. Is it not better to maintain an eternal, ongoing creation than [to have] the belief that [God] acted in the world and then withdrew? . . . God acted, continues to act, and will act, both above and below. In this He constantly maintains the existence [of the universe]. This corresponds to the beliefs of our ancient sages.[92]

Here Isaac argues that the true understanding of religion comes only from philosophy. Upholding the Averroean position that God constantly maintains the existence of the world, a position referred to as "eternal creation,"[93] he argues that this better protects God's omnipotence and omniscience than does the position of creation ex nihilo, which essentially turns God into a deus otiosus. This leads Isaac into a discussion of God's will, something that becomes central to the forthcoming debate between the philosopher and the astrologer. It was the issue of will, it should be recalled, that was of central importance to Abner's decision and justification to convert to Christianity. Although I will deal with this more fully in the following section, suffice it to say here that the issue revolves around what God can and cannot do. The religious position, at least as articulated textually by the critic of philosophy, is that God can do whatsoever he desires simply because he is God. If he could not do that which was logically impossible, then God would cease to be God. Here Isaac distinguishes between that which is possible in action (*be-poʿal*) and that which is possible in the acted (*be-nifʿal*). So even though God can in theory do anything that he desires, he voluntarily restricts his will for the benefit of humanity. However, if God should so desire to break natural laws, as for example in the case of miracles, then he is certainly able to do so.

As is typical with Polleqar's use of the dialogue, whenever he introduces weighty philosophical matters in favor of his textual stand-in, the character who was originally steadfastly opposed to the truth begins to come around and gradually accept Polleqar's way of thinking:

> After the man had heard my words, he examined and began to understand my discourse. His face lit up, his ideas began to settle, and he opened his eyes widely. . . . His sword was beaten into a ploughshare, his spear into a pruning hook, and all of the war instruments that he had brought with him were shattered. He began to increase his praises to the Lord of heaven, he bowed and prostrated to the ground, because he realized that wiser men than he had gotten the better of him.[94]

By the end of book two, then, we have essentially witnessed two separate but overlapping dialogues. The structure is surely significant. The first dialogue begins with philosophy and religion diametrically opposed to each other. This is followed by the introduction of the character of a king, whose ruling attempts to bring the two sides together. It does so briefly, but then a new dialogue is introduced that is more vitriolic than the previous one because it deals with the real issues that are at stake in the dispute, and not just with creating antagonistic caricatures. This dialogue is resolved through a character named Isaac, who explains the traditional vocabulary of religion (e.g., creation, will) philosophically, in at least what he considers to be a manner that is satisfactory to a religious person. At this point, the firm defender of religious belief realizes his errors and admits that philosophy and religion can coexist in harmony.

An Irresoluble Debate between Astrology and Philosophy

The second dialogue, that between a philosopher (*ḥaver*) and an astrologer (*hover*), is both more vitriolic and less amenable to resolution than the previous one. This is because astrology was, at least according to Polleqar, the main phenomenon that Abner appealed to in order to justify both his own conversion and the obduracy of the Jews. Yet Charles Manekin adds the important caveat that Polleqar, like all of those in the Judeo-Islamic philosophical tradition, always tended to frame the issue of determinism in light of astrology, whereas it seems that Abner's theory of determinism was motivated more by theological considerations such as protecting divine omnipotence and omniscience.[95] Manekin also suggests, again correctly in my opinion, that we need not necessarily regard the debate between Polleqar and Abner, at least on the theory of will and determinism, as that between Jew and apostate or even between libertarian and determinist. Even though this seems to be the way Polleqar conceived of it, what was really at stake was an emerging tension between the older paradigm of Islamic philosophy and that of the new scholastic-influenced philosophy.[96]

Abner's critique in many ways strikes at the heart of the medieval Judeo-Islamic philosophical tradition. He argued, for instance, that, unlike the Maimonidean system of which Polleqar was apart, true faith emerges from the love of God. Only this love is not contingent on rational knowledge or intellectual perfection, as it was for Polleqar, but on beliefs that need not be rational at all.[97]

Abner's discussion of will is certainly not simplistic. He argues that all things on earth derive from a causal contingency that emanates from the heavenly spheres. Here I quote from Manekin's convenient summary:

> Combining a strict determinism with a belief in the primacy of the will over the intellect, Abner defined a voluntary agent as one who can, by his nature, equally perform one of two alternatives, that is, one who is not constrained by his nature, or by virtue of himself, to perform just one alternative and not the other is a combination of the motivating stimulus (sense image, cognition, or "intelligible imagination"), which stretches back in a causal chain to the movement of the spheres, and the imaginative faculty; this conjunction yields a new assent which Abner calls the "complete will." So actions are voluntary in so far as the will is part of a rigid causal chain. If there are various outcomes, it is only because the will can be determined in various ways.[98]

Also significant to this debate, at least in Polleqar's account of it, is biblical interpretation. Both the astrologer and the philosopher make frequent appeals to the biblical narrative, especially the book of Qoheleth, in order to justify their arguments. Each individual, then, seeks to ground his truth claims in the same source, the Bible, in order to claim victory over his opponent.[99]

Central to Polleqar's deployment of the dialogue, as I noted earlier, is his ability to create a rich description that naturally attracts the reader's interest in the debate to follow. As in the previous dialogue (indeed, as in every other dialogue recounted in the *Ezer*), the narrator again uses the trope of leaving his home in order to search out wisdom in foreign lands:

> I roamed deserts, wandered in foreign lands until the compassion of heaven led me to a beautiful city [*ʿir shalem;* i.e., Jerusalem], a city great to God. Roaming its streets, I heard the voice of a crowd emerging from the middle of a square. I approached and beheld a group of philosophers [*ḥakhamim*] and magicians [*nivonei laḥash*] discussing [the nature of] wisdom and what constituted true sciences.[100]

As with the description of the two protagonists in the previous debate, Polleqar again provides a thick description of each of the potential antagonists. Especially rich is his description of the astrologer, which again borders on caricature:

> In the midst [of the crowd] was a man looking up to the heavens. He claimed to look at the stars and to be able to predict future events. He stood up and hanging from his finger was a copper instrument [i.e., an astrolabe]. . . . In front of him was a long table upon which were open books that were illustrated with [various] patterns in all types of colors. There were also [instruments to chart] the works of God—quarters, circles, a compass, a drafting instrument, and various other implements. He said to the crowd that was sitting at his feet: "How long will you occupy yourselves with nonsense and lies? What gain is there in spending your days studying logic, physics, and meta-

> physics? [Such sciences take] a lot of work, but provide no advantage; you toil in vain and waste your time! I, however, am able to see visions of God. I look into the stars and can predict the future, just like the prophets of God, who occupy a level far superior to that of philosophers [*baʿalei ḥokhmah*], who are unable to grasp with the help of their science anything that is hidden or concealed.[101]

In many ways, this initial speech of the astrologer echoes the same criticisms leveled against philosophy by the philosophically uninformed talmudist in the previous dialogue. Only now, this criticism is no longer anchored solely in the knowledge that scripture offers, but on the proactive ability of the astrologically informed to predict and subsequently manipulate divine decree through the principles of astral magic.[102] The subsequent disputant of the astrologer, the philosopher, is described in not nearly the same detail:

> Hearing the speech of this man, and his admonitions, some members of the crowd were afraid and accepted his words unconditionally, yet others were surprised and upset by them. However, there was also in their midst one of our associates, a scholar who occupied himself with wisdom and the sciences of justice. He was steadfast to God, His Torah, and to the Truth. He answered [the astrologer]: "What exactly is it that you do? How is your knowledge different from mine?"[103]

With this introduction of the philosopher, the debate begins in earnest. Note, though, that this philosopher is not like the first one, introduced in the previous dialogue, who was described as young and arrogant; rather, this individual is characterized as "steadfast to God, His Torah, and the Truth." The astrologer, by contrast, claims that he has derived his technical knowledge directly from the prophets and sages of old, that he practices an esoteric craft based on the mundane reception of the various celestial influences.

> **The astrologer:** Know that [our world] is divided into four quarters, which is subdivided by two circles, [called] longitude and latitude. Each quarter is in turn divided into three parts, each one of which is called a "house." Each "house" is limited by two hours.[104]

After listing the properties of each "house" in addition to the various planets, the philosopher takes exception to the naivete of the astrologer's account.

> **The philosopher:** Certainly heat and dampness are essential properties of the sun and the moon, but they are not caused simply by their movements. We already know that all of the heavenly bodies are made of fifth matter and that it is impossible to find in them any of the four elements which comprise our world. . . . What you mentioned concerning the coolness of Saturn, the

> heat of Mars, and the intermediacy of Jupiter which sits between them is nothing but dreams . . . [such opinions] can lead to idolatry. . . . How can the distance between the planets cause hatred or love? From where are you getting these crazy ideas? Are you making them up or receiving them from others? . . . These forms [of the zodiac] that you mention, how can we see or perceive them? Who can rise to the heavens and see the form of a ram and why is it not a ewe? Why is it a bull as opposed to a cow? Or, a lion and not a lioness? A virgin as opposed to an old maid? . . . We have eyes so why can we not see them? . . . How can you argue that the ancients can see what we cannot? . . . Did they have better sense perception than we do?[105]

The philosopher here critiques the principles of the astrologer based on sense experience and common sense. If knowledge is based on that which cannot be perceived or does not derive from rational principles, then it does not deserve to be called knowledge. The dialogue between the philosopher and the astrologer continues in this vein, going back and forth, until it culminates in the debate concerning free will and determinism:

> **The astrologer:** How can you say that the authority of man can pick or choose one thing over another? Yet the will of God is able to hinder or prevent the will of man from doing what he wants!
> **The philosopher:** . . . We know that the outermost sphere encircles everything—it is like one man and all that is inside [this sphere] is like this man's limbs. This is the universal will of God, which organizes this world just as the soul organizes the body, it comes anew simultaneously with the will of man who is like a part or limb of God. You see that the nerve moves the finger at its own will, yet one also says that the man moves his finger at his will. The two wills are simultaneous and concordant. This is just as the sage said that all is revealed and liberty has been given to men to act according to their wish and will [Avot 3: 17].[106]

Polleqar's account of the debate here may be, as Manekin suggests, overly simplistic or, at least, a misreading of what was at stake for Abner. Whereas it seems that Abner's true opinion was that predestination need not necessarily render human deliberation meaningless, that human deliberation can play a role as an intermediate link in a causal chain going back to the motion of the celestial spheres.[107] Polleqar, however, criticizes this by developing a theory of will that some regard as pantheistic.[108] According to this theory, human will is intimately connected to divine will so that when an individual acts, the completion of this action is ordained by divine will at the exact same time. Philosophically, this can be problematic, as Abner's criticisms make clear, because what God knows can only come to be at the moment a specific human action occurs or else God's foreknowledge would be seriously jeopardized. In response, Polleqar argues that God's knowledge does not change because God's knowledge of particulars comes from his knowledge of universals, which, in turn, is identical to his essence. In the following exchange, the astrologer and the philosopher further debate the interconnection or synergy between human will and divine will when it comes to the nature of choice:

> **The astrologer**: You boast and praise yourself too much in your attempt to grasp alone what is good without the help of God! You too easily throw off the yoke of the kingdom of heaven. How can you deny such a great thing! Did you not listen to what the prophet said. . . . All the deeds of humans are determined by God. . . .
> **The philosopher:** Heaven forbid that I should be so bold as to think that my will alone has absolute freedom. I already explained to you that my will unites with divine will and that these two wills unite. At the time when I desire something or want to do something, I alone make the choice.[109]

The philosopher adds, "The Creator has chosen to impress upon matter an order and a form."[110] Creation, therefore, implies orderliness and predictability, not that which is arbitrary. The astrologer, the philosopher intimates, is actually prepared to deny the predictability of natural phenomena, for example, the fact that a stone will always fall to earth or that fire will always rise, in order to protect God's freedom.

The philosopher firmly objects to the astrologer's claim that the planets, qua material objects, can have any influence whatsoever on the human intellect, which is not composed of matter:

> That which does not exist in matter is superior to that which exists in matter; the actions of that which is not in matter are superior to that which is in matter; that which isn't in matter acts and that which exists in matter is acted upon. The soul of man, in which is located the will and desire, is not in matter.[111]

As a result, humans cannot come under the influence of the stars. To illustrate the absurdity of the astrologer's claim, the philosopher recounts a parable (*mashal*):

> To what is this similar? To two men who are walking on a path and encounter a deep river . . . they find there a man sitting and ask him if there is a safe place to cross. He says to them, know that this river is very deep, if you go over there you will see a bridge that crosses it and you can go in peace. The one man did as he was told and made it over safely. The other, however, against his better judgment waded into the river, was swept into the deep water, and died.[112]

The key to success, according to the philosopher's *mashal,* does not reside in the arbitrary and predetermined will of God, but in the actions that humans choose based on their own volition. The Torah, he subsequently informs the astrologer, teaches us to follow that which is good and to refrain from that which is evil. And it is precisely this axiom that corresponds with reason. Whereas the young philosopher in the previous dialogue was extremely critical of religion, the philosopher that we encounter in this book accepts the position that philosophy and religion, reason and faith, are mutually inclusive. In so doing, Polleqar constructs the dialogues in the *Ezer* in such a manner that they naturally build on one another. The astrologer, a character who is a stand-in for Abner, is thus not merely an enemy of philosophy and reason, but also one of true religion and true faith.

Central to the debate between the astrologer and the philosopher over determinism and the nature of God's will is the role of biblical, and to a lesser extent rabbinic, interpretation. Both sides, then, are determined to anchor their respective positions in sacred scripture, and they frame their debate in such a manner that each claims to be reading this scripture properly, whereas their antagonist misreads it.

Here it is important to recall that biblical citations formed the basis of Christian argumentation.[113] Of particular importance in the Jewish arsenal was the emphasis on proper understanding of the biblical narrative in Hebrew, and the overwhelming importance of contextual understanding.[114] Jewish polemicists were highly critical of Christian readings of the Bible that purported to start of with a literal reading of the biblical text, often in translation, but that quickly gave way to highly metaphorical and allegorical readings. Even though the astrologer is not advocating a Christocentric reading of the biblical narrative, it is, especially if we regard this as a literary setting that archives for posterity the debate between Polleqar and Abner, a position that could easily emerge, the author hints, from such a reading.

Much of the debate surrounding the exchange between the astrologer and the philosopher revolves around how to interpret the Bible properly. This book is so central to the debate not only because of its many cryptic statements that seem to imply occasionalism, but also because it formed the cornerstone of post-Maimonidean philosophical exegesis of the Bible.[115]

> **The astrologer:** Do you not see that King Solomon who was wiser than all others confirmed and upheld this [belief in determinism], as is evident from many places in [Qoheleth]: "I realized, too that whatever God has brought to pass will recur evermore; nothing can be added to it, and nothing taken from it" [3:14]. Know that all that happens in this world [occurs] from the actions of God based on decree and prior affirmation. It is impossible to change this custom (*minhag*) and law (*ḥuq*) by addition or subtraction, and that the fear of God is the best response in the hearts of humans: "God has brought to pass that men revere Him" [3:14] . . . also from the following: "If you see in a province oppression of the poor and suppression of right and justice, don't wonder

> at the fact . . ." [5:7]. This teaches us that all things that occur are based on the emanation of causes, one after the other, that come from the highest things, which are the heavenly bodies.[116]

To this, the philosopher responds, also framing his argument in the proper interpretation of the book of Qoheleth:

> **The philosopher:** Heaven forbid that a man should stumble on such an evil opinion! Certainly you use the words of Solomon and these are indeed his verses. One has to understand the opposite of what you intend and see the truth. . . . I have already explained these matters in my commentary to the book of Qoheleth, where I showed how to understand the affairs of the world and all of its troubles, and I revealed that everything changes and turns over without ever settling into one [permanent] standard. This is because [everything in this world] cleaves to matter, which is always willing to receive a different form. In order that man is not seduced by the futilities of [this world's] imaginary delights, [Solomon] said: "I realized, too, that whatever God has brought to pass will recur evermore; nothing can be added to it, and nothing taken from it" [3:14]. In other words, do not think that everything will change at this time, it will do so only in the future when things will settle upon a [permanent] standard without change . . . for everything exists according to the nature of possibility: "Only that shall happen which has happened; only that shall occur which has occurred" [1:9].[117]

As is typical with polemical biblical interpretation of the Middle Ages, the philosopher, clearly Polleqar now, argues that his opponent fails to grasp properly the context of the verse that he cites. Because the astrologer cites a verse, namely, 3:14, out of context, he is quite simply unable to appreciate the full meaning of Solomon's intention. After quoting and explicating several more verses from Qoheleth, the philosopher concludes:

> [Solomon] also said: "Indeed he does not know what is to happen; even when it is on the point of happening" [8:7], "who knows whether he will be wise or foolish" [2:19], and "Do not boast of tomorrow, for you do not know what the day will bring" [Prov. 27:1].[118] After all of this evidence and commentary that I have cited, how can anyone possibly suspect Solomon of believing in this worthless faith, such as Abraham ibn Ezra or Rabbi Isaac the Ḥasid did, or even as my well-known disputant [i.e., Abner of Burgos] did? The good reader of my aforementioned commentary to Qoheleth will understand the truth of the matter.[119]

Much of the subsequent debate between the two antagonists revolves around how to interpret the Bible, and also rabbinic aggadot, properly.

Despite the nuanced discussion regarding divine will, human freedom, and strict determinism, the dialogue, as in the previous one between the talmudist and the philosopher, quickly moves to its finale. The lengthy and sustained appeal of the philosopher to biblical and rabbinic prooftexts that dismiss astrology, and concomitantly determinism, begins to wear down the arguments of his opponent and to have an effect on the astrologer. The philosopher, turning to the crowd, announces that one should only respect that which corresponds to the truth, and that one should not believe something that cannot be verified by the intellect. The astrologer slowly begins to admit the weakness of his argument and, now essentially becomes the pupil of the philosopher,[120] asking him to explain various philosophical positions regarding the ability of matter to receive forms, God's knowledge of particulars, and so on.

Unlike the previous dialogue between the talmudist and the philosopher, which is ultimately reconciled by the king, here there is no resolution between the two disputants. This is because in Polleqar's worldview there is quite simply no room whatsoever for the position of determinism: it is irreconcilable with philosophy. This is, to reiterate, based on two factors. The first is that, qua philosopher, Polleqar claims that a belief in the strict deterministic properties of the stars and planets makes a mockery of human freedom to choose. Here we can point to his criticism of one of the greatest biblical exegetes and Jewish Neoplatonists, Abraham ibn Ezra.[121] Secondly, Polleqar is all too aware that his real life, not just textual, disputant, Abner of Burgos, appealed to determinism to justify his apostasy to Christianity. Any attempt to reconcile philosophy and astrology is therefore tantamount to an endorsement of Abner's position, including of course his condemnation of Judaism.

The dispute between the two comes to an end with the astrologer admitting his complete defeat and admitting that one of the reasons he was so attracted to astrology in the first places was because of the respect with which it is treated by others, especially kings and princes who would seek out his advice.[122] With this, Polleqar completely undermines the principles of astrology, considering them based on nothing more than the desire for a high social standing. We should read this, again, as directed at Abner of Burgos in particular, and all those others who converted to Christianity in general, based on their desire to improve their social positions in their new faith. Anyone who converts to Christianity and then tries to justify this conversion as based on predetermined forces generated by the movement of the heavenly bodies, according to Polleqar, is quite simply lying.

Conclusions

As I suggested earlier in this chapter, some argue that Polleqar was out of his league in trying to respond to the criticisms of Abner; that the latter was much more philosophically sophisticated than the former. Such a charge is difficult to answer. There can be no doubt that Abner possessed a first-rate intellect, and that his concept of will was something with which subsequent Jewish philosophers would be forced to wrestle. Despite this, however, we should not undermine the philosophical competence of Polleqar or simply write him off as an epigone, holding on to outdated Maimonidean principles in a changing intellectual landscape.

Polleqar's *Ezer ha-Dat* is, as I have argued in this chapter, one of the most pleasing attempts to combine the literary and the philosophical. His use of humor, sarcasm, poetry, and dialogues that open up onto other dialogues certainly provides the most dynamic example of the genre examined in this study. As with all of the other dialogues examined here, however, he employs the genre not simply to show off his literary talents, but to respond to other ideas, whether Jewish or non-Jewish. In Polleqar's case, the dialogue became a useful means not only to disseminate a rationally constructed understanding of Judaism—one that refused to admit any astrological, kabbalist, or naive elements—to a larger audience. In so doing, Polleqar archives for us a dispute between a purveyor of a rational Judaism and a series of individuals who marshaled these other elements to undermine it.

As the medieval period gradually gave way to the Renaissance, the canons of aesthetics, including the nature of the relationship between the artist and the creative act, changed significantly. Although Jews continued to write dialogues in Hebrew, all of the dialogues examined in the remainder of this work examine the genre as composed in different European vernaculars. The first such work I shall examine in this context is the Italian Renaissance dialogue composed by Judah Abravanel.

5

JUDAH ABRAVANEL: THE DIALOGUE OF DESIRE

JUDAH ABRAVANEL (CA. 1465–AFTER 1521), ALSO KNOWN AS LEONE Ebreo,[1] is an important transitional figure in the history of Jewish philosophy. A common trait of any transitional figure, however, is the problem of contextualization. In the case of Judah Abravanel, do we regard him as the last of the medieval Jewish philosophers or the first of the early modern ones? His work, for example, is certainly in conversation with a number of themes found in Renaissance Platonism and Humanism. Yet at the same time he freely draws upon the cosmology and metaphysics of his Jewish and Islamic predecessors. Judah Abravanel, then, occupies two distinct intellectual worlds, that of medieval Judaism and that of the Renaissance, each of which implies a different set of commitments. It is the tension between these commitments that not only makes his work so dynamic, but also contributes to the difficulty in classifying it today.

Of all the figures examined in this study so far, Judah Abravanel was the earliest to encounter the dialogues of Plato firsthand. Here it is important to remember that the Florentine academy played a large role in the renewal of Platonic translation and philosophy. As we shall see in this chapter, the figure most responsible for this was Marsilio Ficino (1433–1499), who both translated the entire Platonic corpus into Latin and also wrote a multivolume work outlining the shape of a Christianized "Platonic theology." It is thus important that we not forget that "Renaissance Humanism was a thoroughly Christian phenomenon."[2] A main argument of this chapter holds that we need to read Judah Abravanel's *Dialoghi* as a response to the "christianizing" work of Ficino and other Renaissance Humanists.

Abravanel's life is, in many ways, the foil to that of Halevi. Halevi, as we witnessed in chapter 2, was an elite individual deeply entrenched in the Judeo-Arabic culture of his day, and, at first blush, seems likely to have framed, as so many of his literary and philosophical colleagues did, Judaism in universal terms. Abravanel, with the trauma of 1492[3] and the forced conversion of his firstborn still painfully etched in his memory, would have been a likely candidate to rebel against non-Jewish society, preferring to take solace in the suffering of the Jewish community of his day. Yet both thinkers, perhaps as testaments to their creativity, overturn such initial expectations. Faced with destruction of Jewish life on the Iberian Peninsula, Judah Abravanel chose to stress the universalistic dimensions of his tradition.

Despite all of the personal and communal misfortunes that he witnessed, Judah Abravanel embraced the new paradigms supplied by the Italian Renaissance: Humanism, Platonism, Aristotelianism, Neoplatonism, aesthetics, astrology, and mythology. Like many of his medieval Jewish philosophical predecessors, he argued that Judaism was most relevant and most poignant when it fully engaged other civilizations. Judaism, for him, was the universal tradition par excellence, a religion that nourished the main trajectories of Western civilization, and whose ancient literature anticipated the high rhetorical and aesthetic standards of the Italian Renaissance. However, unlike earlier Jewish philosophers, Abravanel chose to compose his work not in Hebrew or in another language written in Hebrew characters, but in the vernacular for all, Jew and non-Jew alike, to read.

These two features—embracing Renaissance ideals, and writing in Italian—have led many to debate the "Jewishness" of the work. Because Abravanel seems to have been completely unconcerned with the venerable medieval philosophical antagonism between faith and reason, and because of the overwhelming positive reception of the *Dialoghi* among a non-Jewish reading public (and concomitant rejection by his immediate Jewish contemporaries), some have questioned whether this work belongs in the "canon" of Jewish philosophical works.[4] In what follows I want to make a case that if such a "canon" exists, then this work clearly belongs in it, and also to demonstrate how, despite the virtually unprecedented universalism that we encounter in it,[5] the *Dialoghi*—like every other dialogue considered in this study—represents a distinctly Jewish response to trends in the larger intellectual cultures in which Jews found themselves.

Although I shall make the case that the *Dialoghi* is a work of Jewish philosophy, it is nevertheless imperative not to gloss over a number of highly innovative features that we encounter in the treatise. Most interesting from my perspective is that of all the dialogues discussed here, no other work employs a female protagonist. Moreover, Abravanel ascribes to his female character, Sophia, a number of traditionally male features, in addition to giving the male character in the dialogue, Philo, traditionally female characteristics. It is the conversation between these two characters, fraught with erotic and sexual tension, that gives Abravanel's philosophical treatment of love and desire a highly literary quality, something that seems to have been one of the many features that contributed to the *Dialoghi*'s popularity in Renaissance cultures.

In addition, and in contrast to the dialogues we have encountered so far, or indeed will encounter later in the book, the *Dialoghi d'amore* recounts an intellectual encounter between equals. Unlike the *Kuzari*, *Meqor Ḥayyim*, *Ḥay ben Meqitz*, *Iggeret ha-Vikuaḥ*, and *Phaedon*—all of which present a dominant character whom we can identify, at least on one level, with the author himself—we are never sure with which character Judah Abravanel identifies. In this regard, the *Dialoghi* presents two Jewish courtiers who debate, inter alia, the nature of love, beauty, and desire, the ontological status of the universe, and the various intersections between classical mythology and the biblical narrative. And although on one level it seems as if Philo chauvinistically tries to instruct Sophia about the true nature of things, in many ways it is actually Sophia who comes across as the true Renaissance thinker, with her unwillingness either to succumb to Philo's advances or to accept his arguments simply because this is what inherited intellectual traditions demanded.

From what we can reconstruct of Abravanel's biography, we witness a number of fractures and joys that are, in many ways, exemplary of Italian Jewry's relationship to the Renaissance.[6] On the one hand, Abravanel drank plentifully from the stream of the Renaissance. This enabled him to absorb many of its vocabularies, categories, and themes. In so doing, he possessed an uncanny ability to wrap some of the major philosophical issues of the era (e.g., love, beauty, desire) in a very attractive and almost unprecedented literary form. The end result is that a wandering Jew—banished from Spain, traumatized by the forced conversion of his firstborn son, and subsequently exiled to Italy where he had to live a peripatetic life—created one of the finest and most popular Renaissance treatises on love. This paradox carries through into the pages of the *Dialoghi d'amore*.[7] Although this treatise only makes sense when contextualized within the various intellectual and literary currents associated with the Florentine school inaugurated by Ficino, it nonetheless expands and popularizes many of these currents, taking them in new and interesting directions.

The Shifting Foundations of Aesthetics and Rhetoric

Renaissance Humanism ushered in new ways of thinking about rhetoric. Whereas the medieval Islamicate tradition was primarily confined to the texts and commentaries on Aristotle's work by the same name, the fifteenth century witnessed the revival of other classical sources, most notably those of Cicero and Quintilian, coupled with the new spirit of Humanism.[8] Rhetoric, now defined as the art of effective communication and ornamental speech, increasingly became associated with the Renaissance ideal of putting the individual at the center of the universe by undermining the fixed hierarchies of medieval cosmology.[9] This newly elevated position of rhetoric, in turn, was inseparable from emerging developments in anthropology, arts, and science.

To appreciate the novelty of this approach to rhetoric, let me briefly juxtapose it with that of the medieval period.[10] Following the lead of philosophers from late antiquity, medieval Islamic and Jewish thinkers included Aristotle's *Poetics* as part of his logical system (the so-called *Organon*).[11] This subsequently made its way into certain Arabic and Judeo-Arabic understandings of the place and function of literature.[12] For instance, Moshe ibn Ezra (ca. 1055–1138)—whose *Kitāb al-muhādara wa al-mudhākara* represents the main work devoted to rhetoric composed by a Jew living under the sphere of Islamicate cultural and literary forms[13]—follows the Aristotelian definition of rhetoric as one of the five logical arts concerned primarily with suasion and, therefore, "inferior to consensus or firm opinion."[14] For many medieval Islamic and Jewish thinkers, literature was not simply a form of entertainment, but played an important role in the noetic and emotional development of the nonphilosopher, who was otherwise unable to discern truth from falsity.[15] This became an important feature of medieval theories of prophecy, in which the prophet, who possessed an uncanny ability to create wonderful images, put philosophical truths in pleasing literary forms.

In the Renaissance, by contrast, rhetoric was increasingly dislodged from the logical corpus of Aristotle in favor of the Ciceronian and Quintilianic tradition.[16] Language now became a central component of philosophy since proper linguistic expression was held up as the ideal to which the *uomo universalis* aspired. With this emphasis on elegant expression, rhetoric shifted to the center of the Humanist educational curriculum. Eloquence, in other words, was not regarded as the prolegomenon to knowledge, but reflected its telos: the good orator was someone regarded as proficient in all branches of human knowledge. Rhetoric now enabled the individual to display his wisdom and, in so doing, persuade others of his position. The perfect orator became synonymous with the perfect man.

The first Jewish response to the new understanding of rhetoric associated with Renaissance Humanism may be found in Judah Messer Leon's *Sefer Nopheth Ṣufim* (The Book of the Honeycomb's Flow). In this work, Messer Leon takes ideas about beauty and rhetoric gleaned from the classical sources and subsequently applies them to the Hebrew Bible:

> For when I had studied the words of the Torah in the way now common amongst most people, I had no idea that the science of rhetoric or any part of it was included therein. But once I studied and investigated rhetoric, "searched for her as for hidden treasures" [Prov.2:4] out of treatises written by men of nations other than our own, and afterwards came back to see what is said of her in the Torah and the holy scriptures, then the eyes of my understanding were opened, and I saw that it is the Torah which was the giver. Between the Torah's pleasing words and stylistic elegancies—and, indeed, all the statutes and ordinances of rhetoric which are included with the Holy Scriptures—and all of the like that all other nations possess, the difference is so striking that to compare them is like comparing "the hyssop . . . in the wall" with "the cedar that is in Lebanon" [1Kings 5:13].[17]

With this passage, Messer Leon signals his desire to discover deep within the Bible a rhetorical core that is synonymous with the writings of the Italian Humanists. Moreover, in order to counter potential criticisms for reading non-Jewish works, he cleverly implies that only those with a firm grasp of rhetoric truly and fully understand the Bible.[18] In a passage typical of the work, Messer Leon weaves biblical prooftexts throughout his discussion:

> The art of rhetoric is one that it is fitting and proper to preserve in writing; and that the sound orator should possess three general qualifications: he must be wise, ethically sound, and one "that orders his words rightfully" [Ps. 112:5] in every possible pertinent respect. This has also been stated by King Solomon in the verses: "The lips of the righteous know what is acceptable, but the mouth of the wicked is all forwardness" [Prov. 10:32], "the heart of the wise teaches his mouth, and adds learning to his lips" [Prov. 16:23]; and many others besides. Thus the eminent in rhetoric were the elect of the nation and its special treasure, in whom all the virtues were very nearly perfect—I mean the prophets, who are without compare.[19]

Here it becomes readily apparent that Messer Leon's goal, as it will subsequently also be Judah Abravanel's, is to take Renaissance ideals and show how they are found most perfectly in the prophetic tradition associated with the Hebrew Bible. Not only is biblical rhetoric every bit as good as that found in classical and Renaissance sources, it is also prior in time to the linguistic embellishments found among Greek and Latin authors.

Unlike his medieval philosophical predecessors who tended to equate rhetoric with lower forms of logic, Abravanel, taking his lead from Messer Leon, subsumed rhetoric into the higher sciences, such as cosmology and epistemology. The beautiful and the pleasing speech of the Torah no longer becomes, as it was for Maimonides, a concession that Moses had to make for the masses; it is now part and parcel of the divine fabric.[20]

Moreover, in keeping with the pride of place put on rhetoric in the

Renaissance, Abravanel contends that the philosopher takes on the role of an orator, someone whose eloquence enabled him to reproduce the beautiful language of the Bible for philosophical purposes. The goal of the philosopher–aesthete–artist is thus to imitate the beautiful speech of the Bible to the best of his ability.[21] The ideal philosopher is someone who is able to create a beautiful and aesthetically pleasing product that leads his audience to an understanding of the beauty found within the universe.[22] This is precisely what we encounter in the *Dialoghi d'amore* when, for example, Abravanel argues that human language is "neither sufficient to express perfectly that which our intellects sense, nor can corporeal sounds reproduce the purity of divine things."[23] Writing, therefore, must imitate cosmology. In other words, writing itself becomes an act of creation in which the images of beautiful language must be beautiful in and of themselves, in addition to pointing beyond themselves to intelligible beauty. Mythopoesis thus becomes the art form par excellence of the philosopher. Abravanel contends that the individual's encounter with celestial beauty occurs indirectly or obtusely (*in enigmate*):[24]

> Our human intellect perceives the incorporeal in the corporeal, and understands well that although this first cause is measureless and infinite, this knowledge is derived from the effect of this cause, which is the corporeal universe: Thus the Master is known by his works, and not by direct perception of the design of His art [*arte*] in His mind.[25]

This is why true philosophical language must be aesthetically and sensually appealing, reflecting human embodiment:

> . . . by mixing delightful history-writing and fable [*dilettabile istoriografo e fabuloso*] with intellectual truth, and the easy with the difficult, in such a way that entices human frailty with delight and ease of the story, it might wisely receive the truth of science. . . . it is especially in poetic fictions [*finzione poetiche*] that such combinations [of pleasure with truth] are possible, one lodged in the rind [*scorza*], the other in the kernel [*medolla*].[26]

Abravanel thus creates his *Dialoghi* as a pleasing treatise that must be read on a number of different levels—philosophical, artistic, and literary. The aesthetic component of the work is not simply for effect, but is inseparable from the message of the work.

The Renaissance Revival of the Platonic Dialogue

The fifteenth century witnessed a rapid increase in the dissemination and study of the Platonic corpus in the Latin West. As we saw in chapters 1 and

2, despite the fact that many medieval Islamicate thinkers knew the name of Plato and could identify many of his central ideas, the latter tended to circulate in the form of Galenic epitomes as opposed to the literary masterpieces that we now acknowledge the Platonic dialogues to be. Before the period under discussion, the non-Arabic speaking Latin West possessed two partial translations of the *Timaeus* made by Cicero and Calcidus, some unintelligible versions of the *Phaedo* and the *Meno* made by Henricus Aristippus in Sicily during the twelfth century, and a partial copy of the *Parmenides,* including Proclus' commentary, translated by William of Moerbeke in the late thirteenth century.[27]

At the beginning of the fifteenth century, in part to counter what they considered to be the pernicious influence of Aristotelian-inspired Scholasticism, Italian Humanists were determined to make the thought of Plato available to a Latin readership. Leonardo Bruni, Umberto Decembrio, and Cencio de' Rustici translated ten dialogues between them in the early fifteenth century.[28] The translation work of Ficino, however, made much of this earlier translation activity redundant: in 1484 he published the first complete Latin translation of Plato's dialogues, and in 1496 he published his annotations and commentaries to the major dialogues in this corpus. Within less than a century, then, Italy went from possessing just a few complete dialogues and several garbled ones to having the entire Platonic canon.

This revival of Platonism and the accessibility of the Platonic dialogues seem to have led various Humanist thinkers to adopt the genre in order to articulate their own intellectual agendas.[29] Since the Humanists put especial emphasis on ornamental style and Plato was generally regarded as the master of elegant writing, it was not long before they began to imitate both his style and also the genre in which he expressed himself.[30] Petrarch (1304–1374) is perhaps indicative of the age when he sees in the dialogue a flexibility and an openness to various opinions, something he perceived to be the opposite of medieval dogmatism.[31] Moreover, the teachings of Plato, often expurgated to conform to contemporaneous values, especially those of the creation of the universe and the immortality of the human soul, fitted nicely with the sensibilities of the Humanists, the great majority of whom still maintained ties, often close, to the Church.

One of the earliest Jewish dialogues of the Renaissance—*Ḥai ha-Olamim* (Eternal Life) by Yohanan Alemanno (1435–ca. 1504)—was composed in this environment sometime in the late Quattrocento. This dialogue is between two characters—one of whom speaks poetically using numerous linguistic embellishments, the other of whom speaks the philosophical language of the Maimonidean-Averroistic tradition.[32] Each topic these two characters discuss thus appears twice: once philosophically and once poetically. The subsequent conversation between the two is eclectic and far-ranging,[33] essentially providing a description of the various stages of human development. It is uncertain whether or not Judah Abravanel ever read this work; however, Alemanno's long philosophical introduction to his allegorical commentary on the Song of Songs, *Shir ha-maʿalot li-Shlomo* (The Song of Solomon's Ascents),[34] provides an important precursor to the *Dialoghi*, yet it is again unclear whether or not Abravanel would have had access to it. Although not written in the form of a dialogue, this work translates the erotic impulse of the Song of Songs into the language of Florentine Humanism and Neoplatonism, something not unlike what Abravanel will subsequently do in the *Dialoghi*.

Although Judah Abravanel may have visited Florence, he spent the majority of his time in southern Italy. Let me therefore focus, in broad strokes, on the composition of dialogues in the Kingdom of Naples. Before Abravanel arrived in Naples,[35] the Aragonese kings there cultivated and employed Humanists in a number of capacities. Many of these individuals composed at least part of their work using the genre of the dialogue, though in Latin as opposed to the vernacular. For example, Bartolemeo Facio (ca. 1405–1457) composed *De humanae vitae felicitate*, which was instrumental in defining certain aspects of human happiness and freedom in the light of Renaissance categories.[36] Lorenzo Valla (1407–1457) composed his *De vero falsoque bono* as a dialogue celebrating Epicurean morality and values. Yet the most famous Neopolitan Humanist of all, and an individual whom Abravanel more than likely knew, was Giovanni Pontano (1426–1503), who composed as least five dialogues (*Charon, Antonius, Asinus, Actius*, and *Aegidius*). From 1471 until the mid-1490s Pontano presided over the Neapolitan Academy, which frequently met in his own house and to which the major political, philosophical, and religious thinkers of the day were invited.[37]

An insight into the composition of dialogues comes from Torquato Tasso (d. 1595), whose *Discorso dell'arte del dialogo* (Discourse on the Art of the Dialogue) proved very influential. Although written after the *Dialoghi*, it nevertheless still provides an interesting window onto why authors would choose this genre.[38] Tasso defines the dialogue as "an imitation of a discussion (*imitazione de ragionamento*), written in prose, not intended for performance, and designed for the benefit (*giovamento*) of civil and speculative men."[39] For Tasso, "the writer of dialogues ought to resemble the poets in his expression and in his effort to make us see the things he describes."[40] The author, in other words, must strike a balance between poet and philosopher, presenting his case in as pleasing an ornamental style as the subject allows.

It should by now be readily apparent that when Abravanel decided to compose his treatise on love in the form of a dialogue, he was by no means original in choosing this genre. If anything, he was picking up a literary style that many major Renaissance thinkers had already chosen to express at least some of their ideas. However, there is a crucial difference between much of the work discussed in this section and the *Dialoghi*. Primary is the fact that many of the aforementioned dialogues, with the obvious exception of *Ḥai ha-Olamim*, were written in Latin, and not the then emerging literary Italian. Moreover, as I shall show in the following section, the dialogue, especially as embodied in Abravanel's work, would come to play a large role in replacing Latin with the vernacular.

TRATTATI D'AMORE

Renaissance Humanists seem to have found the dialogue particularly useful when it came to articulating a theory of love. Of particular importance for contextualizing the *Dialoghi d'amore* is the literary genre known as the *trattato d'amore* (treatise on love). Unlike the dialogues mentioned in the previous section, many of the *trattati d'amore* were composed in the emerging Italian vernacular. These *trattati* were dialogues that often took place in a courtly setting, and many of them tended to elaborate upon the theme of love as a universal principle.

The genre itself was inaugurated by Marsilio Ficino's commentary on Plato's *Symposium*. Yet despite the centrality of this work to the subsequent development of the genre, it was neither written as a dialogue nor originally composed in the vernacular (although he later translated it into Tuscan).[41] Rather, it consists of seven orations attributed to various participants who were summoned to a villa at Careggi by Lorenzo de'Medici to commemorate November 7th, the day considered to mark both Plato's birth and death. In each oration, a speaker expatiates on one of the speeches made in praise of love by a character in the *Symposium*. The result is essentially the christianization of Plato's concept of love as a cosmic principle.

Another important early contribution to the genre, though published posthumously in the early sixteenth century,[42] was Giovanni Pico della Mirandola's commentary to Benivieni's *Canzone d'amore*. This work of commentary,[43] articulating a more pessimistic view of love and human nature, and not enjoying the same popularity as Ficino's treatment, nevertheless also examines love and beauty as cosmic principles. And, like Ficino, Pico spends a considerable amount of time in christianizing ancient myths and terms, including many kabbalistic principles.[44] To take but one example:

> Our author [Benivieni] also wanted to give the epithet "living" to the Ideas in order to follow John the Evangelist, who said "And all created things in him were life," meaning that whatever was created by God existed previously within him in its Ideal being. The secret mysteries of the Cabalists[45] agree with this, for they attribute the name of "life" to the second *seferot* [*sic*], which proceeds from the First Father and is in itself the first ideal wisdom.[46]

Without subscribing to the Christianizing trends found in the likes of Ficino and Pico, Abravanel not only absorbs, but is also limited by, the ideas and vocabulary inherent to the genre of the *trattato d'amore*. Essentially, he develops and expands a number of the philosophical and literary themes that are already in place. His work, however, is not simply the sum of its sources. Abravanel's text is innovative in that it intersperses lighter conversation of a personal and highly literary nature into a philosophical discussion.[47] In this regard, Abravanel's *Dialoghi*, although loosely based on the work of philosophers such as Ficino and Pico, became a model for subsequent emulation by later *trattatisti*.

By the mid-sixteenth century, the dialogue on love had become a very popular genre. Well-known examples include those by, inter alia, Giuseppe Betussi (1523–1560),[48] Sperone Speroni (1500–1588),[49] and Tullia d'Aragona (ca. 1510–1556).[50] This genre was, in turn, related to the emerging ideal of creating a pure Italian literary language.[51] Yet many of the treatises associated with this genre were not particularly philosophical. Although influenced by the Platonic notion of Love—which emphasized its metaphysical principles while denigrating its more sensual or physical aspects—many tended to be fairly popular, focusing primarily on the courtly ideal of love.[52]

Judah Abravanel's *Dialoghi* does not so much rebel against these non-Jewish dialogues as present a more decidedly Jewish alternative to them. Unlike Renaissance *trattatisti* who composed dialogues, Abravanel's work tends to be more theoretical and philosophical. And, unlike the work of Renaissance philosophers, Abravanel's *Dialoghi*, although espousing most of the same themes, presents them in a much more literary and engaging style. For example, the love that Philo feels for Sophia frames the dialogue and serves as a leitmotiv running through the three dialogues.[53] As a result, the philosophical discussion of love, desire, and beauty is embodied in the various interactions of the main characters. Abravanel thus succeeds in creating a treatise on love that works on a number of different levels, with the main characters of his dialogue functioning as points of entry into increasingly abstract philosophical discussions. It is in Abravanel's ability to balance the philosophical and the literary that undoubtedly led to the popularity that the *Dialoghi* would subsequently enjoy.

JUDAH ABRAVANEL: LIFE AND TIMES[54]

Judah Abravanel was born in Lisbon, sometime between 1460 and 1470. He was the firstborn of Don Isaac Abravanel (1437–1508), the well-known financier, diplomat, biblical exegete, and informed critic of philosophy.[55] In many ways, Don Isaac is regarded as the "Judah Halevi" of the fifteenth-century, someone well acquainted with the philosophical system of his day, but who choose to mount a well-informed critique of its central principles. The Abravanel family had moved from Spain to Portugal, and immediately began to play an important role in international commerce, quickly becoming one of the most prominent families in Lisbon. Despite the conservative tendencies in his own thought, Don Isaac insured that his children received educations that included both Jewish and non-Jewish subjects. Rabbi Joseph ben Abraham ibn Hayoun, the leading rabbinic figure in Lisbon, was responsible for teaching religious subjects (e.g., Bible, commentaries, and halakhic works) to Abravanel and his brothers. As far as non-Jewish works and subjects were concerned, Abravanel, like most elite Jews of the fifteenth century, would have been instructed in both the medieval Arabo-Judaic tradition (e.g., Maimonides, Averroes), in addition to Humanistic studies imported from Italy.[56]

By profession, Abravanel was a doctor, one who had a very good reputation and who served the royal court. In 1483, his father was implicated in a political conspiracy led by the Duke of Braganza against João II, and was subsequently forced to flee to Seville, Spain, with his family.[57] Shortly after his arrival, undoubtedly on account of his impressive connections and diplomatic skills, Isaac was summoned to the court of Ferdinand and Isabella, where he became a financial advisor to the royal family. Despite his favorable relationship with them, Isaac was unable to influence them to rescind their infamous edict of expulsion—calling on all Jews who refused to convert to Christianity—to depart from the Iberian Peninsula.

Abravanel seems also to have been well connected at the Spanish court and was one of the physicians who attended the royal family. After the edict of expulsion had been issued, Ferdinand and Isabella requested that he remain in Spain. To do this, however, he still would have been expected to convert to Christianity. In order to try and keep Abravanel in Spain, a plot was hatched to kidnap his firstborn son, Isaac ben Judah. Abravanel, however, discovered the plot and sent his son, along with the child's Christian nanny, on to Portugal, where he hoped to meet up with them.[58] Upon hearing that a relative of Isaac Abravanel had re-entered Portugal, João II had the young boy seized and forcefully converted to

Christianity. It is uncertain whether or not Abravanel ever saw or heard from his son again. In his moving autobiographical poem, *Telunah ʿal ha-zeman,* we witness just what an impact this event, in addition to the impact of exile, had on him:

> Time with his pointed shafts has hit my heart
> and split my guts, laid open my entrails,
> landed me a blow that will not heal
> knocked me down, left me in lasting pain . . .
> He did not stop at whirling me around,
> exiling me while yet my days were green
> sending me stumbling, drunk, to roam the world . . .
> He scattered everyone I care for northward,
> eastward, or to the west, so that
> I have no rest from constant thinking, planning—
> and never a moment's peace, for all my plans.[59]

Like many Jews who refused to convert, Abravanel and his immediate family, including his father, made their way to Naples. There, Ferdinand II of Aragon, the king of Naples, warmly welcomed the Abravanel family, owing to its many contacts in international trade. It is not entirely clear what Abravanel did in the years immediately following his arrival there. Cecil Roth suggests that he was a professor of medicine at the University of Naples.[60] And, as I intimated earlier, there seems to be no compelling reason to believe that Abravanel would not have taken part in the literary and philosophical meetings that took place at the Neapolitan Academy under the directorship of Giovanni Pontano. Despite the acceptance of the *Dialoghi* among a non-Jewish readership and the fact that Abravanel himself seems to have composed the work, in part, for such a readership, his autobiographical poem is surprisingly bitter, especially when it describes what appear to be his feelings of marginality. In the following passage, he highlights his father as his main intellectual influence and surprisingly writes off the influence of Italian Humanists. Once again, though, we witness how all of this is filtered through the lament for his son:

> For you, my son, my heart is thirsting, burning;
> in you I quell my hunger and my thirst.
> My splendid skills are yours by right, my knowledge,
> and the science that has gotten fame for me.
> Some of it my mentor, my own father bequeathed to me—
> a scholar's scholar he.
> The rest I gained by struggling on my own, subduing wisdom
> with my bow and sword, plumbing it with my mind.
> Christian scholars are grasshoppers next to me;
> I've seen their colleges—they've no one who can best me in the
> duel of words.[61]

In 1495, however, the French took control of Naples, and Abravanel was again forced to flee, first to Genoa, then to Barletta, and subsequently to Venice. It seems that he also traveled around Tuscany, and there is some debate as to whether or not he actually met the famous Florentine Humanist, Giovanni Pico della Mirandola (it seems unlikely that he did).[62] In 1501, after the defeat of the French in Naples, Abravanel was invited back to be the personal physician of the Viceroy of Naples, Fernandez de Córdoba. During these peregrinations, Abravanel still found the time to write (but not publish) his magnum opus, the *Dialoghi d'amore.* He seems to have died sometime after 1521. Other than these basic facts, we know very little about his life.

Especially enigmatic are his last years, between 1521 when he was requested to give medical attention to Cardinal San Giorgio until 1535 when Mariano Lenzi published the *Dialoghi* posthumously in Rome. There is some evidence that Abravanel moved to Rome near the end of his life; some suggest that he fell in with a Christian group of Neoplatonists.[63] Indeed, the 1541 edition of the work mentions that Abravanel converted to Christianity (*dipoi fatto christiano*). This, however, seems highly unlikely as (1) it is not mentioned in the first edition, the one on which all subsequent editions and translations were based, and (2) there is no internal evidence in the *Dialoghi* to suggest this. In fact, both of the characters in the work imply the exact opposite, stating on more than one occasion that "all of us believe in the sacred Mosaic law" (*noi tutti che crediamo la sacre legge mosaica*).[64] It seems, then, that either a careless or overzealous editor inserted the phrase *"dipoi fatto christiano"* into a later edition of the *Dialoghi.*

The only major work that we possess by Judah Abravanel is the *Dialoghi d'amore.* There is some debate as to when the work was actually written. Many point to the year 1501–1502 owing to a phrase in the third book: "According to the Jewish tradition, we are in the year 5262 from the beginning of creation" (*Siamo, secondo la veritá ebraica, a cinque milia ducento sessanta due del principio de la creazione*).[65] The year 5262 of the Jewish calendar corresponds to 1501–1502 of the Gregorian calendar, which would predate his autobiographical poem. Yet manuscripts other than that based on the 1535 edition have the date of 5272 (i.e., 1511–1512). This is significant because many who argue that the *Dialoghi* could not possibly have been written in Italian point to the fact that Abravanel would not have been fluent in Italian. Yet, if we assume the 1511–1512 date to be correct, this would place him in Italy for close to twenty years, more than enough time to gain proficiency in Italian (especially given the fact that he would have already known at least one Spanish vernacular and, as a physician, Latin).

In addition to his biographical poem, Abravanel also composed poetic introductions to three of his father's last works: *Rosh Amanah, Zevaḥ Pesaḥ,* and *Naḥalat Avot.* Finally, we possess a letter dating to 1566 from one Amatus Lusitanus, a physician who wrote that he attended to a patient by the name of Judah "who was the grandson of the great Platonic philosopher, known as Judah or Leon Abravanel, who gave to us the most beautiful dialogues on love." Further in this letter, he mentions that Abravanel also composed a work entitled *De Coeli Harmonia* (On the Harmony of the Spheres) and that, according to the introduction, he dedicated it to *Divinus Mirandulensis Picus* (the "divine Pico della Mirandola"). Unfortunately, this work has not survived. If, as the letter indicates, he dedicated to Pico, who died in 1494, it would most likely have been composed before the *Dialoghi* and also, based on the title, would have been composed in Latin. There is also the possibility, however, that since a first name is not mentioned, this *Divinus Mirandulensis Picus* might well have been Giovanni's well-known Humanist nephew Giovanni Francesco (d. 1533).

Dialoghi d'Amore and the Question of Language

The central question concerning the language of the *Dialoghi*'s composition is, How could a Jewish refugee from Portugal show such facility with Italian, let alone the Tuscan dialect, since Abravanel seems to have spent very little time in Tuscany?[66] Those who argue for a Latin original point to the fact that (1) Abravanel was a physician and would have known Latin, and (2) a phrase by Yoseph Shlomo Delmedigo (1591–1655) in *Mikhtav Ahuz* suggests that the latter was going to translate Abravanel's work from Latin.[67] Those who argue for a Hebrew original point to another phrase, this time by Claudio Tolemei (1492–1556), a non-Jew, which states that Abravanel composed his treatise in *sua lingua* (his own language).[68] Note, however, as others have pointed out, that such a phrase could quite easily refer to "his own style."

Given the evidence, an Italian original for the work seems most likely since (1) all the manuscripts, including Mariano Lenzi's edition of 1535, are in Italian; (2) it seems that Abravanel had lived in Italy for close to twenty years by the time that he wrote the *Dialoghi*; (3) neither later Jewish authors, e.g., Azaria de' Rossi,[69] nor non-Jewish authors, e.g., Tullia d'Aragona,[70] had any reason to suspect that the work was written in a language other than Italian; (4) if we assume the later date of 1511–1512, many non-Tuscan Italian authors of this period called for the adoption of Tuscan as a literary language, owing primarily to the fact that this was the language of Petrarch (1304–1374) and Boccaccio (1313–1375);[71] and, (5) as for the question of the Tuscan dialect of the work, many Italian printers of the early sixteenth century "Tuscanized" Italian according to set criteria.[72]

Moreover, many Jewish authors in the fifteenth and sixteenth centuries increasingly resorted to Romance vernaculars in order to attract a Jewish audience (including *conversos* and ex-*conversos*), who no longer understood Hebrew. In sixteenth-century Italy, larger trends in rhetoric increasingly led to the creation of the ideal of a pure Italian language. In this regard, Abravanel became an important transitional thinker in the encounter between Judaism and the Italian Renaissance. Whereas his father, Don Isaac, could still adapt Humanistic themes to his Hebrew writings, which were still primarily in conversation with medieval thought,[73] increasingly in Abravanel's generation the only way to engage in a full-scale examination of the universal tendencies associated with Humanism was to write in the vernacular.

Finally, the very genre of the *Dialoghi*, that of the *trattato d'amore*, was the product of the Italian vernacular of the late fifteenth and early sixteenth centuries. When, for example, Abravanel discusses the concept of love as a universal or cosmic principle he draws upon, as will be made clearer below, a particular vocabulary and set of concepts that only make sense when contextualized within this already existing discourse.[74]

ESTABLISHING THE JEWISH CREDENTIALS OF THE *DIALOGHI D'AMORE*

Although several of the dialogues examined in this study are regarded as "noncanonical" in terms of the central works of Jewish philosophy, very rarely if ever are their Jewish credentials debated. The same case, however, cannot be made for Abravanel's *Dialoghi*, a work whose relationship to Jewish thought is tenuous at best.[75] Even though a Jew composed the *Dialoghi*, this fact does not necessarily make it a work of Jewish philosophy. According to Ze'ev Levy, for instance, the strange fate of Jewish philosophical works composed in a Platonic, as opposed to an Aristotelian, key was that they tended to be ignored by Jews yet embraced by non-Jews.[76] Certainly, there exist several Jewish referents[77] and prooftexts[78] scattered throughout the *Dialoghi*, and both of the characters express matter-of-factly that they believe in the "sacred Mosaic law" (*la sacra legge mosaica*).[79] Yet in order to demonstrate that this is a work of Jewish philosophy, it is important to show that there exists more than such passing comments, and that the overwhelming tenor of the work is concerned with articulating a reading of Judaism in light of a larger philosophical system.

Maimonides' *Guide of the Perplexed* is often, and quite rightly, held up as the quintessential work of Jewish philosophy. This is due to the work's sustained attempt to reconcile Jewish sources with Aristotelian science by showing that the truths of the former, when properly understood and interpreted, are identical with those of the latter. Just as Maimonides sought to show the correspondence between Judaism and Greco-Arabic philosophy, Abravanel, I contend, sought to do something similar, only now the philosophical system was that of Renaissance Platonism and Humanism as opposed to that of the Middle Ages.

For example, Abravanel is interested in exactly the same themes as classical and medieval Jewish philosophy. These themes include creation,[80] revelation and prophecy,[81] and redemption.[82] And, if we define Jewish philosophy as the interpretation of Jewish sources according to non-Jewish philosophical principles, then the following is what Abravanel does, to an extent: he reads these aforementioned themes in light of contemporaneous intellectual concerns. To take but one example, in his discussion of the synergy between celestial beauty and wisdom, he grounds his argument in the Biblical narrative, particularly that of the Song of Songs:

> Just as the beauty of the light of the sun is received more perfectly [*s'imprime piú perfettamente*] in the rare and the diaphanous than in the opaque, so the first beauty, the highest wisdom [*prima bellezza, soma sapienzia*] is impressed more truly and perfectly on the created angelic and human intellect than on all other bodies that it informs in the universe. Solomon in his wisdom not only declared this emanation and idea to be the beginning of the creation under the form and name of highest wisdom but also in his Song of Songs under the form and name of beauty: "You are all fair my love; there is no spot in you."[83]

However, unlike the *Guide* and other works of medieval Jewish philosophy, Abravanel is not interested in showing how Judaism and Jewish sources must be properly interpreted, often esoterically, in order to correspond to philosophical truths. Indeed one of the most surprising features that we encounter in the *Dialoghi* is Abravanel's contentment to let Judaism and philosophy sit side by side without feeling the need to reconcile them. For instance, rather than try to prove that the world is created from nothing (as the account in Genesis was interpreted by orthodoxy in the medieval period), Abravanel is content to claim that this is what he must believe because this is what is required of him as a Jew, even though he subsequently implies that the world was not created ex nihilo, but out of preexistent matter.[84] This contentment or lack of desire on his part to make *esoteric* interpretations of scripture might well be one of the main reasons for the hesitation in regarding the *Dialoghi* as a "Jewish work."

We also encounter in the *Dialoghi* a, for lack of a better term, more subtle "Jewish orientation" when it comes to matters of the body and sexuality. This may be seen, for example, in Abravanel's discussion of love as both a sensual and a cosmic principle. Whereas other Renaissance thinkers tended to denigrate love between humans, Abravanel actively celebrates human, procreative love in and of itself, but also as the gateway to understanding divine love.[85] Although, and I will have more to say about this below, Ficino and many other *trattatisti* who follow in his footsteps equate human love with sensual love between humans, Abravanel resignifies human love as that which individuals have for God and vice versa.

Moreover, when comparing the *Dialoghi* to works written by various Renaissance thinkers, one frequently notices the overt Christianizing references in the latter. In his *Heptaplus,* a work that I shall discuss in more detail below, Giovanni Pico della Mirandola uses imagery from the Hebrew Bible, kabbalah, and Platonic sources to articulate a decidedly apologetic reading:

> Just as man is the absolute perfection of all lower things, so Christ is the absolute perfection of all men. If, as the philosophers say, all perfection in each class is derived by the other members from the most perfect one as from a fountain, no one may doubt that the perfection of all good in men is derived from Christ as a man. To him alone the spirit was given without measure, so that we all might receive it from his fullness. See how without any doubt this prerogative is due to him as God and man, which also, so far as he was a man, was peculiar to him and became him as a legitimate privilege.[86]

On a fundamental level, then, we can read the *Dialoghi* as a subtle attempt to free both the Hebrew Bible and Jewish truths from such overly Christianized interpretations.[87] An example may be found in Abravanel's treatment of the myth of the androgyne, which is "originally" found in Plato's *Symposium:*

> **Sophia:** The story is beautiful and ornate [*la favola è bella e ornata*], and it is impossible not to believe that it signifies some philosophical beauty [*bella filosofia*], more especially since it was composed by Plato himself, in the *Symposium,* in the name of Aristophanes.
>
> Tell me, therefore, Philo what it signifies?
>
> **Philo:** The myth was handed down by earlier writers than the Greeks—in the sacred writings of Moses, concerning the creation of the first human parents, Adam and Eve. . . . it was from [Moses] that Plato took his myth, amplifying and polishing it after Greek oratory, thus giving a new and confused account of the Hebrew version [*facendo in questo una mescolanza inordinata de le cose ebraiche*].[88]

Abravanel then reads the garden story as a universal and Humanistic drama that was subsequently plagiarized by Plato. In so doing, he completely ignores a reading that stresses the concept of original sin that was provided by others, including Ficino and Pico.

Further evidence of the "Jewish" nature of Abravanel's work may be witnessed in Abravanel's debt to earlier Jewish philosophers on the one hand, and his influence on subsequent Jewish thinkers on the other. For example, he is familiar with the thought of Maimonides (d. 1204),[89] and his discussion of the intellectual love of God draws heavily on that of Maimonides.[90] Abravanel also employs the works of Ḥasdai Crescas (d. 1410/11), the important critic of Aristotle and Aristotelianism. And although he never mentions Crescas by name, Abravanel's discussion of divine love seems to presuppose the discussion found in *Or ha-shem*.[91] Looking forward, the *Dialoghi*—especially its interest in post-Aristotelian physics and the intersection of mythology, astrology, and kabbalah—would exert influence on subsequent Jewish thinkers of the sixteenth and seventeenth centuries, such as Yoseph Delmedigo (also known as Yashar of Candia; d. 1655),[92] Menasseh ben Israel (d. 1657),[93] Simone Luzzatto (d. 1663),[94] and even Baruch Spinoza (d. 1677).[95]

It therefore seems safe to state that the *Dialoghi* is indeed a work of Jewish philosophy; my conclusions are based on (1) the self-identification of each of the textual protagonists as Jewish; (2) Abravanel's juxtaposition of the classical themes of Judaism with contemporaneous non-Jewish philosophical categories; (3) his desire to show the explicit correspondence between the Hebrew Bible and Greek myth, in addition to arguing that the latter was a plagiarized version of the former; (4) his engagement with the earlier Jewish philosophical tradition; and (5) his subsequent role in speculation about the natural world in seventeenth-century Jewish thought. As a result of these features, I contend that it is quite appropriate to call Judah Abravanel a Jewish philosopher and the *Dialoghi d'amore* a work of Jewish philosophy.

Yet this does not mean that we do not encounter a number of novel features in the work. For one thing, as I alluded to above, Abravanel is largely uninterested in the venerable tensions between faith and reason that so plagued earlier Jewish philosophers. This coincides with a virtually unprecedented universalism in the *Dialoghi*. Although an emphasis on universalism— Judaism's openness and willingness to learn from other religious and intellectual traditions—is certainly one of the hallmarks of Jewish philosophy, in Abravanel's thought we encounter this feature to an even greater degree. Increasingly as we move out of the medieval period, and as Jewish thinkers more and more resorted to writing in the vernacular, there existed a growing desire to narrow the distance between Judaism and Western civilization.

This, in turn, is related to the audience of the *Dialoghi*. Whereas other works of Jewish philosophy, with the possible exception of ibn Gabirol's

Fons Vitae, were written largely for Jewish audiences, Abravanel wrote his *Dialoghi* in Italian and thus for an audience that would have included not only his coreligionists versed in this language, but also, and it seems primarily, for a largely non-Jewish audience. Abravanel, in other words, never hesitated to present Judaism to a non-Jewish audience, and in such a manner that was naturally in accord with the teachings of the Renaissance. In this regard, the intended audience of the *Dialoghi* is the exact opposite of Halevi's *Kuzari,* a work—written in Arabic, but in Hebrew characters—that was highly critical of non-Jewish culture and that was meant solely for Jewish readers.

Philo and Sophia: The Battle of the Genders

The *Dialoghi* is a revolutionary work both in its deployment of a female character and in her overwhelmingly positive portrayal. As I mentioned in the introduction to this chapter, of all the dialogues examined in this study, the *Dialoghi* is the only one that has a female protagonist. Moreover, moving beyond the confines of Jewish philosophical dialogues, Judah Abravanel subverts the traditional portrayal of women in Western philosophy, where they tend to be equated with evil and privation.[96] Good and evil, form and matter, in other words, are often described metaphorically using the respective gender categories of masculine and feminine.[97] For Abravanel, as I shall show in this section, the female no longer is a passive object of male love and desire, but an active participant in the dialogue, someone who is conscious of Philo's intention to seduce her and sexually conquer her, and who thwarts his advances at every opportunity.[98]

Although neither time nor space permits for a full-scale survey of the portrayal of female characters in either the history of Western philosophy in general or philosophical dialogues in particular, several features are worth highlighting. For example, in the Platonic dialogues—including the *Symposium,* which in many ways functioned as the literary and philosophical precursor to the genre of the *trattato d'amore*—women do not participate, and when Plato does mention women, males always mediate their words.[99] By the time we arrive at the Renaissance, the situation is not radically different. Neither Ficino nor Pico, in their commentaries, are interested in the feminine, and women's discussions of desire are completely sublimated. Even though more literary *tratattti d'amore,* such as Pietro Bembo's *Gli Asolani* or Baldassare Catiglione's *Il Cortigiano,* tend to give the female characters a more active voice in the dialogue, such characters still tend to mediate and comment on what is essentially a dialogue between male characters.[100]

In his positive portrayal of Sophia, however, Abravanel not only rebels against the earlier philosophical tradition, but also, it would seem, against contemporaneous nonphilosophical treatments of women. Writing a little later than Abravanel, the physician Abraham Yagel (1553–1623),[101] who lived in northern Italy, writes of the ideal woman that her

> voice must never be heard in public like a screaming virago [*kolanit*]; all the women who want to be like men raise their voices to speak assertively [*ledaber gevohah*] like cocks croak, raising their voices so their tongue becomes a sharp sword. But [the woman of valor—*eshet ḥayyil*] does not dare to open her mouth except with wisdom "as words of the sages are heard quietly" [Qoh 9:17]. In addition she will not give in to much speech or the idle chatter of women. Rather, all her speech will be leveled with proper correction, and her words will be in suitable conformity to the rest of her ways.[102]

Based on descriptions such as these, Abravanel's portrayal of Sophia as active and publicly vocal contradicts or subverts contemporaneous conceptions of what constitutes a "woman of valor." Further contributing to this subversion is the fact that Sophia, presumably an unmarried woman, interacts with Philo, also probably unmarried, in a series of social spaces that are never clearly defined and, thus, ambiguous.[103] Clearly unrelated to each other, their constant meeting in such ambiguous social spaces borders on the risqué and clearly adds to the sexual tension of the work.

This sexual tension between Philo and Sophia is introduced right at the beginning, in the opening lines of the work:

> **Philo:** My acquaintance with you, Sophia, brings about love and desire in me [*causa in me amore e desidario*].
> **Sophia:** This discordance of opinions about me, Philo, seems to be the effect that the knowledge of me produces in you; perhaps it is passion that makes you speak like this.[104]

Sophia immediately realizes that Philo is attempting to seduce her, and much of what follows can be read, on one level, as Sophia's constant attempt to tire Philo out, to fend off his sexual advances by asking more and more questions of him. At the end of the first dialogue, for example, this pattern is recounted in a humorous way:

> **Sophia:** If you wish to leave me contented you will tell me more about this.
> **Philo:** It is too late for such a narration. It is the hour for you to rest your gentle person even though my mind continues its vigilance. . . .[105]

Leaving the philosophical arguments of the *Dialoghi* aside for the moment, we encounter a narrative that describes a male's constant attempt to conquer a female sexually. The transparency of his intentions, and ultimately the female's own playful reactions, are evident. Read on this level, Philo's philosophical articulations of the interconnections between cosmic and sensual love, between true love and erotic desire, is an elaborate ruse to persuade Sophia that two types of love and desire are in fact the same. The result is an elaborate philosophical justification for why she should consummate their relationship. Yet Sophia never gives in to Philo's advances. Her constant questioning and her unwillingness to accept at face value his comments subsequently create a philosophical treatise in which, spurred on by Sophia's comments and questions, Philo must constantly justify his arguments.

Another novel feature of the *Dialoghi* is in the nature of the relationship between the two protagonists. Whereas all of the other Jewish dialogues that I have discussed or will subsequently discuss involve a conversation between two men, often a teacher and a student, we here have people of equal standing. Sophia does not simply feed Philo convenient questions to move the treatise along. On the contrary, she frequently disagrees with him, calls on him to elaborate his arguments, or else offers alternative positions. To give but one example,

> **Sophia:** Be it as you will, can you not understand that what I want from you is the theory of love [*teorica de l'amore*], and what you want from me is the practice [*pratica*]. You cannot deny that cognition of the theory should always precede it, as it is reason that rules man's actions. Though you have already given me notice of love, both of its essence and its universality, my knowledge will be cut off if I remain ignorant of its origin and effects. Without more ado, then, you should perfect that which you have already begun, and satisfy my remaining desire, because if, as you allege, you feel true love for me, you must love the soul more than the body. Do not leave me on the brink of knowledge of such a price; for you must admit that in this respect, as well as on account of your promise, you are truly indebted to me, so that it is you who should make the first payment. And if mine does not follow you will then have the more reason to complain.
> **Philo:** Sophia, you are irresistible: when I think I have barred your every way of flight, you flee by a new path so that you can have your pleasure. . . .[106]

Although on a superficial level it is Philo who teaches Sophia, on a deeper level it is Sophia who actually does the instructing. We witness this in their very names: Philo (i.e., "love") is portrayed as someone who desires knowledge, whereas Sophia (i.e., "wisdom") possesses such knowledge or wisdom. Nowhere is this more evident than in Philo's constant reliance on "all the great ancient authorities" (*tanti eccellenti antichi*), whereas Sophia is often unwilling to accept such authority, preferring to rely on the unaided human intellect. For example:

> **Sophia:** Has this ancient saying that nothing can be made out of nothing any other reason in its support than the approval and agreement of the ancients?

> **Philo:** If it had no other reason in its favor, it would not have been known and accepted by so many worthy ancient thinkers.
> **Sophia:** Give me this reason, and let us cease discussing ancient authority.[107]

This unwillingness of Sophia to accept ideas or principles simply because "ancient authorities" held them culminates in the following exchange on the nature of Platonic Ideas:

> **Sophia:** How, therefore, will you explain to me what is certain by what is ambiguous, and what is evident by what is mysterious?
> **Philo:** The Ideas are none other than the knowledge of the created universe with all its parts in the mind of the highest Craftsman and Creator of the world, the existence of which no reasonable person can deny.
> **Sophia:** Tell me why it cannot be denied.[108]

Whereas Philo is characterized as the quintessential medieval thinker, someone who relies on the chain of traditional authority, Sophia emerges as someone unwilling to accept such authority. Unlike Philo, she argues that prime emphasis should be put on the unaided human intellect. The result is that Sophia, the female character of the *Dialoghi,* is the metaphor for the new mode of thinking associated with Renaissance Humanism.[109] That Abravanel makes this metaphor a female character is truly interesting and virtually unprecedented.[110]

In the remainder of this chapter, I will examine the *Dialoghi* from one particular perspective. Since I have tried to establish that we need to conceive of this work explicitly as a work of Jewish philosophy, and since I have also made the case, more broadly in this study, that Jewish philosophy is essentially a response to trends in non-Jewish thought, it becomes necessary to examine against what or whom Abravanel responds. I contend that we can read many of the philosophical innovations that occur in the work as the outcome of specifically Jewish responses to Renaissance Humanism. Although here it is worth noting that even though Jewish philosophers responded to non-Jewish ideas and genres, their responses to these were certainly not uniform or monolithic. For example, Halevi was an informed critic of philosophy, and he adopted the genre of the dialogue as a convenient literary form to counter, and ultimately subvert, those who would tune Judaism in a philosophically inspired key. Abravanel, on the contrary, is not a critic of philosophy. Rather than criticize a philosophically informed reading of Judaism, he offers a sustained engagement with some of the main intellectual themes of his day.

Yet on a fundamental level, it is possible to read the *Dialoghi* as treatise that, like the *Kuzari,* revolves around the conception of authenticity. The larger question that each author faced—and that indeed every author in this study faced—is how to respond to non-Jewish ideas in such a manner that the response can take into consideration Jewish sources and, at the same time, be intellectually acceptable. Judah Abravanel, much like Judah Halevi, will contend that philosophy was originally Jewish, but that for a variety of reasons it was transplanted to Greece (and subsequently to the Arabs). When a Jew engages in philosophy, according to Abravanel, he or she is doing nothing more than reclaiming his or her birthright.

PHILOSOPHICAL INNOVATION IN THE *DIALOGHI*

It seems that one of the main reasons behind the *Dialoghi*'s popularity was Abravanel's ability to build on the work of earlier Renaissance Humanists, elaborating on certain trajectories of their thought, marginalizing others, and thereby making philosophical ideas of that era more accessible to a larger reading public. In so doing, he serves as an important link between such figures and the later Italian Platonists of the sixteenth century. In this and the following section, I focus not so much on the dialogic aspects of the *Dialoghi,* but on putting the work in counterpoint with non-Jewish works. In doing this, I argue that Abravanel used a predominantly non-Jewish genre, the dialogue or *trattato d'amore,* to undermine Christian claims to authenticity.

Abravanel's work differs from that of other *trattatisti* in ways that are more than simply literary. A comparison of the *Dialoghi,* for example, with the two major works—those of Ficino and Pico—that inaugurated the genre of the *trattato d'amore,* shows that both function as commentaries: Ficino claims to comment on Plato's *Symposium,* whereas Pico claims to explicate a poem of Benivieni. Abravanel is critical not so much of the fact that both comment on the works of others, but that they confine their discussions to a sublimated human love and thereby ignore both sensual love and God's love for what is below. In the following passage, for example, Abravanel criticizes Plato (and, by extension, Ficino):

> **Sophia:** It is indeed pleasant to talk of these matters; but what comfort can you give for the fact that Plato, with all his genius, denies the existence of love in God?
> **Philo:** The species of love that Plato discusses in his *Symposium,* and he says truly that it cannot exist in God; but it would be false to deny that the universal love, of which we are speaking, is not found in the Divinity.
> **Sophia:** Explain this difference to me.
> **Philo:** Plato in his *Symposium* discusses only the kind of love that is found in men, which has its final cause in the lover but not in the beloved [*terminato ne*

> *l'amante ma non ne l'amato*], for this kind mainly is called love, since that which ends in the loved one is called friendship and benevolence [*amicizia e benivolenzia*]. He rightly defines this love as a desire of beauty. He says that such love is not found in God, because that which desires beauty and doesn't have it is not beautiful, and God, who is the highest beauty, does not lack beauty nor can he desire it, whence he cannot have love, that is, of such a kind [*però che quel che desia bellezza non l'ha né è bello, e a Dio, che è sommo bello, non gli manca bellezza né la può desiare, onde non può avere amore, cioè di tal sorte*].[111]

Abravanel, according to this and other passages, seeks to provide a more comprehensive theory of love than those of his contemporaries. Whereas Ficino and many other *trattatisti* who follow in his footsteps equate human love with sensual love between humans, Abravanel resignifies human love as that which individuals have for God.[112] This has important repercussions, as many of the *trattatisti* denigrated sensual love, identifying it with animality and thereby ignoring "the existence of emotional, psychological, and aesthetic factors" in such love.[113] For example, Castiglione argues that sensual lovers experience pleasures similar to those enjoyed by irrational animals.[114] In like manner, Mario Equicola claims that all sensual love is ultimately sullied by the "filth of coitus."[115]

Abravanel, on the other hand, celebrates sensual love as the gateway to cosmic or spiritual love. Such love, for him, becomes that which orientates the individual toward the Divine.[116] The goal of Abravanel's system is to ascend through the cosmic hierarchy; in order to accomplish this one must first enter through the gate provided by the sensual enjoyment that one derives from physical objects. Only after this can one appreciate spiritual beauty, an appreciation that culminates in basking in the divine presence. Abravanel discusses this process in the following manner:

> God has implanted His image and likeness in His creatures through the finite beauty imparted to them from His surpassing beauty [*ché ne la creature è l'immagine e similitudine di Dio per quella bellezza finita participata da l'immenso bello*]. And the image of the infinite must be finite otherwise it would not be a copy, but that of which it is the image. The infinite beauty of the Creator is depicted and reflected in finite created beauty like a beautiful face in a mirror and although the image is not commensurate with its divine pattern, nonetheless it will be its copy, portrait, and true likeness [*Si depinge e immagina la bellezza infinita del creatore ne la bellezza finita creata come una bella figura in uno specchio: non però commisura l'immagine il divino immaginato, ma bene gli sará simulacro similitudine e imagine*].[117]

The result is the celebration of physical beauty and, by extension, of this world. Significantly, in making such a claim, Abravanel not only moves beyond the conception of beauty and love found in other Renaissance Humanists, but also that found among medieval Jewish philosophers.[118] Even though the corporeal is indispensable, the higher that one moves up the hierarchy, the less important the material becomes. Yet, and this will have important repercussions on his theory of aesthetics, Abravanel does not regard this hierarchy to be one simply of ascent. Within this context, near the end of the third dialogue he introduces the concept of the circle of love, *il circulo degli amari,* an important feature that is lacking in the thought of Ficino, Pico, or other *trattatisti.*[119] This circle begins with the divine, whose love creates and sustains the universe:

> **Sophia:** I understand how this wondrous circle of being is made whole in passing through each degree in turn. And although you told me of this before, in another connection, such delight and satisfaction does it bring me that it is always new to me. Now will you not show me the circle of love in its several degrees. For this is the true subject of our discussion.
> **Philo:** . . . each degree of being with paternal love procreates its immediate inferior [*causa la produzione del suo succedente inferiore*], imparting its being or paternal beauty to it, although in a lesser degree as is only fitting.[120]

This emanative framework, the love of that which is more beautiful for that which is less beautiful, comprises the first half of the circle. Every thing in the universe exists on a hierarchical chain of being, from the pure actuality of the divine to the pure potentiality of prime matter. Just as the superior desires the perfection of the inferior, so does the inferior desire to unite with the superior. The first half of the circle spans from God to utter chaos, whereas the second half works in reverse. It is the love of the inferior for the superior, predicated on the former's privation and subsequent desire to unite with the superior. As far as the individual is concerned, the highest felicity resides in the union with God, which the Italian describes erotically as *felice coppulativa* ("union" in the sexual and erotic sense). The Italian source is worth quoting in full:

> Because the love of the human soul is twofold, it is directed not only toward the beauty of the intellect, but also toward the image of that beauty in the body. It happens that at times the love of intellectual beauty is so strong that it draws the soul to cast off all affection for the body; thus the body and soul in man fall apart, and there follows the joyful death in union with the divine. [*Essendo adunque l'amor de l'anima umana gemino, non solamente inclinato a la bellezza de l'intelletto ma ancora a la bellezza ritratta nel corpo, succede qualche volta che, essendo grandemente tirata da l'amore de la bellezza de l'intelletto, lassa del tutto l'amorosa inclinazione del corpo, tanto che si dissolve totalmente da quello e ne segue a l'uomo la morte felice coppulativa.*][121]

This theory of sensual love also affected the way in which Abravanel envisaged this world. Once again, we see differences when we compare him to other *trattatisti.* Abravanel celebrates this world, describing it as the primogeniture of God, the male principle, and intelligible beauty, personified as a female. Since this world is intimately connected to God, it cannot be negated, but rather must become part of the path that leads the soul back to God. Sensual objects thus become mimetic representations of celestial beauty.

THE *DIALOGHI* AS A JEWISH RESPONSE TO RENAISSANCE HUMANISM

In the previous section I tried to show, using specific examples of his positive valorization of sensual love and of the desire that pervades all levels of the universe, that Abravanel's *Dialoghi* departs from many of the intellectual conventions inherent to the *tratatti d'amore.* In this section, I wish to draw this out further by examining some of the decidedly Christocentric features of Renaissance Humanism, demonstrating how we can envisage, on a fundamental level, the *Dialoghi* as a Jewish response to such features. Much like the Andalusi Hebrew poets from the eleventh and twelfth centuries, we can read the *Dialoghi* as a form of cultural nationalism,[122] an attempt to show that Israel and the Bible not only predate contemporary philosophical and literary trends, but that they also provide the ultimate ground of such trends. And, as was the case with Judah Messer Leon at the beginning of this chapter, so too with Judah Abravanel we encounter the subtle point that for Jews truly to appreciate the biblical narrative, they must be conversant with these larger themes and issues. The crucial difference between Judah Abravanel on the one hand, and the Andalusi Hebrew poets and Messer Leon on the other is that Abravanel, by not composing his work in Hebrew, did not write solely for a Jewish reading public, but, by writing in Italian, for as large an audience as possible.

It seems to me that a convenient point of departure for this section is the line from his autobiographical poem that I cited earlier. This line—"Christian scholars are grasshoppers next to me; I've seen their colleges—they've no one who can best me in the duel of words"—reveals a tension that is missing, at least on the surface, in the *Dialoghi.* The universalism of the philosophical treatise is surprisingly and potentially undermined by the personal circumstances of its author, especially as recounted in this poem, wherein he lashes out not only at fate that has thrown him into his tenuous existence, but also at "Christian scholars" whom he does not regard as his equals.

Yet even if the *Dialoghi* lacks the bitterness and the anger of *Telunah ʿal ha-zeman,* we nevertheless still encounter in the former work a response to these "Christian scholars." This response is apologetic, designed to show to as broad an audience as possible that Judaism, the Jewish people, and the Hebrew Bible are not, to use the words of Halevi, "despised." On the contrary, all represent the true spirit of the Renaissance because they represent a form of universalism that is paradoxically lacking in Renaissance Humanists, the so-called purveyors of such universalism. Read in this manner, there exists a distinct apologetic thread that weaves throughout the *Dialoghi*. Just as Halevi tried to subvert contemporaneous philosophically informed Islamicate dialogues, so does Abravanel attempt to subvert *certain* elements or features of dialogues associated with the Renaissance.

It is important, then, not to lose sight of the Christocentric dimension of Renaissance Humanism and Platonism. Although many of the Renaissance thinkers were critical of what they considered to be the undue emphasis put on medieval authority, especially that of the scholastics, they were nevertheless still subject to censorship and excommunication (or worse) from the Church. Moreover, many of these thinkers did not see a major discrepancy between Christian—or at least what they considered to be "authentic" Christian teaching—and Humanism. In the proem to his *Platonic Theology*, for example, Ficino writes that

> anyone who reads very carefully the works of Plato that I translated in their entirety into Latin some time ago will discover among many other matters two of utmost importance: the worship of God with piety and understanding, and the divinity of souls. On these depend our whole perception of the world, the way we lead our lives, and all our happiness. Indeed it was because of these views that Augustine chose Plato out of the ranks of the philosophers to be his model, as being closest of all to Christian truth. With just a few changes, he maintained, the Platonists would be Christians.[123]

Not only did Ficino attempt to make Plato into a proto-Christian, but he also tried to demonstrate that Platonism was the key to the renewal of Christian belief because it showed the intimate correspondence between the spiritual truths of Christianity and those of philosophy. To use the words of Paul Oskar Kristeller, Ficino sought to "give Christian doctrine a philosophical confirmation."[124] Moreover, in a letter to Pico, Ficino praised this Platonized Christianity as providing a new way to convert people.[125]

Although the notion of *prisca theologia* ("ancient theology") mitigated much of the anti-Judaism of both antiquity and the medieval period, we should not assume that the Renaissance suddenly changed its opinion of Judaism and, especially, Jews. Although certain thinkers were willing to posit that Judaism possessed eternal truths, they still sought to reestablish "the truths of Christianity and ultimately disassociated [these truths] from those of Judaism."[126]

In his commentary to the *Symposium,* for example, Ficino, without explicitly mentioning the figure of Jesus, writes:

> The Pythagorean philosopher believed that the Trinity was the measure of all things, for the reason, I think, that God governs things by the ternary number, and also that things themselves are completed by the ternary number. Hence Virgil said, "God rejoices in the odd number." Certainly the supreme author first creates all things, second attracts them to Himself, and third, perfects them. . . . Orpheus sang this when he called Jupiter the beginning, the middle, and end of the universe.[127]

Here we clearly see how Ficino takes a principle associated with Christianity—the Trinity—and shows how it exists in other traditions. Moreover these other traditions, in doing so, further attest, in his view, to the inherent truths of Christianity. A further example of this may be found later in the same speech:

> Zoroaster posited three princes of the world, the lords of the three orders: Ohrmazd, Mithra, and Ahriman. These Plato called God, Mind, and Soul. The three orders, however, he placed in the divine species: the Ideas, Reasons, and Seeds. The first therefore, that is the Ideas, revolve around the First, that is around God, since they were given to the Mind by God, and they lead back to Him the Mind to which they were given.[128]

In this context, it might be worthwhile to compare Abravanel's work briefly with Pico's *Heptaplus,* a posthumously published (1489) Latin prose commentary on Gen 1:1–27, that I mentioned briefly above. As the name suggests, *Heptaplus* is a Latin work composed of seven "expositions," each one of which is further subdivided into seven chapters. The goal of the treatise, as a whole, is to provide a commentary to the first creation account in Genesis in order to show the correspondence between biblical doctrine and philosophical teachings. In many ways, then, this is not significantly different from what we see in Abravanel's *Dialoghi.* For example, Abravanel will follow Pico in examining the tripartite dimension of the cosmos, the role of nature and humanity's place within it, and the intimate relationship that exists between the individual and God.

Indeed, each of the first six chapters of each one of the seven expositions reads much like the account of creation that we will witness in the *Dialoghi,* minus the attention to rhetorical flourish and the dialogue form. However, in the seventh chapter of each exposition, Pico grounds the preceding discussions explicitly in the figure of Jesus and the concept of the Trinity. For Pico, then, both the Genesis account of creation and the philosophical teachings expounded by the ancients necessarily lead to an endorsement of Christian truths. In the proem to the work, for instance, Pico claims that

Just as with Moses the seventh day is the Sabbath and a day of rest, so we have taken care that every exposition of ours will always in the seventh chapter be turned to Christ, who is the end of the law and is our Sabbath, our rest, and our felicity.[129]

So although Pico is interested in Moses and Mosaic theology, this interest begins and ends in the figure of Jesus. In the first exposition, for example, entitled "On the Elemental World," Pico argues that "nature never acts by chance but only for the sake of some resulting good."[130] After showing the relationship between biblical and Platonic doctrines, Pico discusses how each day of creation introduces us to the increasing perfection of matter, culminating in the seventh day associated with the perfection of Jesus.[131]

Pico uses the biblical account of creation in much the same way that he uses the teachings of kabbalah: both, according to his interpretive strategy, become the sources for a mystical and apologetical reading of Christianity.[132] As a final example, Pico deals in the seventh, and last, exposition primarily with the centrality of Jesus and the perception that he represents the culmination of creation on the one hand, and his intermediary position between the physical and metaphysical worlds on the other. Only now Pico engages in a brief dialogue with an unknown Jewish antagonist. This Jew is a metonym for all those Jews who are unwilling, because of their stubbornness, to acknowledge Jesus' messiahship.[133] Indeed, much of this discussion takes us out of our at least stereotyped view of the Humanism that Pico and the Renaissance are so famous for and puts us squarely back in the arena of medieval Christian Jew-baiting. Using prooftexts from the Bible and the Talmud, Pico shows his Jewish interlocutor how Jesus is the Messiah foretold by the ancient Israelites, and that the lowly status of the Jews is their punishment for the crucifixion:

I am not inventing or dreaming up this interpretation for myself. Elijah himself teaches it to me, and the Talmudists teach it also. It will soon become clear to you also, Jewish viper, unless you close your ears.[134]

This, for obvious reasons, bears no resemblance to that which we find in Judah Abravanel. For Abravanel, in true Humanist fashion, the individual is the epitome of creation. Whereas Pico reserves this position for Jesus, Abravanel locates this potential in every individual.

Although not nearly as vituperative as *Heptaplus*, we nevertheless still encounter in Pico's commentary to Benivieni's *Canzone d'amore* a subtle Christocentrism. In the following example, for instance, Pico is quick to differentiate that the term *son of God* as used by other religio-intellectual traditions (e.g., those of Hermes Trismegistus, Zoroaster, and Platonism) differs from that employed by the Catholic Church:

For what we mean by "the Son" is of one and the same essence as the Father, is equal to Him in everything, and, lastly, is a creator and not a creature; whereas what the Platonists call "the son of God" must be identified with the first and noblest angel created by God.[135]

It is against such passages that we need to situate Judah Abravanel's *Dialoghi d'amore*. In providing such a universal reading of the Jewish tradition in this work, Abravanel can be regarded as reacting negatively to those "Christian scholars" who so desire to read the Bible apologetically and to argue that such apologetics are tantamount to universal human truths. Abravanel shows throughout the *Dialoghi* that the all of the constitutive elements of the Renaissance are preexistent in the Hebrew Bible and Rabbinic literature, and thus it is the Jews that truly embody Renaissance ideals. In the following exchange, for example, he writes:

Sophia: What is the bow of Apollo?
Philo: I could say to you that it is the circumference of the sun's body . . . but I can tell you another more ancient, learned and wiser allegory in the birth of Diana and Apollo.
Sophia: Please tell it to me.
Philo: It refers to their birth at the creation of the world in agreement for the most part with the holy scripture of Moses.
Sophia: How so?
Philo: Moses writes that when God was creating the upper world of heaven and the lower terrestrial world, the spirit of God breathed upon the waters of the abyss and made light, and the evening and the morning were the first day. This refers to the legend of Laton. . . .
Sophia: I am very pleased with this allegory and its agreement with the narrative of creation in the sacred scripture of Moses [*sacra scrittura mosaica*], with its protraction of the work through six consecutive days. Truly it is a wonder how such great and exalted matters could be hidden under the veil of Jupiter's carnal loves.[136]

Here, Abravanel once again shows the correspondence between what he held to be Greek myth and biblical truth. If the former is read properly, it corresponds to the meaning of scripture, which has no need to cover up the truth with allegory. Note that both Philo and Sophia say that Greek myth corresponds to the Bible, and not vice versa. What exists on the surface of the Hebrew Bible must be teased out of other sources—sources that formed the bedrock of Renaissance Humanism.

In many ways, then, we can read Abravanel's *Dialoghi* as an attempt to wrestle back the teachings of Moses from what he perceived to be the distorted readings given to such teachings by the Renaissance Humanists. In this regard, when Abravanel interprets Plato's myth of the androgyne in the *Symposium* as being a corrupt version of the second creation account in Genesis,[137] we can, on one level, read this as showing how Plato "studied" with and learned from biblical prophets in Egypt. However, on a more fundamental level, we can also read such an analysis as a response to Pico's and others' overt Christianization of the Genesis narrative. Similar to the medieval polemics between Christians and Jews, Abravanel provides a Jewish reading of the text to counter those offered by Christians. Interestingly, his "Jewish" reading ultimately proves to be more universal than that of many of the Humanists.

Conclusions

In this chapter, I have situated Judah Abravanel's *Dialoghi d'amore* within the context of Renaissance Humanism and the various literary forms used to articulate it. I argued that central to Humanism was the *trattato d'amore,* the treatise, or dialogue, on love, that proved to be a popular genre in developing and disseminating Renaissance theories of love and desire as philosophical categories. Abravanel's *Dialoghi* was one of the foremost examples of this genre, enjoying an unprecedented popularity among non-Jews that, for earlier Jewish philosophical dialogues, was simply unimaginable. By framing his philosophical discussion of love using the erotically charged exchanges between Philo and Sophia, Abravanel was able to popularize Renaissance philosophical ideals among a general non-Jewish reading audience.

I have also argued that we need to see in the *Dialoghi* a subtle Jewish apologetic. Even though he writes in Italian and primarily for a non-Jewish audience, Abravanel nonetheless attempts to undermine many of the Christocentric ideas found in the work of his contemporaries, the so-called "Christian scholars" that he mentions in *Telunah ʿal ha-zeman*. Caught between the philosophical ideals of medieval Islamicate philosophy and Renaissance Humanism, between being part of a barely tolerated minority and spending a life marked by forced travel and loss, Abravanel channeled these personal and intellectual tensions into creating, arguably, the most popular and widely read work of Jewish philosophy. The tension brought about by occupying two distinct cultural and intellectual worlds is something that we shall witness again in the life and work of Moses Mendelssohn.

6
MOSES MENDELSSOHN: THE DIALOGUE OF FRAGILITY

In the present chapter we again encounter a dialogue, composed by a true master of the genre, whose literary and philosophical features made it a non-Jewish best-seller. Only now the general backdrop is that of the German Enlightenment as opposed to the Italian Renaissance, and the intellectual light that illumines it is supplied by Leibniz and Wolff, not Ficino and Pico della Mirandola. Indeed, so popular was this dialogue, *Phaedon,* that it quickly transformed its author, Moses Mendelssohn (1729–1786), from "Moshe mi-Dessau" (Moses from Dessau) to "the Socrates of Berlin." Yet the clash of these two personae—that of the barely tolerated Jew and that of the towering Enlightenment thinker—created a series of unresolved tensions from which Mendelssohn could never fully escape. Content to engage the Enlightenment ideals as a philosopher whose religious commitment should have no bearing on his argumentation, he was nevertheless frequently called upon to justify his religion and his continued commitment to its law.

In general histories of philosophy, Mendelssohn is often footnoted as the individual whose theory of the soul's permanence Kant criticized in the second book of the *Critique of Pure Reason.*[1] Yet Mendelssohn is, not surprisingly, much more than this. Contemporaries regarded him as one of the finest interpreters of the work of Gottfried Wilhelm Leibniz (1646–1716) and Christian Wolff (1679–1754), two of the leading thinkers associated with the *Frühaufklärung,* the so-called "early phase of the Enlightenment (*Aufklärung*)."[2] Others viewed him as one of the preeminent German literary critics, belletrists, and prose stylists of the eighteenth century. This is all the more amazing when it is remembered that German was not his first language. Still others, notably Gotthold Ephraim Lessing (1729–1781), saw in Mendelssohn the symbol of an age: a virtuous person whose commitment to the shining light of reason was in no way hampered by his religious or ethnic background. These were the same individuals who came out publicly in his support when Johann Caspar Lavater challenged Mendelssohn to either refute Charles Bonnet's *Palingénésie philosophique*—a book which he had just translated into German—or do "what Socrates would have done, had he read this treatise and found it irrefutable," viz., convert to Christianity.[3] In addition to his many contributions to German culture and society, many regard Mendelssohn as the founder of the Jewish Enlightenment or *Haskalah*,[4] and, as such, the first modern Jewish philosopher.

Mendelssohn's *Phaedon*, like much of his early work, is largely uninterested in matters of revelation or ethnicity. It is a dialogue modeled on Plato's work by the same name and, like its predecessor, deals with the last hours of Socrates, recounting the various conversations that he had with his most loyal disciples just before being put to death by the Athenian state. Although this was not the first time that Mendelssohn had employed the genre of the dialogue or used other literary devices in his writings, a number of features—its pleasing style, its poetic prose, the role that Socrates played in the eighteenth-century popular imagination, the treatment of the soul's immortality—all seemed to crystallize in this work. It proved to be so popular that it underwent many editions and was translated into numerous languages during his lifetime.[5] *Phaedon* subsequently secured for Mendelssohn a predominant place in Enlightenment thought and brought him into intimate contact with the luminaries of that intellectual tradition, individuals such as Nicolai, Lessing, and Kant. In retrospect, however, the relative tranquil period in which he composed *Phaedon*—just prior to the Lavater affair, which seems to have triggered in him a nervous-neurological ailment, followed by other periodic open letters publicly challenging him to convert to Christianity—would be short-lived. Despite the fact of *Phaedon*'s popularity (or more likely because of it), Mendelssohn's perceived uncanny ability to write so knowledgably, articulately, and rationally, yet still remain Jewish, bothered many.

When Moses Mendelssohn put pen to paper and wrote *Phaedon*, he was quite content to write as a philosopher, one who happened to be Jewish, and not necessarily as a Jewish philosopher. However, on another level, the case could be made that the major themes of *Phaedon*—the centrality of natural religion, the existence of God, the soul's immortality—are not fundamentally different from what we encounter in Mendelssohn's more specifically Jewish works. In his *Jerusalem, oder über religiöse Macht und Judentum* (Jerusalem, On Religious Power and Judaism), published much later in 1783, Mendelssohn argued that it was Judaism, not Christianity, that most closely resembled natural religion[6] because Judaism was in essence a "revealed legislation" that had no need of a special divine revelation in order to impart truths to humans. This was the opposite of Christianity that, according to him, rested upon a set of dogmas requiring assent, often contrary to reason, on the part of the believer. The major premise of *Jerusalem,* I shall argue in this chapter, is not significantly different from that which we encounter in the *Phaedon.*

The central themes that we encounter in *Phaedon,* especially their concomitant relationship to ideas that preoccupied Mendelssohn later in life, should alert us to the fact that this is not an Enlightenment work of belles lettres designed solely for the entertainment of a non-Jewish reading audience. Rather, on a fundamental level, and much like Judah Abravanel's *Dialoghi, Phaedon* becomes a polemical work designed to demonstrate to a predominantly Christian audience that Christianity was not a prerequisite to the felicity of the soul after corporeal death. By making Socrates, neither Jew nor Christian, the protagonist of the work, Mendelssohn wrestles the concept of natural religion out of the hands of any particular religion or religious claim. The implications of this move are surely significant. For instance, the doctrine of the universal salvation of righteous individuals that we encounter in this work means that Jews cannot be regarded as inferior or be reduced to potential converts. Moreover, reading *Phaedon* from the perspective of his later works, we hear in the utterances of Socrates the echo of later articulations in which Mendelssohn argues that it is Judaism, requiring neither dogma nor faith, that alone enables its practitioners to live well.

On this reading, then, *Phaedon,* perhaps controversially, becomes a work of "Jewish philosophy," despite the fact that there is not one single Jewish reference found in its pages. Furthermore, reading this early work of Mendelssohn's through the prism of his later work, it becomes possible to avoid the temptation to bifurcate his thought neatly into the "Hebrew" and the "German," the "early" and the "later," or the "particular" and the "universal." Rather, viewed from this alternative perspective, we witness a consistent vision that links up all of Mendelssohn's diverse and multifaceted writings irrespective of language of composition, date, or intended audience. *Phaedon,* when read as one part of his oeuvre, shows that the true essence of Judaism most closely approximated the universal truths of the Enlightenment. Judaism, in other words, was not a despised religion, but one that neatly fitted with the rationalist claims of Leibniz and Wolff.

Yet the great paradox of *Phaedon* is that Mendelssohn, in a private correspondence with Raphael Levi, did not think it possible to translate the work into Hebrew and believed that the "literary form" of the dialogue was inappropriate to communicate ideas to fellow Jews.[7] Unlike all the previous thinkers discussed in this study, then, Mendelssohn did not regard the dialogue as suitable for a Jewish audience. Instead, he wrote a Hebrew version of *Phaedon* as a private correspondence, published posthumously by David Friedländer (1750–1834) as *Sefer ha-nefesh* (The Book of the Soul).

In this work, not intended for public consumption, Mendelssohn essentially gives all the same arguments as he does in the *Phaedon*—although minus the character of Socrates, divested of its dialogue form, and replete with many biblical and rabbinic prooftexts.

Situating *Phaedon:* Literary Trends in Eighteenth-Century Philosophy

The Enlightenment, traditionally viewed as the Age of Reason, has in recent years come under assault from a number of disparate constituencies. Relatively recent studies, for example, have called into question the thesis that this period developed and sustained a relatively unified intellectual movement that stressed reason over superstition.[8] Others have called into question the nature of the Enlightenment's commitment to values such as freedom, toleration, and liberty.[9] Despite such well-founded concerns, however, it is still possible to delineate a number of features and commonalities that define a phenomenon that we can recognize as Enlightenment philosophical thought. Such features include, but are certainly not limited to, the importance of rational and secular knowledge, the perceived unity of humanity based on the principles of natural law, and the importance of religious toleration. The concepts of natural religion and natural law, in particular the notion that there exist universal norms irrespective of country of birth or ethnicity, in theory if not always in practice, denoted that all peoples shared basic levels of humanity.

The Enlightenment thinker was distinct from both his medieval and Renaissance counterparts. To use the words of Lois Dubin,

> More critic than philosopher, a man of Enlightenment saw himself as a committed social actor engaged in the essentially practical work of enlightening, that is, of combating ignorance and prejudice by means of all important critique and education. . . . they set themselves up as an alternative lay authority to the clergy, indeed as the new "clerks"—as moral arbiters and interpreters of conscience. In fact this secular intelligentsia did represent a new social type, not identifiable with any particular order in the old regime.[10]

These Enlightenment thinkers stressed rationalism, common sense, scientific inquiry, and were determined to remake society in ways that were bound neither to tradition nor Church, but to reason. In German-Jewish circles, the *maskilim* (sg. *maskil*)—or practitioners of the *Haskalah*[11]—were equally concerned with using reason to illumine various superstitions, but they also had concerns unique to their status as a tolerated minority with few legal privileges. As such, many *maskilim* emphasized the internal correspondences between Judaism and Enlightenment culture, but always with an eye toward improving the legal and social conditions of Jews. This led especially to the reconsidering of the role of education in Jewish life,[12] creating, inter alia, a desire to renew Hebrew at the expense of Yiddish, learn German, and, more generally, educate fellow Jews according to the ideals of *Bildung*.[13] Perceived by some to be calling into question the traditional authority of the rabbis, the early *maskilim*, of which Mendelssohn was one of its first and most important representatives, sought to wed Enlightenment ideals to a more modern, but not necessarily less observant, understanding of Judaism.

We must now attempt to situate Mendelssohn more specifically into this general intellectual milieu. Intellectually, the thinkers who made a tremendous impact on Mendelssohn were the two great names of the early German Enlightenment: Leibniz and his most famous pupil, Christian Wolff. Mendelssohn encountered the works of these two individuals when he first arrived in Berlin as a young student, and, in one of his earliest philosophical works, *Über die Empfindungen* (On the Sentiments), Mendelssohn, in an undoubtedly autobiographical moment, has one of the characters, Theocles, say:

> Thanks be to those true guides who have guided me back to true knowledge and to virtue. Thanks to you, Locke and Wolff! To you immortal Leibniz! I erect an eternal monument to you in my heart. Without your help I would have been lost forever. I have never made your acquaintance, but in my solitary hours I implored your immortal writings for help, writings which remain to this day unread by the wider world, and it was they which steered me on the sure path to genuine philosophy, to knowledge of my very self and my origin. In my soul your writings have planted the holy truths on which my happiness is based; they have inspired me.[14]

When Mendelssohn arrived in Berlin in 1743, Wolff was arguably the most influential philosopher in Germany.[15] Although Mendelssohn never hesitated to dissent from Wolff or Leibniz in his own writings, he nevertheless remained committed to their basic principles throughout his life, and is often regarded as "the last great representative of the Leibniz-Wolffian school."[16] Despite the fact that both Leibniz and Wolff upheld the fundamental tenets of Christian revelation, they nonetheless argued that eternal truths could not be revealed because they had to be accessible to the unaided human intellect, and that revelation could not contradict the truths of reason. Of especial importance to them was the establishment of "natural" (natural being the opposite of revealed) truths that were generally accessible to human reason, viz., God's existence, his providence, and the immortality of the soul. Such concepts, regarded as "natural," became the unassailable truths that formed the bedrock of all morality and belief.

Leibniz and Wolff also composed some of their philosophical work in the vernacular as opposed to Latin. Wolff, in particular, is generally credited with developing a German philosophical idiom and creating a new vocabulary for various terms previously expressed solely in Latin.[17] Writing in the vernacular, as we saw in the previous chapter, played a large role in the dissemination of philosophy, enabling a more general reading public to encounter the concepts of the Enlightenment. Increasingly, Enlightenment ideals were popularized in the vernacular through various literary genres, which included open letters, moral weeklies, church sermons, and other "popular" literary treatises and genres.[18]

Although Leibniz and Wolff probably exerted the greatest influence on Mendelssohn, he still read widely and broadly in the European philosophical tradition. Mendelssohn, however, was not just a passive consumer of philosophy in his early years; he also translated philosophical works into German. Such translations or partial translations included parts of Plato's *Republic*, the Third Earl of Shaftesbury's *Sensus Communis*,[19] and Rousseau's *Discours*. The literary form of such works seems to have left a major impression on the young Mendelssohn, as many of his earliest treatises—especially his *Philosophische Gespräche* (Philosophical Dialogues) and his *Phaedon*—could be described as the dynamic encounter between Lebnizian and Wolffian ideas with the more popular philosophical style of the English and French Enlightenment. Mendelssohn's philosophical style, unlike that of his German contemporaries, included an ornate and poetic literary sense, a general concern with aesthetics,[20] and, most important for my study, the ability to create and sustain a well-crafted dialogue.

In terms of literary form and style, Mendelssohn seems to have been particularly fond of Anthony Ashley Cooper, better known as the Third Earl of Shaftesbury (1671–1713).[21] Shaftesbury's major philosophical work, *Characteristicks of Men, Manners, Opinions, Times*, published in 1711, is a wide-ranging collection of essays that employs a number of different literary genres, including the dialogue. Many of the essays in the collection are written in a highly rhetorical style, and are full of digressions that reflect on contemporaneous culture and ideas.[22] One of the defining features of the Earl of Shaftesbury's highly literary and rhetorical style, according to Lawrence Klein, is that of dialogue, which was a genre that

> assumed the equality of participants and insisted on a reciprocity in which participants were sometimes talkers and sometimes listeners. It provided an opportunity for self-display at the same time that its norms disciplined self-expression for the sake of domestic peace.[23]

It was the writings of the Earl of Shaftesbury that seem to have acquainted the young Mendelssohn with the philosophical potential inherent to the dialogue. Alexander Altmann, the foremost biographer of Mendelssohn, describes the latter as "one of the first in Germany to be enchanted by the great Englishman."[24] Nowhere is this more evident than in Mendelssohn's very first philosophical work, *Philosophische Gespräche,* published anonymously in 1754, which was deeply indebted to *The Moralists.* According to an anecdote of his own son, Joseph, Mendelssohn borrowed from Lessing a treatise, indeed most likely *The Moralists.* When Lessing asked Mendelssohn how he enjoyed it, the latter replied that he had done so very much, but thought that he himself could produce an equally good text. When Lessing dared him to do just that, shortly thereafter Mendelssohn presented him with his own dialogue—the aforementioned *Philosophische Gespräche.* Several months later, Mendelssohn asked Lessing how he enjoyed the work, at which point Lessing handed him a published copy of the dialogue.[25]

Mendelssohn's second philosophical work, *Über die Empfindungen* (On the Sentiments), published in 1755, also reveals the literary influence of the Earl of Shaftesbury. This work recounts a series of epistolary exchanges between Euphrenor and Palemon, the latter of whom Mendelssohn describes as "an English philosopher who inherited the name of that dear enthusiast known to us from the Earl of Shaftesbury's *The Moralists.*"[26] In a later edition of the work, Mendelssohn renamed Palemon as Theokles, another character in *The Moralists,* but one who was more influenced by the principles of deism.[27]

In *Über die Empfindungen* the influence of the Earl of Shaftesbury is immediately palpable both in terms of the characters that Mendelssohn employs in the work, and also in the epistolary style and the various rhetorical devices that he uses (e.g., the use of rural portraits). Unlike the prototype, however, Mendelssohn's version has the main character "renounce his fatherland, his tranquility, and his friends' embrace in order to search for a people that treasures *accurate* thinking more than *free* thinking."[28] Despite the fact that Mendelssohn took over the characters and the genres that he encountered in Shaftesbury's work, he transformed the conversational aspects between the two protagonists—Palemon/Theokles and Euphrenor—in such a manner that reflects his own understanding of the nature of epistolary correspondence. Indeed, Altmann argues that we can read the exchange between the two characters in the work as reflecting the epistolary correspondences between Mendelssohn himself and his good friend Lessing.[29] Finally, the main philosophical ideas that the two literary protagonists share and debate in Mendelssohn's work are not those of Shaftesbury, but those of the German Enlightenment, particularly of Leibniz and Wolff.

Mendelssohn's philosophical oeuvre was, as many have noted, indebted to the Leibnizian-Wolffian context that played such a formative role in shaping the eighteenth-century German Enlightenment. Nevertheless, as important as the thought of these two thinkers was, we must not lose sight of Mendelssohn's desire to express German thought in new and creative literary forms. In exploring the contours between literature and philosophy, he found the philosophical styles that Shaftesbury and Plato employed so amenably. Both of these individuals used forms—the epistolary exchange in the case of the former, and the dialogue in the case of the latter—other than the straightforward expository treatise to give voice to their philosophical ideas. It is certainly no coincidence that when Mendelssohn was composing his earliest philosophical writings he was also engaged in translating parts of both of these authors' works into German.[30]

Mendelssohn experimented with a number of literary genres in his early philosophical work. These included dialogues, epistolary exchanges between fictional characters, essays written in the guise of a Christian author, and, together with Lessing, the publication of the literary and playful *Pope ein Metaphysiker* (Pope, A Metaphysician).[31] Moreover, Mendelssohn was also engaged in highly literary correspondences with people such as Lessing and Thomas Abbt. And in addition to his philosophical and literary achievements, Mendelssohn also wrote poetry, was a well-known literary critic, and was a theoretician of the arts. The thread that seems to link all of these diverse types of writings is his overarching concern with aesthetics, something that I shall discuss in greater detail below. This undoubtedly contributed to Mendelssohn's ability to find the delicate balance between philosophical ideas and literary expression that insured for him a receptive audience, and which would establish a place for him, an individual who had to learn German as a second language in his teens,[32] in German belles lettres. And as we shall shortly see with his *Phaedon*, Mendelssohn was able to take a commonly discussed and analyzed aspect of natural religion, the topic of the immortality of the soul, and give it a novel treatment by essentially rewriting Plato's own dialogue of the same name.

Moses Mendelssohn: Life and Times

Mendelssohn's life has been told many times,[33] and need not be retold here. Rather than attempt to provide an overarching account of his life and times—his role in the early *Haskalah*, his location at the fragile intersection of German and Jewish cultures, ultimately his unsuccessful attempt to reconcile the various demands of each culture—I focus here only on those features of his early life that potentially illumine the composition of his *Phaedon*. Yet, because this early work possesses key motifs that reappear in his later, decidedly more Judaic work, it is impossible to ignore certain aspects of his later life.

Mendelssohn's literary fame, his ability to frame philosophical ideas in universal terms, and his friendship with the major figures of the German Enlightenment make his life story not only remarkable but virtually sui generis. Although there had been many "Jewish philosophers" preceding him, the great majority of them either had written in Hebrew or in the vernacular but in Hebrew characters. This factor immediately confined their reading audience to other elite Jews, with the corollary that they rarely found a voice outside of their own religioethnic communities. One of the few figures who seems to have anticipated the literary and philosophical fame, not to mention the ability to connect with a non-Jewish audience, was Judah Abravanel. As was the case in the previous chapter, it again becomes necessary to ask: for whom was the author writing? And, equally importantly, why that audience in particular?

Mendelssohn was born in 1729 in Dessau, a city that was one of the centers of the early *Haskalah*. In particular, it was in Dessau that Maimonides' *Guide of the Perplexed* was republished, in Hebrew translation, after almost two centuries of neglect. This text, which has reappeared frequently, if tangentially, in these pages, became an important vehicle for demonstrating to young and potential *maskilim* that there were Jewish alternatives to the traditional dialectic found in the Talmud and taught in the traditional schools (*hederim*) throughout Central and Eastern Europe. The republication of the *Guide*, a work that when originally written attempted to show the implicit harmonious relationship between Judaism and Aristotelianism, proved instrumental in introducing many eighteenth-century students to the fact that medieval Judaism possessed a rationalist tradition, and even more importantly that there was no good reason why such a harmonious relation between religion and contemporary philosophy could not recur in the present.

One of the central figures responsible for giving institutional approval to the *Guide*'s republication was David Fränkel,[34] the chief rabbi of Dessau, and one of the earliest teachers of the young Moses Mendelssohn. The latter seems to have found in Fränkel an early model for a life committed to both tradition and philosophy. Reflecting back on his earliest years, prior to his association with Fränkel, Mendelssohn lamented the type of educational activity that he, like so many of his generation, had undergone. He was particularly critical of the traditional rabbinic method of *pilpul* (dialectic), in which students reenact the arguments of the ancient sages of the Talmud. In a letter of March 15, 1784, near the end of his life, Mendelssohn writes to Herz Homberg concerning the education of his own son, Joseph:

> My son Joseph has all but given up his Hebrew studies. Immediately following your tutelage, he unfortunately fell into the hands of a scholar who proved to be a hollow *baʿal pilpul;* and as much as Joseph loves intellectual activity and scholarly disputation, he lacks a sense for real *pilpul.* As you know, it takes a very special kind of instruction to develop a taste for this type of mental exercise. And though both you and I underwent this training, [you will recall that] we agreed Joseph's mind should rather remain a little duller than be sharpened in so sterile a manner.[35]

Despite Mendelssohn's revulsion for this type of educational process, he consciously composed much of his own early work in a way that, on one level, imitated the dialectic exchanges of characters from antiquity. In part, then, Mendelssohn's use of dialogue was related to his larger project, although not formulated fully until much later, to reevaluate and rearticulate the role and function of Jewish education. His general educational goal for Jews was to get them to leave behind traditional paradigms and embrace the rational forms provided by the Enlightenment. Yet according to Mendelssohn's friend and publisher, Friedrich Nicolai, intellectual sterility was not simply a Jewish problem, but also a German one. According to him, Mendelssohn

> learned in his early youth the art of Talmudic disputation and he acquired facility in it. This deplorable training increases the mind's subtlety but not sustained thinking, a deficiency that may be said to attach also to many a German speculative philosopher who indicate only endless and empty arguing.[36]

It is perhaps no coincidence that Mendelssohn spent much of his early philosophical writings experimenting with various literary forms and genres. Both traditional Jewish education and traditional German philosophical expression were, according to him, in need of recasting. Following the lead of Shaftesbury, Mendelssohn became interested in the art of polite conversation. Accordingly, Mendelssohn consciously shifted his emphasis from rote dialectic to a living dialogue that captured the dynamic, interpersonal encounter between individuals.

When Fränkel moved to Berlin in order to serve as rabbi there, the fourteen-year-old Mendelssohn followed him to continue his studies.[37] Once in Berlin, Mendelssohn boarded with a prominent family, where other like-minded Jews gradually introduced him to the themes, ideas, and tastes of the German Enlightenment. These included individuals such as Israel ben Moses Ha-Levi Zamosc (ca. 1700–1772),[38] with whom the young Mendelssohn continued to study the medieval Jewish philosophical tradition, especially the thought of Maimonides. Zamosc is also significant because he composed a line-by-line commentary to the *Kuzari,* one that mitigates the antirationalism of the work and that also shows his own desire to link medieval thought to modern European philosophy by translating key terms in the *Kuzari* into German.[39] Another individual, Abraham Kisch (1728–1803), tutored Mendelssohn in Latin; and yet another, Aaron Solomon Gumpertz (1723–1769),[40] taught him French and English, and it was from him that the young Mendelssohn "acquired the taste for humane letters."[41] Most significantly, however, Gumpertz was responsible for, to use the words of Altmann, setting an example on the impressionable Mendelssohn: "Here was a young Jew, rooted in community and tradition, who had ventured into the intellectual world and society outside them."[42]

The other formative figure in the young Mendelssohn's life was the aforementioned Gotthold Ephraim Lessing. It was Lessing who, inter alia, encouraged Mendelssohn to write one of his earliest works, the *Philosophische Gespräche,* and who would become his best friend, not only on a personal level but on a literary and public one. More generally, it was through his *Die Juden* (The Jews) and especially *Nathan der Weise* (Nathan the Wise), whose protagonist was modeled on Mendelssohn, that Lessing championed the cause of a "noble Jew," hitherto deemed an oxymoron, in German society.

Although his earliest philosophical work was favorably received, it was Mendelssohn's *Phaedon* that truly cemented his reputation as an Enlightenment thinker, establishing for him a place in German belles lettres, and giving him the role of the "Socrates of Berlin." Indeed, the first edition of the book was sold out within months of its publication; second, third, and fourth editions came out in 1768, 1769, and 1776 respectively.[43] Editions published by other presses came out in 1768, 1769, 1776, 1778, 1780, 1784, and 1785. *Phaedon* was subsequently translated into Dutch in 1769, into French in 1772 and 1773, into Italian in 1773, and into Danish and Russian in 1779. All of these publications and re-publications testify to the work's ability to find a receptive audience among a European reading public.

Phaedon, like much of Mendelssohn's so-called early work, was produced in an environment of personal optimism for the writer. Despite his legal status as a "Protected Jew" (*Schutzjude*) in Berlin, he was largely accepted by the leading intellectual figures of Germany: individuals such as Kant, Lessing, Nicolai, and Abbt, to name but a few. He was frequently invited into people's salons and homes to engage in conversation, and, in turn, welcomed visitors to his own parlor. Mendelssohn was frequently asked to join special clubs then being formed in Berlin,[44] to read his papers in front of their audiences, and to enter into correspondence with countless individuals. During this period, he was quite content to be an observant Jew who wrote philosophical works for non-Jews. Yet, as Michael Meyer argues, such a bifurcation could not last:

> as long as he was not a figure of the first rank on the intellectual scene, the enlightened Jew was welcomed even by those of a less universalistic outlook. But could a Jew be one of the dominating spirits of Western European culture and still remain a Jew? For those whose surface devotion to *Aufklärung* thinly overlay deep commitment to orthodox Christianity, it was inconceivable that the noble Mendelssohn should not accept their faith.[45]

The spirit of optimism that characterized Mendelssohn's earliest philosophical writings did not last long after *Phaedon*'s publication. Mendelssohn had always been conscious of the fact that, despite his friendships and reputation, many were intolerant of him because he was a Jew. This may be witnessed, for example, in his dismay and disappointment with Michaelis's critique of Lessing's *Die Juden,* which denied that even one Jew, much less the entire Jewish people, could be virtuous.[46] Yet, Mendelssohn's friendship with Lessing and others, and the general favorable reception of his work, seemed to mitigate such prejudice.

However, this would all change in 1769 when Johann Caspar Lavater, a Swiss theologian, issued a public challenge to Mendelssohn to either refute Christianity publicly or convert to it.[47] Although Lavater's challenge was spurred more by messianism than reason, it nevertheless became apparent to Mendelssohn that he could no longer be perceived simply as a philosopher who, while Jewish, wrote solely for non-Jews. Although many defended Mendelssohn from what they perceived to be Lavater's rabid zealousness, the challenge nevertheless struck at the points where the Enlightenment was most fragile.

The aftermath of the Lavater affair left many marks, both physiological and intellectual, on Mendelssohn. In terms of the former, the affair seems to have precipitated a nervous debility that, in his own words, prevented him from engaging in abstract speculative philosophy. As for the latter, Mendelssohn increasingly felt that he had no option but to demonstrate to both his distracters and his friends that Judaism was a religion of reason. Although he continued to write various reviews and criticisms during and after the affair, his main energies, in the words of Willi Goetshel, became devoted "to explaining and legitimizing Judaism as a culture that was fully qualified to participate in the project of enlightenment and modernity."[48]

Although the Lavater affair eventually dissipated, it was but one in a series of public confrontations that constantly put Mendelssohn on the defensive. Probably the best example of Mendelssohn's new position as defender of a rational Judaism rather than as simple spokesperson for the German Enlightenment is found in his response to the two-pronged pamphlet entitled *The Searching For Light and Right in a Letter to Mr. Moses Mendelssohn Occasioned by his Remarkable Preface to Menasseh ben Israel.*[49] Although written by August Friedrich Cranz, Mendelssohn incorrectly believed it to have been written by a much more serious adversary: the Jewish convert to Christianity and the leader of the Enlightenment in Austria, Joseph Edler von Sonnenfels.[50] In essence, Cranz challenged Mendelssohn to demonstrate how a Jew could remain a Jew *and* a citizen of a modern European nation state. Attached to the pamphlet was a postscript by an obscure chaplain named David Ernst Mörshel challenging Mendelssohn either to clarify his position on revelation or to claim himself a naturalist. It was this "two-pronged" attack that was directly responsible for Mendelssohn's publication of *Jerusalem,* his attempt to argue both for the separation of church and state, and to gain equal rights for Jews.[51]

Plato, Socratic Dialogue, and Mendelssohn's *Phaedon*

In chapter 1, we saw how the figure of Socrates in medieval Islamicate thought was a pliable figure, a convenient literary trope, upon which a thinker or a community articulated or reinforced a particular worldview. Despite the fact that, as mentioned in the previous chapter, the dialogues of Plato increasingly became more accessible, the figure of Socrates remained cloaked in romance and mystique. Socrates—his quest for truth, his unwillingness to accept either opinion or tradition, and his mistrust of revealed religion—now served as a model for Enlightenment thinkers. A large part of the Enlightenment's fascination with him concerned the circumstances surrounding his death: with no separation between church and state, Socrates was condemned to death by the state for corrupting its religion. That Socrates showed neither remorse nor distress, but rather genuine joy at the prospects of an immortal existence, would have delighted proponents of natural religion. Eighteenth-century philosophers sought to emulate the Socrates who was a gifted teacher and who sought to educate his fellow citizens. In this regard, Socrates was often juxtaposed with Aristotle, someone who wrote technical treatises that were largely inaccessible to those who were not philosophically inclined.

In the introduction to *Phaedon,* Mendelssohn, typical of his age, crafts a Socrates based heavily on Enlightenment ideals. This Socrates, unblemished by revealed religion, had to put trust in his intellect and its ability to discover the tenets of natural religion. Mendelssohn's Socrates, in turn, was not a solitary individual but someone engaged in making metaphysical and ethical truths accessible to those around him. Upon returning from the field of battle, Socrates

> began to oppose sophistry and superstition with success, and to teach his fellow citizens virtue and wisdom [*Tugend und Weisheit*]. In the open streets, in the public walks and baths, in private houses, in the workshops of artists or wherever he found men whom he thought he could make better, he entered into conversation with them [*ließ sichmit ihnen in Gespräche ein*], explained what was right and wrong, good and evil, holy and unholy. He talked to them about the providence and government of God [*Vorsehung und Regierung Gottes*], of the means of pleasing God [*von den Mitteln ihm zu gefallen*], of the duties of a citizen [*von der Glückseligheit des Menschen*], a father, and a husband. He spoke not in the arrogant tone of the sophists, but addressed them in the accents of a friend who desired to search for the truth with them, to which he led them by a series of simple questions in order that they might follow him step by step without any strain to their understandings until he brought them imperceptibly to the point they desired.[52]

Socrates here engages his fellow citizens, leading them from error to truth by getting them to cast off superstition in favor of reason. Although he speaks a lot about God and how to please him, Socrates' only appeal is to a reason unmediated by any sort of monotheistic revelation. This, of course, is the opposite of Halevi's *ḥaver* who, it will be recalled, put pride of place on the authoritative chain of tradition over any type of ratiocination. But whereas Halevi recoiled from the dominant philosophical ideas of his time, Mendelssohn, in the name of Socrates, embraced such ideas. The Socrates of Mendelssohn's *Phaedon* is clearly not a simple replica of the individual found in Plato's dialogue by the same name. The vocabulary and categories that we encounter in Mendelssohn's work are clearly those of the Enlightenment, not classical Athens. Mendelssohn's Socrates, in other words, becomes the voice for natural religion.

It is also possible to read Mendelssohn's portrait of Socrates in semi-autobiographical terms:

> So powerfully had reason impressed his mind with the existence of the Deity that he made a sacrifice of health [*Gesundheit*], reputation and peace to virtue, and at last he gave up life itself in the most exemplary manner for the welfare of his neighbors [*das Wohl seiner Nebenmenschen*].[53]

Socrates, in other words, was so committed to ascertaining and disseminating truth to his countrymen that his health suffered. Mendelssohn intimates that Socrates was frail, unhealthy, and generally unconcerned with the ways in which others perceived him: his only goal in life was to help his fellow citizens acquire their natural perfection. Mendelssohn, perhaps not coincidentally, was himself a frail individual, and this frailty would soon be exacerbated during his public debate with Lavater in the early 1770s. Although Mendelssohn could certainly not foretell the manner of his own death, from our vantage point, the brief allusion to Socrates' fate, dying while trying to help his fellow citizens overcome the damaging influences of superstition and imagination, bears an uncanny resemblance to his own end.[54]

For many in the eighteenth century, Socrates embodied the ideals of the Enlightenment. As a result, there was a tendency to uncover the "real" Socrates, unmediated by Plato, someone who was somehow deemed more authentic and who, not surprisingly, upheld contemporaneous values. Shaftesbury, for example, planned to compose, but never did, a work entitled "Socratik History," which would include translations of the sources on Socrates' life, expository essays, and a series of notes.[55] According to Lawrence E. Klein, because "Socrates put philosophy at the center of human activity as the pursuit of moral wisdom . . . , Shaftesbury looked to Socrates as an exemplar of moral philosophy pursued in the midst of humanity."[56]

In 1760, Mendelssohn himself reviewed and published three writings that dealt with Socrates. The first of these works, Johann Georg Hamann's anonymously published *Socratic Memorabilia for the Boredom of the Public,* Mendelssohn reviewed positively, but noted that he was not entirely convinced by the words and arguments that were put in Socrates' mouth by Plato.[57] The second work he reviewed was *The Last Dialogue of Socrates and His Friends* by W**, whom Mendelssohn mistakenly believed was Christoph Martin Wendel, but was in fact Jakob Wegelin. Mendelssohn, who would subsequently compose his own *Phaedon* as the last reported dialogue between Socrates and his friends, was extremely critical of this work. In particular, he took its author to task for his artificial use of dialogue and juxtaposed the modern work against Plato's own mastery of the genre.[58] The final review was of *Abhandlung von der dramatischen Dichtkunst* (Treatise on Dramatic Art), a German translation of Diderot's treatment of the death of Socrates. This review, generally positive, praised Diderot for his use of dramatic narrative to contextualize Socrates' statements. Mendelssohn writes, however, as follows:

> In fact, there are two horns of a dilemma that cannot be avoided. Should Socrates convince his disciples by philosophical arguments, most of the audience will yawn; should he move the audience by his eloquence, philosophers will be dissatisfied. I also say, like Diderot, let him who so desires try his hand at this scene. I hurry to my purpose.[59]

The review of these three works, in addition to showing his perennial interest in the works of Plato and Shaftesbury, seems to have inspired

Mendelssohn to compose his own Socratic dialogue. Although he had always been interested in the intersection of philosophy and aesthetics, especially in genres that could show this intersection, the review essay seems to have put into focus for him the importance of Socrates' final conversation. The style (or lack thereof) of the works under review, in other words, highlighted for Mendelssohn just how important it was to present such a conversation in a pleasing, engaging, and philosophically respectable literary style. In a letter to Abbt dated July 4, 1762, Mendelssohn comments on the artistic skill of Plato:

> Plato has a manner of writing that combines all the merits of Shaftesbury's style with an inimitable ease of phrasing. His prose, even where it becomes poetic, flows with such tranquil majesty that a non-expert might think the phrase had cost him no effort. I never read Plato without feeling ashamed at ever having put pen to paper, for I have written enough in my life at least to be able to see the busy hand of the artist through the veil of naturalness.[60]

Mendelssohn, following Shaftesbury—whose work, we should not forget, Mendelssohn was concomitantly translating into German—was particularly fond of the ancients' ability to employ dialogue in their philosophical writings in order to give their work a sense of real discourse and free debate. It is by these criteria—a philosophical acceptable literary style, the ability to recreate a real, living dialogue—that Mendelssohn judged the three aforementioned works. Not coincidentally, at approximately the same time (July 1762) that he penned the letter to Abbt, he also sketched a preliminary outline of the *Phaedon*.[61] And although he does not make reference to the dialogue form in this preliminary outline, we get a sense from the review article and various correspondences, such as that to Abbt,[62] that the literary form the work should take was of paramount importance to him.

Finally, at the same time that Mendelssohn was conceptualizing the *Phaedon* he was also engaged in translating some of Plato's work into German. Mendelssohn had learned Greek in 1759–1760 with the help of Rector Damm,[63] and we know that he read both Homer and Plato with him. In a letter dated July 5, 1763, Mendelssohn writes that he had already translated three books of the *Republic* into German.[64]

In addition to Mendelssohn's literary fascination with the form of the Socratic dialogue, Socrates also provided Mendelssohn with a literary fiction to develop ideas that would otherwise have been very difficult for a Jew to articulate. To use the words of Goetschel,

> Mendelssohn turned his own experience of exclusion from the center of discourse into the project of emancipation and participation. His own form of writing critically reflects the problematic nature of his marginalized position. By staging his philosophical conversations in an underhanded manner, Men-

delssohn artfully broaches the question of the rules and stipulations of the discursive play in which he strives to participate.[65]

Both Socrates and the Platonic model of writing philosophy, then, afforded Mendelssohn the freedom to articulate the soul's immortality in ways that were completely divorced from contemporaneous theological (i.e., Christian) perspectives. This might well be one of the reasons that so much of his other early philosophical writings were published anonymously. The dialogue, like the epistolary genre he had used earlier, was a form in which a Jew, under the cloak of relative secrecy, could explore certain topics with a primarily non-Jewish audience in mind. Within this context, for a Jew to argue that every soul, as opposed to every Christian soul, was immortal would not have been particularly well received by a general reading public in the eighteenth century. So even though Mendelssohn could never have argued effectively for such a position in his own name, it became possible to articulate such a position in the name of Socrates. Equally important, the figure of Socrates also enabled Mendelssohn to disagree implicitly with certain of the Christocentric metaphysical assumptions of Leibniz and Wolff. Socrates, as someone who lived prior to Jesus, could employ Leibinizan and Wolffian arguments, but in ways devoid of their original religious assumptions.

The dialogue also permitted Mendelssohn to explore his interest in aesthetics, a subject in which neither Leibniz nor Wolff were particularly interested. Wolff's primary concern with aesthetics involved grounding beauty solely in the faculty of desire, thereby circumscribing aesthetics to metaphysics.[66] Mendelssohn, by contrast, was interested in the psychological interpretation of beauty, in particular the various ways in which a work of art produced pleasure in the human soul,[67] he argued that "the essence of the fine arts and sciences consists in an artful, sensuously perfect representation or in a sensuous perfection represented by art."[68]

Mendelssohn's aesthetics, in other words, located the sublime not in the world of nature but in the work of art qua human creation.[69] The work of art—music, visual arts, poetry, etc.—was what enabled humans to perceive and interact with the sublime through the concrete. This encounter, moreover, could not be artificial or contrived, but had to occur through the living and dynamic contexts of lived experience. The dialogue, then, is not just a convenient literary style, but becomes part and parcel of Mendelssohn's theory of how we encounter the sublime through the recognition of a living dialogue between humans. The foundation of the sublime, for Mendelssohn, was God, providence, and the immortality of the soul. All three of these principles formed the bedrock not only of natural religion, but more importantly of his *Phaedon,* which, on one level, we can read as the practical expression of his theory of aesthetics. This theory also had an important practical aspect: to educate the reader, to contribute to his or her *Bildung*.

Dialogue in *Phaedon*

Phaedon—or, more fully, *Phaedon öder über die Unsterblichkeit der Seele in drey Gesprächen* (Phaedon: On the Immortality of the Soul in Three Dialogues)—is, as the title reveals, divided into three dialogues, all of which revolve around the soul's immortality. The setting for the dialogue is based on Plato's account of the last hours of Socrates, and at times Mendelssohn's work literally follows its predecessor.[70] Mendelssohn begins with a lengthy preface describing, in autobiographical and romantic strokes, the life and times of Socrates. Following this he provides the three dialogues, all of which take place between Socrates and a number of his students—Phaedon, Appollodorus, Cebes, Crito, and Simmias. The leitmotif that runs throughout the work is Socrates' desire to convince his students that the soul is immortal and that a better life awaits it on the other side of death.

More specifically, the first dialogue witnesses Socrates' declaration of his commitment to the philosophical life: "I have said, dear Cebes, that wisdom of the world is the most excellent music [*die Weltweisheit die vortrefflichste Musik*] because it teaches us to direct our thoughts and actions so as to make them accord as perfectly as possible with the views of our master [*den Absichten des allerhöchsten Eigenthumsherrn*]."[71] This declaration leads Socrates to defend his belief in the soul's immortality against the objections of his interlocutors:

> **Simmias:** Cebes directs his objections principally against your present conduct: You who can with so much unconcern not only take leave of all your friends, to whom your death is afflicting, but remove yourself also from under the superintendence of a governor, whom you have taught us to believe is the wisest and most benevolent of beings.
> **Socrates:** Listen Simmias and Cebes, in the first place, if I had not hopes that I am going to continue to exist under the care of the same all-kind providence, and to meet the spirits of the departed, whose society is preferable to any friendship we enjoy here on earth. . . . I am not grieved to die, as I know that at death all is not over with us [*mit dem Tode noch nicht alles für uns aus ist*]; another life follows [*es folgt ein anderes Leben*], and one, as has been said of old, which will prove happier for the virtuous than for the wicked.[72]

In order to prove this, however, Socrates must show that the soul does not perish with the death of the body. Since Mendelssohn (and, thus,

Socrates) takes God's existence for granted, he argues that only God, not nature, can destroy phenomena because there is no intermediate state between existence and nonexistence.[73] Since nature cannot destroy souls, only God potentially can. However, following Leibniz, Mendelssohn contends that this world is the best of all possible ones or else God would not have chosen to create it. Since God is good, then, he would not want to destroy souls, not even by a miracle.[74]

Socrates must now prove that the soul does not somehow change into something else, that it is not like the body that changes into dust after death:

> **Socrates:** The body dies; that is to say, all its motions appear no longer to tend to the life and preservation of the whole. . . . The parts which till now had one common aim [*gemeinschaft Endzweck*], and made the body a single machine [*einzige Maschine*], take now quite different aims, and become parts of entirely different machines. And the soul, Cebes, what shall we do with her? . . . Will her sensations, thoughts, imagination, desires, aversions, inclinations, and passions disappear, and not leave the least trace behind [*und nicht die geringste Spur hinterlassen haben*]?
> **Cebes:** Impossible! What would this be but total annihilation [*völlige Zernichtung*]? And no annihilation, as we have already seen, is in the power of nature [*dem Vermögen der Natur*].
> **Socrates:** What shall we conclude then, my friends? The soul cannot be totally lost; for the last step, if we place it as far off as possible, would be a leap from existence to nothing [*vom Daseyn zum Nichts*]: a transition that is inconsistent with the nature of a single being or the general system of beings. The soul must therefore exist and endure forever.[75]

In the second dialogue, Simmias and Cebes object to Socrates' argument. Simmias's objection revolves around our experience, which tells us that thinking seems to be dependent upon the body.[76] Cebes, on the other hand, argues that although Socrates may have proved that the soul survives the death of the body, he has not shown that such a soul will retain its individuality. If it does not maintain such individuality, Cebes further argues, then how or why should we desire such a state?

Socrates spends the rest of the second dialogue taking up Simmias's charge, and responds directly to Cebes in the final dialogue. In response to Simmias, Socrates argues that the act of thinking, the primary activity of the immortal soul, is what is responsible for combining, comparing, and contrasting various phenomena (e.g., musical tones).

> **Socrates:** the Origin [*Ursprung*] of all compositions, numbers, greatness, harmony, symmetry, etc. in so far as they require combination and comparison, must only be looked for in the thinking power [*in dem denkenden Vermögen*]. As this must be taken for granted, the faculty of thinking, the cause of all comparisons and contrasts, cannot possibly arise from its own operations,

> cannot possibly consist in proportion, harmony, symmetry, nor in a whole, which is composed of parts that exist independent of each other; since all these things presuppose the operation and action of a thinking being, and could not become real without it.[77]

Unthinking parts, according to Socrates, cannot give rise to a thinking whole. The soul, in other words, cannot be a composite, for example, of material elements, since the thinking soul is necessary to explain that a composite must be different from its parts.

In the third dialogue, Socrates takes up Cebes' charge. Here, with his Leibnizian and Wolffian colors again showing, Mendelssohn's Socrates describes a harmonious universe ordered and governed by a benevolent Creator:

> **Socrates:** Is it consistent with the supreme wisdom to produce a world in order to make the happiness of the creatures that inhabit it arise from the contemplation of its beauties and then, a moment later, deprive them of that enjoyment forever? Can the divine author have made such a phantom of bliss the whole aim of their being? No, my friends, nature has not given us the desire of eternal happiness in vain. Our wishes can and will be satisfied. The design of creation [*das Ziel der Schöpfung*] will subsist as long as the things are created; and the admirers of the divine perfections will subsist as long as the work where those perfections are visible.[78]

Socrates' arguments here turn on the consistency of God's goodness and the ability of the universe to run harmoniously. He establishes that it is not in keeping with the goodness, justice, and wisdom of the Creator to give humans reason and then simply grab it back from them when the body dies. Based on this knowledge, Socrates informs his friends, he can peacefully go to his execution.

None of Mendelssohn's arguments in *Phaedon* are particularly novel; in fact, the great majority of them derive from other Enlightenment thinkers such as Leibniz and Wolff. Yet, unlike such thinkers, Mendelssohn succeeds in putting such arguments in a very pleasing literary prose that borders on the poetic. It is this latter feature, in particular, that established Mendelssohn's reputation both as one of the most important philosophers of his day, and that also carved out a niche for him in German belles lettres. Despite this, no other work took Mendelssohn so long to bring to completion.[79] Nearly seven years separated Mendelssohn's first mention of the project and the time of its initial publication in 1767. The long prehistory of the work might very well have been related to Mendelssohn's desire to find not only an appropriate genre but also the right character to express his views on natural religion. His off-again, on-again desire to translate the philosophical texts of Shaftesbury and Plato seems to have convinced him of the intrinsic merits to be derived from using a literary genre in a vernacular composition. In fact, in one letter, Mendelssohn calls his *Phaedon* "something intermediate between a translation and a work of my own."[80]

Regardless of how it came to be composed, the sheer success of the work belied authorial expectations. The overwhelming reasons for its success, to reiterate, resided in the form of the work, perhaps to an even greater extent than its actual content. Since the immortality of the soul was one of the main principles, if not the central one, of natural religion, many other authors, including Wolff himself, composed treatises devoted to elucidating this topic.[81] Yet none of these authors' works met with nearly the same degree of popular success as Mendelssohn did with his *Phaedon*. Mendelssohn alone seems to have found the ability to wed a sophisticated philosophical treatise to a very pleasing literary and artistic style.[82]

Mendelssohn succeeded in "translating" Plato's work of the same name, but also in couching his own original arguments for the soul's immortality in ways that appeared natural to the reader.[83] The reader of *Phaedon*, in turn, encountered a work brimming with the optimism of the age: the world was a just and moral place created by its benevolent and just Maker, a universe in which souls only reached their full perfection after the death of the body. And although Mendelssohn's Socrates lived in Athens and contemplatively awaited his execution there, the language and the categories that he bespeaks are those of eighteenth-century Germany.

Phaedon as Precursor to *Jerusalem*: A Brief Comparison

As I have argued throughout this chapter, Mendelssohn composed his *Phaedon* at a very optimistic point in his life. As a Jew he was, according to the noblest teachings of the Enlightenment, accepted as a philosopher and as a belletrist. The Lavater controversy, not to mention the others that followed in its wake, however, put an abrupt end to this youthful optimism and sense of belonging. And although he could take pride in his friendships with individuals such as Lessing, Nicolai, and Abbt, these individuals were by no means characteristic of the larger population.

Despite the fact that *Phaedon* was the product of Mendelssohn's early career and that it met with tremendous critical and popular success, we nevertheless encounter in it a number of themes that will later emerge in his more overtly polemical writings. Although he nowhere mentions Judaism or even revelation in *Phaedon*, he still articulates a position that, in true Enlightenment fashion, puts pride of place on the tenets of natural religion: God's existence, divine providence, and the souls' immortality. The goal of *Phaedon*, in other words, was to demonstrate to the Sophists of his day (i.e., skeptics) that the soul was, without any shadow of a doubt, an immortal substance different from the body.

In his later work, most notably *Jerusalem,* Mendelssohn argues that Judaism alone most closely coincided with the Enlightenment ideal of natural religion because Judaism, although possessing revelation, did not infringe upon the beliefs of its practitioners. The tenets of natural religion, articulated so well in *Phaedon,* now become those of Judaism. Near the beginning of the second section of *Jerusalem,* Mendelssohn writes his famous statement:

> I recognize no eternal truths other than those that are not merely comprehensible to human reason but can also be verified by human powers. . . . I believe that Judaism knows of no revealed religion in the sense in which Christians understand this term. The Israelites possess a divine *legislation*—laws, commandments, ordinances, rules of life, instruction in the will of God as to how they should conduct themselves in order to attain temporal and eternal felicity . . . but not doctrinal opinions, no saving truths, no universal propositions of reason. These the Eternal reveals to us and to all other men, at all times, through nature and thing, but never through word and script.[84]

Here Mendelssohn contends that "true" or "ancient" Judaism—a Judaism from which all later historical accretions have been removed—provides its practitioners with a set of laws to conduct themselves, but not beliefs that tell them how to think.[85] Judaism was thus different from other religions, especially Christianity, because it relied neither on abstract doctrines nor on creedal statements, but upon human will and action:

> Among all the prescriptions and ordinances of the Mosaic law, there is not a single one which says: *You shall believe or not believe.* They all say: *You shall do or not do.* Faith is not commanded, for it accepts no other commands than those that come to it by way of conviction. All the commandments of the divine law are addressed to man's will, to his power to act. . . . Hence, ancient Judaism has no symbolic books, no *articles of faith.* No one has to swear to symbols or subscribe, by oath, to certain articles of faith. Indeed, we have no conception at all of what are called *religious oaths.*[86]

Judaism, according to Mendelssohn, provides an outlet for proper action without curtailing the rational capacities of its practitioners by forcing them to believe anything, least of all propositions based on faith or ones that contradict reason. Judaism, then, contains no truths except those that are accessible to reason and, thus, accessible to all peoples at all times.[87] Judaism, to use his oft-quoted statement, is not a revealed religion but a revealed legislation. So although Mendelssohn agrees with Spinoza that God did not reveal eternal truths at Sinai, he nevertheless sees the religious aspects of this law, and not simply political dimensions, as did Spinoza.[88]

Because eternal truths cannot be revealed, Mendelssohn's polemical thrust in *Jerusalem* is not just to challenge, but actually to subvert, the claims of any religion that is based on revealed doctrine or irrational dogma (viz., Christianity). According to Altmann, Mendelssohn's

> severe rationalism was a refuge from the challenge thrown at him. It amounted to a rebuttal of Christian dogma as irreconcilable with natural religion and, at the same time, to an affirmation of Judaism as totally in accord with the eternal truths of reason.[89]

Read from the vantage point of *Jerusalem*, one can detect the faint echoes of Mendelssohn's critique of Christianity as early as *Phaedon*. In many ways this latter work, which upholds the rational faculty's ability to grasp eternal truths, is part and parcel of Mendelssohn's larger project to establish Judaism's superiority over Christianity. Although this is certainly not the overarching goal of *Phaedon*, it is no coincidence that Mendelssohn uses the character of Socrates. Much like Halevi's or Polleqar's king, Socrates is the perfect spokesperson or arbiter. As neither Christian nor Jew, Socrates can best articulate the principles of the soul's immortality in such a manner that cannot offend Christian ears. Near the end of *Phaedon*, for example, as Socrates approaches his final minutes on earth, he says:

> Whoever adheres to the performance of his duties [*seine Pflicht erfüllet*] with fortitude and constancy of temper, and bears adversity with patient resignation to the divine will [*göttlichen Willen*], will deserve and enjoy at last the recompense of his virtues.[90]

Mendelssohn here, as he will later in *Jerusalem*, puts pride of place not on belief, but on performance—actions—that allows one's will "the power to act." One encounters neither dogma nor belief in *Phaedon;* Socrates' comments are based on the principles of reason, the same principles upon which Mendelssohn will develop his understanding of Judaism. Although Socrates' religion is never stated beyond the fact that he is strongly committed to the principles of reason, Socrates, on one level, is the ideal Jew. Only as an "authentic" Jew, as an individual guided solely by reason and not dogma, can Socrates articulate his arguments for the immorality of the human soul. Indeed, as Mendelssohn himself admits in the preface to the work, "Socrates speaks almost like an eighteenth-century philosopher. I preferred to use an anachronism rather than omit any convincing arguments."[91]

Again near the very end of the dialogue, Socrates informs his friends, from whom he is about to depart:

> **Socrates:** With respect to myself, I am content with feeling a conviction that the eye of heaven is perpetually upon me; that its divine providence and justice will watch over me in the next, as it has protected me in this life; and that my real happiness consists in the beauties and perfections of my soul. These

> perfections are temperance, justice, charity, benevolence, knowledge of the supreme being, unceasing efforts to accomplish his views and resignation to his divine will.[92]

Here again we encounter Socrates uttering the central tenets of natural religion, tenets that we know, especially from Mendelssohn's later work, are embedded most perfectly in Judaism. Even though Mendelssohn nowhere mentions "Judaism" in his *Phaedon,* he nevertheless sets the stage in this dialogue for arguments that will emerge in subsequent works. Only later, however, will Mendelssohn make the connections explicit between Judaism and natural religion. What exists subtly in the narrative of *Phaedon* will become explicit in later works like *Jerusalem.* If Mendelssohn had never been called upon to defend his Jewishness, then perhaps the ideas that we encounter only nascently in *Phaedon* might very well have remained so. But, brought on by his antagonists' refusal to accept that an individual could be committed to Judaism and reason, he would come to emphasize those features of "true" Judaism, now the natural religion par excellence, one that not only made it Christianity's equal, but—in its aversion to dogma and irrationality—its superior.

German vis-à-vis Jew: *Phaedon* and *Sefer ha-Nefesh*

In a letter to Raphael Levi, composed near the end of 1767, Mendelssohn makes a rather curious statement:

> I wish I were able to write a treatise on the immortality of the soul in the Hebrew language. The *Phaedon* does not allow itself to be translated [into Hebrew]. At any rate, I am convinced that it would no longer be intelligible in a Hebrew version. For this reason I would like to choose another literary form in which to make our coreligionists understand these matters. We shall see. As yet, my Hebrew is not good enough.[93]

This statement is curious for a number of reasons. Presumably Mendelssohn means by his first statement—that *Phaedon* is not amenable to a Hebrew translation—something to the effect that a Socratic dialogue would be of little interest to a Hebrew-reading audience. Although this may certainly be true, more surprising is his implication that the dialogue is somehow un-Jewish, and that Jews, to appreciate his arguments, would need to encounter them in "another literary form." Mendelssohn, in other words, seems to regard the dialogue as an inauthentic vehicle for Jewish speculation, even despite the fact that someone like his teacher, Zamosc, would well have argued that a dialogue, such as Halevi's *Kuzari,* was a very Jewish work. Moreover, as I have tried to argue throughout this study, the dialogue is in fact the opposite of what Mendelssohn here claims: it was a form that had provided numerous Jewish thinkers with a literary venue in which to articulate a Jewish response to larger ideas that circulated in the intellectual circles of the majority cultures in which Jews found themselves. Even if Mendelssohn had thought that Socrates, as an ancient Athenian, might not resonate with a Hebrew reading public, surely he could have composed another dialogue using other characters that would.

Equally surprising is his final statement, that his "Hebrew is not good enough," especially given the fact that Mendelssohn was one of the preeminent Hebrew stylists of the eighteenth century. His *Koheleth Musar* (Preacher of Morals), written in the latter half of the 1750s, for example, was a Hebrew weekly journal that, according to Sorkin, was modeled on English language weeklies, such as *The Tatler* and *The Spectator*.[94] Here, Mendelssohn's Hebrew showed itself articulate and dynamic enough to be used to compose letters, essays, *and dialogues* using the guise of a fictional narrator! This journal represented the first modern journal in Hebrew, and if its author was not up to the task of writing a Hebrew treatise on the soul, then surely no one was.

In another letter, this time in a letter to Hartwig Wessely, written late in the summer of 1768, Mendelssohn claims:

> Originally it occurred to me to write in Hebrew, and it was not my intention to attribute the statements to Socrates—for what have we, the followers of the true religion, to do with the son of Sophronicus [i.e., Socrates]? I wanted to depart completely from the way of Plato and write my own book on the nature and immortality of the soul. My idea was to base my teaching on the utterances of our rabbis of blessed memory as found in the haggadic portions of the Talmud and in the Midrashim, for most of them agree to a very large extent with what I have expounded philosophically [*be-derekh ha-emet*] and in no way contradict the [philosophical] truth. Yet many obstacles prevented me from carrying out my intention.[95]

According to this letter, Mendelssohn had first wanted to write his work demonstrating the soul's immortality in Hebrew, not German. Why did he change his mind? Mendelssohn gives no hint about this matter. Perhaps he thought that there was such a small Hebrew-reading audience, especially one that was familiar with philosophy, that his work would have made little or no impact. If this was his assumption, he was probably correct since his *Koheleth Musar* had a very short life; only two issues appeared.[96] Another reason is suggested by Noah Rosenbloom, who argues that Mendelssohn's conceptualization of the soul's immortality without any mention of corporeal resurrection would be regarded as heretical.[97] He cites as evidence the fact that Mendelssohn, despite his comments in the above letter, did not find it necessary to quote or utilize references to the Talmud or Midrashim in his *Biur* (commentary).[98]

These two letters provide vignettes through which we can glimpse at Mendelssohn's hesitation to compose a Hebrew-language treatise on the fate and career of the human soul. This does not mean, however, that he did not write one. Several of Mendelssohn's colleagues (e.g., Hartwig Wessely, David Wagenaar) had offered to do what Mendelssohn said he could not: to translate *Phaedon* into Hebrew.[99] Mendelssohn, however, refused such offers (although the work was translated by Isaiah Beer Bing and published posthumously in 1787, with an introduction by Wessely).[100]

Despite Mendelssohn's unwillingness to see *Phaedon* appear in Hebrew, he did compose a private letter, in Hebrew, to Hartog Leo, in either 1770 or 1772, on the nature and immortality of the human soul. As secretary of the Berlin Jewish community, Leo was someone versed in both traditional and philosophical topics. Although Mendelssohn wrote the letter as a private correspondence, it was subsequently collated with another treatise that was edited and published by his self-styled successor David Friedländer in 1787, the year after Mendelssohn's death, who gave it the name *Sefer ha-nefesh* (The Book of the Soul).[101] In this work, Mendelssohn does what he said he would do in his letters to both Levi and Wessely: he composes a version of the *Phaedon* shorn of its dialogue form, replete with Jewish references, with no mention whatsoever of "the son of Sophronicus."

Since it was not meant for public consumption, it is difficult to know what to make of *Sefer ha-nefesh*. Does the work simply represent Mendelssohn's private musing on the topic of the soul? Alternatively, it reads as a very carefully thought-out treatise. In the introduction to the work, it is apparent that his goal is certainly no different than it was in *Phaedon:*

> This study of the soul's departure, according to what is the foundation [*yesod*] of the Torah and belief [*emunah*], is divided into three parts. It is necessary to speak about all of them in order to establish the truth of this matter. Part one consists of [establishing] that the soul is not the body, that it is a simple substance: [this part] is called the "spirituality of the soul." The second part [establishes] that the soul is not harmed by the death of the body, because it is immortal: [this section] is called the "eternality of the soul." The final part [establishes] that the soul lives on after the death of the body, and that it continues to know and remember everything when it was conjoined with the body: it is called the "true life of the soul."[102]

The subject matter of these three parts, then, is that of *Phaedon*. What is different, of course, is Mendelssohn's desire to show how these are not just Socratic or philosophical arguments, but the "foundation" of the Torah and proper Jewish belief. Although his arguments may not be significantly different from that which we encounter in *Phaedon,* the mode of presentation most certainly is. For example, he uses biblical prooftexts when talking about possible relationships between the soul and the body:

> If we believe that the soul partakes of true life, does this mean that it is a substance endowed with reason and will, and possessed of all its acquired perfections? How, then, can we say that at death it will separate from the body? It cannot be separated from all the acquisitions and the perfections that it acquired in this world when it used the [corporeal] senses and limbs. Or, is it possible that [the soul] descends from its greatness and its lofty height where it was a substance already endowed with thoughts and desiring the good? In which case the soul would descend to the level of an infant "before knowing to refuse the evil and choose the good" [Is. 7.15]. It would then be like the soul of an animal that only desires, like the "untimely births of a woman that have not seen the sun" [Psalm 58.9].[103]

Mendelssohn, as passages such as this attest, does not hesitate to make appeals to revelation to buttress his claims, something that he did not do at all in *Phaedon.* In *Sefer ha-nefesh,* he cites biblical prooftexts, in addition to Maimonides' *Guide of the Perplexed:*

> Because all of the deeds of God, blessed is His name, are essentially good, even though they may sometimes appear as evil to us. . . . It is certainly true that what may seem evil as a part of creation can be good as far as the whole is concerned. If we knew all of this in the way that God does, we would thank and praise Him, for they only appear evil. I will explain this in greater detail in another place, just as the Rav did in his book *The Guide of the Perplexed.*[104]

In addition to such quotations, citations, and prooftexts, there is also a greater "Jewish feel" to *Sefer ha-nefesh.* In the following example, for instance, Mendelssohn coins a *mashal* (parable) in traditional rabbinic fashion in order to understand better that God creates by way of the miraculous, and that that which is truly simple cannot be created in time:

> By way of a *mashal* [*derekh mashal*]: At the time of creation, God commanded that all beings should arise in "their beauty and full stature" [BT Rosh ha-Shana 11a] out of nothing [*min ha-efes*]. [Explanation:] when something's parts are destroyed, then so too is the composite; just as the composite is created and ordered through the coming together of its parts. The composite is created in time, and in so far as it is composed of parts, it is destroyed in time.[105]

Although he calls this a *mashal,* and introduces it in the same manner that *meshalim* are introduced in rabbinic literature, there is really nothing traditional about this. Yet, the fact that Mendelssohn sets this argument up in the same manner—by using the technical phrase "by way of a *mashal*"—is significant in that it signals to the reader that what follows will be familiar, even if its contents may not be.

A comparison of *Sefer ha-nefesh* and *Phaedon,* then, reveals a similarity of content, if not of actual genre. Mendelssohn designed both treatises to demonstrate to his audience—one German, the other Jewish—that the soul is immortal, separate from the body, and will enjoy a blissful afterlife, especially if properly taken care of.

Moreover, since the two independent treatises that comprise *Sefer ha-nefesh* were composed roughly at the same time as the Lavater affair, we can regard them, on one level, as responses to this. For instance, if I am correct in arguing that in *Phaedon* we witness several ideas that we will later encounter in more polemical works such as *Jerusalem,* then we can also see in *Sefer ha-nefesh* Mendelssohn's desire to show explicit connections between the themes of *Phaedon* and the Jewish tradition. With Lavater challenging Mendelssohn's decision to remain a Jew, the composition of *Sefer ha-nefesh,* in Hebrew and stripped of non-Jewish protagonists, provides additional evidence that we can read *Phaedon* as a Jewish work. What *Sefer ha-nefesh* does, however, is make the Jewishness of *Phaedon* explicit, showing how the latter's themes are the "foundation" of the Torah and Jewish belief.

Since I began this section with excerpts from two letters, it is perhaps appropriate to end it with another excerpt. In the same letter to Hartwig Wessely, Mendelssohn seems to apologize for ever having written *Phaedon:*

> In the next few days a copy of a small treatise on the immortality of the soul, which I wrote in German, will reach you. Truly speaking, I was afraid to present it to you until now because I thought you might hold me in derision for having propounded and demonstrated a truth that is not doubted by anyone "called by the name of Israel," since it is an integral part of the principles of our holy faith.[106]

With this quotation, we again witness the fragility of Mendelssohn's intellectual program. On the one hand, as an Enlightenment thinker he attempted to demonstrate beyond any measure of a doubt the soul's immortality; yet, as a Jew, according to this passage, he should have accepted the soul's immortality simply on the authority of tradition. The sense of unease that emerges from this letter is indicative of Mendelssohn's unique, though often ambiguous, position between Jewish and non-Jewish cultures.

Conclusions

Mendelssohn's ability to conjoin Judaism and natural religion was a fragile endeavor, with the points at which he sought to bind them held together tenuously by gossamer threads.[107] Perhaps nowhere is this more on display than in his need to compose one work on the fate of the soul in German, using the form of a dialogue, and meant primarily for a non-Jewish reading audience, and a completely different one in Hebrew, shorn of dialogic exchange, and meant solely for Jews. Although both works may well have shared a similar structure and basic line of argumentation, that Mendelssohn believed that he could not adequately express himself using the dialogue in Hebrew or for a Jewish audience is significant. For him, as for most in the eighteenth-century philosophical tradition, the dialogue was a genre that was intimately connected to the name of Socrates. Had Mendelssohn looked to the various forms utilized by earlier Jewish philosophers, he might well have found "Jewish" precursors or models of philosophical dialogues. Yet because he did not, the way he conceived of the dialogue was destined to be non-Jewish, further contributing to the fragility inherent in his larger intellectual project.

Although he may well have been one of the great representatives of the Leibnizian-Wolffian school, Kant, whom Mendelssohn dubbed "the all-crushing," was in Mendelssohn's own lifetime already dismantling speculative metaphysics and the arguments concerning the soul's immortality. By the end of Mendelssohn's life, the religion of reason and other Enlightenment principles in which Mendelssohn had so much invested, both personally and intellectually, were gradually being questioned and undermined by the new Romantic movement. This movement was highly critical of reason, and in its place emphasized the roles of emotions and feelings. Mendelssohn's fragile synthesis, in other words, was rapidly becoming out of date. This was true to the extent that after Mendelssohn, the only way for Jews to be accepted in German society was not so much through their intellectual ability, but through their willingness to convert to the dominant religion.

Mendelssohn's place in Jewish intellectual history was truly unique. Very few, if any, Jewish philosophers had the ear of a non-Jewish reading public in the manner that he did. Yet, as I argued, even when Mendelssohn did write an ostensibly non-Jewish work such as *Phaedon,* it is possible to see in it the specter of his later concerns and various ideas that could readily be emphasized to equate Judaism with the tenets of natural religion. Moreover, because Mendelssohn occupied such an important place in philosophical and artistic circles, even his decidedly apologetic works such as *Jerusalem* were meant primarily for non-Jews, to demonstrate to them the superiority of Judaism over other faiths.

EPILOGUE: FROM DIALOGUE TO DIALOGIC

This epilogue charts, in broad strokes, the fate of the genre of dialogue in modern Jewish philosophy.[1] Although in the years following Mendelssohn the genre would prove popular among various Galician and Russian *maskilim* in their quest to disseminate the teachings of the *Haskalah*,[2] the use of the literary dialogue to express philosophical ideas largely fell out of favor in the German-Jewish philosophical tradition. Yet as the genre itself was gradually losing appeal, the concept of dialogue *as a philosophical principle* became of paramount concern. This new principle, which I refer to here as dialogic, replaced both the specific characteristics and the generic features of the textual dialogue. In these last few pages, then, I would like to provide a brief examination of this transformation, if for no other reason than to bring a sense of closure to the discussion in the previous six chapters.

If and when a premodern Jewish philosopher employed the genre of the dialogue, as this study has shown, he did so primarily to confront those whose readings or understandings of Judaism he disagreed with. The opponents in these dialogues, as we have seen, were often metonymic figures, textual devices in which an individual could conveniently represent a particular school of thought. Many, though by no means all, of these textual antagonists were—as in the case of Halevi's introduction to the *Kuzari*, Falaquera's *Iggeret ha-Vikuaḥ*, and Polleqar's *Ezer ha-dat*—caricatures as opposed to real-life, flesh-and-blood individuals.

In the modern period, by contrast, Jewish philosophers tended to conceptualize dialogue as a living, ongoing process. Dialogue now became the face-to-face encounter between idiosyncratic equals, with the goal being not so much to convince the other of his or her errors, but to arrive at a sense of completeness or authentic existence through an unfolding relationship with an other. Unlike their premodern literary incarnations, these living dialogic encounters could not be scripted; to be effective, they had to be spontaneous. Modern Jewish philosophers also expanded the borders of their premodern predecessors by envisaging dialogue as occurring on many different and overlapping levels: between humans and God, between humans and humans, and, especially in the case of Martin

Buber, even between humans and the natural world. True dialogue, not to be confused with its many imitators,[3] is the encounter between an individual, wrenched away from the generic casing of his or her species, and an other. The outcome of this dialogue is authenticity of both self and other, including the nature of the relationship that links the two together.

The modern conception of dialogue thus represents a major rupture from that of the premodern period. If the latter was often bound to the generic characteristics of the dialogue's form, the former refuses to be confined by such characteristics because to be authentic, it must be unpredictable. Whereas the outcome of the premodern dialogue was rarely surprising since it often coincided with the author's own construction of Judaism, for the former to be effective it has to be transformed out of the sphere of the written word to that of the spoken, living encounter. And it is precisely within this spoken encounter that the realm of the possible occurs for the partners in the dialogue.[4] There cannot be a victor now because it is the process that is of central concern.

Yet this certainly does not imply that modern Jewish thinkers are not interested in the relationship between form and content or that they do not acknowledge the importance of the literary in presenting a philosophical argument. Two individuals that figure highly in this epilogue, Martin Buber and Franz Rosenzweig, were true literary masters, and, as their thought makes clear, the nexus between philosophy and literature was instrumental to their thinking. Characteristic of both Buber and Rosenzweig is the notion that the paradigms that German Idealism had bequeathed to them, especially their modes and forms of presentation, prevented the individual from self-realization. Drawing impetus from the thought and style of the likes of Nietzsche and Schelling, these modern Jewish thinkers sought to articulate new philosophical *and* literary paradigms in order to move beyond traditional philosophical concerns.

Perhaps the best example of the transition from dialogue to dialogic is Martin Buber's *Daniel,* an early work published in 1913 and generally regarded as representative of his so-called pre-dialogic, or mystical stage.[5] This work played a large role in Buber's formative years, in which the young Buber, under the influence of Nietzsche,[6] began to explore various literary forms of presenting philosophy. It was also during this period that Buber was, at least according to his own account written later, on the verge of understanding the existential importance of dialogue (what I refer to here as *dialogic*). Yet, paradoxically, once Buber developed these initial thoughts on dialogic, he ceased to employ the genre.

The work—whose full title is *Daniel, Gespräche von der Verwirklichung* (Daniel: Dialogues on Realization)—consists of five successive dialogues, between Daniel and various named individuals, which revolve around a particular theme (direction, reality, meaning, polarity, and unity). Each dialogue takes place *in* a particular locale: in the mountain, above the city, in the garden, after the theater, by the sea. Although it is a highly literary work, with certain passages verging on the protagonists' mystical union with nature, from a literary perspective many of the dialogues actually involve long monologues by Daniel in response to questions put to him by his interlocutors. The fifth and last dialogue, between Daniel and Lukas, is essentially two lengthy monologues in which the protagonists do not so much speak to, but alongside each other. It is perhaps no coincidence that, on the level of ideas, we witness Daniel, in this last dialogue, speaking at great length about the actualization of "I." Unlike Buber's later work, this actualization does not require a Thou for its validation.[7]

Despite the overtly mystical emphasis in *Daniel,* we nevertheless encounter the importance of dialogue and dialogic in the work. In the introduction, for example, Buber writes that he realized the importance of these principles by touching a tree with a walking stick:

> At that time dialogue appeared to me. For the speech of man, wherever it is genuine speech, is like that stick; that means: truly directed address. Here where I am, where ganglia and organs of speech help me to form and to send forth the word, here I "mean" him to whom I send it, I intend him, this one unexchangeable man. But also there, where he is, something of me is delegated, something that is not at all substantial in nature like that being-here, rather pure vibration and incomprehensible; that remains there, with him, the man meant by me, and takes part in the receiving of my word. I encompass him to whom I turn.[8]

Here Buber intimates that the goal of dialogue is the establishment of the principle of unity, between the individual and him- or herself, between the individual and the world of nature, in the constant face of plurality. Yet even though he mentions the term *dialogue,* including the principles that such a dialogue must take, Buber's main concern in *Daniel* is, as the title makes clear, the notion of "realization" (*Verwirklichung*), and especially how it differs from its antithesis, "orientation." In the second dialogue, entitled "On Reality: Dialogue above the City," Daniel and his companion, Ulrich, expatiate on the meaning and contents of these two terms. As the title intimates, the city is associated with "orientation," something that is tantamount to inauthenticity. Juxtaposed against this is nature and the natural world, the locus of self-realization, experience, and individuality:

> **Daniel:** If I may say it to you as simply as I know it; he remains unreal who does not realize.

> **Ulrich:** You will probably have to say it to me more complexly if I am to understand it.
> **Daniel:** Indeed we already spoke once of the fact that there is a twofold relation of man to his experience: the orienting or classifying and the realizing or making real. What you experience, doing and suffering, creating and enjoying, you can register in the structure of experience for the sake of your aims or you can grasp it for its own sake in its own power and splendor.[9]

In this passage, Daniel informs Ulrich that the goal of life is self-realization, something that emerges only when one embraces experience while refusing to mediate such experiences through analytical or intellectual categories. The goal of life is a turning from orientation to realization through nature, art, and literature. Unlike his later thought, as articulated in works such as *I and Thou*, realization—despite the fact that it is expressed in the formal structures of the dialogue in *Daniel*—does not necessarily require dialogue with another.

Invoking Nietzschean terminology, Daniel describes orientation in the following manner:

> And everywhere where orienting knowledge ruled autonomously it was robbery, for it took place at the cost of the mothering, nourishing juices of life-experience [*Erlebnis*] and was only able to transpose the realization in the greater into a little need or a little security. And it was this predominance of the orienting from which I suffer and against which I rebel—for the sake of realizing which creates out of the life-experience of reality.[10]

In "orienting" oneself to the world, one creates a network of relationships based upon quotidian needs. Orientation, which he will subsequently rename as the "relation" (*Verhaltnis*) between I and It in his later work, involves a way of relating to people that is contingent upon utility as opposed to authenticity. This difference between realization and orientation is not just about the intentionality behind the encounter, but is a characteristic of the very language we employ. The language that characterizes city life, for example, is that of discursive prose, whereas that above the city is poetic:

> **Ulrich:** What do you think about the common usage of speech to which reality is simply the totality of the perceived and the perceivable which is experienced as existing?
> **Daniel:** It seems to me that we should pay attention to it because the life of men together is erected upon it. . . . And we shall accept it again as soon as we have returned into the enclosure of the city . . . but now has it not often struck you that in a poem, Hölderlin's perhaps, a word is employed in a heightened meaning that the common usage does not know.[11]

It is the language of poetry that shatters the mundane speech that seeks to orientate us. Only by transgressing such speech—that which filters, categorizes, and removes—can one fulfill one's potential for self-realization. It is the creative language of poetry, however, that enables one to cultivate a spontaneous and creative relationship with the world.

Although it is clear that *Daniel* played a large role in the development of the importance of dialogic as a philosophical principle, the style of the work also permitted Buber to chart an independent philosophical path. Despite this, however, the later Buber had an ambiguous relationship to this work. He refused to publish a second German edition because he did not think that the text adequately reflected his mature thought.[12] Buber also refused to assent to an English translation of the book until 1964, a full fifty years after its original German publication. He only consented so long as the translator, Maurice Freedman, would

> write an introduction explaining, even at some length, that this is an early book in which there is already expressed the great duality of human life, but only in its cognitive and not yet in its communicative and existential character. This book is obviously a book of transition to a new kind of thinking and must be characterized as such.[13]

Hence, despite the importance of dialogic to his later thought, Buber seems to have been uncomfortable with the mystical origins of the concept. It is a great irony that as Buber began to develop the concept of dialogic, he gradually came to the realization that the genre of the dialogue was not particularly suited to the principle. For example, in a much later work entitled *Zwiesprache* (Dialogue), written in 1929, Buber devotes significant space to the concept of dialogic, but does not employ the genre. For him, dialogue is no longer a textual expression between literary characters, but is something that can only be framed when two like-minded individuals encounter each other spontaneously:

> A time of genuine religious conversations is beginning—not those so-called but fictitious conversations where no one regarded and addressed his partner in reality, but genuine dialogues, speech from certainty to certainty, but also from one open-hearted person to another open-hearted person. Only then will genuine common life appear, not that of an identical content of faith which is alleged to be found in all religions, but that of the situation, of anguish and of expectation.[14]

In a much later work, "Dialogue between Heaven and Earth," published in 1952, Buber again has no interest in dialogue as a literary genre and once again focuses his attention on the principle of dialogic.[15] In particular, he asks how dialogue can be possible after the Shoah:

> In this our own time, one asks again and again: how is a Jewish life still possible after Auschwitz? I would like to frame this question more correctly: how is a life with God still possible in a time in which there is an Auschwitz?

> The estrangement has become too cruel, the hiddenness too deep. One can still "believe" in the God who allows those things to happen, but can one still speak to Him? Can one still hear His word? Can one still, as an individual and as a people, enter at all into a dialogic relationship with Him? Dare we recommend to the survivors of Auschwitz, the Job of the gas chambers: "Give thanks unto our Lord, for He is good; for His mercy endureth forever"?[16]

At around the same time that the young Buber was publishing his dialogue *Daniel,* Buber's former teacher, Hermann Cohen (1842–1918), was also working out a philosophy of alterity. Unlike his student, however, Cohen was not interested at all in either the formal characteristics or generic features of the genre of dialogue.[17] In many ways, the young Buber and the senior Cohen could not have been more different: Whereas the young Buber was interested in both myth and mysticism, the elder Cohen was an arch-rationalist, stressing that at Judaism's core resided a religion of reason; whereas Buber was highly critical of reading Judaism through the lenses of Kant, Cohen was the founder of the neo-Kantian school at Marburg, and argued that Judaism was essentially the ethical monotheism par excellence; and unlike Cohen who was critical of Jewish nationalism, for Buber it was Zionism that led him back to Judaism, after his alienation from the tradition in his youth.[18]

Because of the overwhelming popularity of Buber's later dialogic philosophy, especially the way it revolves around the I-Thou relationship, there is a tendency to overlook how other contemporaneous Jewish philosophers employed this relationship. In his *Religion of Reason Out of the Sources of Judaism (Religion der Vernunft aus den Quellen des Judentums),* published posthumously in 1919, Cohen argues that central to individual realization is the social and ethical relationship that opens up between individuals. Only when the individual realizes that he or she is a being in relationship with God and with others, does that individual truly fulfill his or her duties as a moral agent.[19] This leads to a situation in which the individual must act to perfect the world through the particular dialogic relationships that he or she forms with others:

> The love for man has therefore to be the beginning, because although God created man, man must create the fellowman for himself. And religion must assist in this creation. Thus God must become the creator a second time when, through the share of reason in religion, he teaches man himself to create man as fellowman.[20]

Here Cohen states that the individual must become a partner in creation. Just as God created humans and the world order, so must the individual create or re-create human order through the various relationships that he or she forms with others on a daily basis. The dialogic relationship that forms between individuals is, according to Cohen, ultimately more important than the ethical relationship, something that deals solely with universals, in which humans become nothing more than "a number among other numbers."[21] It is only by experiencing the pathos of the other person that he or she moves out of the realm of a number to become a Thou.[22] As the title of his work suggests, Cohen is quick to ground this idea in the "Sources of Judaism":

> The prophets are not theoretical moralists. Therefore, for them there cannot be even a temporary difference between theory and practice. Their problem is religion, monotheism, the correlation between man and God. And this correlation is intertwined with the correlation between man and man. The first, between God and man, may seem to be merely theoretical; the other, however, between man and man is immediately practical. And the fellowman belongs to this second correlation. Therefore the prophet cannot allow any doubt to divert him from the problem: How the fellowman is to originate out of pity for the poor man.[23]

It is in the feeling of pity and the movement from a generic humanity to a Thou, Cohen will argue, that the idea of seeing oneself as an "I" emerges.[24] It is in the subsequent I-Thou relationships that one forms that is responsible for moving one from sinfulness to goodness, something that ultimately develops in one the humility to approach God.[25]

Cohen's idea on the nature of language, I and Thou, and the concept of the dialogic relationship that unfolds between them, is taken in a different direction by another of his students, Franz Rosenzweig.[26] In an attempt to move beyond the arch-rational system of German philosophy, Rosenzweig refuses to locate the relationship between God and human solely on the level of intellect. As a consequence, he stresses a number of phenomena that traditional philosophy had marginalized: death, experience, poetry, metaphor, vision, and imagination. To signal both his displeasure and departure from what went before, he labels his thought as *das neue Denken,* or "the New Thinking."

In his essay by the same name, Rosenzweig defines the importance of *Sprachdenken,* or "speech-thinking," in which, following the lead of Cohen, humans are transformed by opening themselves up to the call of others, both God and other humans.[27] Language, accordingly, should not just be private between for example, individuals, or translator and text, but should expand into the world through such concepts as prayer and liturgy.[28]

Yet despite the centrality of both language and dialogic to his thought, Rosenzweig suggests that the ultimate form of communication is one that is characterized not by language, but by the erasure of language, by silence, a return to Naught.[29] Redemption—the third part of his second triad, and the point which the other parts, creation and revelation, anticipate—is engulfed in silence. Dialogue and dialogic must accordingly give way to silence. Yet, it is a silence that, paradoxically, we can only glimpse from the vantage point of anticipation, and, because this anticipation can only take place in the confines of the temporal, it requires speech for articulation. It is, thus, a language that, paradoxically, both speaks and unspeaks, says and unsays, at the same time:

> Thus the We must say Ye, and the more its own volume increases, the louder the Ye resounds out of its mouth as well. The We must say it, though it can only say it by way of anticipation and must await the ultimate confirmation out of another, an ultimate mouth.[30]

This ultimate mouth is what utters an ultimate word that, paradoxically, ceases to be a word. This "word" no longer anticipates because it does not need another to complete it. This anticipation of language for speaking, of a silence that articulates, is at the heart of Rosenzweig's thought. Moreover, it is the anticipation of both unspeaking and silence that he locates the genius of Judaism. For Rosenzweig, this anticipation is constitutive of Judaism's ability to exist at the extreme point of history, occupying the Archimedean point between the historical and the eternal, between the linguistic and nonlinguistic. As a consequence Judaism alone anticipates the silence that characterizes the arrival of Redemption, which he also calls Eternity.[31] So, despite the fact that Eternity exists beyond time, Jews uniquely experience it in time, in, for example, the weekly liturgical structure of the week, that culminates and begins in the Sabbath:

> Six days he has worked and attended to all his affairs; now, on the seventh, he rests. Six days he has uttered the many useful and useless words the workday demanded of him, but on the seventh he obeys the command of the prophet: he lets his tongue rest from the talk of everyday, and learns to be silent, to listen. And this sanctifying of the day of rest by listening to God's voice in silence must be shared by all members of his house. . . . The Sabbath is the feast of creation, but of a creation wrought for the sake of redemption.[32]

Just as the sanctity of the Sabbath must define the profanity of the rest of the week (and vice versa), so, too, must the silence of eternity be understood, mirrored by the nonsilence of creation and revelation.

It is the dialogic relationship—between humans, between creation, revelation, and redemption, between, God, humans, and the world—that, for Rosenzweig, sustains us and makes thinking possible in the first place. Perhaps nowhere is Rosenzweig's dismissal of early philosophical forms and content more obvious than in his criticism of Plato's dialogues:

> Speech is bound to time, nourished by time. . . . it does not know beforehand where it will emerge; it lets itself be given its cues from others; it actually lives by another's life, whether that other is one who listens to a story, or is the re-

> spondent in a dialogue, or the participant in a chorus; thinking, by contrast, is always solitary, even if it should happen in common, among several "symphilosophers": even then, the other is only raising objections I should actually have made myself—which accounts for the tediousness of most philosophical dialogues, even the overwhelming majority of Plato's. In actual conversation something really happens. I do not know beforehand what the other will say to me, because I do not even know beforehand what I will say.[33]

Although this epilogue has not done justice to the complexity of the thought of Buber, Cohen, and Rosenzweig, that was not its point. On the contrary, my goal here has been to show a transformation—not necessarily an evolution or a development—from dialogue to dialogic. It is a transformation because modern Jewish philosophy has a different set of concerns than premodern Jewish philosophy. Whereas medieval Jewish philosophy was an enterprise based upon showing the compatibility between Torah and philosophy, modern Jewish philosophy is less interested in compatibility than in using Jewish sources to undermine, to show the problems with certain features of non-Jewish thought, and to take this thought in new directions.[34] Modern Jewish philosophy, less interested in metaphysics, tends to focus more on the alterity that emerges from interhuman encounters, the so-called "dialogic."[35] Whereas medieval thinkers equated love of God with the knowledge of God, modern thinkers are more concerned with how one encounters God through the mundane encounters between self and others.

Medieval Jewish philosophers, by contrast, were much less interested in dialogic encounters. They primarily used the generic aspects of the dialogues either to popularize and disseminate philosophical truths or to create narrative encounters between themselves and various critics of philosophy. Many of the dialogues that I examined in the first six chapters of this study, with the exception of Halevi's *Kuzari,* were concerned primarily with articulating a rational vision of Judaism, one in which a protagonist could confront a number of antagonists who were highly critical of such a vision. In the case of Falaquera and Polleqar, these antagonists were Jewish and textual, whereas in the work of Abravanel and Mendelssohn they were often non-Jewish (e.g., Pico in the case of Abravanel; Leibniz in the case of Mendelssohn) and, thus, only implied. Certainly each author employed a number of literary features and devices, and they did so to such an extent that, as I mentioned in the first chapter, it becomes impossible to speak about a, much less *the,* Jewish philosophical dialogue.

The various philosophical dialogues that were composed by Jews over the centuries were written in different languages, different cultural and intellectual contexts, and for different audiences. Only by analyzing and understanding each dialogue in its specific temporal, intellectual, and geographic milieu does it become possible to understand it fully. This study, however, also tried to take this to the next level: after having contextualized these dialogues, I briefly pulled them out of their specific environments in order to see if and how they can contribute to a broader understanding of the role and function of genre in Jewish philosophy. The results are, I hope, illuminating. Through an examination of one genre I have tried to recover some of the dynamics inherent to Jewish philosophical production, thereby contributing to the elucidation of the complete history of Jewish philosophy.

NOTES

1. Expanding the Canon of Jewish Philosophy

Citations of sources are abbreviated, giving only the author's surname and the main title of the work. Full publication details of primary and secondary sources may be found in the bibliography.

1. See, for example, the comments in Jacobi, "Einleitung," 15–21.

2. Robinson, "Secondary Forms of Transmission."

3. Although I disagree with the central premise of his analysis—that Halevi recognized that the law of reason is the ultimate truth and that this is something to which the person of faith cannot agree—one of the earliest scholars sensitive to the literary aspects of the *Kuzari* was Leo Strauss. See his comments in "The Law of Reason in the *Kuzari*."

4. I certainly do not claim to be reinventing the wheel here. Excellent examples of secondary studies that examine so-called "less important" or "epigonic" thinkers and treatises include Ravitzky, "The Thought of Zeraḥiah ben Isaac ben She'altiel Ḥen and Maimonidean-Tibbonid Philosophy in the Thirteenth Century"; idem, *Crescas' Sermon on the Passover and Studies in His Philosophy;* Eisen, *Gersonides, Providence, Covenant, and the Chosen People;* idem, *The Book of Job in Medieval Jewish Philosophy;* Steven Harvey, ed., *The Medieval Hebrew Encyclopedias of Science and Philosophy;* Kellner, trans., *Gersonides' Commentary on the Song of Songs;* Robinson, "Philosophy and Exegesis in Ibn Tibbon's Commentary on Ecclesiastes"; Fraenkel, *From Maimonides to Samuel Ibn Tibbon.*

5. On the importance of epigonic figures in the history of Jewish cultures, see Berger and Zweip, eds., *Epigonism and the Dynamics of Jewish Culture.*

6. Requisite secondary literature on the problematics of this term may be found in Seeskin, *Jewish Philosophy in a Secular Age,* 1–14; the collection of essays in Samuelson, *Studies in Jewish Philosophy;* Frank, "What is Jewish Philosophy?"

7. Hughes, *The Texture of the Divine,* e.g., 3–5.

8. For Saadia's reading of the Book of Job, See Eisen, *The Book of Job in Medieval Jewish Philosophy,* 17–41.

9. Rubenstein, *Talmudic Stories,* 3.

10. See, for example, Hasan-Rokem, *The Web of Life,* 78–100; Rubenstein, *The Culture of the Babylonian Talmud,* 16–38.

11. E.g., *BT Sanhedrin* 91a–91b; *Avodah Zarah* 10a.

12. Tarrant, "Style and Thought in Plato's Dialogues," 28–30; D. Hyland, "Why Plato Wrote Dialogues," 38–42; Kahn, *Plato and the Socratic Dialogue.*

13. *Meno* 82b–85b.

14. Merlan, "Form and Content in Plato's Philosophy," 406–410.

15. Seeskin, *Dialogue and Discovery,* 7.

16. Rosenthal, "On the Knowledge of Plato's Philosophy in the Islamic World," 393.

17. Bergsträsser, *Neue Materielien zu Hunain ibn Ishāq's Galen-Bibliographie,* 1–24. This is a critical edition and translation of Ḥunayn ibn Isḥāq's epistle documenting the translations that he had made. A convenient description of forms and genres found within the medieval Arabic philosophical literature may be found in Gutas, "Aspects of Literary Forms and Genre in Arabic Logical Works."

18. Alfarabi's (870–895) knowledge of Plato's *Laws* has been the subject of a debate between Joshua Parens and Dimitri Gutas. Parens has argued that Alfarabi in his summary to the *Laws* had access to the entire Platonic text, one that was "similar, if not identical, to our own." He cites, inter alia, as "likely" evidence that Alfarabi studied in Byzantium. See Parens, *Metaphysics as Rhetoric,* xxviii–xxxi. Gutas, however, argues that such evidence is highly unlikely based on (1) Alfarabi's own comments at the end of his summary, and (2) the intricacies of the Greco-Arabic translation process. Instead, Gutas argues that Alfarabi most likely used Galen's synopsis of the *Laws.* See his comments and textual evidence in "Review of *Metaphysics as Rhetoric.*" Because of its implications for my argument, I tend to side with the evidence presented by Gutas.

19. More generally, see *Plato Arabus,* vol. 1; Steinschneider, *Die arabischen Übersetzungen aus dem Griechischen,* 54–64.

20. Perhaps not coincidentally, this is also the way that hadith literature ("Sayings of the Prophet") was forming during this period. On the latter, see the classic study in Schacht, *The Origins of Muhammedan Jurisprudence.*

The term "Islamicate," coined by Marshall Hodgson, refers "not directly to the religion, Islam, but to the social and cultural complex historically associated with Islam and Muslims, both among Muslims themselves and even when found among non-Muslims." See Hodgson, *The Venture of Islam,* vol. 1, 59.

21. Alon, *Socrates in Medieval Arabic Literature,* 29.

22. This and further examples may be found in Alon, *Socrates in Medieval Arabic Literature,* 25.

23. ʿUsāma ibn Munqidh, *Lubāb al-ʾadab* (Cairo: n.p., 1935), 432, qtd. in Alon, *Socrates in Medieval Arabic Literature,* 131.

24. For Ghazālī's criticisms of Socrates in particular and of Greek philosophy in general, see his *Tahāfut al-falāsifa.* A convenient English translation with facing Arabic text may be found in *The Incoherence of the Philosophers.*

25. E.g., al-Ghazālī, *al-Naṣīhat al-mulūk,* 139.

26. Hankins, *Plato in the Italian Renaissance,* vol. 1, 3–7.

27. E.g., Altmann, *Moses Mendelssohn,* 151–152.

28. al-Tawḥīdī, *Al-Imtāʿ wa al-muʾānasa,* 108–128. An English translation of this work may be found in Margoliouth, "The Merits of Logic and Grammar," *Journal of the Royal Asiatic Society.* Also see Mahdi, "Language and Logic in Classical Islam."

29. Pines, "On the Term *Ruḥaniyyot* and Its Origin and on Judah Halevi's Doctrine"; Lewis, *The Origins of Ismailism,* 44–54; Fenton, "The Arabic and Hebrew Versions of the *Theology of Aristotle*"; Wasserstrom, *Between Muslim and Jew,* 122–135.

30. For an attempt to do this, see Walbridge, *The Leaven of the Ancients: Suhrawardī and the Heritage of the Greeks.*

31. An English translation may be found in *The Case of the Animals Versus Man before the King of the Jinn.* On the relationship between the *Ikhwān* and the Ismaʿilis, see, for example, Nasr, *An Introduction to Islamic Cosmological Doctrines,* 35–37; Fakhry, *A His-*

tory of Islamic Philosophy, 164. For a dissenting opinion, see Netton, *Muslim Neoplatonists,* 94–104.

32. Here it is important to note that Ismaʿilis proselytized not just among Jews and Christians but primarily among other Muslims. See, for example, Daftary, *The Ismāʿīlīs,* 186–196; van Ess, *Chiliastische Erwartungen und die Versuchung der Göttlichkeit der Kalif al-Ḥākim (386–411A.H.).*

33. Although as I will try to argue in chapter 6, we can, on one level, see in some of these companions metaphors or metonyms for, e.g., the French skeptical tradition.

34. See the comments in, e.g., Strauss, "Law of Reason in the *Kuzari,*" 118–119.

35. The classic study of these controversies remains Silver, *Maimonidean Criticism and the Maimonidean Controversy 1180–1240;* a convenient selection of primary sources may be found in Halkin, ed., *After Maimonides: An Anthology of Writings by His Critics, Defenders, and Commentators;* more recently, see the discussion in Tirosh-Samuelson, *Happiness in Premodern Judaism,* ch. 6.

36. E.g., Harvey, "Falaquera's *Epistle of the Debate* and the Maimonidean Controversy of the 1230s"; Levine, "Falaquera's Philosophy."

37. E.g., Gershenzon, "A Tale of Two Midrashim."

38. Although as I shall discuss in chapter five this may be a problematic assertion.

39. Goodman comments that Halevi puts a lot of "thuses" and "therefores" into the philosopher's speech as a form of sarcasm. See his "Judah Halevi," 197.

40. Halevi, *Kitāb al-radd wa al-dalīl fī al-dīn al-dhalil,* I:1. A problematic English translation may be found in Hirschfeld, trans., *The Kuzari: An Argument for the Faith of Israel,* 36. For the sake of convenience, future citations will be from the book and section of the Judeo-Arabic edition of Baneth and Ben-Shammai, with the page number from the English translation in parentheses. Mention should also be made in this context of an excellent French translation: Judah Hallévi, *Le Kuzari: Apologie de la religion méprisée,* trans. Charles Touati.

41. Although, as the dialogue progresses, Halevi's relationship to philosophy, especially that of Avicenna, is not so easily dismissed. In this regard, see Pines, "Shiʿite Terms," 215–217.

42. See the comments in Strauss, "The Law of Reason in the *Kuzari,*" 98–103. Another important study that is sensitive to the literary claims of the *Kuzari* is found in Schweid, "The Literary Structure of the First Book of the *Kuzari.*"

43. See the evidence cited in Harvey, "Falaquera's *Epistle of the Debate* and the Maimonidean Controversy of the 1230s," 76–81; Dahan, "Epistola Dialoghi," 56–57.

44. E.g., Schweid, "The Literary Structure of the First Book of the *Kuzari,*" 259–260; Strauss, "The Law of Reason in the *Kuzari,*" 102–103.

45. Melamed, "The Woman as Philosopher," 122–123. I would like to thank Prof. Melamed for calling this article to my attention, and for sending me an offprint of it.

46. E.g., *Dialoghi* III. 233–234. An English translation of this may be found in Friedeberg-Seeley and Barnes, trans., *The Philosophy of Love,* 273–277. For the sake of convenience, future citations will be from the book and page number of the Italian edition with the page number from the English translation in parentheses. See the comments in Melamed, "The Woman as Philosopher," 113–130.

47. See Tirosh-Rothschild, "Jewish Philosophy on the Eve of Modernity," 557, n. 101.

48. *Dialoghi* III. 391 (Friedeberg-Seeley and Barnes, 468).

49. E.g., *Falaquera's Epistle of the Debate.*

50. E.g., Jospe, *Torah and Sophia.*

51. al-Ḥarizi, *The Book of the Taḥkemoni.* See the comments in Brann, *Power in the Portrayal,* esp. 140–159.

52. Ibn Verga, *Shevet Yehudah.* For secondary literature, see Yerushalmi, *The Lisbon Massacre of 1506 and the Royal Image in the Shebet Yehudah.*

53. Ibn Daʿud, *The Exalted Faith,* 40.

54. See, e.g., Melamed, "The Hebrew Encyclopedias of the Renaissance," esp. 448–454; Lelli, "La Retorica Nell'Introduzione del Hay ha-'Olamim."

55. E.g., Mendes-Flohr, *From Mysticism to Dialogue,* 93–126; Kepnes, *The Text and Thou,* 19–40; Schmidt, *Martin Buber's Formative Years,* 21–47.

56. For instance, in an excellent local analysis of the Jewish community of Valencia at the time of the anti-Jewish riots of 1391, Mark D. Meyerson argues: "a history that privileges philosophical, theosophical, and polemical texts often overlooks crucial details of Jewish socioeconomic life and the complexities of Jewish coexistence and conflict with non-Jews." See his *A Jewish Renaissance in Fifteenth-Century Spain,* 7. Although on one level I agree with him—intellectual history has been traditionally unconcerned with socioeconomic life—on another, I completely disagree, as philosophical texts, when read with a different set of concerns, have the potential to tell us much about "socioeconomic" life and the relationships between Jews and non-Jews.

57. Boyarin, *Carnal Israel,* 12, qtd. in Rosen, *Unveiling Eve,* 26.

58. Biale, "Preface," in *Cultures of the Jews,* xxvi.

59. See, for example, Lerner, *Maimonides' Empire of Light,* 3–13; Seeskin, *Searching for a Distant God,* 142–175.

60. In using the term *Jewish cultures* I am influenced by the discussion in Shmueli, *Seven Jewish Cultures,* who writes, for example, that "By culture I mean a set of shared symbols which represent an organized collective attempt to express the meaning, or meanings, of life and to make the world habitable by transforming its impersonal vastness and frightening dimensions into an understandable and significant order" (3). In Judaism, these "shared symbols" include God, Torah, chosenness, etc.; yet, for Shmueli, while "these concepts have endured, their meanings have changed, the inevitable result of the changes occurring in the ontologies underlying these concepts and experiences" (4). To this discussion of Jewish cultures should also be added the essays in Biale, ed., *The Cultures of the Jews.*

61. By employing the term *nationalist* here, I certainly do not refer to the modern concept of Zionism, but to a form of biblical nationalism, in which certain Jewish thinkers appealed to the supremacy of the cultural and literary forms of ancient Israel. See, for example, the rich discussion in Brann, *The Compunctious Poet,* 23–58.

62. See the cautionary comments in Eisen, *The Book of Job in Medieval Jewish Philosophy,* 10.

63. See, for example, Whitman, *Allegory;* Heath, *Allegory and Philosophy in Avicenna (Ibn Sīnā).*

64. E.g., Boyle, "The Setting of the *Summa Theologiae* of St. Thomas"; Jordan, "The Protreptic Structure of the *Summa Contra Gentiles.*"

65. E.g., Evans, "Boethian and Euclidean Axiomatic Method in the Theology of the Later Twelfth Century."

66. E.g., Eisen, *Gersonides on Providence, Covenant, and the Chosen People;* idem, *The Book of Job in Medieval Jewish Philosophy.*

67. See, for example, the collection of essays in Jacobi, ed., *Gespräche lesen: Philosophische Dialogue im Mittelalter.*

68. Heath, *Allegory and Philosophy in Avicenna,* 6–7.

2. Judah Halevi

1. See chapter 1 n. 20 for explanation of "Islamicate."

2. For a good survey of this topic, see Bonebakker, "Adab and the Concept of Belles-Lettres"; also see my *Texture of the Divine*, 10–12.

3. On his recidivism, about which I will say more below, see Goitein, "The Biography of Rabbi Judah Ha-Levi in Light of the Cairo Genizah Documents," esp. 50–52.

4. Although not referring directly to Halevi, the work of Elliot R. Wolfson is most sensitive to the *ẓāhir/bāṭin* hermeneutic in medieval Jewish thought. See, for example, his "Beautiful Maiden Without Eyes"; idem, "Occultation of the Feminine and the Body of Secrecy in Medieval Kabbalah." On Wolfson's reading of Halevi, see, inter alia, his "Merkabah Traditions in Philosophical Garb."

5. The full title of the *Kuzari—Kitāb al-radd wa al-dalīl fī al-dīn al-dhalīl*, or *The Book of Refutation and Proof in Defense of the Despised Religion*—better contextualizes the work, revealing its scope and intent.

6. The story of the Khazars would have played an important role in the Jewish imagination of the twelfth century. In the middle of the tenth century, emissaries from Khorasan came to Cordoba and there told Hasdai ibn Shaprut (912–961), an important adviser to the Muslim caliph Abd al-Raḥman III, about the Jewish kingdom of Khazaria. The existence of a mysterious kingdom located somewhere in the East in which Jews held power would have undoubtedly had a tremendous effect on Jewish self-understanding because Jews had not held any type of political power since the destruction of the Second Temple in 70 CE. On the correspondence between Hasdai ibn Shaprut and the King of the Khazars, see Kobler, ed., *Letters of Jews Through the Ages*, vol. 1, 97–116. On the history of the Khazars, see Brook, *The Jews of Khazaria;* Golb and Ptisak, *Khazarian Hebrew Documents of the Tenth Century;* Peter B. Golden, *Khazar Studies.*

7. On the role of dreams in Islamicate civilization, especially when it comes to undertaking momentous decisions, see Goldziher, "The Appearance of the Prophet in Dreams"; Hughes, "Imagining the Divine," 38–41.

8. The "identity" of the philosopher is a matter of some debate in the secondary literature. Herbert Davidson argues that the views attributed to this individual are, for the most part, imprecise and eclectic. See his "The Active Intellect in the Kuzari and Hallevi's Theory of Causality," 352–374. Pines, however, argues that the philosopher resembles ibn Bājja; see his "Shiᶜite Terms and Conceptions in Judah Halevi's *Kuzari,*" 211–215. I tend to side more with Langermann, who argues that it is the generic spirituality of the philosopher that Halevi finds most bothersome. As a result, Langermann argues that this individual bears more than a passing resemblance to an informed Ismaᶜili *dāᶜī* ("missionary"). See Langermann, "Science and the *Kuzari,*" 497–501.

9. It was in Ismaᶜili circles, for instance, that the longer version of the mystico-philosophical *Theology of Aristotle* most likely originated. See Pines, "La longe recension de la Theologie d'Aristote." Fritz Zimmerman, however, thinks that the Ismaᶜilis might only have adapted this recension. See his "The Origins of the So-Called Theology of Aristotle." Paul Fenton contends that it may actually have been the product of Jewish Neoplatonists influenced by Ismaᶜilis. See his "The Arabic and Hebrew Versions of the *Theology of Aristotle.*"

10. On the relationship between form and content of literature in medieval Arabo-Judaic literary composition, see my "A Case of Twelfth-Century Plagiarism?"

11. What follows by no means claims to be an exhaustive account of Judah Halevi's life, much of which has been minutely studied by others. Biographical accounts of Halevi may be found in Goitein, *A Mediterranean Society,* vol. 5, 448–468; idem, "Autographs of Judah Halevi from the Genizah"; Baneth, "Some Remarks on the Autographs of Judah Halevi and the Genesis of the *Kuzari*"; Schirmann, "The Life of Judah Halevi," vol. 1, 250–341; Gil and Fleischer, eds., *Judah Halevi and His Circle;* Brann, *The Compunctious Poet,* 84–118; idem, "Judah ha-Levi."

12. This ambiguity revolves around the manuscript tradition. See the comments in Schirmann, "Where Was Judah Halevi Born?" in his *Studies in the History of Hebrew Poetry and Drama,* vol. 1, 247–249.

13. See, for example, "A Letter of Rabbi Judah Halevi to Rabbi Moses ibn Ezra," 404–407. A poetic version of ibn Ezra's invitation may be found in "*Yaldei yamim*" in *Secular Poems,* vol. 1, 22–23.

14. Goitein, *A Mediterranean Society,* vol. 5, 448; Brann, *The Compunctious Poet,* 84–85.

15. Brann, *The Compunctious Poet,* 94–106.

16. Long regarded in secondary scholarship as the "Golden Age," this has in recent years come under increasing interrogation. See, for example, Cohen, *Under Crescent and Cross,* 3–14; Brann, *Power in the Portrayal,* 1–21; Hughes, "The 'Golden Age' of Muslim Spain."

17. *The Jewish Poets of Spain,* trans. Goldstein, 137–138.

18. Pines argues, for example, that book five of the *Kuzari,* generally regarded as a later addition to the work, was written at a time when Halevi began to know and look favorably upon the work of Avicenna, and that he subsequently reworked a number of his earlier ideas in the light of Avicennian categories. See Pines, "Shiᶜite Terms and Conceptions in Judah Halevi's *Kuzari,*" 215–217. Also on the subject of the *Kuzari*'s "stratigraphy," Yohanan Silman argues that there exist two distinct layers in the *Kuzari,* an "early" one that is influenced by philosophy, and a "later" one that rejects philosophy in favor of experience and history. See his *Philosopher and Prophet,* 159–165, 289–307.

19. Goitein, "The Biography of Rabbi Judah ha-Levi," 55–56; Touati, introduction to *Le Kuzari,* viii.

20. This is the opinion of Guttmann, "The Relationship between Religion and Philosophy According to Judah Halevi," in his *Religion and Knowledge,* 66. See the comments in Berger, "Towards a New Understanding of Judah Halevi's *Kuzari.*"

21. E.g., Pines, "Shiᶜite Terms," 165–167.

22. Lobel, *Between Mysticism and Philosophy,* 21–30.

23. Lewis, *The Origins of Ismailism,* 23–43; Daftary, "The Earliest Ismaᶜilis"; idem, *The Ismāᶜīlis,* 91–143.

24. See Pines, "On the Term '*ruḥaniyyot*'"; Wasserstrom, *Between Muslim and Jew,* 122–135.

25. For appropriate secondary literature, consult Stern, "The Earliest Cosmological Doctrines of Ismāᶜīlism"; Halm, "The Cosmology of the pre-Fatimid Ismāᶜīliyya."

26. Walker, *Ḥamid al-Dīn al-Kirmānī,* 22–23.

27. Gohlman, ed. and trans., *The Life of Ibn Sina,* 18–21. Also witness the hostile criticism of al-Ghazālī (d. 1111) directed against the Ismaᶜilis in his own autobiography, "*Al-Munqidh min al-dalāl.*" For an English translation, see *Deliverance from Error,* 71–77. On the complicated relationship between Ghazālī and the Ismaᶜilis, see Mitha, *Al-Ghazālī and the Ismaᶜilis,* 19–27.

28. al-Ṭūsī, *Contemplation and Action,* 24.

29. See my *Texture of the Divine,* 25–30.

30. An important exception is Fierro, "Bātinism in al-Andalus."

31. Asín-Pallacios, *The Mystical Philosophy of Ibn Masarra and His Followers.* A circle that formed around the teachings of ibn Masarra is believed to be the environment that produced one of the most famous mystico-philosophers in Islam, ibn Arabi (1165–1240).

32. Ibn Ḥazm's heresiographical work, *Faṣl fī al-milal wa al-ahwāʾ wa al-nihal,* although obviously ideological, is nevertheless concerned with accurate representations of those who deviate from "mainstream" Islam. See Ormsby, "Ibn Hazm."

33. Ghazali's work was known in Spain. See my comments in "The Three Worlds of Ibn Ezra's *Ḥay ben Meqitz,*" 16, n. 87.

34. al-Rāzī, *Kitāb al-ʿalām wa al-nubuwwa.*

35. *Kitāb al milal wa al-nihal,* vol. 2, 117–201. Interestingly, though, al-Shahrastānī, was accused by others of harboring Ismaʿili sympathies. See the comments in Steigerwald, *La pensée philosophique et théologique de Shahrastānī,* 64–65.

36. Corbin, "L'initiation Ismaélienne ou l'ésotérisme et le Verbe"; Halm, "The Ismaʿili Oath of Allegiance (*ʿahd*) and the 'Sessions of Wisdom' (*majālis al-ḥikma*) in Fatimid Times"; idem, *The Fatimids and their Traditions of Learning,* 41–45.

37. An Arabic text and English translation may be found in al-Yaman, *The Master and the Disciple.*

38. A critical edition and an English translation may be found in *The Advent of the Fatimids: A Contemporary Shiʿi Witness.*

39. Halevi, *Kuzari* I:1 (Hirschfeld, 35).

40. al-Sijistānī, *The Wellsprings of Wisdom,* 40; my italics.

41. al-Yaman, *The Master and the Disciple,* 63.

42. Lane, *An Arabic-English Lexicon,* vol. 1, 35. Also see Morris's comments in al-Yaman, *The Master and the Disciple,* 172.

43. Al-Yaman, *The Master and the Disciple,* 75.

44. Ibid., 83.

45. See my *Texture of the Divine,* 40–42, 61–64.

46. Al-Yaman, *The Master and the Disciple,* 84.

47. *Kuzari* 2:26 (Hirschfeld, 106).

48. Ibid., 3:10–11 (Hirschfeld, 142–143).

49. Ibid., 3:22–23 (Hirschfeld, 161–162).

50. Ibid., 3:37 (Hirschfeld, 168–169).

51. For elaboration, see below.

52. See Walker, *Early Philosophical Shiism,* 27–29.

53. Al-Sijistānī, *Kitāb al-maqālīd,* 189, qtd. in Walker, *Early Philosophical Shiism,* 127.

54. Al-Sijistānī, *Kitāb al-yanābīʿ,* qtd. in Walker, *The Wellsprings of Wisdom,* 47.

55. Al-Yaman, *The Master and the Disciple,* 156–157.

56. *Kuzari* 2:56 (Hirschfeld, 117).

57. Pines, "Shi'ite Terms," 167–172.

58. *Kuzari* I:44–47 (Hirschfeld, 49).

59. Ibid., 4:3 (Hirschfeld, 201).

60. See my *Texture of the Divine,* 25–30. Also see the discussion in Halm, "The Ismaʿili Oath of Allegiance (*ʿahd*) and the 'Sessions of Wisdom' (*majālis al-ḥikma*) in Fatimid Times."

61. ibn al-Ḥaytham, *The Advent of the Fatimids,* 95–96.

62. Al-Yaman, *The Master and the Disciple,* 79.

63. *Kuzari* 3:17–19 (Hirschfeld, 155–157).

64. Ibid., 3:53 (Hirschfeld, 183).

65. Ibid., 2:1 (Hirschfeld, 82–83).

66. Halevi, of course, does argue that native-born Jews do form the core of Judaism in Khazaria. This, however, does not have anything to do with the fact that they possess some form of secret wisdom. Rather, it is connected to Halevi's ontology that those who convert to Judaism occupy a level just below that of Jews. See Lasker, "Proselyte Judaism, Christianity, and Islam in the Thought of Judah Halevy"; Eisen, "The Problem of the King's Dream and Non-Jewish Prophecy in Judah Halevi's *Kuzari*."

67. See my *Texture of the Divine*, 51–81.

68. *Kuzari* 1:1 (Hirschfeld, 37–38).

69. ibn Gabirol, *Sefer Meqor Ḥayyim*, 3. For general background on ibn Gabirol, see Loewe, *Ibn Gabirol*.

70. Ibid., 6.

71. E.g., ibn Gabirol, *Sefer Meqor Ḥayyim*, 106–137.

72. Also of interest is the fact that ibn Gabirol mentions neither Jewish ideas nor prooftexts in his *Fons Vitae*. Indeed, because the work circulated in Arabic, it was long thought that its author, now referred to as Avicebron, was not a Jew but a Muslim.

73. See my discussion in "Two Approaches to the Love of God in Medieval Jewish Thought."

74. Langermann, "Some Astrological Themes in the Thought of Abraham ibn Ezra," 65–74.

75. I provide a critical translation of the entire poem in the appendix to my *Texture of the Divine*, 189–207. This passage comes from 195.

76. Baḥya, *The Book of Direction to the Duties of the Heart*, 181.

77. Ibid., 102. See, in this regard, Tirosh-Samuelson, *Happiness in Premodern Judaism*, 176–180.

78. Ibid., 102–107.

79. Ibid., 405.

80. Ibid., 200.

81. Ibid., 213–215.

3. Shem Tov ibn Falaquera

1. This was done primarily through Falaquera's "encyclopedias," about which I will have more to say below.

2. Even Falaquera's biographers tend not to dispute this appellation. Henry Malter, for example, writes that "the thirteenth century was not, indeed, an age of originality," and that Falaquera "did not aspire to lead forth on new paths, but was content to follow classic models." See his "Shem Tov ben Joseph Palquera," 152, 162. According to Guttmann, "The voluminous writings of Shem Tob ibn Falaquera testify to great philosophic erudition; but his originality did not measure up to his learning." See his *Philosophies of Judaism*, 196. Even Sirat, who is usually more sympathetic to "marginal" thinkers, writes of Falaquera that he "did not look for any original solution; he proposed nothing new, as if all were settled and the philosophical tradition were united and coherent." See her *A History of Jewish Philosophy in the Middle Ages*, 237. The sole positive treatment in a survey of Jewish philosophy is found in Zonta, *La filosofia ebraica medievale*, 155–156: "Più originale è forse, in questo autore, l'eclettismo, che lo spinge a

farsi divulgatore di tutti gli asppetti della filosofia greca e Arabo-islamica (fisica, metafisica, etica), con la sola eccezione della logica. . . ."

3. The most scathing remarks against Falaquera's poetry may be found in Graetz, who writes: "Falaquera tat fich auch viel aus seine dichterische Begabung zugute. Von seiner Jugend an bis in sein spätestes Alter hat er viel Reime geschmiedet; aber die von ihm bekannt gewordenen Verse legen ein schlechtes Zeugnis für seine dichterische Fahigkeit ab; sein Prosa ist jedenfalls besser." See his *Geschichte der Juden*, vol. 7, 217; in this regard, also see Sirat, *A History of Jewish Philosophy in the Middle Ages*, 234. For a refreshing and alternative account, see Brann, *The Compunctious Poet*, 124–137.

4. Brann, *The Compunctious Poet*, 19–22.

5. Although, as Moshe Halbertal has convincingly argued, Maimonideanism had indeed made many strong inroads into thirteenth-century halakhic circles. See his *Between Torah and Wisdom*, 22–49.

6. E.g., Jospe, *Torah and Sophia*, 46–48; Sirat, *A History of Jewish Philosophy in the Middle Ages*, 234.

7. Steven Harvey, "Introduction," in *The Medieval Hebrew Encyclopedias of Science and Philosophy*, 9.

8. In this regard, see the collection of essays in Binkley, ed., *Pre-Modern Encyclopaedic Texts*. There is, however, an important difference between Christian and Jewish encyclopedias. The Christian encyclopedia, for instance, was primarily intended for preachers in order to give them moral instruction; Jewish encyclopedias, on the other hand, were meant for a socially mobile lay audience. For a comparison between the two types, see Voorbij, "Purpose and Audience."

9. For requisite secondary literature on these controversies in general, and which my discussion relies upon, see Baer, *A History of the Jews in Christian Spain*, vol. 1, 96–110; Sarachek, *Faith and Reason*, 66–103; Touati, "La controverse de 1303–1306"; Septimus, *Hispano-Jewish Culture in Transition*, 39–60; Dobbs-Weinstein, "The Maimonidean Controversy," 331–349; Stern, "The Crisis of Philosophic Allegory in Languedocian-Jewish Culture (1304–1306)"; idem, "Menahem ha-Meiri and the Second Controversy over Philosophy"; Tirosh-Samuelson, *Happiness in Premodern Judaism*, 246–290.

10. See the comments in Twersky, "Aspects of the Social and Cultural History of Provençal Jewry."

11. Septimus, *Hispano-Jewish Culture in Transition*, 63. Also see idem, "Piety and Power in Thirteenth-Century Catalonia," 206–211.

12. See, e.g., Robinson, "The Ibn Tibbon Family."

13. See, e.g., Halbertal, *Between Torah and Wisdom*, 152–180.

14. The general cultural milieu of this transmission is discussed in Freudenthal, "Science in the Medieval Jewish Culture of Southern France"; idem, "Les sciences dans les communautés juives médiévales de Provence." More specifically, see Zonta, "Hebrew Transmission of Arabic Philosophy and Science."

15. Robinson, "Secondary Forms of Transmission." More generally on the role of Hebrew in medieval Jewish culture, see Halkin, "The Medieval Jewish Attitude towards Hebrew," 233–238.

16. See the comments in Halbertal, *Between Torah and Wisdom*, 16–17; Tirosh-Samuelson, *Happiness in Premodern Judaism*, 253–254. A collection of philosophical sermons may be found in Saperstein, *Jewish Preaching*.

17. This is nicely formulated in Tirosh-Samuelson, *Happiness in Premodern Judaism*, 267–268.

18. My examination here relies on the more detailed studies of Sarachek, *Faith and Reason*, 73ff.; Shatzmiller, "Towards a Picture of the First Maimonidean Contro-

versy"; Shoḥat, "Concerning the First Controversy on the Writings of Maimonides"; Septimus, *Hispano-Jewish Culture in Transition,* 61–72; Tirosh-Samuelson, *Happiness in Premodern Judaism,* 267–277.

19. See Shatzmiller, "Towards a Picture of the First Maimonidean Controversy," 128–129.

20. On the importance of Kimḥi see the pioneering study of Talmage, *David Kimḥi,* 23–42.

21. See Sarachek, *Faith and Reason,* 10ff., 85–87; Cohen, *The Friars and the Jews,* 52–60; Tirosh-Samuelson, *Happiness in Premodern Judaism,* 274–275.

22. There is some debate as to what actually happened. Urbach suggests that the whole story was exaggerated by the pro-Maimonideans to discredit their opponents. See his "The Participation of German and French Scholars in the Controversy about Maimonides and His Works," 156–157. Shoḥat suggests that the *Guide* and *Sefer ha-Madda* were handed over to the Church and that parts of these works were probably burned but it is doubtful if it was a public display or that all of Maimonides' writings were destroyed. See his "Concerning the First Controversy on the Writings of Maimonides," 50. In this regard, also see Cohen, *The Friars and the Jews,* 56–58.

23. Cohen, *The Friars and the Jews,* 59.

24. A good example of just how pervasive these Controversies were can be gleaned from contemporaneous poetry. See, in this regard, Lehmann, "Polemic and Satire in the Poetry of the Maimonidean Controversy."

25. As before, the opponents of this ban issued their own counter ban. Much of this internecine activity subsided, however, in 1306 when the Jews of France were expelled from the royal territories.

26. This letter, in addition to many others surrounding the Maimonidean Controversy, can be found in Abba Meri ben Joseph ha-Yarḥī, *Minḥat Qenāʾot,* 182–185.

27. On the many ways that this name has been spelled in both Hebrew and English, see Jospe, *Torah and Sophia,* 2–4. The origins of the name are by no means clear. Malter thinks that it derives from the French city Beucaire. See his "Shem Tov Ben Joseph Palquera," 155, n. 3. Others think that it comes from the French term "flochiedre" ("wool carder"). See, e.g., the discussion in Jospe, *Torah and Sophia,* 3. Interestingly, although highly unlikely, Isadore Loeb argues that the name Falaquera might be related to, or be a derivation from, the name Pulgar or Polleqar. See his "Polémistes Chretiens et Juifs en France et en Espagne," 63.

28. Full and detailed biographies of Falaquera may be found in Malter, "Shem Tov Ben Joseph Palquera"; Jospe, *Torah and Sophia,* 1–30.

29. This, of course, might well be another literary trope that he employed.

30. Sirat claims matter-of-factly that Falaquera's "poetry is in contemporary taste, without further distinction." See her *A History of Jewish Philosophy in the Middle Ages,* 234. However, I tend to side with the comments of Ross Brann: "As a consequence of his notoriety as a transmitter of and commentator on philosophical thought, Falaqera's poetry, artistic prose, and the belletristic style in which his early philosophical writings are couched have elicited virtually no attention." See his *The Compunctious Poet,* 125.

31. Shem Tov ibn Falaquera, *Sefer ha-Mevaqqesh,* 11. Part one of this work has been translated into English in *The Book of the Seeker by Shem Tob ben Joseph ibn Falaquera,* 7. In subsequent notes, I will, at least when citing from part one, give the page number from each text.

32. *Sefer ha-Mevaqqesh,* 7; *Book of the Seeker,* 2.

33. Brann, *The Compunctious Poet,* 126–127; Jospe, *Torah and Sophia,* 11.

34. Jospe, *Torah and Sophia,* 31–33; he gives a brief summary of the contents of each in 33–76.

35. He also wrote commentaries to the biblical narrative, only fragments of which survive in the work of Samuel ibn Zarza. See the comments in Jospe and Schwartz, "Shem Tov ibn Falaquera's Lost Bible Commentary."

36. *Sefer Moreh ha-Moreh.*

37. This is published in Kaufmann, *Studien über Salomon ibn Gabirol,* 17–51.

38. *Meqor Ḥayyim,* 435–452.

39. See 18 above.

40. For a breakdown of the correspondence between the original and the translation, see Jospe, *Torah and Sophia,* 69–74.

41. Jospe, *Torah and Sophia,* 69.

42. Steven Harvey makes the interesting, though ultimately unprovable, suggestion that Falaquera might have dispensed with the dialogue form of ibn Gabirol's work because he translated it for the few as opposed to the many. See his *Falaquera's Epistle of the Debate,* 132. Harvey thus regards the dialogue as a genre that is particular suited to explicating philosophy to the masses.

43. *Sefer Reshit Ḥokhmah.* For the structure of the work's contents, see Jospe, *Torah and Sophia,* 37–42. There also exists a Latin translation of this work, presumably made by a non-Jew. This translation exists in a manuscript that includes the *Iggeret ha-Vikuaḥ.* See Gilbert Dahan, "Epistola Dialoghi," 47–49.

44. Zonta, *Un dizionario filosofico ebraico del XIII secolo.* This work provides a critical edition and Italian translation of the philosophical lexicon that Falaquera included at the beginning of the work.

45. Harvey, *Falaquera's Epistle of the Debate,* Hebrew, 79; English, 51.

46. Evidence for this is the fact that at the end of the *Iggeret,* he writes that he has yet to compose such works.

47. Harvey, *Falaquera's Epistle of the Debate,* ix.

48. An English translation of the Arabic text may be found in Hyman and Walsh, eds., *Philosophy in the Middle Ages,* 297–316. For a Hebrew version, see Golb, "The Hebrew Translation of Averroes' *Faṣl al-maqāl.*" See the comments in Harvey, *Falaquera's Epistle of the Debate,* 83–98.

49. E.g., *Sefer ha-Maʿalot,* 75; *Moreh ha-Moreh,* 131.

50. *Epistle of the Debate,* Heb., 56; Eng., 14–15.

51. This proved particularly popular among authors of *maqāmāt,* particularly by Judah al-Ḥarizi (b. 1170) and Isaac ibn Sahula (b. 1244).

52. E.g., *Epistle of the Debate,* Heb., 68; Eng., 32

53. See the comments in Harvey, "Falaquera's *Epistle of the Debate* and the Maimonidean Controversy of the 1230s," 75–76.

54. See Brann, *The Compunctious Poet,* 119–124. However, there were, as Brann notes, important differences between Andalusi poetry composed in the eleventh century and that in the thirteenth. For further elaboration, see Pagis, *Change and Tradition in the Secular Poetry of Spain and Italy,* 173–198.

55. Those who fall into this camp include, inter alia, R. Solomon ben Abraham of Montpellier (fl. middle of the 13th century), R. Moses ben Naḥman (Naḥmanides; d. ca. 1270), and R. Solomon ben Adret (Rashba; ca. 1235–ca. 1310).

56. Those who fall into this camp include, inter alia, Judah ibn Alfakar (d. 1235), the youthful Meshullam da Piera (fl. first half of the 13th century), and Solomon Petit (fl. late 13th century).

57. From the talmudic statement "Great matters mean the account of the chariot, small matters the disputes of Abbaye and Rabba" (*BT Baba Batra* 134b). The philosopher in Pollaqar's *Ezer ha-Dat* uses this exact same phrase, although much more condescendingly.

58. *Epistle of the Debate*, Heb., 56; Eng., 16.

59. Ibid., Heb., 68; Eng., 32.

60. See the evidence cited in Harvey, "Falaquera's *Epistle of the Debate* and the Maimonidean Controversy of the 1230s," 76–81; Dahan, "Epistola Dialoghi," 56–57; Tirosh-Samuelson, *Happiness in Premodern Judaism*, 274–276.

61. These letters may be found in Lichtenberg, ed., *Qovets Teshuvot ha-Rambam ve-Iggerotav*.

62. Harvey, "Falaquera's *Epistle of the Debate* and the Maimonidean Controversy of the 1230s," 76.

63. *Epistle of the Debate*, Heb., 62; Eng., 25.

64. Ibid., Heb., 65–66; Eng., 29–30.

65. See, for example, *BT Megillah* 17b.

66. *Epistle of the Debate*, Heb., 67–68; Eng., 32.

67. Ibid., Heb., 72; Eng., 38.

68. Ibid., Heb., 73–74; Eng., 41.

69. For a discussion of the concept of theft in medieval Jewish thought, see Roth, "The 'Theft of Philosophy' by the Greeks from the Jews"; Hughes, "A Case of Twelfth-Century Plagiarism?" 306–315. On this trope in medieval philosophy, see H. A. Wolfson, *Philo*, vol. 2, 167–168.

70. E.g., Ravitzky, "Samuel ibn Tibbon and the Esoteric Character of *The Guide of the Perplexed*."

71. See Vajda, *Isaac Albalag*, 251–266.

72. *Epistle of the Debate*, Heb., 75–76; Eng., 44–46.

73. Ibid., Heb., 78; Eng., 49–50.

74. Jospe dates the work to 1263, when Falaquera would have been somewhere between 35 and 40. See Jospe, *Torah and Sophia*, 46.

75. *Sefer ha-Mevaqqesh*, 8; *Book of the Seeker*, 3.

76. See the important discussion in Brann, *The Compunctious Poet*, 128–136. This paragraph owes much to Brann's comments there.

77. *Sefer ha-Mevaqqesh*, 87; *Book of the Seeker*, 91.

78. Brann, *The Compunctious Poet*, 135; see also the comments in Klar, "Falaquera's *Sefer ha-Mevaqqesh*," 257–258. Similarly, Harvey argues that Falaquera intended the "Book of the Seeker" as a "bill of divorcement from poetry and announcement of his betrothal to wisdom, with the implication that a bigamous attachment to both poetry and wisdom was not desirable and should not be tolerated." See his *Falaquera's Epistle of the Debate*, 129.

79. *Sefer ha-Mevaqqesh*, 13; *Book of the Seeker*, 9–10.

80. According to Schirmann and Jospe, by the time that the seeker finishes with all of these individuals he would be roughly 35 to 40 years old, the same age that Falaquera was when he composed the work, thus making it semiautobiographical. See Schirmann, *Hebrew Poetry in Spain and Provence*, vol. 2, 330; Jospe, *Torah and Sophia*, 48.

81. *Sefer ha-Mevaqqesh*, 33–35; *Book of the Seeker*, 43–45.

82. For example, the physician says, "Maimonides, of blessed memory, said: As Galen has already explained, all Greeks, when overcome by illness would apply no remedy at all, but would rely on nature, for it suffices to cure sickness." See *Sefer*

ha-Mevaqqesh, 35; *Book of the Seeker,* 45. This is verbatim from Maimonides, "Letter to the Sultan," 15.

83. *Sefer ha-Mevaqqesh,* 51; *Book of the Seeker,* 51.

84. *Sefer ha-Mevaqqesh,* 53; *Book of the Seeker,* 54.

85. *Sefer ha-Mevaqqesh,* 75; *Book of the Seeker,* 79–80.

86. *Sefer ha-Mevaqqesh,* 83; *Book of the Seeker,* 88.

87. *Sefer ha-Mevaqqesh,* 82; *Book of the Seeker,* 88.

88. *Sefer ha-Mevaqqesh,* 83; *Book of the Seeker,* 89.

89. E.g., al-Fārābī, *The Attainment of Happiness,* 70–77.

90. *Sefer ha-Mevaqqash,* 145.

91. For requisite secondary literature concerning this enigmatic chapter in the *Guide,* see Harvey, "Maimonides in the Sultan's Palace," 63; Hughes, "The Torah Speaks in the Language of Humans," 237–252; Kellner, *Maimonides on Human Perfection,* 13–39; Kasher, "The Parable of the King's Palace"; Kreisel, *Maimonides' Political Thought,* 189–224.

92. *Sefer ha-Mevaqqesh,* 145.

93. Ibid., 146–147.

94. Ibid., 146.

95. Ibid., 146.

4. Isaac Polleqar

1. A convenient survey of the entire treatise may be found in Belasco, "Isaac Pulgar's 'Support of the Religion.'"

2. Guttmann, for example, argues that Polleqar was unable to attain his philosophical goals, especially regarding the problem of will. Subsequent philosophers, however, offered "more penetrating" solutions. See his *Philosophies of Judaism,* 233. Husik characteristically overlooks the contribution of Polleqar to the story of medieval Jewish philosophy, not even mentioning him in his survey. Sirat, however, is one of the few who appreciates Polleqar's treatise. She writes that the *Ezer ha-Dat* is "a work in which touches of contemporary interest, lively descriptions and reflections full of good sense abound; moreover, the style is remarkable, and poetical passages enliven the prose. Unfortunately, the work has not been translated into any occidental language. . . ." (*A History of Jewish Philosophy in the Middle Ages,* 322).

3. On the problematic nature of the spelling of the name "Polleqar" (also Pulcher or Polgar), see Levinger's introduction to his critical edition, 9.

4. This assumes that we take as the standard for importance in medieval philosophy the composition of a modern biography. In addition to the literature devoted to Abner in the following notes, see the biography in Baer, "Abner von Burgos."

5. See, e.g., Chazan, *Daggers of Faith,* 25–37; idem, *Fashioning Jewish Identity in Medieval Western Christendom,* 67–87.

6. For requisite bibliography, see Baer, *A History of the Jews of Christian Spain,* vol. 1, 78–110; Chazan, *Daggers of Faith,* ch. 1.

7. Rationalism played a large role in the medieval disputations. See, for instance, Chazan, *Fashioning Jewish Identity in Medieval Western Christendom,* 250–277; Lasker, *Jewish Philosophical Polemics Against Christianity in the Middle Ages,* 25–43.

8. As some of these works made their way into Christian circles, which increasingly understood Hebrew, the implications to communities and not just the individual

authors were often major. The prime example is the reception of Naḥmanides' critique of the disputation in Barcelona in 1263. In this regard, see Chazan, *Barcelona and Beyond*, 87–92.

9. "A blow of the rod is a means of directing a boy towards study and good behavior, as Scripture advises: 'Rod and reproof impart wisdom' (Prov. 29:15), and 'By mere words a slave is not disciplined, for though he understands he heeds not' (Prov. 29:19). The book of Ben Sira expresses it this way: 'A wink to the wise, a fist for the fool' . . . When many Jewish communities are massacred and the particular generation of Jews is thereby reduced in numbers, some Jews immediately convert to the dominant Christian faith out of fear, and in that way a handful are saved. . . ." *Teshuvot ha-Meḥaref*, qtd. in Baer, *A History of the Jews in Christian Spain*, vol. 1, 353.

10. Chazan, *Barcelona and Beyond*, 52.

11. For requisite secondary literature, consult Chazan, *Barcelona and Beyond;* Maccoby, *Judaism on Trial: Jewish-Christian Disputation in the Middle Ages;* Berger, *The Jewish-Christian Debate in the High Middle Ages;* Cohen, *The Friars and the Jews.*

12. The Tortosa disputation, which followed the massacres throughout Spain of 1391, lasted twenty-one months. The Jewish participants were more or less prisoners and were not, for example, allowed to return home. See Maccoby, *Judaism on Trial*, 102–146.

13. See Gershenzon, "A Study of *Teshuvot la-Meharef* by Abner of Burgos," 18. These debates, according to her, would have been informal and "not the forced public debates whose repercussions so terrified the Jewish communities."

14. See Gershenzon, "A Study of *Teshuvot la-Meharef* by Abner of Burgos," 18.

15. Graetz, *Geschichte der Juden*, vol. 7, 444. Interestingly, though, this is missing in the English translation.

16. Justin Martyr, *Dialogue with Trypho.* For secondary literature, I have consulted Mach, "Justin Martyr's *Dialogus cum Tryphone Iudaeo* and the Development of Christian Anti-Judaism"; Rajak, "Talking at Trypho."

17. *Dialogus Petri et Moysi*, 535–672. For a study of this work, see Tolan, *Petrus Alfonsi*, 12–41.

18. An English translation may be found in Odo of Tournai, *On Original Sin and a Disputation with the Jew, Leo, Concerning the Advent of Christ, the Son of God.*

19. I have consulted the medieval French translation in *Le Livre du gentil et des trois sages.*

20. This paragraph owes much to Chazan, *Fashioning Jewish Identity in Medieval Western Christendom*, ch. 4.

21. An English translation may be found in *The Book of the Covenant.* For requisite secondary literature, consult Talmage, "R. Joseph Kimḥi"; Chazan, "Joseph Kimḥi's *Sefer ha-Berit.*"

22. For requisite secondary literature, consult Berger, "Gilbert Crispin, Alan of Lille, and Jacob ben Reuben"; Robert Chazan, "The Christian Position in Jacob ben Reuben's *Milḥamot ha-Shem.*"

23. For requisite secondary literature, consult Stein, *Jewish-Christian Disputations in Thirteenth-Century Narbonne;* Chazan, "Confrontation in the Synagogue of Narbonne"; idem, "Polemical Themes in the *Milḥemet Miẓvah.*"

24. Rabbi Moses ben Nahman, *Vikuaḥ Barcelona*, in *Kitvei Rabbenu Moshe ben Naḥman*, vol. 1, 302–320. An English translation may be found in Maccoby, *Judaism on Trial*, 102–146. For requisite secondary literature, consult the collection of essays in Twersky, ed., *Rabbi Moses Nahmanides (Ramban);* Chazan, *Barcelona and Beyond*, esp. ch. 1.

25. For socioeconomic background see Baron, *A Social and Religious History of the Jews,* vol. 10, 139–151; Cantera, "La Juderia de Burgos."

26. Baron, *A Social and Religious History,* 146.

27. I am well aware of the many layers and voices in the Zohar, and here follow Wolfson, who writes, "I still think the zoharic anthology preserves multiple voices, including ideas either absent from or contradictory to treatises of Moses de León, but I nevertheless maintain on hermeneutical grounds that it is possible to continue to speak of a unifying factor that allows for difference. . . ." See Wolfson, *Language, Eros, Being,* 48.

28. E.g., Liebes, *Studies in the Zohar,* 99–105.

29. Scholem, *The Kabbalah in Gerona,* 25–32.

30. See Gershenzon, "A Tale of Two Midrashim," 134–135.

31. E.g., *Ezer ha-Dat,* 157–158.

32. Baer, *A History of the Jews of Christian Spain,* vol. 1, 331.

33. It also seems likely, for example, that Isaac Albalag studied with Abner. In this regard, see Vajda, *Isaac Albalag,* appendix 2, 275–276. Moreover, Moses Narboni is also familiar with Abner's work and directed some of the criticisms in his *Ma'amar ha-Beḥira* ("Treatise on Free Will") against him.

34. Abner of Burgos, *Teshuvot la-Meḥaref,* 13b, qtd. in Gershenzon, "A Study of *Teshuvot la-Meharef,*" 15.

35. Norman Roth, for example, intimates that Polleqar's response to Abner was unsatisfactory as it did not successfully refute Abner's often superior arguments. See his "Isaac Polgar y su libro contra un converso."

36. Baer, *A History of the Jews of Christian Spain,* vol. 1, 329–330; idem, "Abner von Burgos," 20–24.

37. Baer, *A History of the Jews of Christian Spain,* vol. 1, 280; Carlos Saiz de la Maza, "Aristóteles, Alejandro y la polemice antijudaica en al signo xiv," 146.

38. See Valle Rodriguez, "*El Libro de la Batalla de Dios,* de Abner de Burgos," 78–79.

39. Baer, *A History of the Jews of Christian Spain,* vol. 1, 333.

40. Ibid., vol. 1, 330.

41. This is, for example, the opinion of Chazan, "Maestre Alfonso of Valladolid and the New Missionizing"; Valle Rodriguez, "*La Contradicción del Hereje* de Issac ben Polger."

42. This is especially true of his *Libro de las tres creencias* (Book of the Three Creeds), which has key biblical quotations transliterated into Spanish presumably for polemicists who did not speak Hebrew to employ against Jews. See Carpenter, "The Language of Polemic."

43. See the comments in Yuval, "Yitzhak Baer and the Search for Authentic Judaism."

44. Baer, "*Sefer Minhat Qenaot* of Abner of Burgos and Its Influence on Hasdai Crescas." For a dissenting opinion, however, see Feldman, "Crescas' Theological Determinism."

45. Manekin, "Hebrew Philosophy in the Fourteenth and Fifteenth Centuries," 366–368; Tirosh-Samuelson, *Happiness in Premodern Judaism,* 373–379; Gershenzon, "The View of Maimonides as a Determinist in *Sefer Minhat Qenaot* by Abner of Burgos," 94–97; idem, "A Tale of Two Midrashim."

46. Gershenzon, "A Study of *Teshuvot la-Meharef,*" 24–26.

47. Ibid., 25.

48. E.g., "Once I was engaged in a dispute with a man who was knowledgeable

and wise in the way of religion and philosophy, but he ultimately decided to fulfill his desire and his heart turned from the ways of our Torah, his name was Rabbi Abner" (*Ezer ha-Dat,* 60).

49. Gershenzon, "A Study of *Teshuvot la-Meharef,*" 25–26.

50. For requisite background literature on the role of principles of faith, see Kellner, *Dogma in Medieval Judaism.*

51. Also see the comments in Melamad, *The Philosopher-King in Medieval and Renaissance Jewish Political Thought,* 93–101.

52. *Ezer ha-Dat,* 70.

53. Ibid., 93.

54. Manekin, "Hebrew Philosophy in the Fourteenth and Fifteenth Centuries," 366–369.

55. *Ezer ha-Dat,* 142.

56. In addition to the *Ezer* and the three treatises from which it is compiled, we also know that Polleqar composed a commentary on Genesis, Qoheleth, and Psalms. In this regard, see *Ezer ha-Dat,* 121, 131. He also continued Albalag's commentary to Alghazali's *Maqāsid al-falasifa* (Intentions of the Philosophers). See Valle Rodriguez, "*La Contradicción del Hereje* de Isaac ben Polgar," 554. For a list of Abner's various publications, see J. Rosenthal, "Mi-tokh sefer Alfonso," 620f.

57. E.g., Chazan, *Fashioning Jewish Identity in Medieval Western Christendom,* ch. 15; Lasker, *Jewish Philosophical Polemics against Christianity,* 25–43.

58. Cohen, *The Friars and the Jews,* 97.

59. Ibid., 156.

60. Ibid., 156–160.

61. Another well-known Jewish response to a disputation is found in *Sefer ha-Ikkarim* by Joseph Albo (1380–1444), a work that he wrote partly in response to his involvement at that Disputation of Tortosa (1413–1414).

62. A good summary of these debates may be found in Chazan, *Barcelona and Beyond,* 4–12.

63. Baer, "On the Disputations of R. Yeḥiel of Paris and R. Moses ben Naḥman."

64. Maccoby, *Judaism on Trial,* 74–75.

65. Chazan, *Barcelona and Beyond,* 13–16.

66. Ibid., 107–115.

67. *Ezer ha-Dat,* 166–167.

68. Ibid., 87.

69. Ibid., 142.

70. Ibid., 142.

71. Ibid., 143

72. On the difference between *hamon* and *kahal* in the dialogue, see Belasco, "Isaac Pulgar's 'Support of the Religion,'" 48.

73. In this, Gabriel functions much as the king does in the second dialogue of *Ezer ha-Dat.*

74. *Ezer ha-Dat,* 176.

75. Ibid., 178.

76. For a dissenting voice, one based on a fascinating local analysis of the Jews of Valencia, see Meyerson, *A Jewish Renaissance in Fifteenth Century Spain.*

77. *Ezer ha-Dat,* 35.

78. Ibid., 35.

79. Ibid., 69.

80. Ibid., 70.

81. Ibid., 71–72.

82. The term that the old man applies for alliance is *berit,* a religious term denoting a covenant or covenantal agreement.

83. *Ezer ha-Dat,* 84–87.

84. Ibid., 88–89.

85. In many ways, this is similar to the *ḥaver*'s critique in the *Kuzari.*

86. Here I differ from Pines, who regards the youth as the "mouthpiece" of Polleqar. See his "Spinoza's *Tractatus Theologico-Politicus* and the Jewish Philosophical Tradition," 502. Pines argues that Polleqar's position on prophecy is very radical, anticipating Spinoza, because Polleqar negates the Maimonidean principle that the prophet does not have to have a perfected intellectual faculty. In this regard, also see Pines, "Some Topics Dealt with in Polleqar's Treatise 'Ezer ha-Dat' and Parallels in Spinoza." Disagreeing with Pines, I regard the young man certainly as a radical philosopher, but not the "mouthpiece" of Polleqar, whose own position only becomes clear as the dialogue progresses.

87. *Ezer ha-Dat,* 92–93. I quoted the second part of this passage in another context above.

88. Ibid., 93–94.

89. Ibid., 100.

90. Such, at least, is the opinion of Levinger in his critical edition.

91. *Ezer ha-Dat,* 101.

92. Ibid., 101–102.

93. On the various views concerning creation in post-Maimonidean Jewish philosophy, see Seeskin, *Maimonides on the Origin of the World,* 182–198.

94. *Ezer ha-Dat,* 104.

95. Manekin, "Hebrew Philosophy in the Fourteenth and Fifteenth Centuries," 367.

96. Ibid., 368.

97. See the discussion in Tirosh-Samuelson, *Happiness in Premodern Judaism,* 375.

98. Manekin, "Hebrew Philosophy in the Fourteenth and Fifteenth Centuries," 367.

99. See Chazan, *Fashioning Jewish Identity in Medieval Western Christendom,* 188.

100. *Ezer ha-Dat,* 105.

101. Ibid., 106.

102. On the role of magic and astral magic in medieval Jewish thought, see Schwartz, *Astral Magic in Medieval Jewish Thought,* 219–261; Sela, *Astrology and Biblical Exegesis in the Thought of Abraham Ibn Ezra,* 11–26.

103. *Ezer ha-Dat,* 107.

104. Ibid., 108.

105. Ibid., 109–111.

106. Ibid., 119. The last two sentences of this have been adapted from Sirat, *A History of Jewish Philosophy in the Middle Ages,* 320.

107. Manekin, 367.

108. Guttmann, *Philosophies of Judaism,* 205.

109. *Ezer ha-Dat,* 120.

110. Ibid., 135.

111. Ibid., 138.

112. Ibid., 129–130.

113. See, for example, D. Berger, "Jewish-Christian Polemics"; idem, "Mission to the Jews and Jewish-Christian Contacts in Polemical Literature of the High Middle Ages"; Chazan, *Fashioning Jewish Identity in Medieval Western Christendom,* 122–140.

114. See, for example, Joseph Kimḥi, *Sefer ha-Berit,* 44–46; *The Book of the Covenant,* 54–56.

115. See the introductory sections of Robinson, "Philosophy and Exegesis in Ibn Tibbon's Commentary on Ecclesiastes."

116. *Ezer ha-Dat,* 120–121.

117. Ibid., 121.

118. The book of Proverbs, like that of Qoheleth, was also thought to be composed by Solomon.

119. *Ezer ha-Dat,* 122–123.

120. See the block quotation above, 89.

121. E.g., *Ezer ha-Dat,* 122–123.

122. Ibid., 141.

5. Judah Abravanel

1. I prefer to use the form Judah Abravanel for the simple reason that this was his name. Leone Ebreo (or Hebreo), on the other hand, is a generic name given to many Jews in the Renaissance. See, for example, the discussion in Dorman, "Introduction: Judah Abravanel, His Life and Works," in *Sihot 'al ha-Ahavah,* 14.

2. Tirosh-Rothschild, *Between Worlds,* 4.

3. Note, however, as Idel cautions, that the tragedy of the Spanish exiles did not necessarily alter radically the dynamics of Jewish culture, especially those found in Italy. See his "Religion, Thought, and Attitudes"; idem, "Encounters between Spanish and Italian Kabbalists in the Generation of the Expulsion."

4. Perhaps the most extreme comment comes from Sirat, who writes that it was "written in a secular language and represent[s] a work of profane philosophy" (*A History of Jewish Philosophy in the Middle Ages,* 408).

5. I say unprecedented because even Maimonides' *Guide,* although published in Arabic, was nonetheless written in Hebrew characters, thereby keeping out a non-Jewish reading public. The *Dialoghi,* on the contrary, was composed in Italian for all and sundry to read. And read it they did, for, as will become apparent, the work subsequently became a non-Jewish best-seller throughout Europe.

6. On the various ways in which the term *Renaissance* has been deployed, see Hay, "Historians and the Renaissance during the Last Twenty-Five Years"; Celenza, *The Lost Italian Renaissance,* xi–xx. As for Jews and the Renaissance, it is important not to romanticize the relationship. According to Tirosh-Rothschild, "The Renaissance was not an epoch of tolerance, secularism, and individualism as Jewish historians from the late nineteenth century to the 1960s portrayed it, neither did the Renaissance anticipate the Emancipation or the beginning of modernity for Jews" (*Between Worlds,* 3). See further, idem, "Jewish Culture in Renaissance Italy," 63–68. For an argument that is highly critical of the view that Jews simply adopted and adapted to the Renaissance, see Bonfil, "The Historian's Perception of the Jews in the Italian Renaissance." Bonfil is particularly critical of the "harmonistic" portrayal in the work of, e.g., Ruderman, references to whose work may be found in subsequent notes.

7. For a somewhat outdated English translation, see *The Philosophy of Love.* All translations from this work are my own. For convenience, though, subsequent citations from this work will give the page number from the standard Italian edition of Caramella, with the page number from the English translation in parentheses.

8. Trinkaus defines *Humanism* as "deeply concerned with the dignity of man, giving new importance to human values while taking full account of human limitations. This approach, which was central to the Renaissance, gave expression to a renewed interest in man in his historical setting and to a heightened appreciation of the qualities and achievements, the 'wonders' of man, without any repudiation of the Creator in whose image man was wrought." See Trinkaus, *The Scope of Renaissance Humanism,* 22. On Humanism more generally, see idem, "Renaissance Humanism, Its Formation and Development," in *The Scope of Renaissance Humanism,* 3–31; Garin, *Italian Humanism,* 18–36. On different constructions and understandings of Humanism in contemporary secondary literature, see Weinstein, "In Whose Image and Likeness"; Celenza, *The Lost Italian Renaissance,* 16–57.

9. Tirosh-Rothschild, "Jewish Philosophy on the Eve of Modernity," 519.

10. Although it is worth pointing out here that I fully concur with Kristeller who argues that rather than see in the Renaissance a sharp break from the medieval period, we need to envisage the former as continuing a number of trends and trajectories of the latter. See in particular Kristeller, "Humanism and Scholasticism in the Italian Renaissance," in his *Renaissance Thought and Its Sources,* 85–105; idem, "Renaissance Philosophy and the Medieval Tradition," in *Renaissance Thought and Its Sources,* 106–133.

11. E.g., Black, *Logic and Aristotle's Rhetoric and Poetics in Medieval Arabic Philosophy,* 1–51.

12. E.g., Cantarino, *Arabic Poetics in the Golden Age.*

13. This is so, even though he wrote this work when he had lived for many years as an exile from Granada and Islamdom.

14. Ibn Ezra, *Kitāb al-muhādara wa al-mudhākara,* 12. See the comments in Melamed, "Rhetoric as Persuasive Instrument in Medieval Jewish Thought," 166–167.

15. E.g., al-Fārābī, *Risāla fī qawānīn sināʿa al-shʿir,* 149–158; Avicenna, *Kitāb al-majmuʿ: al-ḥikma al-ʿarūdiyya fī maʿānī kitāb al-shʿir.* See the discussion in my *Texture of the Divine,* 45–46.

16. Altmann, "*Ars Rhetorica* as Reflected in Some Jewish Figures of the Italian Renaissance."

17. Judah Messer Leon, *The Book of the Honeycomb's Flow,* 144–145.

18. See the discussion in Tirosh-Rothschild, *Between Worlds,* 66–73.

19. Judah Messer Leon, *The Book of the Honeycomb's Flow,* 40–41. On the specific role of rhetoric in this work, see Abraham Melamed, "Rhetoric and Philosophy in *Nofet Ṣufim* by R. Judah Messer Leon."

20. See my "Transforming the Maimonidean Imagination," 479–483.

21. Here I follow the lead of Brian Vickers, "Rhetoric and Poetics." A useful discussion can also be found in Panofsky, *Idea: A Concept in Art Theory.*

22. Tirosh-Rothschild, "Jewish Philosophy on the Eve of Modernity," 522–524.

23. *Dialoghi* I. 43 (Friedeberg-Seeley and Barnes, 46).

24. Ibid., III. 274 (Friedeberg-Seeley and Barnes, 324).

25. Ibid., III. 274 (Friedeberg-Seeley and Barnes, 323).

26. Ibid., II. 100 (Friedeberg-Seeley and Barnes, 113).

27. See the comments in Hankins, *Plato in the Italian Renaissance,* vol. 1, 4–5.

28. A dated, though still highly useful, study remains Garin, "Ricerche sulle traduzioni di Platone nella prima metà del sec. XV."

29. Kristeller, "Renaissance Platonism," in his *Renaissance Thought and Its Sources*, 48–69; Hankins, *Plato in the Italian Renaissance*, 3–26.

30. See the comments in Garin, *La cultura filosofica del Rinascimento italiano*, 93–102; idem, *Il ritorno dei filosofi antichi*, 21–30.

31. E.g., Trinkaus, *The Poet as Philosopher*, 1–26; Foster, *Petrarch*, 23–47; O'Rourke Boyle, *Petrarch's Genius*, 44–70.

32. Alemanno, *Hay Ha'Olamim*. For secondary works, consult Lelli, "L'educazione ebraica nella seconda metà del '400"; idem, "Umanismo Larenziano nell'opera di Yohanan Alemanno."

33. Melamed argues that the work belongs to the genre of the "Hebrew Encyclopedia." See his "The Hebrew Encyclopedias of the Renaissance," 448–454.

34. For Hebrew texts and English translation, see Lesley, "*The Song of Solomon's Ascents* by Yohanan Alemanno."

35. The best short history of Neapolitan history remains Croce, *History of the Kingdom of Naples*.

36. Bentley, *Politics and Culture in Renaissance Naples*, 102–103.

37. Percopo, *Vita di Giovanni Pontani*, 106–119; Santoro, "La cultura umanistica," 159–171.

38. Tasso, "Discourse on the Art of the Dialogue," in *Tasso's Dialogues*. The suggestion to look at this work comes from Lesley, "Proverbs, Figures, and Riddles," 220–221.

39. Tasso, "Discourse on the Art of the Dialogue," 25.

40. Ibid., 37.

41. Ficino, *El Libro dell'amore;* translated in English as *Commentary on Plato's Symposium*.

42. Pico della Mirandola, *Commento sopra una canzone d'amore*. An English translation may be found in *Commentary on a Canzone of Benivieni by Giovanni Pico della Mirandola*. On the details surrounding its publication, see the comments in Garin, "Marsilio Ficino, Girolamo Benivieni e Giovanni Pico"; Jayne's introduction to his English translation of the Commentary, 1–20.

43. Although this is not the place to analyze in detail the work of Pico, it is worth pointing out that although published as a commentary, it was in fact anything but. Rather, it was three unfinished treatises—a treatise on love, a treatise on mythology, and a commentary on Plato's *Symposium*—all wrapped into one. Moreover, the "commentary" was published so much later because Benivieni suppressed it owing to his high regard for Ficino and his account of love.

44. See Wirszubski, *Pico della Mirandola's Encounter with Jewish Mysticism*, 121–185.

45. I retain the term *Cabala* and *Cabalist* in these obviously Christian or christianizing contexts in order to differentiate from the "kabbalah" practiced in a Jewish context by "kabbalists."

46. *Commentary on a Canzone by Benivieni*, 143.

47. Nelson, *Renaissance Theory of Love*, 130; also see my "Epigone, Innovator, or Apologist?"

48. "Il Raverta" and "La Leonare," in *Trattati d'amore del Cinquecento*.

49. "Dialoghi d'amore," in his *Opere*, vol. 1, 1–45.

50. "Della infinitá di amore," in *Trattati d'amore del Cinquecento*, 187–247.

51. See, for example, Guidotti, *Tre Inventari di Bicchierai Toscani fra Cinque e Seicento;* Giovanardi, *La Teoria Cortigiana e il Dibattito linguistico nel Primo Cinquecento*.

52. E.g., Bembo, *Gli Asolani.* An English translation may be found in Gottfried, trans., *Gli Asolani.*

53. E.g., *Dialoghi* I. 5–6; II. 61–62; III. 171–172, 391 (Friedeberg-Seeley and Barnes, 3–4; 67–68; 197–198, 468). In this regard, see Yavneh, "The Spiritual Eroticism of Leone's Hermaphrodite."

54. This section draws on the biographical section of my "Abrabanel, Judah."

55. For recent literature on Isaac Abravanel, see Lawee, *Isaac Abarbanel's Stance Toward Tradition,* 9–57; Feldman, *Philosophy in a Time of Crisis,* 3–31.

56. For an examination of the typical education curriculum of an elite Jew at this time, see Idel, "The Study Program of R. Yohanan Alemmano."

57. This is the way that Judah writes of the scandal in his autobiographical poem, *Telunah ʿal ha-zeman* ("The Travails of Time"), composed in 1503:

> His courtiers and his brother schemed revolt.
> He thwarted them and killed his brother: then,
> alleging that my father was with them,
> he tried to kill him too! But God,
> the Rider of the clouds, preserved his life.
> My father fled to Castile, home of my ancestors,
> my family's source. But as for me,
> The King seized all my gold and silver,
> took as forfeit everything I owned.

See Abravanel, "*Telunah ʿal ha-zeman,*" 216–222. The English translation comes from Scheindlin, "Judah Abrabanel to His Son," 195.

58. Again, he describes this poetically:

> The day the King of Spain expelled the Jews
> he ordered that a watch be set for me
> so that I not slip away through mountain passes,
> and that my child, still nursing, should be seized
> and brought into his faith on his behalf.
> A good man got word to me in time, a friend;
> I sent him with his wet-nurse in the dark
> of midnight—just like smuggled goods!—
> to Portugal, then ruled by a wicked king
> who earlier had nearly ruined me.
> . . .
> My darling boy was taken, and his good name,
> the name of the rock from which I was hewn,
> changed!
> He's twelve years old; I haven't seen him since—
> so are my sins repaid!
> I rage, but only at myself:
> there's no one else but me to bear the blame.
> I chased him from mere troubles to a trap,
> I drove him from mere sparks into a flame.
> I hope to see him, heartsick with my endless hope. (Scheindlin, 195)

59. Scheindlin, 193.

60. Roth, *The Jews of the Renaissance,* 129.

61. Scheindlin, 198; see the comments in Veltri, "'Philo and Sophia,'" 60–62.

62. Those who insist that he did also argue that he might have met Pico when he first arrived in Italy, and that, perhaps, he made his way north. See, for example, Roth, *The Jews in the Renaissance,* 130–131.

63. See the discussion in Sonne, "On the Question of the Original Language of the *Dialoghi d'amore* of Judah Abravanel," 146–148; Dorman, "Introduction," 86–95.

64. *Dialoghi* III. 239, 351 (Friedeberg-Seeley and Barnes, 280, 418).

65. Ibid., III. 245 (Friedeberg-Seeley and Barnes, 289).

66. See the comments in Ruderman, "Italian Renaissance and Jewish Thought," 407–412.

67. On the debates surrounding the language of the *Dialoghi* in the secondary literature, see Dorman, "Introduction," 86–95.

68. Such is the opinion of Sonne, "On the Question," 147–148; Lesley, "The Place of the *Dialoghi d'Amore* in Contemporaneous Jewish Thought."

69. Azaria de' Rossi, *Meqor Einayim,* 10.

70. Tullia d'Aragona, *"Della Infintà de amore,"* in *Trattati d'amore del Cinquecento,* 225. The work itself was originally published in 1547.

71. Of particular interest is Pietro Bembo (1470–1547) a contemporary of Judah Abravanel, and someone who also wrote an important dialogue of love. In his *Prose della volgar lingua,* Bembo made the case that Italian writers of his generation should write in Tuscan rather than in other dialects. Although he did not publish this work until 1525, he nevertheless wrote some time between 1497 and 1502 his *Gli Asolani,* itself a dialogue on love, in Italian, and which was subsequently published in 1505. This was one of the earliest examples of a prose work written in Italian. This, in turn, was intimately related to the emerging role of Tuscan nationalism. In this regard, also see Sansone, *Da Bembo a Galiani,* 24–36.

72. Garvin, "The Language of Leone Ebreo's *Dialoghi d'Amore,"* 194.

73. For general background, see Tirosh-Rothschild, *Between Worlds,* 85–90.

74. For a dated though still useful analysis of where and how Judah's work fits into the Renaissance genre of the *trattato d'amore,* see Nelson, *Renaissance Theory of Love,* 67–162

75. Arthur Lesley, for example, writes that "the *Dialogues of Love* by Yehuda Abravanel has attracted more attention from historians of Jewish philosophy than its influence on later Jewish thought deserves." See his "Proverbs, Figures, and Riddles," 204. Also see the comments in Sirat, *A History of Jewish Philosophy in the Middle Ages,* 408, qtd. above, 194, n. 4.

76. As examples he cites the work of Philo, ibn Gabirol's *Meqor ḥayyim,* and Abravanel's *Dialoghi.* See his "On the Concept of Beauty in the Philosophy of Judah Abravanel," 28.

77. *Dialoghi,* II. 111 (Friedeberg-Seeley and Barnes, 126). Further examples may be found in II. 122–123, 126–127; III. 178, 186, 245–246, 248–251, 275–277, 279–280, 291–305, 336–337, 345–350, 385 (Friedeberg-Seeley and Barnes, 139, 143–145, 205, 215, 289, 292–296, 325–327, 330–331, 345–362, 400–401, 424, 460).

78. E.g., *Dialoghi* III. 178, 264, 291–295, 300, 302, 303, 304, 351, 352, 353, 354, 355, 382, 383, 385, 386 (Friedeberg-Seeley and Barnes, 205, 312, 345–350, 357, 359, 360, 361, 419, 420 [5 times], 421 [4 times], 422, 423 [4 times], 424, 456, 457 [4 times], 460 [3 times]). The Hebrew translation of Dorman is especially useful in this regard as it lists in the footnotes all of the biblical and rabbinic prooftexts employed.

79. *Dialoghi* III. 239 (Friedeberg-Seeley and Barnes, 280). Also see the comments in *Dialoghi* III. 351 (Friedeberg-Seeley and Barnes, 418).

80. E.g., *Dialoghi* II. 126–127; III. 351–358 (Friedeberg-Seeley and Barnes, 139–140; 418–427).

81. E.g., *Dialoghi* III. 275–277 (Friedeberg-Seeley and Barnes, 325–327).

82. E.g., *Dialoghi* II. 178 (Friedeberg-Seeley and Barnes, 205–206).

83. *Dialoghi* III. 355 (Friedeberg-Seeley and Barnes, 422). Other examples may be found in *Dialoghi* II. 122, 126–127; III. 178, 245–246, 248–251, 264, 300–304, 352, 382–383 (Friedeberg-Seeley and Barnes, 139, 143–145, 205, 289, 292–296, 312, 357–361, 420, 456–457).

84. *Dialoghi* III. 351–355 (Friedeberg-Seeley and Barnes, 418–427).

85. E.g., *Dialoghi* I. 52; III. 183, 226–229 (Friedeberg-Seeley and Barnes, 57; 212, 264–268). See McGinn, "Cosmic and Sexual Love in Renaissance Thought."

86. The English translation comes from *Heptaplus,* found in *On the Dignity of Man, On Being and the One, and Heptaplus,* 92–93.

87. Lesley, "The Place of the *Dialoghi* in Contemporaneous Jewish Thought," 182.

88. *Dialoghi* III. 291 (Friedeberg-Seeley and Barnes, 345).

89. E.g., *Dialoghi* III. 348 (Friedeberg-Seeley and Barnes, 415).

90. Compare, for example, *Dialoghi* III. 367–375 (Friedeberg-Seeley and Barnes, 438–444) and *Guide of the Perplexed* III. 51.

91. E.g., *Dialoghi* III. 382–387 (Friedeberg-Seeley and Barnes, 456–462). See the comments in Harvey, *Physics and Metaphysics in Hasdai Crescas,* 114–117.

92. Barzilay, *Yoseph Shlomo Delmedigo (Yashar of Candia),* 31–32.

93. See, for example, Idel, "Kabbalah, Platonism and Prisca Theologia."

94. See the comments in Ruderman, *Jewish Thought and Scientific Discovery in Early Modern Europe,* 153–163.

95. Solmi, *Benedetto Spinoza e Leone Ebreo,* 34–53; Ze'ev Levy, *Baruch or Benedict,* 2–25.

96. In saying this, however, I am well aware of the difficulty, if not impossibility, of understanding women and gender through male-authored texts. See, in this regard, Rosen, *Unveiling Eve,* 20–29.

97. Here I base my comments on Tirosh-Samuelson, "Editor's Introduction: Jewish Philosophy in Conversation with Feminism," in *Women and Gender in Jewish Philosophy,* 5–11.

98. Many of my comments in this section draw on Melamed, "The Woman as Philosopher." For valid criticism of Melamed's approach to the Maimonidean treatment of women, see Rosen, *Unveiling Eve,* 239–240, n. 49.

99. The best example of this is Diotima, the Mantinean woman, in *Symposium* 201d–212b.

100. E.g. Bembo, *Gli Asolani,* 21, 81, 97.

101. For a detailed discussion of his life and times, see Ruderman, *Kabbalah, Magic, and Science.*

102. Abraham Yagel, *Eshet Hayyil,* qtd. in Adelman, "Finding Women's Voices in Italian Jewish Literature," 53; see also idem, "The Educational and Literary Activities of Jewish Women in Italy during the Renaissance and the Catholic Restoration."

103. Melamed, "The Woman as Philosopher," 123.

104. *Dialoghi* I. 5 (Friedeberg-Seeley and Barnes, 3).

105. *Dialoghi* I. 58 (Friedeberg-Seeley and Barnes, 64). See the comments in Melamed, "The Woman as Philosopher," 125.

106. E.g., *Dialoghi* III. 200–201 (Friedeberg-Seeley and Barnes, 233–234).

107. *Dialoghi* III. 222–224; 241 (Friedeberg-Seeley and Barnes, 259–262; 283).

108. *Dialoghi* III. 336 (Friedeberg-Seeley and Barnes, 400).

109. Melamed, "The Woman as Philosopher," 129.

110. This is not to say, of course, that one does not find more stereotypical comments on the passivity of females vis-à-vis the activity of males. See, for example, *Dialoghi* II. 79–80 (Friedeberg-Seeley and Barnes, 89–90).

111. *Dialoghi* III. 217–218 (Friedeberg-Seeley and Barnes, 254).

112. E.g., *Dialoghi* I. 52; III. 183, 226–229 (Friedeberg-Seeley and Barnes, 57; 212, 264–268). See McGinn, "Cosmic and Sexual Love in Renaissance Thought," 191–195.

113. Nelson, *Renaissance Theory of Love,* 70.

114. Castiglione, *Il Cortigiano,* book IV, liii, 476–477.

115. Equicola, *Libro di natura d'amore,* 71. For requisite secondary literature, see Burke, *The Fortunes of the Courtier,* 19–38.

116. See my "Transforming the Maimonidean Imagination," 474–479.

117. *Dialoghi* III. 269 (Friedeberg-Seeley and Barnes, 318).

118. See Hughes, *The Texture of the Divine,* 146–187.

119. *Dialoghi* III. 377 (Friedeberg-Seeley and Barnes, 450). The source of this concept has been the subject of some debate. According to Suzanne Damiens, Abravanel would have derived this from Ficino by way of the Alexandrian mystics, especially Pseudo-Dionysius. See her *Amor et Intellect chez Léon L'Hébreu,* 162–166. Zimmels sees in it a kabbalistic influence. See, in particular, his *Leone Hebreo,* 39. Idel, however, claims that Judah Abravanel's source is al-Batalyawsi, perhaps as received from his father's commentary to Genesis, or from Yohanan Alemanno. See Idel, "The Source of the Circle of Love in the *Dialoghi d'amore,*" 156. I should also like to add to this conversation that we find as early as Proclus, who lived in the fifth century, the notion of mutual attraction of the imperfect for the perfect and the perfect for the imperfect. See, for example, his *Commentary on Plato's Parmenides,* 53–54.

120. *Dialoghi* III. 378 (Friedeberg-Seeley and Barnes, 451).

121. Ibid., II. 195–196 (Friedeberg-Seeley and Barnes, 227).

122. Brann, *The Compunctious Poet,* 58.

123. I have consulted the Latin text with facing English translation in Ficino, *Platonic Theology,* vol. 1, 8–11.

124. Kristeller, *The Philosophy of Marsilio Ficino,* 27.

125. Ibid., 322.

126. Ruderman, *The World of a Renaissance Jew,* 45.

127. Ficino, *Commentary on Plato's Symposium,* trans. Sears Jayne, Speech II, ch. 1 (45).

128. Ibid., Speech II, ch. 4 (50).

129. Carmichael, trans., in *On the Dignity of Man, On Being and the One, and Heptaplus,* 84.

130. *Heptaplus,* 85.

131. See *Heptaplus,* 92–93, which is quoted above on 123.

132. See the discussion in Ruderman, *The World of a Renaissance Jew,* 47–52.

133. Here I tend to agree with parts of Craven's argument, which stresses the apologetic and proselytizing agenda of Pico's work. See his *Giovanni Pico della Mirandola, Symbol of His Age.*

134. *Heptaplus,* 161.

135. Pico della Mirandola, *Commentary on a Canzone of Benivieni,* 81.

136. *Dialoghi* II. 126–127 (Friedeberg-Seeley and Barnes, 143–145).

137. Ibid., III. 289–291 (Friedeberg-Seeley and Barnes, 342–345). Parts of this section are quoted above, 123.

6. Moses Mendelssohn

1. Examples of such secondary literature include Beck, *Early German Philosophy,* 414–416; Roberts, *German Philosophy,* 163; Beiser, *German Idealism,* 39.

2. See the comments in Altmann, *Moses Mendelssohn,* 638–653. On the periodization of the Enlightenment, and how the Jewish Enlightenment either relates to or departs from it, see Feiner, *The Jewish Enlightenment,* 33.

3. An exhaustive account of the Lavater affair complete with translations of the requisite source material may be found in Altmann, *Moses Mendelssohn,* 194–263.

4. As recent scholars have argued, however, it is important to separate Mendelssohn the individual from Mendelssohn the symbol. The latter was the larger-than-life figure that later *maskilim* (practitioners of *Haskalah*) credited with leading German Jewry from darkness to light. His disciples (e.g., David Friedländer) and early biographers (e.g., Isaac Euchel) were largely responsible for the creation of this legend. See the comments in Feiner, *Haskalah and Historiography,* 27–60. But, if some regarded Mendelssohn as the symbol of transformation, others saw in him the symbol of German Jewry's assimilation. See the comments in Sorkin, *Moses Mendelssohn and the Religious Enlightenment,* xviii–xix. Yet, despite the fact that Mendelssohn was certainly the most famous Jew of the eighteenth century, it is important to recognize that he was but one individual, albeit a very important one, in the emergence of the *Haskalah.*

5. A convenient list of the various editions and translations appears in Meyer, *Moses Mendelssohn Bibliographie,* 39–44.

6. Natural religion refers primarily to a set of religious beliefs, grounded solely in reason. The opposite of natural religion is "revealed religion," whose beliefs emerge not from reason but from a particular scripture. The best attempt to show the impossibility of "natural religion" was expressed in the form of a series of dialogues by a contemporary of Mendelssohn, the Scotsman David Hume (1711–1776), whose *Dialogues Concerning Natural Religion* was published posthumously in 1779.

7. Mendelssohn, *Gesammelte Schriften,* vol. 5, 446–449.

8. This view is argued most persuasively in Cassirer, *The Philosophy of the Enlightenment;* also see Gay, *The Enlightenment.*

9. E.g., the collection of essays in Gordon, ed., *Postmodernism and the Enlightenment.* On Judaism's place in this, see Sutcliffe, *Judaism and Enlightenment,* 1–19.

10. Dubin, "The Social and Cultural Context," 640.

11. Here it is important to nuance the various "waves" of the *Haskalah,* with each wave having concerns unique to its particular time. For example, the early *maskilim,* which included the likes of Mendelssohn and Wessely, tended to be very conservative, arguing, for example, that *halakhah* was an essential part of Jewish life. Later *maskilim,* for example, Friedländer and Euchel, were much less likely to hold this position. See the important comments in, e.g., Sorkin, *The Transformation of German Jewry,* 41–62; Lowenstein, *The Berlin Jewish Community,* 69–73.

12. This was especially the case with Naphtali Herz Wessely's *Divrei shalom ve-emet* (Words of Peace and Truth) published in 1782, which set out, in practical terms, just how to go about reforming the traditional education curriculum. An English translation of this work may be found in Mendes-Flohr and Reinharz, eds., *The Jew in the Modern World,* 70–74. For appropriate contextualization, its reception, and the *Kulturkampf* it set off, consult Feiner, *The Jewish Enlightenment,* 87–104.

13. See the comments in Sorkin, *The Transformation of German Jewry,* 13–40.

14. Moses Mendelssohn, "On the Sentiments," in *Philosophical Writings,* 27.

15. Sorkin, *Moses Mendelssohn and the Religious Enlightenment,* 6.

16. Arkush, *Moses Mendelssohn and the Enlightenment,* 37.

17. See the comments in Beck, *Early German Philosophy,* 45–46, 376–382; on the role of German, see Blackall, *The Emergence of German as a Literary Language,* 26–48.

18. Feiner, *The Jewish Enlightenment,* 34.

19. In a letter of February 22, 1762, Mendelssohn writes to Thomas Abbt:

> My Shaftesbury translation has bogged down in the last few weeks. It is, however, to be continued shortly. This labor is of little benefit. The lord is a self-willed Englishman who many a times refuses to don a German outfit. How the company of a professor and a Jew will suit him I do not know. (*JubA* 11, letter 178, 296, qtd. in Altmann, *Moses Mendelssohn,* 110)

The truth of the matter is that Mendelssohn never finished the translation. Although, as I shall argue below, Shaftesbury's highly literary and dialogic style would nevertheless leave an indelible mark on Mendelssohn's thought.

20. See the comments in Sorkin, *Moses Mendelssohn and the Religious Enlightenment,* 8–9.

21. For Mendelssohn's high regard for Shaftesbury, see, e.g., *JubA* 11, letter 81, 181.

22. The *Characteristicks* would subsequently exert an important influence on British literature and the arts. See the comments in Yaffe, "Earl of Shaftesbury," 425.

23. Klein, *Shaftesbury and the Culture of Politeness,* 4.

24. Altmann, *Moses Mendelssohn,* 44.

25. *GS,* vol. 1, 13. For what seems like a more accurate picture of the events surrounding the publication of Mendelssohn's first work, see the comments in Altmann, *Moses Mendelssohn,* 38.

26. Mendelssohn, "On the Sentiments," in *Philosophical Writings,* 7.

27. *JubA* 16, letter 129 (to Elkan Herz), 153.

28. Mendelssohn, "On the Sentiments," in *Philosophical Writings,* 7.

29. Altmann, *Moses Mendelssohn,* 45.

30. See, e.g., his letter to Isaak Iselin from July 5, 1763, qtd. in Altmann, *Moses Mendelssohn,* 144–145.

31. For the details of this essay—submitted to a competition on the topic of what exactly did Alexander Pope mean by the phrase "all is good"—see Altmann, *Moses Mendelssohn,* 46–50.

32. Nicolai, Mendelssohn's publisher, writes of Mendelssohn's prose in the *Philosophische Gespräche:* "He labored with incredible tenacity to grasp, little by little, the character of this language, which was by no means his mother tongue. It is all the more admirable that, left entirely to his own devices, he achieved such considerable progress as the result of his exertions." *GS,* vol. 5, 205, qtd. in Altmann, *Moses Mendelssohn,* 39.

33. The most impressive of these is the exhaustive 900-page biography in Altmann, *Moses Mendelssohn.* A brief survey of other treatments of his life may be found, chronologically, in Michael A. Meyer, *The Origins of the Modern Jew,* 11–56; Schoeps, *Moses Mendelssohn;* Sorkin, *Moses Mendelssohn and the Religious Enlightenment;* Simon, *Moses Mendelssohn;* Bourel, *Moses Mendelssohn;* Feiner, *Moses Mendelssohn.*

34. Details of Fränkel may be found in Altmann, *Moses Mendelssohn,* 12–15.

35. *GS* vol. 5, 671–672, qtd. in *Moses Mendelssohn: Selections from His Writings,* 65–66.

36. Ibid., vol. 5, 206, qtd. in Altmann, *Moses Mendelssohn,* 15.

37. Berlin, and especially Jewish Berlin, of the mid-eighteenth century was undergoing major and rapid transformations. See the important study of Lowenstein, *The Berlin Jewish Community,* 10–22.

38. Biographical details may be found in Altmann, *Moses Mendelssohn,* 21–22.

39. Shear, "Judah Halevi's *Kuzari* in the *Haskalah*"; Ruderman, *Jewish Thought and Scientific Discovery in the Early Modern Europe,* 332–338.

40. Biographical details may be found in Altmann, *Moses Mendelssohn,* 23–25.

41. Mendelssohn, *GS,* vol. 5, 526.

42. Altmann, *Moses Mendelssohn,* 24.

43. See Meyer, *Moses Mendelssohn Bibliographie;* also, see the comments in Altmann, *Moses Mendelssohn,* 148.

44. In 1771, Mendelssohn was elected to become a member of the Royal Academy of Berlin; the king, however, vetoed his appointment.

45. Meyer, *The Origins of the Modern Jew,* 27.

46. The details of Michaelis's criticism and both Mendelssohn's and Lessing's response may be found in Altmann, *Moses Mendelssohn,* 40–44.

47. I have no intention of going into the details of this debate. Secondary literature that I have drawn upon includes Altmann, *Moses Mendelssohn,* 194–263; Meyer, *The Origins of the Modern Jew,* 29–40.

48. Goetshel, *Spinoza's Modernity,* 123.

49. *Nach Licht und Recht in einem Schreiben an Herrn Moses Mendelssohn auf Veranlassung seiner merkwürdigen Vorrede zu Manasseh Ben Israel* (Berlin, 1782), and republished in *JubA* 8.

50. See the comments in Katz, "To Whom Did Mendelssohn Reply in His *Jerusalem?*"

51. Details of the controversy may be found in Altmann, *Moses Mendelssohn,* 511–513; Arkush, *Moses Mendelssohn and the Enlightenment,* 222–229; Sorkin, *Moses Mendelssohn and the Religious Enlightenment,* 136–137; Goetshel, *Spinoza's Modernity,* 147–150.

52. *JubA* 3.1, 17. An early English translation of this work was made by Charles Cullen in 1789, which has recently been reprinted as *Phaedon, or the Death of Socrates,* intro. Curtis Bowman, xii–xiii. In following citations to this work, I shall, for the sake of convenience, put the page number from the English translation in parentheses.

53. *JubA* 3.1, 16 (Cullen, ix).

54. On the circumstances surrounding Mendelssohn's own death, which seems to have been precipitated by his own lack of concern for his physical well-being when, in a hurry to deliver a manuscript to a publisher, he went out without proper attire and subsequently got sick, see Altmann, *Moses Mendelssohn,* 729–741.

55. See Klein, *Shaftesbury and the Culture of Politeness,* 107–111.

56. Ibid., 42.

57. See the comments in Altmann, "Die Entstehung von Moses Mendelssohns *Phädon,*" 91–93.

58. *GS,* vol. 4.2, 128–129.

59. Ibid., vol. 4.2, 129.

60. *JubA* 11, letter 217, 346, qtd. in Altmann, *Moses Mendelssohn,* 111.

61. Ibid., vol. 3, 3–4.

62. Altmann, "Die Entstehung von Moses Mendelssohns *Phädon,*" 86–87.

63. Altmann, *Moses Mendelssohn,* 112.

64. See the comments in Schwarz, "Briefe Moses Mendelssohns an Isaak Iselin," 65. Fragments of the translation are extant and, according to Altmann, in the possession of a private collector (Altmann, *Moses Mendelssohn,* 780 n. 80).

65. Goetschel, *Spinoza's Modernity*, 87.

66. Krüger, *Christian Wolff und die Äesthetik*, 72–80.

67. *JubA* 1, 427. This paragraph owes much to Sorkin, *Moses Mendelssohn and the Religious Enlightenment*, 46–52.

68. Moses Mendelssohn, "On the Main Principles of the Fine Arts and Sciences," in *Philosophical Writings*, 172–173.

69. See, for example, "On the Main Principles of the Fine Arts and Sciences," 169–173. It is this principle, according to Sorkin, that was behind Mendelssohn's translation project (*Moses Mendelssohn and the Religious Enlightenment*, 50).

70. Compare, for example, the openings of both dialogues, in which Mendelssohn's (*JubA* 3.1, 40–43 [Cullen, 1–8]) follows Plato (57a–59d) virtually word for word.

71. *JubA* 3.1, 47 (Cullen, 18–19).

72. Ibid., 48–49 (Cullen, 22–24).

73. Ibid., 67–68 (Cullen, 66–67).

74. Ibid., 70 (Cullen, 74).

75. Ibid., 72–73 (Cullen, 78–80).

76. Ibid., 82–83 (Cullen, 102–103). Altmann posits that he is in fact a stand in for the French materialists, of whom Mendelssohn was so often critical. See his *Moses Mendelssohn*, 153–154.

77. Ibid., 93 (Cullen, 127–128).

78. Ibid., 114–115 (Cullen, 180–181).

79. Altmann, "Die Entstehung von Moses Mendelssohns *Phädon*," 84.

80. *JubA* 3.1, 8.

81. These include Christian Wolff, *Vernünftige Gedanken von Gott, der Welt und der Seele des Menschen* (1719); Johann Gustav Reinbeck's *Philosophical Thoughts on the Rational Soul and Its Immortality* (Berlin, 1740); Hubert Hayer, *La Spiritualité et l'immortalité de l'âme* (Paris, 1757).

82. As Altmann proclaims, "Nobody before him had hit upon the magnificent idea of rewriting Plato's *Phaedon*" (*Moses Mendelssohn*, 149).

83. For the reviews that accompanied the work's publication, see Altmann, *Moses Mendelssohn*, 149–150.

84. *JubA* 8, 157. For an English translation, see Mendelssohn, *Jerusalem*, 89–90. Emphasis in the original.

85. For requisite secondary literature on this aspect of Mendelssohn's thought, see Altmann, *Moses Mendelssohn*, 531–552; A. Eisen, "Divine Legislation as 'Ceremonial Script'"; Sorkin, *Moses Mendelssohn and the Religious Enlightenment*, 128–132; Morgan, "Mendelssohn," 666–677.

86. *JubA* 8, 166 (Arkush, 100). Emphasis in the original.

87. Which, of course, brings up numerous problems: Why were these laws given only to Israel? Or, on the other hand, if Christians can obtain salvation without this law, why should Jews require it? See the criticisms in Altmann, *Moses Mendelssohn*, 547–550; Guttmann, "Mendelssohn's *Jerusalem* and Spinoza's *Theologico-Political Treatise*," in *Studies in Jewish Thought*, 374–375; Seeskin, *Autonomy in Jewish Philosophy*, 142–143.

88. See the comments in Guttmann, "Mendelssohn's *Jerusalem* and Spinoza's *Theologico-Political Treatise*," 364.

89. Altmann, "Moses Mendelssohn's Concept of Judaism Re-examined," in his *Von der mittelalterlicher zur modernen Aufklärung*, 235–236.

90. *JubA* 3.1, 123 (Cullen, 200).

91. An English translation of this preface may be found in *Moses Mendelssohn: A Selection from His Writings,* 184.

92. *JubA* 3.1, 124 (Cullen, 202–203).

93. *GS,* vol. 5, 449, qtd. in Altmann, *Moses Mendelssohn,* 179.

94. Sorkin, *Moses Mendelssohn and the Religious Enlightenment,* 15.

95. *JubA* 16, 119 (letter 98), qtd. in Altmann, *Moses Mendelssohn,* 180.

96. On the work, see Gilon, *Mendelssohn's "Koheleth Musar" in Its Historical Context,* 83–91.

97. Rosenbloom, "Theological Impediments to a Hebrew Version of Mendelssohn's *Phaedon,*" 66–67. However, I am not sure I agree with this, since the goal of Mendelssohn's entire Hebrew oeuvre was to educate his fellow Jews by showing the mutual affinities between Judaism and Enlightenment thought.

98. Ibid., "Theological Impediments," 58.

99. See the comments in Rosenbloom, "Theological Impediments," 60–61; Altmann, *Moses Mendelssohn,* 191–193.

100. Wessely writes in the preface:

> [Beer Bing] translated this German treatise into our holy tongue. In some places he added words so as to render more intelligible some difficult expressions therein. He sent the translation, through one of his friends who resides here, to the learned author (may the memory of the righteous be for a blessing), while he was still alive, in order to obtain his judgment, and it did not find grace in his eyes. The author told me that he found it satisfactory and that he considered it a good piece of work. (qtd. in Altmann, *Moses Mendelssohn,* 192)

101. *JubA* 14, 123–144.

102. Ibid., 123.

103. Ibid., 128.

104. Ibid., 127.

105. Ibid., 126.

106. Qtd. in Altmann, *Moses Mendelssohn,* 190.

107. Perhaps the fragility of Mendelssohn's own project may be witnessed in the very fate of his own family: despite Mendelssohn's observance of the commandments as defined by traditional Judaism, four of his six children would ultimately convert to Christianity. See Lowenstein, *The Berlin Jewish Community,* 75–88.

Epilogue

1. By "modern Jewish philosophy" I refer primarily to the German-Jewish philosophical traditions and its main representatives: Hermann Cohen (1842–1918), Franz Rosenzweig (1886–1929), and Martin Buber (1878–1965). I am certainly aware that modern, much less contemporary, Jewish philosophy cannot be reduced to these three individuals; however, there can be no doubt that these three names represent the main pillars of philosophical speculation in the twentieth century.

2. E.g., Mieses, *Kinat haʾemet* (1828); Levinsohn, *Efes damim* (Vilna, 1837). For a study of this literature, see Feiner, *Haskalah and History,* 71–150.

3. Perhaps the best way to distinguish these terms is to employ Buber's distinc-

tion between an authentic "I-Thou" dialogue and the many inauthentic "I-It" encounters. See his *I and Thou,* 3–6.

4. E.g., Buber, *I and Thou,* 78–81.

5. Bergman, *Dialogical Philosophy from Kierkegaard to Buber,* 217–218; Horwitz, *Buber's Way to I and Thou,* 216–218; Silberstein, *Martin Buber's Social and Religious Thought,* 108–109.

6. One of Buber's earliest articles was entitled "Ein Wort über Nietzsche und die Lebenswerte"; we also know that, at seventeen, Buber had decided to translate *Thus Spake Zarathustra* into Polish.

7. E.g., Buber, *Daniel,* 140–144.

8. Ibid., 47.

9. Ibid., 64.

10. Ibid., 66.

11. Ibid., 67.

12. See the comments in Bergman, *Dialogical Philosophy from Kierkegaard to Buber,* 217.

13. Letter of Buber to Freedman, qtd. in "Translator's Preface" to Buber, *Daniel,* ix.

14. Buber, "Dialogue," 9.

15. For a critique of this principle along philosophical lines, see Katz, "Martin Buber's Epistemology." Despite the fact that Katz uses the term *dialogue* in his title, he is not at all interested in the genre by the same name.

16. Buber, "Dialogue Between Heaven and Earth," 224.

17. For an account of Cohen's life, times, and general intellectual milieu, see Myers, *Resisting History,* 35–67.

18. For a comparison of Buber's and Cohen's differing use of "I-Thou," see Horwitz, *Buber's Way to I and Thou,* 16–169.

19. See the comments in Seeskin, *Autonomy in Jewish Philosophy,* 178.

20. Cohen, *Religion of Reason out of the Sources of Judaism,* 147.

21. Bergman, *Dialogical Philosophy from Kierkegaard to Buber,* 153–154.

22. E.g., *Religion of Reason out of the Sources of Judaism,* 138–143. In this regard, see Seeskin's introductory essay in Cohen, *Religion of Reason out of the Sources of Judaism,* entitled "How to Read *Religion of Reason,*" 32–36. Also see the comments in Munk, "Who Is the Other?"

23. *Religion of Reason out of the Sources of Judaism,* 143.

24. Cohen expressed this philosophy of alterity in earlier works as well; see, for example, Hermann Cohen, *Ethics of Maimonides,* 152–153.

25. See the comments in Zank, *The Idea of Atonement in the Philosophy of Hermann Cohen,* 207–209, 360–389.

26. Nowhere is the relationship between the thought of Cohen and Rosenzweig clearer than in the latter's introduction to *Hermann Cohens Jüdische Schriften.*

27. Rosenzweig, "The New Thinking," 81–85.

28. E.g., Rosenzweig, *Star of Redemption,* 270–275, 310–314.

29. See the comments in Horwitz, "Franz Rosenzweig on Language," 395; Wolfson, "Facing the Effaced."

30. Rosenzweig, *Star of Redemption,* 237; See Mosès, *System and Revelation: The Philosophy of Franz Rosenzweig,* 145–149.

31. See the comments in Altmann, "Franz Rosenzweig on History," 130–135; Bruckstein, "Zur Phänomenologie der jüdischen Liturgie in Rosenzweig's *Stern der Erlösung.*"

32. Rosenzweig, *Star of Redemption,* 314–315.

33. Ibid., "The New Thinking," 86.

34. Levy, "The Nature of Modern Jewish Philosophy," 579.

35. Perhaps this is discussed most pertinently in the thought of Emmanuel Levinas, someone whom I have not discussed at all in this epilogue. See, for example, his *Difficult Freedom;* idem, *In the Time of the Nations.*

BIBLIOGRAPHY

Primary Sources

Abravanel, Judah. *Dialoghi d'amore.* Edited by Santino Caramella. Bari: Gius. Laterza and Figli, 1929.

———. *The Philosophy of Love (Dialoghi d'Amore).* Translated by F. Friedeberg-Seeley and Jean H. Barnes. London: Soncino Press, 1937.

———. *Siḥot ʿal ha-Ahavah.* Edited and translated by Menachem Dorman. Jerusalem: Mossad Bialik, 1983.

———. "*Telunah ʿal ha-zeman.*" In *Mivhar ha-Shirah ha-Ivrit be-Italyah,* ed. Jefim Hayyim Schirmann, 216–222. Berlin: Schocken, 1934.

Alemanno, Yohanan. *Hay Ha'Olamim (L'Immortale). Parte 1: La Retorica.* Edited by Fabrizio Lelli. Florence: Leo S. Olschki, 1995.

Alfarabi. See al-Fārābī.

Alfonsi, Petrus. *Dialogus Petri et Moysi.* In *Patrologia Latina* 157: 535–672.

d'Aragona, Tullia. "Della Infintà de amore." In *Trattati d'amore del Cinquecento,* ed. Giuseppe Zonta. Bari: G. Laterza e figli, 1912.

Avicenna. *See* ibn Sīnā.

Bembo, Pietro. *Gli Asolani.* Florence: Accademia della Crusca, 1991.

———. *Gli Asolani.* Translated by Rudolf B. Gottfried. Bloomington: Indiana University Press, 1954.

———. *Prose della volgar lingua.* Padua: Liviana, 1955.

Betussi, Giuseppe. "La Leonare." In *Trattati d'amore del Cinquecento,* ed. Giuseppe Zonta, 307–348. Bari: G. Laterza e figli, 1912.

———. "Il Raverta: Dialogo di messer Giuseppe Betussi nel quale si ragiona d'amore e degli effetti suoi." In *Trattati d'amore del Cinquecento,* ed. Giuseppe Zonta, 3–145. Bari: G. Laterza e figli, 1912.

Blumenkranz, Bernhard, ed. *Altercatio Aecclesie contra Synagogam: Texte inédit du Xe siècle.* Strasbourg: Palais de l'Université, 1954.

Buber, Martin. *Daniel: Dialogues of Realization.* Translated by Maurice Freedman. New York: Holt, Rinehart and Winston, 1964.

———. "Dialogue." In Martin Buber, *Between Man and Man,* trans. Ronald Gregor Smith, 1–45. London: Routledge, 2002 [1947].

———. "Dialogue between Heaven and Earth." In Martin Buber, *On Judaism,* ed. Nahum N. Glatzer, 214–225. New York: Schocken, 1995 [1967].

———. *I and Thou.* 2nd ed. Translated by Ronald Gregor Smith. New York: Charles Scribner's Sons, 1958.

Castiglione, Baldassarre. *Il Cortigiano.* 3rd ed. Florence: G. C. Sansoni, 1929.

Cohen, Hermann. *Ethics of Maimonides.* Translated by Almut Sh. Bruckstein. Madison: University of Wisconsin Press, 2004.

———. *Hermann Cohens Jüdische Schriften.* Edited by Bruno Strauss. Berlin: C. A. Schwetschke und Sohn, 1924.

———. *Religion of Reason out of the Sources of Judaism.* Translated by Simon Kaplan. Atlanta: Scholars Press, 1995.

ibn Daʿud, Abraham. *The Exalted Faith.* Translated by Norbert M. Samuelson. Rutherford, N.J.: Fairleigh Dickinson University Press, 1986.

Equicola, Mario. *Libro di natura d'amore.* Edited by Laura Ricci. Rome: Bulzoni, 1999.

ibn Ezra, Moshe ben Jacob. *Kitāb al-muhādara wa al-mudhākara (Sefer ʿiyyunim ve ha-diyyunim).* Edited by A. S. Halkin. Jerusalem: Mekize Niramim, 1975.

———. *Secular Poems* (Hebrew). Edited by H. Brody and D. Pagis. 3 vols. Jerusalem: Schocken Institute, 1935–1977.

ibn Falaquera, Shem Tov ben Joseph. *The Book of the Seeker by Shem Tob ben Joseph ibn Falaquera.* Edited and translated by M. Herschel Levine. New York: Yeshiva University Press, 1976.

———. *Falaquera's Epistle of the Debate: An Introduction to Jewish Philosophy.* Edited and translated by Steven Harvey. Cambridge: Harvard University Press, 1987.

———. *Sefer ha-maʿalot.* Berlin: n.p., 1894.

———. *Sefer ha-mevaqqesh.* Warsaw: n.p., 1923.

———. *Sefer Moreh ha-Moreh.* Edited by Mordecai Leib Bisliches. Pressburg: n.p., 1837. Reprinted in *Sheloshah Qamonei Mefarshei ha-Moreh.* Jerusalem: n.p., 1961.

———. *Sefer Reshit ḥokhmah.* Edited by Moritz David. Berlin, 1902. Reprinted Jerusalem: Maqor, 1970.

al-Fārābī, Abū Naṣr. *The Attainment of Happiness.* Translated by Muhsin Mahdi. In *Medieval Political Philosophy: A Sourcebook,* ed. Ralph Lerner and Muhsin Mahdi, 58–82. Ithaca: Cornell University Press.

———. *Risāla fī qawānīn sināʿa al-shʿir.* In *Arisṭūṭālīs fann al-shʿir.* Edited by ʿAbd al-Raḥman Badawī. Cairo: dār al-thaqāfa, 1973.

Ficino, Marsilio. *Commentary on Plato's Symposium.* Translated by Sears Jayne. Dallas: Spring Publications, 1985.

———. *El Libro dell'amore.* Ed. S. Niccoli. Florence: L. S. Olschki, 1987.

———. *Platonic Theology.* Vol. 1. Edited and translated by James Hankins and Michael J. B. Allen. Cambridge: Harvard University Press, 2001.

ibn Gabirol, Shlomo. *Sefer Meqor Ḥayyim.* Translated into Hebrew by Ya'akov Blubstein. Jerusalem: Mossad ha-Rav Kook, 1926.

Gershom, Levi ben (Gersonides). *Gersonides' Commentary on the Song of Songs.* Translated by Menachem Kellner. New Haven: Yale University Press, 1998.

al-Ghazālī, Abū Ḥāmid. *Deliverance from Error: An Annotated Translation of al-Munqidh min al-Dhalāl and Other Relevant Works by al-Ghazālī.* Edited and translated by Richard J. McCarthy. Louisville: Fons Vitae, 2000.

———. *The Incoherence of the Philosophers.* Translated by Michael E. Marmura. Provo, Utah: Brigham Young University Press, 2000.

———. *al-Naṣīhat al-mulūk.* Edited by F. R. C. Bagley. Oxford: Oxford University Press, 1964.

Goldstein, David, ed. and trans. *The Jewish Poets of Spain, 900–1250.* Harmondsworth: Penguin, 1971.

Halevi, Judah. *Kitāb al-radd wa al-dalīl fī al-dīn al-dhalil.* Edited by David H. Baneth and Haggai Ben-Shammai. Jerusalem: Magnes Press, 1977.

———. *Le Kuzari: Apologie de la religion méprisée.* Translated by Charles Touati. Paris: Verdier, 1994.

———. *The Kuzari: An Argument for the Faith of Israel.* Translated by Hartwig Hirschfeld. New York: Schocken Books, 1964.

———. "A Letter of Rabbi Judah Halevi to Rabbi Moses ibn Ezra." Edited by Sh. Abramson. In *Hayyim Schirmann Jubilee Volume,* ed. Sh. Abramson and A. Mirsky, 397–411. Jerusalem: Schocken Institute for Jewish Research, 1970.

Halkin, A. S., ed. *After Maimonides: An Anthology of Writings by His Critics, Defenders, and Commentators* (Hebrew). Jerusalem: The Zalman Shazar Center, 1979.

al-Ḥarizi, Judah. *The Book of the Taḥkemoni: Jewish Tales from Medieval Spain.* Translated by David Simha Segal. London: Littman Library of Jewish Civilization, 2001.

ibn al-Ḥaytham. *The Advent of the Fatimids: A Contemporary Shiʿi Witness.* Edited and translated by Wilfred Madelung and Paul E. Walker. London: I. B. Tauris, 2000.

Hyman, Arthur, and James J. Walsh, eds. *Philosophy in the Middle Ages.* 2nd ed. Indianapolis: Hackett, 1973.

Ikhwān al-Safāʾ. *The Case of the Animals Versus Man before the King of the Jinn: A Tenth-Century Ecological Fable of the Pure Brethren of Basra.* Translated by Lenn E. Goodman. Boston: Twayne, 1978.

Kimḥi, Joseph. *The Book of the Covenant.* Translated by Frank Ephraim Talmage. Toronto: The Pontifical Institute of Medieval Studies, 1972.

———. *Sefer ha-Berit.* Edited by Frank Ephraim Talmage. Jerusalem: Mossad Bialik, 1974.

Kobler, Franz, ed. *Letters of Jews through the Ages: From Biblical Times to the Middle of the Eighteenth Century.* Vol. 1. New York: East and West Library, 1953.

Levinas, Emmanuel. *Difficult Freedom: Essays on Judaism.* Translated by Seán Hand. Baltimore: Johns Hopkins University Press, 1990.

———. *In the Time of the Nations.* Translated by Michael B. Smith. London: Athlone Press, 1994.

Levinsohn, Issac Baer. *Efes damim.* Vilna, 1837; repr. Warsaw, 1879.

Lichtenberg, Abraham, ed. *Qovets Teshuvot ha-Rambam ve-Iggerotav.* 3 vols. Leipzig: n.p., 1859.

Llull, Ramon. *Le Livre du gentil et des trois sages.* Edited by Armand Llinarés. Paris: Press universitaires de France, 1966.

Martyr, Justin. *Dialogue with Trypho.* Edited by Miroslav Marcovich. Berlin: Walter de Gruyter, 1997.

Mendelssohn, Moses. *Jerusalem, or On Religious Power and Judaism.* Translated by Allan Arkush, with introduction and commentary by Alexander Altmann. Hanover, N.H.: University Press of New England for Brandeis University Press, 1983.

———. *Moses Mendelssohns Gesammelte Schriften.* Leipzig: G. B. Mendelssohn, 1843–1845.

———. *Moses Mendelssohns Gesammelte Schriften Jubiläumsausgabe.* Berlin and Stuttgart-Bad Cannstatt: Friedrich Frommann Verlag, 1929–1984.

———. *Moses Mendelssohn: Selections from His Writings.* Edited and translated by Eva Jospe. New York: Viking Press, 1975.

———. *Phaedon, or the Death of Socrates.* Translated by Charles Cullen, with an introduction by Curtis Bowman. London: Thoemmes Continuum, 2004.

———. *Philosophical Writings.* Edited and translated by Daniel O. Dahlstrom. Cambridge: Cambridge University Press, 1997.

Mendes-Flohr, Paul, and Jehuda Reinharz, eds. *The Jew in the Modern World: A Documentary History.* 2nd ed. New York: Oxford University Press, 1995.

Messer Leon, Judah. *The Book of the Honeycomb's Flow (Sefer Nopheth Ṣufim).* Edited and translated by Isaac Rabinowitz. Ithaca: Cornell University Press, 1983.

Mieses, Judah Leib. *Kinat ha'emet.* Vienna, 1828. Reprinted in *Hebrew Satire in Europe,* ed. Y. Friedlander, vol. 3. Ramat Gan: Bar Ilan University Press, 1994.

Naḥman, Moses ben (Naḥmanides). *Vikuaḥ Barcelona.* In *Kitvei Rabbenu Moshe ben Naḥman,* ed. H. D. Chavel, vol. 1, 302–320. Jerusalem: Mossad ha-Rav Kook, 1971.

Odo of Tournai. *On Original Sin and a Disputation with the Jew, Leo, Concerning the Advent of Christ, the Son of God.* Translated by Irven M. Resnik. Philadelphia: University of Pennsylvania Press, 1994.

ibn Paquda, Baḥya. *The Book of Direction to the Duties of the Heart.* Translated by Menahem Mansoor. London: Littman Library of Jewish Civilization, 1973.

Pico della Mirandola, Giovanni. *Commentary on a Canzone of Benivieni by Giovanni Pico della Mirandola.* Translated by Sears Jayne. New York: Peter Lang, 1984.

———. *Commento sopra una canzone d'amore.* Palermo: Novecento, 1994.

———. *Heptaplus.* Edited by Eugenio Garin. Florence: Vallecchi, 1942.

———. *On the Dignity of Man, On Being and the One, and Heptaplus.* Translated by Charles Glenn Wallis, Paul J. W. Miller, and Douglas Carmichael. Indianapolis: Bobbs-Merrill, 1965.

Polleqar, Isaac. *Ezer ha-Dat.* Edited by Jacob Levinger. Tel Aviv: Tel Aviv University Press, 1984.

Proclus. *Commentary on Plato's Parmenides.* Translated by Glenn R. Morrow and John M. Dillon. Princeton: Princeton University Press, 1987.

al-Rāzī, Abū Ḥātim. *Kitāb al-ʿalām wa al-nubuwwa.* Jinīf: Al-Muaʾassasah al-ʿarabiyya li al-taḥdīth al-fikrī, 2003.

ben Reuben, Jacob. *Milḥamot ha-Shem.* Edited by Judah Rosenthal. Jerusalem: Mossad ha-Rav Kook, 1963.

Rosenzweig, Franz. "The New Thinking." In *Franz Rosenzweig's "The New Thinking,"* edited and translated by Alan Udoff and Barbara E. Galli, 67–102. Syracuse, N.Y.: Syracuse University Press, 1999.

———. *The Star of Redemption.* Translated by Barbara Galli. Madison: University of Wisconsin Press, 2005.

———. *The Star of Redemption.* Translated by William W. Hallo. London: Routledge and Kegan Paul, 1970.

———. *Der Stern der Erlösung.* Frankfurt am Main: J. Kauffmann, 1921.

———. *Understanding the Sick and the Healthy: A View of World, Man, and God.* Translated with an introduction by Nahum Glatzer. Cambridge: Harvard University Press, 1999.

de' Rossi, Azaria. *Meqor Einayim.* Edited by David Cassel. Vilna: n.p., 1886.

ibn Sahula, Isaac. *Fables from the Distant Past.* 2 vols. Edited and translated by Raphael Loewe. Portland, Ore.: Littman Library of Jewish Civilization, 2004.

al-Shahrastānī. *Kitāb al milal wa al-nihal.* Cairo: al-matbaʿa al-ināniyya, 1948.

al-Sijistānī, Abū Yaʿqūb. *The Wellsprings of Wisdom.* Translated by Paul E. Walker. Salt Lake City: University of Utah Press, 1994.

bar Simon, Meir. *Milḥemet Miẓvah.* In *Shitat ha-kadmonim ʿal masekhet nazir,* ed. M. Y. Blau, 305–337. New York: n.p., 1974.

ibn Sīnā, Abū ʿAli al-Ḥusayn (Avicenna). *Kitāb al-majmuʿ: al-ḥikma al-ʿarūdiyya fī maʿānī kitāb al-shʿir.* Edited by M. Salīm Sālim. Cairo: dār al-thaqāfa, 1973.

——. *The Life of Ibn Sina.* A critical edition and annotated translation by William E. Gohlman. Albany: State University of New York Press, 1974.

Speroni, Sperone. "Dialoghi d'amore." In *Opere,* ed. Mario Pozzi, vol. 1, 1–45. Rome: Vecchiarelli, 1989.

Tasso, Torquato. *Tasso's Dialogues: A Selection with the Discourse on the Art of the Dialogue.* Translated by Carnes Lord and Dain A. Trafton. Berkeley: University of California Press, 1982.

al-Tawḥīdī, Abū Ḥayyān. *Al-Imtāʿ wa al-muʾānasa.* Vol. 1. Edited by Aḥmad Amīn and Aḥmad al-Zayn. Cairo: al-Taʾlif, 1939–1944.

al-Ṭūsī, Naṣīr al-Dīn. *Contemplation and Action: The Spiritual Autobiography of a Muslim Scholar.* Translated by S. J. Badakhchani. London: I. B. Tauris, 1998.

ibn Verga, Shlomo. *Shevet Yehudah.* Jerusalem: Mekhon benei Yisakhar, 1991.

Walzer, Richard, and Paul Kraus, eds. *Plato Arabus.* Vol. 1. London: Warburg Institute, 1951.

al-Yaman, Jaʿfar ibn Manṣūr. *The Master and the Disciple: An Early Islamic Spiritual Dialogue.* Edited and translated by James Morris. London: I. B. Tauris, 2001.

ha-Yarḥī, Abba Meri ben Joseph. *Minḥat Qenāʾot.* Pressburg: Druck und Verbag von Anton Edlan v. Schmid, 1838.

Secondary Sources

Adelman, Howard. "The Educational and Literary Activities of Jewish Women in Italy during the Renaissance and the Catholic Restoration." In *Shlomo Simonsohn Jubilee Volume: Studies on the History of the Jews in the Middle Ages and the Renaissance Periods,* 9–23. Tel Aviv: Tel Aviv University Press, 1993.

——. "Finding Women's Voices in Italian Jewish Literature." In *Women of the Word: Jewish Women and Jewish Writing,* ed. Judith R. Baskin, 50–69. Detroit: Wayne State University Press, 1994.

Alon, Ilai. *Socrates in Medieval Arabic Literature.* Leiden and Jerusalem: E. J. Brill and The Magnes Press, 1991.

Altmann, Alexander. "*Ars Rhetorica* as Reflected in Some Jewish Figures of the Italian Renaissance." In *Essential Papers on Jewish Culture in Renaissance and Baroque Italy,* ed. David B. Ruderman, 63–84. New York: New York University Press, 1982.

——. "Die Entstehung von Moses Mendelssohns *Phädon.*" In his *Die trostvolle Aufklärung: Studien zur Metaphysik und politischen Theorie Moses Mendelssohns,* 84–108. Stuttgart: Frommann-Holzboog, 1982.

——. "Franz Rosenzweig on History." In *The Philosophy of Franz Rosenzweig,* ed. Paul Mendes-Flohr, 124–137. Hanover, N.H.: University Press of New England for Brandeis University Press, 1988.

——. *Moses Mendelssohn: A Biographical Study.* University: University of Alabama Press, 1973.

——. *Von der mittelalterlicher zur modernen Aufklärung.* Tübingen: Mohr, 1987.

Arkush, Allan. *Moses Mendelssohn and the Enlightenment.* Albany: State University of New York Press, 1994.

Asín-Pallacios, Miguel. *The Mystical Philosophy of Ibn Masarra and His Followers.* Leiden: E. J. Brill, 1978.

Baer, Yitzhak. "Abner von Burgos." *Korrespondenzblatt der Akademie für Wissenschaft des Judentums* 10 (1929): 20–37.

———. *A History of the Jews in Christian Spain.* 2 vols. Translated by Louis Schoffman. Philadelphia: Jewish Publication Society of America, 1961.

———. "On the Disputations of R. Yeḥiel of Paris and R. Moses ben Naḥman" (Hebrew). *Tarbiz* 2 (1930–1931): 177–187.

———. "*Sefer Minhat Qenaot* of Abner of Burgos and Its Influence on Hasdai Crescas" (Hebrew). *Tarbiz* 11 (1982): 188–206.

Baneth, D. Z. "Some Remarks on the Autographs of Judah Halevi and the Genesis of the *Kuzari*" (Hebrew). *Tarbiz* 26 (1957): 297–303.

Baron, Salo Wittmayer. *A Social and Religious History of the Jews.* 2nd ed. 18 vols. New York and Philadelphia: Columbia University Press and Jewish Publication Society of America, 1952–1983.

Barzilay, Isaac. *Yoseph Shlomo Delmedigo (Yashar of Candia): His Life, Works, and Times.* Leiden: Brill, 1974.

Beck, Lewis White. *Early German Philosophy: Kant and His Predecessors.* Cambridge: Harvard University Press, 1969.

Beiser, Frederick C. *German Idealism: The Struggle Against Subjectivism.* Cambridge: Harvard University Press, 2002.

Belasco, George. "Isaac Pulgar's 'Support of the Religion'." *Jewish Quarterly Review* 27 (1905): 26–56.

Benjamin, Walter. "On Language as Such and on the Language of Man." Translated by Rodney Livingstone. In *Walter Benjamin: Selected Writings,* vol. 1, 1913–1926, 62–74, ed. Marcus Bullock and Michael W. Jennings. Cambridge: Harvard University Press, 1996.

Bentley, Jerry H. *Politics and Culture in Renaissance Naples.* Princeton: Princeton University Press, 1987.

Berger, David. "Gilbert Crispin, Alan of Lille, and Jacob ben Reuben: A Study in the Transmission of Medieval Polemic." *Speculum* 59 (1974): 34–47.

———. *The Jewish-Christian Debate in the High Middle Ages: A Critical Edition of the Niẓẓaḥon Vetus with an Introduction, Translation, and Commentary.* Philadelphia: Jewish Publication Society of America, 1979.

———. "Jewish-Christian Polemics." In *The Encyclopedia of Religion,* ed. Mircea Eliade et al., vol. 11, 389–395. New York: Macmillan, 1987.

———. "Mission to the Jews and Jewish-Christian Contacts in Polemical Literature of the High Middle Ages." *American Historical Review* 91 (1986): 576–591.

Berger, Michael S. "Towards a New Understanding of Judah Halevi's *Kuzari.*" *Religion* 72.2 (1992): 210–228.

Berger, Shlomo, and Irene Zweip, eds. *Epigonism and the Dynamics of Jewish Culture.* Louvain: Peeters, forthcoming.

Bergman, Shmuel Hugo. *Dialogical Philosophy from Kierkegaard to Buber.* Translated by Arnold A. Gerstein. Albany: State University of New York Press, 1991.

Bergsträsser, Gotthelf. *Neue Materielien zu Ḥunain ibn Ishāq's Galen- Bibliographie.* Nendeln, Liechtenstein: Kraus Reprints, 1966 [1932].

Biale, David, ed. *The Cultures of the Jews: A New History.* New York: Schocken, 2002.

Binkley, Peter, ed. *Pre-Modern Encyclopaedic Texts: Proceedings of the Second COMERS Congress, Groningen, 1–4 July, 1996.* Leiden: E. J. Brill, 1997.

Black, Deborah. *Logic and Aristotle's Rhetoric and Poetics in Medieval Arabic Philosophy.* Leiden: E. J. Brill, 1990.

Blackall, Eric A. *The Emergence of German as a Literary Language.* 2nd ed. Ithaca: Cornell University Press, 1978.

Bonebakker, S. A. "Adab and the Concept of Belles-Lettres." In *ʿAbbasid Belles-Lettres,* ed. Julia Ashtiany et al., 16–30. Cambridge: Cambridge University Press, 1990.

Bonfil, Robert. "The Historian's Perception of the Jews in the Italian Renaissance: Towards a Reappraisal." *Revue des Études juives* 143.1 (1984): 59–82.

Bourel, Dominique. *Moses Mendelssohn: La Naissance du Judaïsme moderne.* Paris: Gallimard, 2004.

Boyarin, Daniel. *Carnal Israel: Reading Sex in Talmudic Culture.* Berkeley: University of California Press, 1993.

Boyle, Leonard. "The Setting of the *Summa Theologiae* of St. Thomas: Revisited." In *The Ethics of Aquinas,* ed. Stephen J. Pope, 1–16. Washington: Georgetown University Press, 2002.

Brann, Ross. *The Compunctious Poet: Cultural Ambiguity and Hebrew Poetry in Muslim Spain.* Baltimore: Johns Hopkins University Press, 1991.

———. "Judah ha-Levi." In *The Cambridge History of Arabic Literature,* ed. M. R. Menocal, R. P. Scheindlin, and M. Sells, 265–281. Cambridge: Cambridge University Press, 2000.

———. *Power in the Portrayal: Representations of Jews and Muslims in Eleventh- and Twelfth-Century Islamic Spain.* Princeton: Princeton University Press, 2002.

Brook, Kevin Alan. *The Jews of Khazaria.* Northvale, N.J.: Jason Aronson, 1999.

Bruckstein, Almut Sh. "Zur Phänomenologie der jüdischen Liturgie in Rosenzweig's *Stern der Erlösung:* Ein Versuch über das Schweigen mit Husserl." In *Rosenzweig als Leser: Kontextuelle Kommentare zum Stern der Erlösung,* ed. Martin Brasser, 357–368. Tübingen: Max Niemeyer Verlag, 2004.

Burke, Peter. *The Fortunes of the Courtier: The European Reception of Castiglione's Cortegiano.* University Park: The Pennsylvania State University Press, 1996.

Cantarino, Vicente. *Arabic Poetics in the Golden Age.* Leiden: Brill, 1975.

Cantera, Francisco. "La Juderia de Burgos." *Sefarad* 12 (1952): 59–104.

Carpenter, Dwayne. "The Language of Polemic: Abner of Burgos' Quadrilingual Defense of Christianity." In *Circa 1492: Proceedings of the Jerusalem Colloquium,* ed. Isaac Benabu, 59–77. Jerusalem: Gefen, 1992.

Cassirer, Ernest. *The Philosophy of the Enlightenment.* Translated by F. C. A. Koelln and J. P. Pettegrove. Boston: Beacon, 1955.

Celenza, Christopher. *The Lost Italian Renaissance: Humanists, Historians, and Latin's Legacy.* Baltimore: Johns Hopkins University Press, 2004.

Chazan, Robert. *Barcelona and Beyond: The Disputation and Its Aftermath.* Berkeley: University of California Press, 1992.

———. "The Christian Position in Jacob ben Reuben's *Milḥamot ha-Shem.*" In *From Ancient Israel to Modern Judaism: Essays in Honor of Martin Fox,* ed. Jacob Neusner et al., vol. 2, 157–170. Atlanta: Scholars Press, 1989.

———. "Confrontation in the Synagogue of Narbonne: A Christian Sermon and a Jewish Reply." *Harvard Theological Review* 67 (1974): 437–457.

———. *Daggers of Faith: Thirteenth-Century Christian Missionizing and the Jewish Response.* Berkeley: University of California Press, 1989.

———. *Fashioning Jewish Identity in Medieval Western Christendom.* Cambridge: Cambridge University Press, 2004.

———. "Joseph Kimhi's *Sefer ha-Berit:* Pathbreaking Medieval Jewish Apologetics." *Harvard Theological Review* 85 (1992): 417–432.

———. "Maestre Alfonso of Valladolid and the New Missionizing." *Revue des études juives* CXLIII.1–2 (1984): 83–94.

———. "Polemical Themes in the *Milḥemet Miẓvah.*" In *Les Juifs au regard de l'histoire en l'honneur de Bernhard Blumenkranz,* ed. Gilbert Dahan, 169–184. Paris: Picard, 1985.

Cohen, Jeremy. *The Friars and the Jews: The Evolution of Medieval Anti-Semitism.* Ithaca: Cornell University Press, 1982.

Cohen, Mark R. *Under Crescent and Cross: The Jews in the Middle Ages.* Princeton: Princeton University Press, 1994.

Corbin, Henri. "L'initiation Ismaélienne ou l'ésotérisme et le Verbe." *Eranos Jahrbuch* 39 (1970): 41–142.

Craven, William G. *Giovanni Pico della Mirandola, Symbol of His Age: Modern Interpretations of a Renaissance Philosopher.* Geneva: Droz, 1981.

Croce, Benedetto. *History of the Kingdom of Naples.* Translated by F. Frenaye. Chicago: University of Chicago Press, 1970.

Daftary, Farhad. "The Earliest Ismaᶜilis." *Arabica* 38 (1991): 214–245.

———. *The Ismāᶜīlīs: Their History and Doctrines.* Cambridge: Cambridge University Press, 1990.

Dahan, Gilbert. "Epistola Dialoghi: Une traduction Latine de l'*Igeret ha-Vikuaḥ* de Shem Tov ibn Falaquera." *Sefarad* 39.1 (1979): 47–85 and 39.2 (1979): 237–264.

Damiens, Suzanne. *Amor et Intellect chez Léon L'Hébreu.* Toulouse: E. Privat, 1971.

Davidson, Herbert. "The Active Intellect in the Kuzari and Hallevi's Theory of Causality." *Revue des études juives* 131.3–4 (1971): 351–396.

Dobbs-Weinstein, Idit. "The Maimonidean Controversy." In *History of Jewish Philosophy,* ed. Daniel H. Frank and Oliver Leaman, 331–349. New York and London: Routledge, 1997.

Dubin, Lois C. "The Social and Cultural Context: Eighteenth-Century Enlightenment." In *History of Jewish Philosophy,* ed. Daniel H. Frank and Oliver Leaman, 636–659. New York and London: Routledge, 1997.

Eisen, Arnold. "Divine Legislation as 'Ceremonial Script': Mendelssohn on the Commandments." *Association for Jewish Studies Review* 15 (1990): 239–267.

Eisen, Robert. *The Book of Job in Medieval Jewish Philosophy.* Oxford: Oxford University Press, 2004.

———. *Gersonides, Providence, Covenant, and the Chosen People: A Study in Medieval Jewish Philosophy and Biblical Commentary.* Albany: State University of New York Press, 1995.

———. "The Problem of the King's Dream and Non-Jewish Prophecy in Judah Halevi's *Kuzari.*" *Journal of Jewish Thought and Philosophy* 3 (1994): 231–247.

Evans, Gillian R. "Boethian and Euclidean Axiomatic Method in the Theology of the Later Twelfth Century." *Archives Internationale d'Histoire des Sciences* 30 (1980): 36–52.

Fakhry, Majid. *A History of Islamic Philosophy.* 2nd ed. New York: Columbia University Press, 1983.

Feiner, Shmuel. *Haskalah and Historiography: The Emergence of a Modern Jewish Historical Consciousness.* Translated by Chaya Naor and Sondra Silverston. Oxford: Littman, 2002.

———. *The Jewish Enlightenment.* Translated by Chaya Naor. Philadelphia: University of Pennsylvania Press, 2002.

———. *Moses Mendelssohn* (Hebrew). Jerusalem: Merkaz Zalman Shazar, 2005.

Feldman, Seymour. "Crescas' Theological Determinism." *Da'at* 9 (1982): 3–28.

———. *Philosophy in a Time of Crisis: Don Isaac Abravanel, Defender of the Faith.* London: RoutledgeCurzon, 2003.

Fenton, Paul B. "The Arabic and Hebrew Versions of the *Theology of Aristotle.*" In *Pseudo-Aristotle in the Middle Ages: "The Theology" and Other Texts,* ed. Jill Kraye, W. F. Ryan, and C. B. Schmitt, 241–264. London: The Warburg Institute, 1986.

Fierro, Maribel. "Bātinism in al-Andalus: Maslama b. Qāsim al-Qurtubī (d. 353/964), Author of *Rutbat al-Hakīm* and the *Ghāyat al-Hakīm* (Picatrix)." *Studia Islamica* 84.2 (1996): 87–111.

Foster, Kenelm. *Petrarch: Poet and Humanist.* Edinburgh: Edinburgh University Press, 1984.

Frank, Daniel H. "What Is Jewish Philosophy?" In *History of Jewish Philosophy,* ed. Daniel H. Frank and Oliver Leaman, 1–10. New York and London: Routledge, 1997.

Fraenkel, Carlos. *From Maimonides to Samuel Ibn Tibbon: The Method of the Guide of the Perplexed* (Hebrew). Jerusalem: Magnes Press, forthcoming.

Freudenthal, Gad. "Les sciences dans les communautés juives médiévales de Provence: Leur appropriation, leur role." *Revue des études juives* 152 (1993): 29–136.

———. "Science in the Medieval Jewish Culture of Southern France." *History of Science* 33 (1995): 23–58.

Garin, Eugenio. *La cultura filosofica del Rinascimento italiano: Ricerche e documenti.* 2nd ed. Florence: G. C. Sansoni, 1979.

———. *Italian Humanism: Philosophy and Civic Life.* Translated by Peter Munz. Oxford: Blackwell, 1965.

———. "Marsilio Ficino, Girolamo Benivieni e Giovanni Pico." *Giornali critico della filosofia italiana* 23 (1942): 93–99.

———. "Ricerche sulle traduzioni di Platone nella prima metà del sec. XV." In *Medioevo e Rinascimento: Studi in onore di Bruno Nardi,* vol. 1, 339–374. Florence: G. C. Sansoni, 1955.

———. *Il ritorno dei filosofi antichi.* Naples: Bibliopolis, 1983.

Garvin, Barbara. "The Language of Leone Ebreo's *Dialoghi d'Amore.*" *Italia* 13–15 (2001): 181–210.

Gay, Peter. *The Enlightenment: An Interpretation.* 2 vols. New York: Knopf, 1966 and 1969.

Gershenzon, Shoshanna. "A Study of *Teshuvot la-Meharef* by Abner of Burgos." Ph.D. dissertation, Jewish Theological Seminary, 1984.

———. "A Tale of Two Midrashim: The Legacy of Abner of Burgos." In *Approaches to Judaism in Medieval Times,* vol. 3, ed. David R. Blumenthal, 133–145. Atlanta: Scholars Press, 1988.

———. "The View of Maimonides as a Determinist in *Sefer Minhat Qenaot* by Abner of Burgos." In *Proceedings of the 9th World Congress of Jewish Studies, Division C: Jewish Thought and Literature,* 93–100. Jerusalem: Magnes Press, 1986

Gil, Moshe, and Ezra Fleischer, eds. *Judah Halevi and His Circle: 55 Geniza Documents* (Hebrew). Jerusalem: World Union of Jewish Studies, 2001.

Gilon, Meir. *Mendelssohn's "Koheleth Musar" in Its Historical Context* (Hebrew). Jerusalem: The National Israel Academy for Sciences, 1979.

Giovanardi, Claudio. *La Teoria Cortigiana e il Dibattito linguistico nel Primo Cinquecento.* Rome: Bulzoni, 1998.

Goetshel, Willi. *Spinoza's Modernity: Mendelssohn, Lessing, and Heine.* Madison: University of Wisconsin Press, 2004.

Goitein, Shlomo Dov. "Autographs of Judah Halevi from the Genizah" (Hebrew). *Tarbiz* 25 (1956): 393–412.

———. "The Biography of Rabbi Judah Ha-Levi in Light of the Cairo Genizah Documents." *Proceedings of the American Academy of Jewish Research* 28 (1959): 41–56.

——. *A Mediterranean Society.* Vol. 5. Berkeley: University of California Press, 1988.

Golb, Norman. "The Hebrew Translation of Averroes' *Faṣl al-maqāl.*" *Proceedings of the American Academy of Jewish Research* 25 (1956): 91–113 and 26 (1957): 41–64.

Golb, Norman, and Omeljan Ptisak. *Khazarian Hebrew Documents of the Tenth Century.* Ithaca: Cornell University Press, 1982.

Golden, Peter B. *Khazar Studies: An Historico-Philological Inquiry into the Origins of the Khazars.* Vol. 1. Budapest: Akadémiai Kiadó, 1980.

Goldziher, Ignaz. "The Appearance of the Prophet in Dreams." *Journal of the Royal Asiatic Society* (1912): 503–506.

Gordon, Daniel, ed. *Postmodernism and the Enlightenment: New Perspectives in Eighteenth-Century French Intellectual History.* London: Routledge, 2001.

Goodman, Lenn E. "Judah Halevi." In *History of Jewish Philosophy,* ed. Daniel H. Frank and Oliver Leaman, 188–227. London and New York: Routledge, 1997.

Graetz, Heinrich. *Geschichte der Juden von den ältesten Zeiten bis auf die Gegenwart: Aus den Quellen neu bearbeitet.* 12 vols. Leipzig: O. Leiner, 1894–1908.

Guidotti, Gabriella Cantini. *Tre Inventari di Bicchierai Toscani fra Cinque e Seicento.* Florence: Presso l'Accademia della Crusca, 1983.

Gutas, Dimitri. "Aspects of Literary Forms and Genre in Arabic Logical Works." In *Glosses and Commentaries on Aristotelian Logical Texts: The Syriac, Arabic, and Medieval Latin Traditions,* ed. Charles Burnett, 29–76. London: The Warburg Institute, 1993.

——. "Review of *Metaphysics as Rhetoric* by Joshua Parens." *International Journal of the Classical Tradition* 4.3 (1998): 405–412.

Guttmann, Julius. "Mendelssohn's *Jerusalem* and Spinoza's *Theologico-Political Treatise.*" In *Studies in Jewish Thought,* ed. Alfred Jospe, 361–386. Detroit: Wayne State University Press, 1981.

——. *Philosophies of Judaism: A History of Jewish Philosophy from Biblical Times to Franz Rosenzweig.* Translated by D. W. Silverman. New York: Schocken, 1964.

——. *Religion and Knowledge: Essays and Lectures.* Edited by S. H. Bergman and N. Rotenstreich. Jerusalem: Magnes Press, 1955.

Halbertal, Moshe. *Between Torah and Wisdom: Menaḥem ha-Me᾿iri and the Maimonidean Halakhists in Provence* (Hebrew). Jerusalem: Magnes Press, 2000.

Halkin, A. S. "The Medieval Jewish Attitude towards Hebrew." In *Biblical and Other Studies,* ed. Alexander Altmann, 233–248. Cambridge: Harvard University Press, 1963.

Halm, Heinz. "The Cosmology of the pre-Fatimid Ismāʿīliyya." In *Mediaeval Ismaʿili History and Thought,* ed. Farhad Daftary, 75–84. Cambridge: Cambridge University Press, 1996.

——. *The Fatimids and Their Traditions of Learning.* London: I. B. Tauris, 1997.

——. "The Ismaʿili Oath of Allegiance (*ʿahd*) and the 'Sessions of Wisdom' (*majālis al-ḥikma*) in Fatimid Times." In *Medieval Ismaʿili History and Thought,* ed. Farhad Daftary, 91–115. Cambridge: Cambridge University Press, 1996.

Hankins, James. *Plato in the Italian Renaissance.* 2 vols. Leiden: E. J. Brill, 1990.

Harvey, Steven. "Falaquera's *Epistle of the Debate* and the Maimonidean Controversy of the 1230s." In *Torah and Wisdom: Studies in Jewish Philosophy, Kabbalah, and Halakha in Honor of Arthur Hyman,* ed. Ruth Link-Salinger, 75–86. New York: Shengold Publishers, 1992.

——. "Maimonides in the Sultan's Palace." In *Perspectives on Maimonides,* ed. Joel L. Kraemer, 47–75. Oxford: Oxford University Press for the Littman Library of Jewish Civilization, 1991.

——, ed. *The Medieval Hebrew Encyclopedias of Science and Philosophy.* Dordrecht: Kluwer, 2000.

Harvey, Warren Zev. *Physics and Metaphysics in Ḥasdai Crescas.* Amsterdam: J. C. Gieben, 1998.

Hasan-Rokem, Galit. *The Web of Life: Folklore in Rabbinic Literature* (Hebrew). Tel Aviv: Am Oved, 1996.

Hay, Denys. "Historians and the Renaissance during the Last Twenty-Five Years." In *The Renaissance: Essays in Interpretation,* ed. André Chastel, 1–32. London: Methuen, 1982.

Heath, Peter. *Allegory and Philosophy in Avicenna (Ibn Sīnā).* Philadelphia: University of Pennsylvania Press, 1992.

Hodgson, Marshall G. S. *The Venture of Islam: Conscience and History in a World Civilization.* 3 vols. Chicago: University of Chicago Press, 1974.

Horwitz, Rivka. *Buber's Way to I and Thou: An Historical Analysis and the First Publication of Martin Buber's "Religion als Gegenwart."* Heidelberg: Verlag Lambert Schneider, 1978.

——. "Franz Rosenzweig on Language." *Judaism* 13.4 (1964): 393–406.

Hughes, Aaron W. "Abrabanel, Judah." In the *Stanford Encyclopedia of Philosophy,* ed. Edward N. Zalta. Online at http://plato.stanford.edu/entries/abrabanel.

——. "A Case of Twelfth-Century Plagiarism? Abraham ibn Ezra's *Hay ben Meqitz* and Avicenna's *Hayy ibn Yaqzān." Journal of Jewish Studies* 55.2 (2004): 306–331.

——. "Epigone, Innovator, or Apologist? The Case of Judah Abravanel." In *Epigonism and the Dynamics of Jewish Culture,* ed. Shlomo Berger and Irene Zweip. Louvain: Peeters, forthcoming.

——. "The 'Golden Age' of Muslim Spain: Religious Identity and the Invention of a Tradition in Modern Jewish Studies." In *Historicizing "Tradition" in the Study of Religion,* ed. Steven Engler and Greg Grieve, 51–74. Berlin: Walter de Grutyer, 2005.

——. "Imagining the Divine: Ghazali on Imagination, Dreams, and Dreaming." *Journal of the American Academy of Religion* 70.1 (2002): 33–53.

——. *The Texture of the Divine: Imagination in Medieval Islamic and Jewish Thought.* Bloomington: Indiana University Press, 2004.

——. "The Three Worlds of ibn Ezra's *Hay ben Meqitz." Journal of Jewish Thought and Philosophy* 11.1 (2002): 1–24.

——. "'The Torah Speaks in the Language of Humans': On Some Uses of Plato's Theory of Myth in Medieval Jewish Philosophy." In *Plato Redivivus,* ed. Robert Berchman and John Finamore, 237–252. New Orleans: University Press of the South, 2005.

——. "Transforming the Maimonidean Imagination: Aesthetics in the Renaissance Thought of Judah Abravanel." *Harvard Theological Review* 97.4 (2004): 461–484.

——. "Two Approaches to the Love of God in Medieval Jewish Thought: The Concept of *devequt* in the Works of Ibn Ezra and Halevi." *Sciences Religeuses / Studies in Religion* 28.2 (1999): 139–152.

Husik, Isaac. *A History of Medieval Jewish Philosophy.* Philadelphia: Jewish Publication Society of America, 1940.

Hyland, D. "Why Plato Wrote Dialogues." *Philosophy and Rhetoric* (1968): 38–50.

Idel, Moshe. "Encounters between Spanish and Italian Kabbalists in the Generation of the Expulsion." In *Crisis and Creativity in the Sephardic World: 1391–1648,* ed. Benjamin R. Gampel, 189–222. New York: Columbia University Press, 1997.

——. "Kabbalah, Platonism and Prisca Theologia: The Case of R. Menasseh ben Israel." In *Menasseh Ben Israel and His World,* ed. Y. Kaplan, H. Méchoulan, and R. Popkin, 207–219. Leiden: Brill, 1989.

———. "Religion, Thought, and Attitudes: The Impact of the Expulsion on the Jews." In *Spain and the Jews: The Sephardic Experience, 1492 and After,* ed. Elie Kedourie, 123–139. London: Thames and Hudson, 1992.

———. "The Source of the Circle of Love in the *Dialoghi d'amore*" (Hebrew). *Iyyun* 28 (1978): 156–166.

———. "The Study Program of R. Yohanan Alemmano" (Hebrew). *Tarbiz* 48 (1979): 303–330.

Jacobi, Klaus. "Einleitung." In *Gespräche lesen: Philosophische Dialogue im Mittelalter,* ed. K. Jacobi, 15–21. Tübingen: Gunter Narr Verlag, 1999.

Jordan, Mark D. "The Protreptic Structure of the *Summa Contra Gentiles." The Thomist* 50.2 (1986): 173–209.

Jospe, Raphael. *Torah and Sophia: The Life and Thought of Shem Tov Ibn Falaquera.* Cincinnati: Hebrew Union College Press, 1988.

Jospe, Raphael, and Dov Schwartz. "Shem Tov ibn Falaquera's Lost Bible Commentary." *Hebrew Union College Annual* LXIV (1993): 167–200.

Kahn, Charles. *Plato and the Socratic Dialogue: The Philosophical Use of a Literary Form.* Cambridge: Cambridge University Press, 1996.

Kasher, Hannah. "The Parable of the King's Palace" (Hebrew). *AJS Review* 14 (1989): 1–19.

Katz, Jacob. "To Whom Did Mendelssohn Reply in His *Jerusalem?" Scripta Hierosolymitana* 23 (1972): 214–243.

Katz, Steven T. "Martin Buber's Epistemology: A Critical Appraisal." In his *Post-Holocaust Dialogues: Critical Studies in Modern Jewish Thought,* 1–51. New York: New York University Press, 1985.

Kaufmann, David. *Studien über Salomon ibn Gabirol.* Jahresbericht der landes-Rabbinerschule. Budapest: n.p., 1899.

Kellner, Menachem. *Dogma in Medieval Judaism: From Maimonides to Abravanel.* Oxford: Littman Library, 1986.

———. *Maimonides on Human Perfection.* Atlanta: Scholars Press, 1990.

Kepnes, Steven. *The Text as Thou: Martin Buber's Dialogical Hermeneutics and Narrative Theology.* Bloomington: Indiana University Press, 1992.

Klar, Benjamin. "Falaquera's *Sefer ha-Mevaqqesh*" (Hebrew). *Kiryat Sefer* 16.2 (1939): 257–258.

Klein, Lawrence E. *Shaftesbury and the Culture of Politeness: Moral Discourse and Cultural Politics in Early Eighteenth-Century England.* Cambridge: Cambridge University Press, 1994.

Kreisel, Howard Haim. *Maimonides' Political Thought.* Albany: State University of New York Press, 1999.

Kristeller, Paul Oskar. *The Philosophy of Marsilio Ficino.* Translated by Virginia Conant. Gloucester, Mass.: Peter Smith, 1964.

———. *Renaissance Thought and Its Sources.* Edited by Michael Mooney. New York: Columbia University Press, 1979.

Krüger, Joachim. *Christian Wolff und die Äesthetik.* Berlin: Humboldt Universität, 1980.

Lane, Edward W. *An Arabic-English Lexicon.* Beirut: Librairie du Liban, 1968.

Langermann, Y. Tzvi. "Science and the *Kuzari." Science in Context* 10.3 (1997): 495–522.

———. "Some Astrological Themes in the Thought of Abraham ibn Ezra." In *Rabbi Abraham Ibn Ezra: Studies in the Writings of a Twelfth-Century Jewish Polymath,* ed. Jay Harris and Isadore Twersky, 28–85. Cambridge: Harvard University Press, 1993.

Lasker, Daniel J. *Jewish Philosophical Polemics against Christianity in the Middle Ages.* New York: Ktav, 1977.

———. "Proselyte Judaism, Christianity, and Islam in the Thought of Judah Halevy." *Jewish Quarterly Review* 81 (1990): 75–92.

Lawee, Eric. *Isaac Abarbanel's Stance Toward Tradition: Defense, Dissent, and Dialogue.* Albany: State University of New York Press, 2001.

Lehmann, James H. "Polemic and Satire in the Poetry of the Maimonidean Controversy." *Prooftexts* 1 (1981): 133–152.

Lelli, Fabrizio. "L'educazione ebraica nella seconda metà del '400: Politica e scienze naturali nel *Hay Ha'Olamim* di Yohanan Alemanno." In *Rinascimento,* seconda serie 36 (1996): 75–136.

———. "La Retorica Nell'Introduzione del Hay ha-Olamim." In *Hay Ha-Olamim (L'immortale): Parte I: La Retorica,* ed. F. Lelli, 29–55. Florence: Leo S. Olschiki, 1995.

———. "Umanismo Larenziano nell'opera di Yohanan Alemanno." In *La cultura ebraica all'epoca di Lorenzo il Magnifico,* a cura di Dora Liscia Bemporad e Ida Zatelli, 49–67. Florence: Leo S. Olschki, 1998.

Lerner, Ralph. *Maimonides' Empire of Light: Popular Enlightenment in an Age of Belief.* Chicago: University of Chicago Press, 2000.

Lesley, Arthur M. "The Place of the *Dialoghi d'Amore* in Contemporaneous Jewish Thought." In *Essential Papers on Jewish Culture in Renaissance and Baroque Italy,* ed. David B. Ruderman, 170–188. New York: New York University Press, 1992.

———. "Proverbs, Figures, and Riddles: The *Dialogues of Love* as a Hebrew Humanist Composition." In *The Midrashic Imagination: Jewish Exegesis, Thought, and History,* ed. Michael Fishbane, 204–225. Albany: State University of New York Press, 1993.

———. "*The Song of Solomon's Ascents* by Yohanan Alemanno: Love and Human Perfection According to a Jewish Colleague of Giovanni Pico della Mirandola." Ph.D. dissertation, University of California, 1976.

Levine, M. Hershel. "Falaquera's Philosophy." In *Proceedings of the Association of Orthodox Jewish Scientists,* vol. 3–4, ed. Fred Rosner, 191–196. New York: Feldheim, 1976.

Levy, Zeᶜev. *Baruch or Benedict: On Some Jewish Aspects of Spinoza's Philosophy.* New York: Peter Lang, 1989.

———. "The Nature of Modern Jewish Philosophy." In *History of Jewish Philosophy,* ed. Daniel H. Frank and Oliver Leaman, 577–588. New York and London: Routledge, 1997.

———. "On the Concept of Beauty in the Philosophy of Judah Abravanel" (Hebrew). In *The Philosophy of Judah Abravanel: Four Lectures,* ed. M. Dorman and Z. Levy, 27–42. Haifa: Hakibbutz Hameuchad, 1985.

Lewis, Bernard. *The Origins of Ismailism.* Cambridge: W. Heffer and Sons, 1940.

Liebes, Yehuda. *Studies in the Zohar.* Translated by Arnold Schwartz, Stephanie Nakache, and Penina Peli. Albany: State University of New York Press, 1993.

Lobel, Diana. *Between Mysticism and Philosophy: Sufi Language of Religious Experience in Judah ha-Levi's Kuzari.* Albany: State University of New York Press, 2000.

Loeb, Isadore. "Polémistes Chretiens et Juifs en France et en Espagne." *Revue des études juives* 18 (1889).

Loewe, Raphael. *Ibn Gabirol.* London: Peter Halban, 1989.

Lowenstein, Steven M. *The Berlin Jewish Community: Enlightenment, Family, Crisis, 1770–1830.* New York: Oxford University Press, 1994.

Maccoby, Hyam. *Judaism on Trial: Jewish-Christian Disputation in the Middle Ages.* London: Littmann Library of Jewish Civilization, 1993.

Mach, Michael. "Justin Martyr's *Dialogus cum Tryphone Iudaeo* and the Development of Christian Anti-Judaism." In *Contra-Judaeos,* ed. Ora Limor and Guy Stroumsa, 27–47. Tübingen: J. C. B. Mohr, 1991.

Mahdi, Muhsin. "Language and Logic in Classical Islam." In *Logic in Classical Islamic Culture,* ed. G. E. von Grunebaum, 102–113. Wiesbaden: O. Harassowitz, 1970.

Malter, Henry. "Shem Tov ben Joseph Palquera: A Thinker and Poet of the Thirteenth Century." *Jewish Quarterly Review* 1 (1910): 151–181.

Manekin, Charles H. "Hebrew Philosophy in the Fourteenth and Fifteenth Centuries: An Overview." In *History of Jewish Philosophy,* ed. Daniel H. Frank and Oliver Leaman, 350–378. New York and London: Routledge, 1997.

Margoliouth, D. S. "The Merits of Logic and Grammar." *Journal of the Royal Asiatic Society* (1905): 111–129.

McGinn, Bernard. "Cosmic and Sexual Love in Renaissance Thought: Reflections on Marsilio Ficino, Giovanni Pico della Mirandola, and Leone Ebreo." In *The Devil, Heresy, and Witchcraft in the Middle Ages,* ed. Alberto Ferreiro, 191–209. Leiden: E. J. Brill, 1998.

Melamed, Abraham. "The Hebrew Encyclopedias of the Renaissance." In *The Medieval Hebrew Encyclopedia of Science and Philosophy,* ed. Steven Harvey, 441–464. Dordrecht: Kluwer, 2000.

———. *The Philosopher-King in Medieval and Renaissance Jewish Political Thought.* Albany: State University of New York Press, 2003.

———. "Rhetoric and Philosophy in *Nofet Ṣufim* by R. Judah Messer Leon" (Hebrew). *Italia* (1978): 7–39.

———. "Rhetoric as Persuasive Instrument in Medieval Jewish Thought." In *Topik und Rhetorik: Ein interdisziplinäres Symposium,* ed. Thomas Schirren and Gert Ueding, 165–176. Tübingen: Max Niemeyer Verlag, 2000.

———. "The Woman as Philosopher: The Image of Sophia in Judah Abravanel's *Dialoghi*" (Hebrew). *Madaei ha-Yahadut* 40 (1990): 113–130.

Mendes-Flohr, Paul. *From Mysticism to Dialogue: Martin Buber's Transformation of German Social Thought.* Detroit: Wayne State University Press, 1989.

Merlan, Philip. "Form and Content in Plato's Philosophy." *Journal of the History of Philosophy* 8.4 (1947): 406–430.

Meyer, Herrmann M. Z. *Moses Mendelssohn Bibliographie: Mit einigen Ergänzungen zur Geistesgeschichte des ausgehenden 18. Jahrhunderts.* Berlin: Walter de Gruyter, 1965.

Meyer, Michael A. *The Origins of the Modern Jew: Jewish Identity and European Culture in Germany, 1749–1824.* Detroit: Wayne State University Press, 1967.

Meyerson, Mark D. *A Jewish Renaissance in Fifteenth-Century Spain.* Princeton: Princeton University Press, 2004.

Mitha, Farouk. *Al-Ghazālī and the Ismaʿilis: A Debate on Reason and Authority in Medieval Islam.* London: I. B Tauris, 2001.

Morgan, Michael L. "Mendelssohn." In *History of Jewish Philosophy,* ed. Daniel H. Frank and Oliver Leaman, 660–681. New York and London: Routledge, 1997.

Mosès, Stéphane. *System and Revelation: The Philosophy of Franz Rosenzweig.* Translated by Catherine Tihanyi. Detroit: Wayne State University Press, 1992.

Munk, Reinier. "Who Is the Other? Alterity in Cohen's *Religion der Vernunft.*" In *Religion der Vernunft aus den Quellen des Judentums: Tradition und Ursprungsdenken in Hermann Cohens Spätwerk,* ed. Helmut Holzey, Gabriel Motzkin, and Hartwig Weiderbach, 275–286. Heidescheim: Georg Olms Verlag, 2000.

Myers, David N. *Resisting History: Historicism and Its Discontents in German-Jewish Thought.* Princeton: Princeton University Press, 2003.

Nasr, Seyyed Hossein. *An Introduction to Islamic Cosmological Doctrines.* Rev. ed. Albany: State University of New York Press, 1993.

Nelson, John Charles. *Renaissance Theory of Love: The Context of Giordano Bruno's Eroici Furori.* New York: Columbia University Press, 1958.

Netton, Ian Richard. *Muslim Neoplatonists: An Introduction to the Thought of the Brethren of Purity.* Edinburgh: Edinburgh University Press, 1991.

Ormsby, Eric. "Ibn Hazm." In *The Cambridge History of Arabic Literature,* ed. M. R. Menocal, R. P. Scheindlin, and M. Sells, 237–251. Cambridge: Cambridge University Press, 2000.

O'Rourke Boyle, Marjorie. *Petrarch's Genius: Pentimento and Prophecy.* Berkeley: University of California Press, 1991.

Pagis, Dan. *Change and Tradition in the Secular Poetry of Spain and Italy* (Hebrew). Jerusalem: Keter, 1976.

Panofsky, Erwin. *Idea: A Concept in Art Theory.* Translated by J. J. S. Peake. New York: Harper and Row, 1968.

Parens, Joshua. *Metaphysics as Rhetoric: Alfarabi's Summary of Plato's "Laws."* Albany: State University of New York Press, 1995.

Percopo, Erasmo. *Vita di Giovanni Pontani.* Edited by M. Manfredi. Naples: I.T.E.A. Industrie Tipografiche, 1938.

Pines, Shlomo. "La longe recension de la Theologie d'Aristote." *Revue des études islamiques* 22 (1954): 7–20.

———. "Shiʿite Terms and Conceptions in Judah Halevi's *Kuzari." Jerusalem Studies in Arabic and Islam* 2 (1980): 165–251.

———. "Some Topics Dealt with in Polleqar's Treatise 'Ezer ha-Dat' and Parallels in Spinoza" (Hebrew). In *Philosophy, Kabbalah and Ethical Literature: Essays in Honor of Isaiah Tishby on His Seventy-Fifth Birthday,* ed. Joseph Dan and Joseph Hacker, 395–457. Jerusalem: Magnes Press, 1986.

———. "Spinoza's *Tractatus Theologico-Politicus* and the Jewish Philosophical Tradition." In *Studies in the History of Jewish Thought,* ed. Warren Zev Harvey and Moshe Idel, 499–521. Jerusalem: Magnes Press, 1997.

———. "On the Term *Ruḥaniyyot* and Its Origin and on Judah Halevi's Doctrine" (Hebrew). *Tarbiz* 57.4 (1988): 511–540.

Rajak, Tessa. "Talking at Trypho: Christian Apologetic as Anti-Judaism in Justin's *Dialogue with Trypho the Jew."* In *Apologetics in the Roman Empire: Pagans, Jews, and Christians,* ed. Mark Edward et al., 59–80. Oxford: Oxford University Press, 1999.

Ravitzky, Aviezer. *Crescas' Sermon on the Passover and Studies in His Philosophy* (Hebrew). Jerusalem: Israel Academy of Sciences and Humanities, 1988.

———. "Samuel ibn Tibbon and the Esoteric Character of *The Guide of the Perplexed." Association of Jewish Studies Review* 6 (1981): 87–123.

———. "The Thought of Zeraḥiah ben Isaac ben Sheʾaltiel Ḥen and Maimonidean-Tibbonid Philosophy in the Thirteenth Century" (Hebrew). Ph.D. dissertation, Hebrew University of Jerusalem, 1979.

Roberts, Julian. *German Philosophy: An Introduction.* Cambridge, U.K.: Polity Press, 1988.

Robinson, James T. "The Ibn Tibbon Family: A Dynasty of Translators in Medieval Provence." In *Be'erot Yitzhak: Studies in Memory of Isadore Twersky,* ed. Jay Harris, 193–224. Cambridge: Harvard University Press.

———. "Philosophy and Exegesis in Ibn Tibbon's Commentary on Ecclesiastes." Ph.D. dissertation, Harvard University, 2002.

———. "Secondary Forms of Transmission: Teaching and Preaching Philosophy in Thirteenth-Century Provence." In *Exchange and Transmission Across Cultural Bound-*

aries: Philosophy, Mysticism, and Science in the Mediterranean World, ed. H. Ben-Shammai, S. Stroumsa, and S. Shaked. Jerusalem: Magnes Press, forthcoming.

Rosen, Tova. *Unveiling Eve: Reading Genre in Medieval Hebrew Literature.* Philadelphia: University of Pennsylvania Press, 2003.

Rosenbloom, Noah H. "Theological Impediments to a Hebrew Version of Mendelssohn's *Phaedon." Proceedings of the American Academy of Jewish Research* 56 (1990): 51–81.

Rosenthal, Judah. "Mi-tokh sefer Alfonso." In *Studies and Essays in Honor of Abraham A. Neuman,* ed. M. Ben-Horin, Bernard Weinryb, and Solomon Zeitlin, 588–621. Leiden: Brill, 1962.

Rosenthal, Franz. "On the Knowledge of Plato's Philosophy in the Islamic World." *Islamic Culture* 14 (1940): 387–422.

Roth, Cecil. *The Jews of the Renaissance.* New York: Harper and Row, 1959.

Roth, Norman. "Isaac Polgar y su libro contra un converso." In *Polémica Judeo-Christiana Estudios,* ed. Carlos del Valle Rodriguez, 67–73. Madrid: Aben Ezra Ediciones, 1992.

———. "The 'Theft of Philosophy' by the Greeks from the Jews." *Classical Folio* 32 (1978): 52–67.

Rubenstein, Jeffrey L. *The Culture of the Babylonian Talmud.* Baltimore: Johns Hopkins University Press, 2003.

———. *Talmudic Stories: Narrative Art, Composition, and Culture.* Baltimore: Johns Hopkins University Press, 1999.

Ruderman, David B. "Italian Renaissance and Jewish Thought." In *Renaissance Humanism: Foundations, Forms, and Legacy,* ed. Albert Rabil, Jr., vol. 1, 382–433. Philadelphia: University of Pennsylvania Press, 1988.

———. *Jewish Thought and Scientific Discovery in Early Modern Europe.* Detroit: Wayne State University Press, 2001.

———. *Kabbalah, Magic, and Science: The Cultural Universe of a Sixteenth-Century Jewish Physician.* Cambridge: Harvard University Press, 1988.

———. *The World of a Renaissance Jew: The Life and Thought of Abraham ben Mordechai Farissol.* Cincinnati: Hebrew Union College Press, 1981.

Saiz de la Maza, Carlos. "Aristóteles, Alejandro y la polemice antijudaica en al signo xiv." *El Olivio* 24 (1986): 145–154.

Samuelson, Norbert M., ed. *Studies in Jewish Philosophy.* Lanham, Md.: University Press of America, 1987.

Sansone, Mario. *Da Bembo a Galiani: Il dibattio sulla lingua in Italia.* Bari: Adriatica, 1999.

Santoro, Mario. "La cultura umanistica." In *Storia di Napoli,* vol. 7, 159–171. Naples, 1975–1981.

Saperstein, Marc. *Jewish Preaching, 1200–1800: An Anthology.* New Haven: Yale University Press, 1989.

Sarachek, Joseph. *Faith and Reason: The Conflict over the Rationalism of Maimonides.* New York: Hermon Press, 1970 [1935].

Schacht, Joseph. *The Origins of Muhammedan Jurisprudence.* Oxford: Clarendon Press, 1979.

Scheindlin, Raymond. "Judah Abrabanel to His Son." *Judaism* 41 (1992): 190–191.

Schirmann, Hayyim. *Hebrew Poetry in Spain and Provence* (Hebrew). 2 vols. Jerusalem and Tel Aviv: Bialik Institute and Dvir, 1960–1961.

———. "The Life of Judah Halevi" (Hebrew). In his *Studies in the History of Hebrew Poetry and Drama,* vol. 1, 250–341. Jerusalem: Mossad Bialik, 1979.

——. *Studies in the History of Hebrew Poetry and Drama* (Hebrew). Vol. 1. Jerusalem: Mossad Bialik, 1979.

Schmidt, Gilya Gerda. *Martin Buber's Formative Years: From German Culture to Jewish Renewal, 1897–1909.* Tuscaloosa: University of Alabama Press, 1995.

Schoeps, Julius H. *Moses Mendelssohn.* Königstein: Jüdischer Verlag, 1979.

Scholem, Gershom G. *The Kabbalah in Gerona.* Jerusalem: Akademon, 1968.

Schwartz, Dov. *Astral Magic in Medieval Jewish Thought* (Hebrew). Ramat Gan: Bar Ilan University Press, 1999.

Schwarz, Ferdinand. "Briefe Moses Mendelssohns an Isaak Iselin." In *Basler Jahrbuch 1923,* ed. August Huber and Ernst Jenny.

Schweid, Eliezer. "The Literary Structure of the First Book of the *Kuzari*" (Hebrew). *Tarbiz* 30 (1961): 257–272.

Seeskin, Kenneth. *Autonomy in Jewish Philosophy.* Cambridge: Cambridge University Press, 2001.

——. *Dialogue and Discovery: A Study in Socratic Method.* Albany: State University of New York Press, 1987.

——. *Jewish Philosophy in a Secular Age.* Albany: State University of New York Press, 1990.

——. *Maimonides on the Origin of the World.* Cambridge: Cambridge University Press, 2005.

——. *Searching for a Distant God: The Legacy of Maimonides.* Oxford: Oxford University Press, 2000.

Sela, Shlomo. *Astrology and Biblical Exegesis in the Thought of Abraham Ibn Ezra* (Hebrew). Ramat Gan: Bar Ilan University Press, 1999.

Septimus, Bernard. *Hispano-Jewish Culture in Transition: The Career and Controversies of the Ramah.* Cambridge: Harvard University Press, 1982.

——. "Piety and Power in Thirteenth-Century Catalonia." In *Studies in Medieval History and Literature,* ed. Isadore Twersky, 197–230. Cambridge: Harvard University Press, 1979.

Shatzmiller, Joseph. "Toward a Picture of the First Maimonidean Controversy" (Hebrew). *Zion* 34 (1969): 126–144.

Shear, Adan B. "Judah Halevi's *Kuzari* in the *Haskalah:* The Reinterpretation and Reimagining of a Medieval Work." In *Rewriting the Jewish Past, Reconfiguring Jewish Culture: From al-Andalus to the Haskalah,* ed. Ross Brann and Adam Sutcliffe, 71–92. Philadelphia: University of Pennsylvania Press, 2004.

Shmueli, Efraim. *Seven Jewish Cultures: A Reinterpretation of Jewish History and Thought.* Translated by Gila Shmueli. Cambridge: Cambridge University Press, 1990.

Shoḥat, Azriel. "Concerning the First Controversy on the Writings of Maimonides" (Hebrew). *Zion* 36 (1971): 27–60.

Silberstein, Lawrence J. *Martin Buber's Social and Religious Thought: Alienation and the Quest for Meaning.* New York: New York University Press, 1989.

Silman, Yohanan. *Philosopher and Prophet: Judah Halevi, the Kuzari, and the Evolution of His Thought.* Translated by Lenn J. Schramm. Albany: State University of New York Press, 1995.

Silver, Daniel J. *Maimonidean Criticism and the Maimonidean Controversy 1180–1240.* Leiden: E. J. Brill, 1965.

Simon, Hermann. *Moses Mendelssohn: Gesetzestreuer Jude und deutscher Aufklärer.* Berlin: Centrum Judaicum, 2003.

Sirat, Colette. *A History of Jewish Philosophy in the Middle Ages.* Cambridge and Paris:

Cambridge University Press and Editions de la Maison des Sciences de l'Homme, 1985.

Solmi, Edmondo. *Benedetto Spinoza e Leone Ebreo: Studio su una Fonte Italiana Dimenticata dello Spinozismo.* Modena: G. T. Vincenzi e Nipoti, 1903.

Sonne, Isaiah. "On the Question of the Original Language of the *Dialoghi d'amore* of Judah Abravanel" (Hebrew). In *Notes: A Collection in Memory of Y. N. Simhoni.* Berlin: n.p., 1928–1929.

Sorkin, David. *Moses Mendelssohn and the Religious Enlightenment.* Berkeley: University of California Press, 1996.

——. *The Transformation of German Jewry: 1780–1840.* New York: Oxford University Press, 1987.

Steigerwald, Diane. *La pensée philosophique et théologique de Shahrastānī.* Sainte-Foy, Quebec: Presses de l'Université Laval, 1997.

Stein, Siegfrid. *Jewish-Christian Disputations in Thirteenth-Century Narbonne.* London: H. K. Llewis, 1969.

Steinschneider, Moritz. *Die arabischen Übersetzungen aus dem Griechischen.* Nendeln, Liechtenstein: Kraus Reprint, 1968 [1902].

Stern, Gregg. "The Crisis of Philosophic Allegory in Languedocian-Jewish Culture (1304–06)." In *Interpretation and Allegory: Antiquity to the Modern Period,* ed. Jon Whitman, 189–210. Leiden: E. J. Brill, 2000.

——. "Menahem ha-Meiri and the Second Controversy over Philosophy." Ph.D. dissertation, Harvard University, 1995.

Stern, Samuel M. "The Earliest Cosmological Doctrines of Ismāʿīlism." In his *Studies in Early Ismāʿīlism,* 3–29. Leiden and Jerusalem: E. J. Brill and The Magnes Press, 1983.

Strauss, Leo. "The Law of Reason in the *Kuzari.*" In his *Persecution and the Art of Writing,* 95–141. Chicago: University of Chicago Press, 1988 [1952].

Sutcliffe, Adam. *Judaism and Enlightenment.* Cambridge: Cambridge University Press, 2003.

Talmage, Frank Ephraim. *David Kimḥi: The Man and the Commentaries.* Cambridge: Harvard University Press, 1972.

——. "R. Joseph Kimḥi: From the Dispersion of Jerusalem in Sepharad to the Canaanites in Zarephath" (Hebrew). In *Tarbut ve-ḥevrah be Toldot Yisraʾel bi-yemei ha-benayim: Kovets meʾamarim le-zikhro shel Haim Hilel Ben-Sason,* ed. Robert Bonfil, M. Ben-Sason, Y. Hacker, 315–332. Jerusalem: Merkaz Zalman Shazar, 1989.

Tarrant, Dorothy. "Style and Thought in Plato's Dialogues." *Classical Quarterly* 42 (1948): 28–34.

Tirosh-Rothschild, Hava. *Between Worlds: The Life and Thought of Rabbi David ben Judah Messer Leon.* Albany: State University of New York Press, 1991.

——. "Jewish Culture in Renaissance Italy: A Methodological Study." *Italia* 9, 1–2 (1990): 63–96.

——. "Jewish Philosophy on the Eve of Modernity." In *History of Jewish Philosophy,* ed. Daniel H. Frank and Oliver Leaman, 499–573. New York and London: Routledge, 1997.

Tirosh-Samuelson, Hava. *Happiness in Premodern Judaism: Virtue, Knowledge, and Well-Being.* Cincinnati: Hebrew Union College Press, 2003.

——, ed. *Women and Gender in Jewish Philosophy.* Bloomington: Indiana University Press, 2004.

Tolan, John. *Petrus Alfonsi: His Medieval Readers.* Gainesville: University Press of Florida, 1993.

Touati, Charles. "La controverse de 1303–1306: Autour des études philosophiques et scientifiques." *Revue des études juives* 127 (1968): 21–37.

Trinkaus, Charles. *The Poet as Philosopher: Petrarch and the Formation of Renaissance Consciousness.* New Haven: Yale University Press, 1979.

———. *The Scope of Renaissance Humanism.* Ann Arbor: University of Michigan Press, 1983.

Twersky, Isadore. "Aspects of the Social and Cultural History of Provençal Jewry." In *Jewish Society through the Ages,* ed. H. H. Ben-Sasson and S. Ettinger, 185–207. London: Valentine and Mitchell, 1971.

———, ed. *Rabbi Moses Nahmanides (Ramban): Explorations in His Religious Virtuosity.* Cambridge: Harvard University Press, 1983.

Urbach, Ephraim. "The Participation of German and French Scholars in the Controversy about Maimonides and His Works" (Hebrew). *Zion* 12 (1947): 149–159.

Vajda, Georges. *Isaac Albalag: Averroïste juif, traducteur, et annotateur d'al-Ghazalī.* Paris: J. Vrin, 1960.

Valle Rodriguez, Carlos del. "*La Contradicción del Hereje* de Issac ben Polger." In *Jewish Studies at the Turn of the Twentieth Century: Proceedings of the 6th EAJS Congress,* vol. 1, ed. Judit Targarona and Angel Sáenz-Badillos, 552–560. Leiden: Brill, 1989.

———. "*El Libro de la Batalla de Dios,* de Abner de Burgos." In *Polémica Judeo-Christiana Estudios,* ed. C. del Valle Rodriguez, 75–103. Madrid: Aben Ezra, 1992.

van Ess, Josef. *Chiliastische Erwartungen und die Versuchung der Göttlichkeit der Kalif al-Ḥākim (386–411A.H.).* Heidelberg: Carl Winter Universitätsverlag, 1977.

Veltri, Giuseppe. "'Philo and Sophia': Leone Ebreo's Concept of Jewish Philosophy." In *Cultural Intermediaries,* ed. David B. Ruderman and Giuseppe Veltri, 55–66. Philadelphia: University of Pennsylvania Press, 2004.

Vickers, Brian. "Rhetoric and Poetics." In *The Cambridge History of Renaissance Philosophy,* ed. Charles B. Schmitt et al., 715–745. Cambridge: Cambridge University Press, 1988.

Voorbij, Johannes B. "Purpose and Audience: Perspectives on the Thirteenth-Century Encyclopedias of Alexander Neckam, Bartholomaeus Anglicus, Thomas of Cantimpré and Vincent of Beauvais." In *The Medieval Hebrew Encyclopedias of Science and Philosophy,* ed. Steven Harvey, 31–45. Dordrecht: Kluwer, 2000.

Walbridge, John. *The Leaven of the Ancients: Suhrawardī and the Heritage of the Greeks.* Albany: State University of New York Press, 2000.

Walker, Paul E. *Early Philosophical Shiism: The Ismaili Neoplatonism of Abū Yaʿqūb al-Sijistānī.* Cambridge: Cambridge University Press, 1993.

———. *Ḥamid al-Dīn al-Kirmānī: Ismaili Thought in the Age of al-Ḥākim.* London: I. B. Tauris, 1999.

Wasserstrom, Steven M. *Between Muslim and Jew: The Problem of Symbiosis under Early Islam.* Princeton: Princeton University Press, 1995.

Weinstein, Donald. "In Whose Image and Likeness? Interpretations of Renaissance Humanism." *Journal of the History of the Ideas* 33 (1972): 165–176.

Whitman, Jon. *Allegory: The Dynamics of an Ancient and Medieval Technique.* Cambridge: Harvard University Press, 1987.

Wirszubski, Chaim. *Pico della Mirandola's Encounter with Jewish Mysticism.* Cambridge: Harvard University Press, 1989.

Wolfson, Elliot R. "Beautiful Maiden Without Eyes: *Peshat* and *Sod* in Zoharic Hermeneutics." In *The Midrashic Imagination: Jewish Exegesis, Thought, and History,* ed. Michael Fishbane, 155–203. Albany: State University of New York Press, 1993.

———. "Facing the Effaced: Mystical Eschatology and the Idealistic Orientation in the

Thought of Franz Rosenzweig." *Journal for the History of Modern Theology* 4 (1997): 39–81.

——. *Language, Eros, Being: Kabbalistic Hermeneutics and Poetic Imagination.* New York: Fordham University Press, 2005.

——. "Merkabah Traditions in Philosophical Garb: Judah Halevi Reconsidered." *Proceedings for the American Academy of Jewish Research* 57 (1990/1991): 179–242.

——. "Occultation of the Feminine and the Body of Secrecy in Medieval Kabbalah." In *Rending the Veil: Concealment and Secrecy in the History of Religions,* ed. Elliot R. Wolfson, 113–154. New York: Seven Bridges Press, 1999.

Wolfson, Harry Austryn. *Philo: Foundations of Religious Philosophy in Judaism, Christianity, and Islam.* 2 vols. Cambridge: Harvard University Press, 1947.

Yaffe, Gideon. "Earl of Shaftesbury." In *A Companion to Early Modern Philosophy,* ed. Steven Nadler, 425–436. Oxford: Blackwell, 1992.

Yavneh, Naomi. "The Spiritual Eroticism of Leone's Hermaphrodite." In *Playing with Gender: A Renaissance Pursuit,* ed. Jean R. Brink, Maryanne C. Horowitz, and Allison P. Coudert, 85–98. Urbana: University of Illinois Press, 1991.

Yerushalmi, Yosef Haim. *The Lisbon Massacre of 1506 and the Royal Image in the Shebet Yehudah.* Cincinnati: Hebrew Union College Press, 1976.

Yuval, Israel Jacob. "Yitzhak Baer and the Search for Authentic Judaism." In *The Jewish Past Revisited: Reflections on Modern Jewish Historians,* ed. David. N. Myers and David B. Ruderman, 77–86. New Haven: Yale University Press, 1998.

Zank, Michael. *The Idea of Atonement in the Philosophy of Hermann Cohen.* Providence, R.I.: Brown Judaic Studies, 2000.

Zimmels, B. *Leone Hebreo, Neue Studien.* Vienna: Waizner, 1892.

Zimmerman, Fritz. "The Origins of the So-Called Theology of Aristotle." In *Pseudo-Aristotle in the Middle Ages: "The Theology" and Other Texts,* ed. Jill Kraye, W. F. Ryan, and C. B. Schmitt, 110–240. London: The Warburg Institute, 1986.

Zonta, Mauro. *Un dizionario filosofico ebraico del XIII secolo: L'introduzione al "Sefer Deʿot ha-Filosofim" di Shem Tob ibn Falaquera.* Torino: S. Zamorani, 1992.

——. *La filosofia ebraica medievale: Storia e testa.* Rome-Bari: Gius. Laterza e Figli, 2002.

——. "Hebrew Transmission of Arabic Philosophy and Science: A Reconstruction of Shem Tov Ibn Falaquera's 'Arabic Library'." In *L'interculturalità dell'ebraismo,* a cura di Mauro Perani, 121–137. Ravenna: Longo Editore, 2004.

INDEX

Abbt, Thomas, 148, 153, 158
Abner of Burgos (Alfonso de Valladolid), 11; Abner's critique of the Judeo-Islamic philosophical tradition, 98–99; antagonist of *Ezer ha-Dat,* 11, 13, 77, 78, 82–85, 91–106; brief biographical sketch of, 80–82; difficulty in classifying, 81–82; influence on subsequent Jewish philosophy, 82. *See also* Polleqar, Isaac
Abravanel, Isaac, 117
Abravanel, Judah, 4, 7, 15, 19, 106, 107–137, 175; brief biographical sketch of, 117–120; compared to Judah Halevi, 107–108, 128–129; compared to Moses Mendelssohn, 175; *De Coeli Harmonia,* 120; *Dialoghi d'Amore,* 10, 11; *Dialoghi d'Amore* compared to *Heptaplus,* 134–135; and enigmatic last years, 119–120; erotic nature of the *Dialoghi,* 108–109; fictional conversion to Christianity, 119; forced conversion of his son, 108, 117–118; influence on later Italian Platonists, 129; Jewish themes in his work, 121–125; language of his composition, 19, 108, 120–121; in Naples, 114; as offering Jewish response to Christianizing trends in Renaissance Humanism, 107, 129–130; 132–137; and Plato's *Symposium,* 123, 136; poetic introductions to father's work, 120; problematic relationship to Jewish philosophy, 16, 121–125; and the protagonists of the *Dialoghi d'Amore,* 109; relationship to the thought of Judah Messer Leon, 111; relationship to the *trattati d'amore,* 115–116; *Telunah ʿal ha-zeman,* 118, 132, 197nn57,58. *See also il circulo degli amari;* Ficino, Marsilio; Messer Leon, Judah; Pico della Mirandola, Giovanni; Plato; Sophia
adab, 26, 28, 34
Adret, Solomon, 54, 75, 77
aesthetics, 3–4, 26, 76, 106, 108, 154; medieval contrasted with Renaissance, 109–112; in the thought of Moses Mendelssohn, 154–155
ʿahd, 31, 35, 41–43, 46
Albalag, Isaac, 64, 191n33
Alemanno, Yohanan, 18–19, 113–114
Alfonsi, Petrus, 79
Alon, Ilai, 6–7
Altmann, Alexander, 144, 160
ʿamal vs. *niyya,* 13, 15, 27, 32–35, 44, 49
al-Andalus (Muslim Spain), 26, 28, 45, 48, 50, 74, 76, 77
d'Aragona, Tullia, 116
Aristotle, 109–110, 124, 150
astral magic, 100–101
astrology, 13, 75, 78, 83, 89, 91, 98–105, 108

AARON W. HUGHES is Associate Professor in the Department of Religious Studies at the University of Calgary, Canada. He is author of *The Texture of the Divine: Imagination in Medieval Islamic and Jewish Thought* (Indiana University Press, 2004), which was a finalist for the Koret Jewish Book Award, and *Jewish Philosophy A–Z*.

Ingram Content Group UK Ltd.
Milton Keynes UK
UKHW010658210523
422080UK00002B/108

9 780253 219442